The
WORLD
Is a
BALL

THE **JOY, MADNESS, AND MEANING** OF SOCCER

JOHN DOYLE

RODALE

For Sean and Mary Doyle, decent people

Rodale books may be purchased for business or promotional use or for special sales. For information, please write to:
Special Markets Department, Rodale Inc., 733 Third Avenue, New York, NY 10017

Printed in the United States of America
Rodale Inc. makes every effort to use acid-free ♾, recycled paper ♻.

The information in this book was previously published by Doubleday Canada, a division of Random House of Canada Limited. This edition is published in 2010 by Rodale Inc.

Library of Congress Cataloging-in-Publication Data

Doyle, John.
    The world is a ball : the joy, madness, and meaning of soccer / John Doyle.
        p.   cm.
    Includes bibliographical references and index.
    ISBN 978-1-60529-146-8   paperback
    1. Soccer—Social aspects—Anecdotes.   2. Soccer fans—Anecdotes.   3. Doyle, John, 1957—Travel—Anecdotes.   I. Title.
    GV843.2.D69   2010
    796.334—dc22   2010032422

Distributed to the trade by Macmillan
2   4   6   8   10   9   7   5   3   1   paperback

RODALE
LIVE YOUR WHOLE LIFE™

We inspire and enable people to improve their lives and the world around them.

CONTENTS

MEANING:
ALL *the* RAMBLING BOYS
of PLEASURE

I HAD NO PLANS to try my hand at being a sportswriter. Honestly, I didn't. I work as the television critic for the *Globe and Mail* in Toronto and I've been blessed with the freedom to write about whatever I see on TV. As long as it's been seen on a TV screen, I can write about it. This means that I write about everything, because everything that happens is shown on television, sooner or later.

On November 15, 2001, this was my TV column for the day:

> As usual, it's all about me watching TV. This morning, while many of you are reading this, around 8 to 9 A.M. in Toronto, I'll actually be in a bar, glued to the TV. It's unlikely there will be much beer drinking, but the place will be crowded, noisy and cheerful. It's where you have to go to see a certain soccer game—Ireland playing Iran, in Tehran, for a place in next year's World Cup.
>
> Last Saturday afternoon I was in the same Irish bar, the bizarrely named McVeigh's New Windsor Tavern, watching the first leg of the two playoff games being broadcast from Dublin. You can't see these games on your regular TV menu, no matter what fancy satellite system you've got. So the place was packed, with about half the crowd there to cheer the Irish team and the

other half to loudly applaud Iran.

Thanks to previous experience in these matters, I was there early to get a seat. Many Iranian supporters were there already, consuming coffee at a fierce rate. Everybody was wound up, cheerful and looking forward to the game. By the time it started, the place was filled to capacity and the doors had to be closed. This left several dozen people outside hoping to get in, most of them supporters of Iran.

I had no idea about this until later, when I had to get to the back of the bar for a drink. There, at the door, were numerous faces pressed to the glass, watching one of the TV screens on the wall. There were more faces at all of the windows. At the table where I sat, a man kept talking into his cell phone while staring at the screen. Eventually I realized he was giving a running commentary on the game to some guy outside who, as far as I could tell, was duly relaying the commentary, shouting it out to the guys outside. You couldn't make this stuff up—it's real life in Toronto on a Saturday.

There was a big cheer when the satellite picture arrived and the first thing we all saw was an Iranian player about to take the field. We all watched the official opening to the game, and I wondered how the players and supporters from a strict Islamic country felt as the Iranian team was greeted by the President of Ireland, a woman named Mary McAleese. The game itself was intense, sometimes beautiful, and followed with bursts of applause and rueful moaning by a weirdly unified crowd in this Toronto bar. Islam met the Irish and we all prospered from the experience, thanks to TV.

At one point, a slickly skilled player for Iran, Ali Karimi, a preening gazelle with the distinctive white boots of the self-conscious star, breezed through the Irish defense. He was stopped at the last second by the Irish goalkeeper Shay Given, a young man famous for crying buckets when Ireland lost a playoff game in Belgium a few years ago and failed to reach the last World Cup. At the next table, an Iranian man who'd been quietly drinking coffee leapt to his feet, banged the table and expressed outrage at the missed opportunity. I knew this without translation. He looked around the crowded bar, as if suddenly surprised to find himself there, and not at a soccer stadium. Everybody smiled back at him.

The guy in charge of entry at the door, a Scot, was highly agitated by halftime. He was trying to keep an eye on the game, and the horde outside was driving him to distraction. He told me that one guy had tried to sweet-talk his way inside with a gambit that included "Canada is a great country." The Scot could only bark, "Fire regulation! Fire regulation!" Everybody was having a marvelous time. Ireland won 2–0 but Iran has the opportunity to overcome that goal deficit with a strong, multi-scoring display in Tehran.

We'll all be back this morning, hoping the satellite picture from Tehran is clear and good. While we watch in Toronto, about 110,000 people will be in the stadium there, including women. You see, women are not allowed to attend soccer games in Iran but after much protest from the Irish end (about 1,000 Irish supporters, some of them women, planned to travel to Tehran) an exception was made. It's a funny old world. Sometimes, watching TV is a profound, polycultural experience as well as being great fun.

A few weeks later, I was asked if I would consider going to Korea and Japan to cover the 2002 World Cup. I said yes. Eight years later, it turns out that I have been to fifteen countries to watch and write about soccer. My writing about it has appeared in the *Globe and Mail*, the *New York Times* and the *Guardian*. I'm still not a sportswriter; in truth, I am pathologically incapable of writing the traditional report on a game—the score,

the comments from the managers, coaches and players afterwards, the attendance in the stadium, the statistics on ball possession and whether the result of the game means that the teams
move up or down in the standings. I write about the travel, the
game, the atmosphere and all the attendant meanings that are
tethered to the game. I take the view that most international
soccer games serve as a metaphor for something else, and all
international soccer games are special occasions.

It is a commonly held view in the newspaper racket that
sportswriting is a genre declining in importance. Once, it is
believed, before television ruined everything, a sportswriter
could be the king of his paper (for they were almost always male)
and a famous figure in his town or city. In the golden age of
big-city newspapers, especially in the U.S. and Canada, certain
sportswriters were celebrities, and some were even prose writers
of great distinction. Professional athletes and sports organizations
deferred to them, treated them with enormous respect. The reading public waited avidly for their reports. They traveled to fara-
way places where important sporting contests happened. They
spoke to the athletes and professional players and told dramatic
tales in the back pages of newspapers. They held readers
enthralled.

. Television changed that. Eventually, almost every important
sports event happening in a particular country, or anywhere on
the planet, could be watched by everyone who wanted to see it.
With the money that television injected into sports, the players—especially soccer players—became very rich, remote figures. They didn't need to talk to guys who hammered at
typewriters for newspapers. They needed to be famous through
television, and it was TV pundits, reporters and sports anchors
who became far more famous, influential and important than
newspaper writers. In fact, it is believed by many that television
makes sportswriting redundant. Anyone who cares has seen the
game, knows the score and has heard the post-game quotes.

Perversely, I've always taken the opposite view, especially
when it comes to international soccer and such tournaments as

the World Cup and the European championships. Television only shows you what happens on the field and offers brief comments, if any at all, from the players. What's seen on the screen is not what actually happened at a stadium holding fifty thousand or ninety thousand people. When I watched the World Cup on TV for the first time, in 1970 when it was held in Mexico, I was immensely curious about what it felt like to be there. I wanted to know what the fans were singing in the stands as the commentator droned on about the game. I wanted to know the whole story of events in the hours before the game and the hours after it. I wanted to know what it felt like to be in a country far from home, among tens of thousands of people who'd traveled long and worked hard to be there. I wanted to see, hear and feel the occasion. I wanted to belong in it.

That's what this book is about, really. It's about the full-throttle experience of attending the biggest sporting events in the world in the twenty-first century. Television has had a profound effect on international soccer tournaments, creating a vast global culture of celebration, joy, bittersweet feelings and, sometimes, despair. When the World Cup unfolds now, the planet is truly a global village, thanks to TV. It makes people giddy and gloriously distracted from all the mundane tasks and problems of daily life. But the intensity of attention created by television has also made the tournaments even bigger and more of a carnival where they happen—in the host country, the host cities and the stadiums. Starting with the 1998 tournament in France, it became stunningly easy to attend and experience the World Cup without having a ticket to a single game. Huge areas in host cities were set aside for visiting fans to show up, eat, drink, party and watch the game on giant screens. This became the norm, and at the World Cup in Korea and Japan in 2002, at Euro 2004 in Portugal, the World Cup in Germany in 2006 and Euro 2008 in Austria and Switzerland, the tournaments became something vaster than anything that could be transmitted in TV reports of individual games. Millions of people pour into the country that hosts the World Cup, and only a fraction actually attend the games.

Figures issued by the Fédération Internationale de Football Association (FIFA), the sport's world governing body, for the 2006 World Cup in Germany are staggering. A total of 3,359,439 spectators attended 64 games in the 12 stadiums. Some 18 million spectators watched the games at the "Fan Festival" sites in Germany. At those, 93,000 gallons of beer were sold, along with 46,000 gallons of non-alcoholic drinks and, by the way, 3.5 million sausages. A total of 18,850 media representatives were accredited. The whole thing lasted four weeks. There is no event in the world that unfolds on such a scale. Little wonder that the cumulative TV audience was 26.29 billion viewers.

When J.B. Priestley described a local soccer match in England in the opening of his 1929 novel *The Good Companions*, he wrote:

> To say that these men paid their shillings to watch twenty-two hirelings kick a ball is merely to say that a violin is wood and catgut, that *Hamlet* is so much paper and ink. For a shilling the Bruddersford United AFC offered you Conflict and Art; it turned you into a critic, happy in your judgment of fine points, ready in a second to estimate the worth of a well-judged pass, a run down the touchline, a lightning shot, a clearance kick by back or goalkeeper; it turned you into a partisan, holding your breath when the ball came sailing into your own goalmouth, ecstatic when your forwards raced away towards the opposite goal, elated, downcast, bitter, triumphant by turn at the fortunes of your side, watching a ball shape *Iliad*s and *Odyssey*s for you; and what is more, it turned you into a member of a new community, all brothers together for an hour and a half, for not only had you escaped from the clanking machinery of this lesser life, from work, wages, rent, doles, sick pay, insurance cards, nagging wives, ailing children, bad bosses, idle workmen, but you had escaped with most of your neighbors, with half the town, and there you were cheering together, thumping one another on the

shoulders, swapping judgments like lords of the earth,
having pushed your way through a turnstile into another
and altogether more splendid kind of life, hurtling with
Conflict and yet passionate and beautiful in its Art.

That is a description of club soccer in England eight decades
ago. There are few more apt evocations of the thrill that accom-
panies being part of the great throng at a game, and it applies
equally—and on an even grander scale—to the international
games of today. One of the great pleasures of being alive is being
part of a large, unruly gathering, the majority of people there
smiling with the joy of being in one convivial, unhindered mass.
It is a deeply gratifying, uplifting feeling, one utterly unfamiliar
to most adults in ordinary life, and, as I discovered and point out
in the tales told here, it frees adults to rediscover the bliss of
childish revelry. The World Cup and other big, international
soccer tournaments are joy-bringers, unique festivals of
congeniality.

This is one of the contradictory aspects of international soccer
today. Soccer simultaneously separates and unites. The games are
hard fought. No team wants to lose or is prepared to accept defeat
with equanimity. Yet the tournaments are about shared passion
and generally unfold in a spirit of peace, amiability and respect.
People support their country's teams ardently, but embrace and
acknowledge the right of others to support their countries too.
An utterly unique kind of kinship is in the air. A groovy kind
of powerful, childlike internationalism is playing out at international tournaments. The multitudes flock and throng from all
over the world to become immersed in a sea of gaiety and
goodwill.

In all the countries and cities I have visited to watch soccer,
in all the stadiums, streets and train stations packed with soccer
fans, I have never once felt afraid. At the major tournaments, the
idea of "soccer hooliganism" has become redundant. At the
World Cup in France in 1998 and at Euro 2000 in Holland and
Belgium, there were serious problems with English supporters.

Since then, the worst that has happened are rare outbreaks of scuffles when police try to clear drunken fans from downtown areas. Much worse has happened after NHL games in Canada, where stores have been smashed and looted and police cars set alight in post-game frenzies. The threat of fan violence at soccer tournaments has essentially been eliminated thanks to the confiscation of passports of established troublemakers, intensified border security, pre-tournament patrols and smart policing plans for host cities. Most of the time I am present at tournaments, as I tell in this book, I am among the happiest people on earth.

Every game has meaning, though. The principle that soccer is a form of ritual combat between tribes and nations holds true. The nexus between social identity and soccer is obvious. Social, political and religious attributes are attached to national teams, and soccer tournaments are, today, among those very rare public events where the expression of these attributes is allowable. When the Republic of Ireland plays England—this always matters to me, deeply, and it seems to happen over and over again—the game is filled with an intensity of meaning that the Irish diaspora, scattered across the continents, understands in a way that no one else can. We, the Irish, are now citizens of a republic, no longer subjects of a monarchy. England is always the old enemy, hopefully defeated on the soccer field as it once was by a people's rebellion. In part, the importance of the game rests not on the result of the contest on the field, but in what happens among the supporters of each country. It is, after all, the English fans who have the reputation of being savages, not us.

This is old-school stuff. When Senegal, a former colony of France, defeated France in the opening game of the World Cup in 2002, the event mocked the facts of history. When, at Euro 2008 in Austria and Switzerland, Turkey stormed through the tournament, winning games late and with an obstinacy that was breathtaking to behold, the team carried the rage, resentment and pride of generations of Turkish workers who had left home to work in menial jobs in Germany, Austria and Switzerland. Those Turkish workers and their sons and daughters were in the stadium, hoarse from singing, chanting and willing, through sheer noise, their country's team to teach the teams of the bosses and the bourgeoisie a lesson. One memorable night in Vienna, after Turkey had defeated Croatia on penalty kicks in the quarter-final game of Euro 2008, I emerged from the subway to find the street filled with dancing Turkish families. Elderly women and small children whirled together on the sidewalk. Then, somehow, the dancing moved from the sidewalk onto the roadway and traffic stopped. For a time, the dancers owned the city. At last, the city in which they had slaved, hustled and traded, always as outsiders, was theirs. It was their right. The result of the game accorded them that right and the spirit of tournament sanctioned it.

A case can be made that the World Cup, like the contemporary Olympic Games, has its origins in ancient religious festivals. The World Cup, though, did not begin, as the modern Olympic movement did, with an attempt to re-create an ancient athletic competition. It began as an idea when FIFA, having had a falling-out with the International Olympic Committee—one reason for which was the IOC's lack of enthusiasm for including soccer in the 1932 Summer Olympics to be held in Los Angeles, where interest in the sport was low—decided to create a tournament independent of the Games. It's ironic, of course, that the World Cup has now become a far bigger event and spectacle than the Olympics.

The fact is that the World Cup and the continental national championships in Europe and South America have become events that transcend athletic competition. These tournaments are festivals, carnivals of revelry, pageantry and celebration, that last for weeks, with vast crowds of people—millions, even— gathering and traveling to and fro in the host country, all of them intent both on supporting their country's team and, intuitively, celebrating soccer itself and its power to draw so many people from distant places together. If the World Cup and the other continental tournaments resemble anything in the planet's past, it is the ancient Greek festival of Dionysus, a large and raucous religious feast in honor of the god Dionysus, and where core ceremonies were the staging of tragedies and comedies. You could say that the soccer tournaments serve as examples of the Dionysian tendency in Western culture—that impulse towards irrationality, frenzy and intoxication. In this too, mind you, there is a powerful contradiction at work, because the opposite of the Dionysian impulse, the Apollonian urge for clarity and structure, is also present. The actual games, with their formal rules, symmetry and standard form, embody the Apollonian impulse. I'm no scholar of ancient Greece and its festivals; nor am I an anthropologist. I travel, observe and write. But in major tournaments I have witnessed, I'd say the Apollonian and Dionysian tendencies of human nature and civilization are, finally, united. Intoxication and exuberance coexist, beatifically, with order and moderation.

It is doubly ironic that a lack of American interest in soccer helped propel the World Cup into existence. Soccer remains the only truly global entertainment force that prospers while happily anchored outside of the United States. There is Major League Soccer in the U.S. these days, and there is a strong national team that is usually underestimated by European and South American countries, but soccer there exists low in the hierarchy behind baseball, basketball, NFL football and hockey. And yet, this might be changing.

For those of us who live outside the United States and pay attention to what happens there—as we must—one word captures everything about the election of Barack Obama as president, and that word is "change." It defined Obama's campaign and victory, and it defined, perhaps, an urge to bury the recent past and move on emphatically towards a more inclusive, tolerant, cosmopolitan America—an America that is less rigid about what it means to be an American.

Well, there was one significant symbol of change during his campaign: the decision by the all-sports cable TV channel ESPN to broadcast all of the Euro 2008 soccer championship from Austria and Switzerland. It was, possibly, a cultural watershed moment, and one that is in sync with that craving for change. Some of the games appeared on the secondary network, ESPN2, while a bunch were shown on the main channel, to which tens of millions of American subscribe. And, incredibly, two games were carried nationally, over the air, by ABC. The final, played in Vienna, was shown on the network on a Sunday afternoon, as part of a doubleheader with an MLS game between the David Beckham–led Los Angeles Galaxy and Washington's D.C. United.

This was near revolutionary. It wasn't the World Cup that was being covered. The U.S. team was not involved, so there was no opportunity for viewers to come upon the tournament by accident and root for the home side, chanting "USA! USA!" every few days as they faced an old enemy—not from soccer, but, usually, politics. The matches involved European teams only: Portugal against Germany, Turkey against the Czech Republic, the effete-looking, speedy Spanish players practically dancing the ball around tall Swedes. It was soccer as Old World sport, a confluence of chess and ballet.

In 2008, of all years, it is surely significant that American broadcasters devoted airtime to all this. Some meaning can be extrapolated from it, because soccer acts as a cultural divide in the U.S.: on the one hand, interest in the game and support for its expansion signal a progressive attitude, a willingness to see the U.S. as part of the larger world, not an isolated place, smug in its status as a world power; on the other, skepticism and even derision for soccer signal American traditionalism, if not patriotism itself. Scorn for soccer is a kind of signifier of "red-state," or Republican, attitudes. That contempt is rooted in a hardline belief that the United States is the biggest, strongest country in the world, and its sports are the best sports. They are manly games that require strength, skill and masculine fortitude. In contrast, soccer is metrosexual. Polished and urbane. Definitely blue state.

It's that metrosexual quality (as epitomized by Beckham) that often alienates followers and pundits of traditional American

sports. Much the same response prevails in Canada, where the
national sport, hockey, is emphatically masculine and nation-
defining. Hockey is a fast, brutal, beautiful and thrilling game.
Around it, there's a mythology that's drenched in sadness, failure
and death. You could speculate that hockey is part of the life-
blood of the Canadian culture precisely because it's about survival on the hard, unforgiving ice in the face of the eternal
enemy of the elements. In this context, some Canadians look
on soccer with a livid abhorrence. But it's in the United States
that soccer has sometimes been seen as truly subversive. Some
Americans are wary of soccer not just because it is the game of
other countries, but because it cannot be seen as a sport that's
passed down from father to son, and therefore traditional and
truly defining of time-honored American qualities.

The American wariness and outright confusion about soccer
was emphatically evident during the 2010 World Cup. An estimated 111.6 million U.S. viewers watched a portion—which might
be mere minutes—of the World Cup on English or Spanish language networks, according to The Nielsen Company. The figure
is a 22 percent increase on the 91.4 million U.S. viewers who
tuned in to some part of the 2006 World Cup. The World Cup
final between Spain and The Netherlands drew the biggest-ever
U.S. audience for a soccer game, with a total of 24.3 million viewers tuning in. Two weeks earlier, the previous biggest-ever audience was measured when 19.4 million viewers watched the U.S.
team lose to Ghana. A comparison is necessary, though. An estimated 106.5 million people in the U.S. watched the Super Bowl
in February 2010. What the millions seeing the final and earlier
games witnessed was exquisite, maddening and, at times, utterly
confusing. The issues that define soccer's status in the U.S. were
everywhere and blatant. Often, such issues raise the question of
whether soccer can be sold to more Americans. There is a lingering feeling in some parts of the U.S. media, in particular, that the
World Cup exists to promote the game to a potential U.S. audience. It doesn't. It's a championship tournament for the world. The
winners, Spain, are not concerned about American TV viewers.

The USA did well in a tough group at the World Cup. A righteous 1–1 tie with England in a game decided by a freakish bounce of the ball in the USA's favor. Then the stunning act of fortitude in the comeback against Slovenia. The sheer resilience of the American players was exciting for anyone—never mind Americans—to watch. But that game ended with the USA scoring a well-taken goal from a free-kick. And the referee waved it off. For even the casual American observer, there was something enraging about the injustice. There was no video-replay technology. There was no stoppage while the referee and his sideline officials determined if the furious American players were correct in their arguments that the goal was legal, which it was. This was international soccer's problem writ large—the game was maddeningly mercurial, illogical even. If the technology is available, why not use it? TV viewers well accustomed to the use of replays in a multitude of professional sports were enraged. To those viewers, the use of replay technology adds a moral purity to a game. The technology decides what is correct and mistakes by mere humans are amended. It was mystifying to see the referee and the Slovenia team walk off the field, seemingly pleased that the game had ended as it should. Some sort of European trickery seemed to be at work and, worse, nobody was bothering to make explanations or apologies to the American team and viewers in the USA.

There is also the seemingly simple matter of time in a soccer game. The referee decides on the amount of extra-time to be added in compensation for stoppages during the game. There is no deference to a clock on the TV screen. The lack of precision seems perverse.

And there was, as there always is at a World Cup, the issue of players diving. It wasn't as headline-grabbing at the 2010 World Cup as it has been in previous tournaments. But it happened: The dive, the play-acting and the outrageous feigning of injury. Nobody admires it and for those watching a World Cup on TV, if the play-by-play commentary originates in England or the U.S., there is resolute tut-tutting. There is bluster and denunciation.

The game is declared to be in disrepute. Standards lowered. Somewhere, in the denunciation, in the outrage or in the subtle subtext, there is usually a suggestion that what the diving, play-acting international soccer player has done is unmanly, unworthy, not sporting. This is always the uncomfortable moment in the U.S., in particular. It's an illumination of a cold, hard fact—soccer is the world's game, not a traditional North American Sport. Nor is it England's game any more. Sure, the rules of the game are the same, wherever the grass grows, but the culture deviates in countries and regions. That's the way the world is, outside of soccer and inside it.

The fact is, in some countries—and it can be Latin nations or Eastern Europe—soccer is as much theater as it is athletic endeavor. A win can be achieved by a cunning ruse, and that's okay. It is part of the game there. The players and the fans really don't care if some Englishman or an American disapproves. They don't care if some barking commentator on American TV or radio believes the ethical standards applied to NHL hockey, Major League Baseball or NFL Football have been breached. The play-acting players in soccer don't need to show that they are "manly" by adhering to some North American guy-code of ethics. They are men. They intend to win. By any means necessary. This flummoxes some American observers.

Mind you, the perplexity of North American sports fans about diving and play-acting is also, maybe, an expression of frustration with multiculturalism. That's an issue that emerges through sports all the time, though few people are willing to admit it. It's all about the difference between the ideals of the melting-pot culture and the mosaic culture. In the melting pot—the preferred American ideal—everyone blends to accept the same rules. But international soccer serves to remind people that differences persist. In some countries and cultures, it is more acceptable to exaggerate, to bluff, to be disingenuous for the sake of saving face, for family or for country. In soccer, that's diving and play-acting, or feigning injury to achieve victory. In ordinary life and business, even in a place where the melting-pot culture is the ideal, people learn to accommodate differences and each other. Allowances are made. But in sports, where the rules are apparently plain, it's not so easy.

In a way, the American confusion and antagonism about soccer are part of a story that is as old as the country itself. It's a story of the conflict, distrust and misunderstanding between European and American cultures. It's a story about American naïveté meeting Old World guile and cunning. And it is has been told countless times, by Henry James and others. In fact, those American sports pundits who rail against soccer bear a close resemblance to little Randolph Miller, the irritating younger brother of Daisy Miller in James's classic short story, first published in 1878 and still studied by millions in U.S. schools, about a young American woman visiting Europe. As anyone who has read *Daisy Miller* knows, little Randolph firmly believes that his hometown, Schenectady, New York, is superior to everything in Europe, especially the candy. In the story, Daisy Miller dies. Maybe that's what some Americans fear about the future of traditional American sports. But she dies essentially because of circumstances caused by her failure to understand European subtleties and nuances that are over her pretty American head. So perhaps ESPN's airing of all that sophisticated European soccer (and it was a superb tournament, an aggressively positive advertisement for the game) signifies that the U.S. culture is flirting again with the mysterious nuances and stratagems of Old World Europe, as Daisy did. It's certainly all connected somehow to that word "change."

Some say that soccer is a religion, and there's truth in that, whether the speaker means that club soccer is literally a sort of civil religion or that soccer at the club and international levels imitates the models of institutional faiths. Most successful clubs in Europe and South America exist and profit from a devotional communication model that promotes the idea of supporters as "the faithful," and they establish shrines to the team's greatest players as if they are saints. And, like all religions, soccer clubs provide a bottomless reservoir of hope—and even the odd miracle—for their devotees. In the case of the greatest and most internationally renowned clubs such as Barcelona or Manchester United, to identify the intensity of support as "religious" is now a cliché. The players are worshipped, the home grounds are temples. International soccer cannot be so easily defined or understood in these terms. What is remarkable about the World Cup and the other major tournaments is that the appeal transcends traditional religious barriers. Few events or emanations of contemporary culture are instantly understood and appreciated in both the Islamic and Judeo-Christian worlds. Soccer is one. The great players are as known, valued and argued about in Saudi Arabia and Iran as they are in Spain or England. In the post–9/11 world, shared, intense interest in soccer and the World Cup is one of the very few things that transcend suspicion and hostility between countries and cultures.

Theories about meaning abound. One night in Berlin during the 2006 World Cup, an elderly Brazilian journalist sat beside me on a bench as we both waited for a bus. Eventually we talked, which surprised me because the journalists from Brazil rarely interact with others. Brazil has the most important soccer culture on the planet so, you know, they don't need to pay the slightest bit of attention to anyone else. It's their thing. The journalist was bored, perhaps, and maybe he wanted to show that he was cosmopolitan and his English was solid enough to hold a good conversation. Also, I think he was amused to meet a journalist from Canada covering the World Cup. We talked of this and that. Of Ronaldo and Ronaldinho. Meandering, he told me that, in Brazil, the young players are sometimes told that the ball is symbolic. It represents Mother Earth, and when players stroke, caress and kick it, they are like gods, tossing the earth around. "They must respect it," he said. "It is the planet we live on." This was delivered to me as a profound truth, and one known mainly to Brazilians.

It was late and he was an interesting character. I was the polite Canadian, too polite to tell him that, in a way, I'd figured it out years ago. On a wet, windy day in Ireland, when I was a boy,

I'd watched two teams of eleven men move the ball around with passion and obvious pleasure in working in unison. It had occurred to me that it's all quite simple, really. If you look at it philosophically, the ball does represent the world. The world keeps turning just as the ball keeps rolling. We have to follow along with the changing, ever-turning world just as the players have to follow the ball and keep it moving. That's the point of the game—of life. That's why soccer is the world's game.

I had no plans to try my hand at being a sportswriter. I set out on a journey, and I liked it. I kept doing it, even when no publication was paying me to do it. This book is about those journeys to the World Cup and the Euro championships. It's not about club soccer and it's not about women's soccer. It's about traveling the world to see international men's soccer games and tournaments. In the end, it's about traveling the road that is the qualifying route for the next World Cup in South Africa in 2010. I was in Italy and in Ireland, and went from Buenos Aires to Bratislava. I soaked up the 2010 World Cup in Canada, at home and in bars and cafes, absorbing it as most of the world does, on TV and in the company of believers and skeptics. In all of those places, and in all of the cities I've been during tournaments, I've really been seeking the feeling—the joy and camaraderie—that I experienced and witnessed that day in a bar in Toronto when Ireland played Iran. And I found it, all over, near and far.

PART I

JOY:
The LONG BALL *from*
LONGFORD *to* IBARAKI

CHAPTER 1

THE FIRST KISS

In my childhood in a small western town, the local soccer club had the status of an illegal organization.
—JOHN WATERS, IRISH WRITER, 2002

IT BEGAN AS MOST illicit affairs in the old Ireland began: after Mass on a Sunday at a place where people gather. It was innocent enough, at the start.

I saw my first soccer game on a sunny summer Sunday in 1967. I was nine years old. The place was Longford, a small town in the middle of nowhere. It's a place people pass through, knowing as they drive along its long, flat main street or see its train station go by that they have almost reached the northern counties of Ireland or are still a long way from Dublin. No matter what direction they're heading, north or south, Longford hardly registers. But Longford is a county, and Longford town is its capital. In 1967, a few thousand people lived there. On Sundays, the shops were open, to accommodate the farming families who lived in outlying areas and came into the town once a week. On other days, most of the business done in the town was administrative. Longford town was, then, where people went to get a license, in order to appear in court or deal with authority in some way. The town had a long history of anchoring authority. For two centuries, during British rule in Ireland, the town had a

British military garrison. Even in the 1960s, forty years after British rule had ended, a former garrison town in Ireland still had a special significance. The hated British army barracks had stood there. Maybe men had died in some assault on the barracks during the War of Independence. Maybe men had died there, imprisoned and shot by British soldiers during that same war. The place was thus tainted. Usually, part of the lingering taint was an appreciation for soccer, a game introduced by British soldiers during the occupation of Ireland.

We didn't live in Longford. We lived a few miles away, in Carrick-on-Shannon. Carrick was a smaller, prettier town, a place where the River Shannon turned and widened. On a sunny summer Sunday it was a quiet, pleasant and relaxed place. We were in Longford because there was an indoor swimming pool, and my sister Máire and the Coughlan girls loved to swim. The Coughlans lived near us in Carrick, and we'd all become great friends. Often on a Sunday, after Mass and the big lunch, Mr. Coughlan would drive the two girls and Máire to Longford and the swimming pool. His son Martin, a year older than me, would go too, and I usually tagged along. While the girls swam, we'd wander around the town in a bored way, looking in the shops for toys we couldn't find in Carrick. On this Sunday, Mr. Coughlan had some business to take care of, so he took us to a tiny, ramshackle stadium and paid a few pennies for us to enter. There were about a hundred other people there.

A soccer game between Longford Town Football Club and Sligo Rovers had just begun. In minutes, I was transfixed. I'd never seen soccer played, in person or on TV. All I knew was that it was an English game and the players couldn't use their hands. The rules were unknown to me. But the role of soccer in Ireland was not. The Christian Brothers railed against it at school, calling it "the garrison game." They sneered at it, saying that the players only played for money, the game was unmanly and foreign, best ignored. They compared it unfavorably with Gaelic football and hurling, the two most popular sports in the country. Gaelic football was played by strong, fit men, and hurling was

for fast-running men who weren't afraid of a clatter on the head
from a flying stick. Gaelic players didn't play for money, they
played for pride. They represented their local area, and if they
were good enough, they played for their county. The Brothers
said that soccer belonged in England, not in Ireland. They said
that soccer players in Ireland and their followers were "Shoneens,"
a word they spoke with a curled lip of contempt. To be a Shoneen
was an awful thing. Sean is the Gaelic for John, and a Shoneen
meant a small John, or Johneen, meaning a toady who wanted
to be something like John Bull. Being a Shoneen was about the
worst thing an Irish person could be. Some of the Brothers said
that half the members of the government up in Dublin were
Shoneens.

Carrick was in County Leitrim, which wasn't famous for its
Gaelic football or hurling. The county was always getting knocked
out in the early stages of the all-Ireland championship in both
sports. We'd only lived in Carrick for a few months, and much
about life there was still new to me. But the Gaelic Athletic
Association was everywhere in Ireland, and its influence was
almost as powerful as that of the Catholic Church. Before Carrick,
we'd lived in Nenagh, a town in County Tipperary where everybody was mad for Gaelic hurling. Tipperary was a great hurling county, everybody knew, and had some legendary players.
The Brothers in Nenagh had hardly mentioned soccer, because
there was no need. Only a few people who had immigrated to
England and returned knew the slightest thing about it.

Attending a soccer game was, therefore, not something done
lightly. And I knew that. My impression was that you could get
in trouble for it. The GAA, which governed Gaelic football and
hurling, had a branch and an organizing committee in every area
of Ireland, no matter how small, and it kept an eye on soccer
games. If you wanted to play Gaelic football or hurling, you
couldn't play soccer—or even watch a game. That was the official rule. You'd be barred forever from playing the Gaelic games.
Even if you weren't a player, but only a member of the GAA or
a volunteer helping out with the Gaelic games, you couldn't have

anything to do with soccer, or you'd be out the door and nobody in the association would have anything to do with you. The only member of the GAA who was allowed to attend soccer games was a member of the committee assigned to take note of the traitors who were playing or watching. The Brothers said that if we boys were tempted to play soccer, or to go off to Longford or some other place to watch a game, we'd better be damn careful. The committee might have somebody there, watching, taking names and reporting back. We'd never play for our home county after that.

This knowledge lent a thrill to the experience of sitting in the little stadium in Longford, watching fellas play soccer. I didn't know the word *illicit* then, but I had all the feelings that came with doing something un-Irish and, God knows, possibly harmful to my future and even that of Ireland. It was like telling a Christian Brother or a priest to go to hell. Yet nobody in the stadium at Longford seemed to be nervous about the GAA taking notes and names, so I relaxed and just watched. Beside me, Martin Coughlan was serene. He'd see soccer played before and said a lot of boys in Carrick played it, behind the Christian Brothers' backs. "It's a bit of fun, " he said. "We might see some good moves here."

The players were young, some had long hair, and they were enjoying themselves. The two teams were in position and I could immediately see the logic of the formation: four defenders in front of the goalkeeper, four more in the middle, with the players on the outside wings moving forward or retreating as the ball was moved around. Two forward, attacking players lined up in front of the middle four, and these were the most active and intense, all the time calling for the ball and seeking space for themselves to rush towards the opposing team. Across the middle of the field, the groups of four players moved tidily, protecting their space, keeping an eye on the forwards and, when they possessed the ball, kicking it forward short distances, waiting for an opening to send it farther forward to the two attackers. At the back, the two groups of four players formed the defense, moving little but shifting position slightly to guard the ground around them from penetration by the attacking players.

The rhythm of the game was easy to follow, almost musical in its pattern of slow, staccato movement followed by sudden rushes of high-energy sprinting. The ball was mostly on the ground, the players' feet caressing it and coaxing it forward or sideways until it had to be sent forward, floating above everyone. Then, the opposing players would rise in the air, trying to change its direction with a glance of the head. There was a simple elegance to it all. I noted that some players were big-boned, hefty men, while others were skinny, almost frail, all legs and lungs, like greyhounds.

I knew that it was a kind of theater I was watching. I was only nine years old, but my dad had been involved with amateur theater for years, and I'd spent many an evening sitting in tiny theaters, church halls or the back rooms of pubs, watching one-act plays about farmers and their wayward sons and daughters, or drunken husbands who came to rue the day they'd tasted their first drop of drink. The intimacy of the theater matched the intimacy of the soccer field, the players enacting their roles with intense concentration. The players had to think fast, with their feet and heads, and probe the space in front of them, searching for ways to move the ball that would cause panic in the other team. I was hypnotized by the rhythm of it.

My dad was also a fiercely Gaelic man, a proud speaker of the Gaelic language and supporter of the Gaelic games. I'd been to hurling matches in Tipperary, and at first been unnerved and then bored by the ferment of the crowd and the packed action on the field, which was hard to follow if you were small and trying to see everything. Gaelic hurling and football were about town against town, village against village or county against county. All everybody did was roar for the local men on the field, men who worked in the local shops or factories and represented them. That was the only point of going to a game—the shouting and braying that Nenagh was the best, or shouting "Come on, Tipp!" when Tipperary played. On the field were two groups of fifteen players, and the contest seemed chaotic. Height and strength mattered, and big lads with barrel chests tore up and down the field. In Gaelic football, the men kicked the ball with all their might; in Gaelic hurling, they whacked the ball hard with their sticks, all frantic energy and force. Yet when somebody scored, he looked self-conscious, as if he hadn't really meant to do that, while the crowd roared in appreciation. It didn't seem to make sense. And for all the intensity and noise of the crowd, I had the feeling that it was inconsequential. Outside of two towns or counties, nobody would really care what happened.

This soccer was different. It seemed aloof, more about tactics and skill than brute strength. The players were of all shapes and sizes. A small man could beat a big man with the skill and speed of his feet. The game had a spare, uncomplicated grace. It seemed to radiate the purest form of exhilaration in running, kicking and following a rolling ball along green grass. And it was more difficult to score than in the Gaelic games because the goal was smaller; yet because it was more difficult, the intensity of effort was greater. The game required thinking, agility and tactics. The cadence and pulse of it seemed connected to something outside of my experience. The players would have to be outlaws of some kind to indulge in a game that was condemned so often by all the priests and teachers. I didn't know what *debauchery* meant any more than I did *illicit*, yet I had a child's unerring sense that what I was watching was forbidden because it had a languid, honeyed pleasure to it. It tasted good, tempting and new. Besides, the Gaelic games seemed to me to be all wrapped up in the rigid tally of things that defined Irishness and we were all supposed to support— the Church, the priests, the Christian Brothers, going to confession on Saturday and Mass on Sunday. Soccer was the forbidden thing. It wasn't hearty and Irish, it was foreign, and on that Sunday, it seemed delicious.

The experience was like the shock and pleasure of the first glancing kiss from a first love, from a woman who could make a man silent, excited, thrilled and always enthralled. I would spend a life in search of that pleasure. I'd seek it out, and everywhere it would be with me, the bliss of it. Here and there, across countries and continents, I'd find it. I'd change, and Ireland would change, but the bliss of that first kiss stayed constant.

CHAPTER 2

IT'S ONLY A GAME

THIRTY-FIVE YEARS LATER, in 2002, that illicit first look at soccer and all the feelings it evoked are coming back to me in a rush, a reverie of emotion and wonder, as I stand outside a huge soccer stadium in Japan.

I'm studying a Japanese police officer who's doing his best to look menacing. In addition to his uniform, heavy boots and cap, he's wearing a sour look on his face. His eyes are fixed in a permanent, hostile glare. His movements are brief and abrupt. With one hand he's directing limousines into the stadium, and with the other he's halting pedestrian traffic. He stares hard at the pedestrians as more and more gather, waiting to be allowed to move on. With his colleagues, he has trained for this—the expected arrival of soccer hooligans and rowdies, giant crowds of deranged young men who might turn violent in the blink of an eye, begin ripping up paving stones and start a riot. He looks every inch the man who's ready for it.

Today, mind you, the menacing look isn't working. It is utterly useless, and he's just beginning to know it. Nobody has prepared him for what he actually faces on this sunny afternoon: elderly women with their grey hair dyed green; entire multigenerational families with the children dressed as leprechauns. As the line of limousines slowly turns, a couple and their young child stand at the front of the group of pedestrians. All three are dressed entirely in green. The father is carrying his daughter on his shoulders;

while he waits to cross, he smiles at the police officer. There is
no response. He smiles again, and I can see the light of mischief
in his face. He says, "Hello. A grand day for it." Nothing doing.
Then he says to the child on his shoulders, "Say hello to the
man, Nora." Nora, aged about eight, pushes her giant green top
hat out of her eyes, smiles a wide smile and waves her little hand.
"Hiya!" she screeches. The police officer looks mortified. The
facade of toughness evaporates. He looks awkward and unsure.
He can't wave back, can't smile—he wasn't trained for that. The
limousines stop coming and he waves the pedestrians across, but
there is no assuredness in his gesture. "Thanks, boss," the father
says as he passes the officer. Nora perks up. "You'll never beat
the Irish!" she says emphatically, looking down at the officer.
The officer stands with his hands on his hips, then hitches up
his trousers and moves uneasily from foot to foot. He looks at
the long approach to the stadium from the nearby city and all
he can see, as far as the horizon stretches, is green. He's looking
at the Green Army on the march, and I can tell that it perplexes
him. He doesn't know what to do with himself. It looks like the
entire population of Ireland, every man, woman and child, has
descended on this small Japanese city to irritate him with their
smiles, their laughter and their songs.

I watch this little tableau unfold from a few feet away. I've just
left the media center at Ibaraki Stadium, next door to the VIP
entrance where the limousines were headed. After being inside
for an hour, sitting among hundreds of journalists who were
writing, gossiping and killing time before the announcement of
the team lineups, I'd grown anxious, hungry for a real taste of
the occasion. It was stultifying in there. So I'd left and wandered
outside. I follow the Irish fans on their march down the street
and across to a park. I have waited years for this.

On this day, I'm at the World Cup, the biggest sporting event
in the world. It's being held in Asia for the first time, Ireland has
qualified for the third time, and after watching the Irish team
play in Dublin through the long, dark years of the 1970s, and
having seen them play on TV from afar in the 1980s, and having

watched in dizzying amazement as the Irish surged to tournament berths in 1990 and 1994, I am finally present at an Ireland game at a World Cup. I'm a journalist and a fan, and I'm a child all over again. Ireland is playing Germany, who are three-time champions, in the first round. Both countries have already played one game: Ireland has drawn 1–1 with Cameroon, while Germany has thrashed Saudi Arabia 8–0. The stakes are high. Ireland needs a win or a draw to stay in the tournament. Germany can't afford to lose, with Cameroon still waiting.

Just a few minutes' walk away from where the comically stern police officer is presiding, I find a fabulous party going on in the park. The local population has welcomed the Irish and Germans with a joyous, welcoming celebration. They're putting on a show with local singers, the children's choir, and Japanese drumming and dancing—and some of them are even dressed up as ninjas, for a laugh. There's beer for sale, and it's cheap, for Japan, but the Irish and the Germans, famous beer drinkers and all, are not getting wildly drunk. Everybody is too busy watching the concert, eating the local food, posing for pictures with the residents, playing soccer with the kids and thoroughly enjoying themselves. There appear to be several thousand Irish supporters and a few hundred Germans. The Irish vastly outnumber the Germans and probably outnumber the welcoming citizens of Ibaraki.

The Irish embassy has even set up a booth to deal with travel problems, explain the local rules and regulations and generally help out. Little wonder—this afternoon, more than the entire population of many Irish towns is hanging around in this part of Japan. The entertainment starts with a gloriously awful pop band doing covers of Beatles tunes. The singer's English is as good as it gets from mastering Beatles lyrics, and he even puts a twist to the lyrics of "All My Loving." He ends by belting out, "And I'll send all my women to you." There are roars of approval from the groups of young men sitting on benches, and considerable giggling from the groups of young Irish women sitting or stretched out on the grass, away from the stage.

There is wild applause for the children's choir, especially when their teacher, a woman dressed in a traditional Japanese outfit, announces that the next song is called "It's a Small World." A group of Germans in lederhosen stamp their feet and shout in agreement. One stands up and ostentatiously shakes hands with all the Irish supporters nearby. There is silence as the little boys and girls sing their song about it being a small world. When it ends, there is a standing ovation, much whistling of appreciation and a cacophony of hollering. For a few seconds, the school-teacher looks terribly uncertain, taken aback, but her hesitant smile becomes a delighted grin as she feels the wave of emotion sweep towards the tiny stage. An Irish supporter, dressed bizarrely as a bishop in flowing green robes and with an orange-colored miter sitting precariously atop garishly green hair, leaps to his feet, calling for an encore.

I wander around, agog at the scene. Some kind of joyous lunacy has been let loose here. Not a harsh word is being spoken. The only rivalry is over the level of friendliness the two sets of fans can exhibit. The Germans are competing with the Irish to charm the locals. A Japanese mother and father watch closely as their son, perhaps five years old, is presented with a giant plastic blow-up hammer by an Irish supporter. Along the side of the hammer are the words, "You'll never beat the Irish." A German asks to pose for a picture with the boy and the Irish supporter. I watch as he takes off his little hat with a feather in it and places it gently on the boy's head. The parents take pictures of the boy with his Irish hammer and German hat and the two grinning soccer supporters beaming at them. Hardly a word is spoken. The scene unfolds in smiles, gestures, handshakes and bows. The field in which all this is taking place is enveloped in a benign energy, swaddled in affability. Even as time passes and the game itself grows closer, no tension surfaces.

I watch a photographer from Agence-France Press take photographs of the Irish and German fans. As far as I can tell, he's the only other reporter there. I see him gather a group of Germans, stocky guys in their leather pants and suspenders, and line them up beside a group of young Irish fans in skimpy bathrobes liberated from their hotel. They're wearing the bathrobes over green underpants and T-shirts. In each case, the hems of the bathrobes are at mini-skirt level. I can see what the photographer wants—a line of Irish and German guys, all with their knock-knees exposed, linked arm-in-arm: German, Irish, German, Irish. The Irish guys, determined to be dead cool, keep a straight face. Then one German starts giggling as he puts an arm around the Irish guy beside him, and in a second they all collapse into giggles. Even the photographer fails to keep his cool and starts laughing.

In a corner of the field, I find that someone in the Irish contingent has produced a soccer ball and proposed a game—Ireland versus Germany. About ten Irish guys rouse themselves and announce that they are ready for it. Two Germans in lederhosen proclaim they are ready to represent Deutschland. One sets off to gather some others. Eventually, it becomes a seven-a-side game. Jackets and sweaters are piled, in the traditional manner, to represent the goal posts. Then they go to it. Seven Germans in lederhosen, one of whom is at least fifty years old, huff and puff in a mad scramble against a team of absurdly outfitted Irish guys, including a very large leprechaun. After a few minutes, one Irish player leaves the game, exhausted either by cramps or laughing, or both. The substitute who takes his place is about ten years old, also dressed as a leprechaun, with a giant top hat, false beard, green shorts, and green socks and shoes. The game lasts about twenty minutes. It is a 2–2 tie, with the junior leprechaun being gallantly allowed to score a goal shortly after his debut. Then it is time for the real game, inside the big concrete stadium that had loomed over the afternoon party.

I make my way back to the media center and frantically write down some impressions of what I have seen. But I know in my heart that I'll never forget it. I'm only afraid that the delight, the feeling that I had just attended the best party I'd ever been at, might eventually evaporate. After writing quickly, it's up the long, steep stairways I climb, to the media seats. There is a magic moment in that journey, at all international games, and it's not confined to the reporters. Everyone who attends a game in some country far from home has the same breathtaking experience. There is the tedious process of lining up and crossing through security and the ticket takers. There is the march up and up the steps towards the entrance to the designated area for the tickets, the noise inside the stadium getting louder with each step. And then there's a moment when the core of the stadium itself is entered, the green field below is suddenly unveiled, the smell of the damp grass rises and the sight and sounds of the crowd come as an all-enveloping sensual shock.

This is the arena where enchantment, mayhem or frustration will unfold. It's an evening game, and under the stadium lights the field looks pristine, lush and soft, awaiting the presence of the two sets of adversaries to devour it. The supporters in the stands are there already, singing and chanting in second gear, flirting with each other as one chant brings a response lesser or stronger than what was expected. They feel each other out, waiting for the moment when the teams march onto the pitch and the real vocal battle begins. As you arrive, the majesty of the occasion is evident and touches every part of the senses. Only the dullest heart would be unmoved by it. When you enter the stadium at a World Cup game, you know that around the world, on every continent, there are tens of millions of people waiting for the television pictures of this place to appear on the screen. They wait and watch, thrilled and tense about the game to come, but if you are there in the stadium, you feel and see what television cannot communicate. You are overwhelmed by the noise, the sights, the sounds and smells—by the spectacle.

I'm seated in a small row of seats reserved for the Canadian press corps. But I'm the only Canadian there, so there are empty seats on either side of me. Below me are journalists from Taiwan; behind me from Malaysia. I can see the Irish reporters away to my right, in the best seats, overlooking the center of the field, and the German journalists beside them. Some Irish reporters, already familiar with the cool nights in Japan, are in jackets and sweaters. One is wearing a scarf and a cloth cap. He looks stonily at the Irish supporters who are beginning to fill the stadium with noise. The Germans start with a few massed shouts of "Deutschland!" The Irish listen to this, measure its volume and, many times louder, begin chanting, "Ireland! Ireland!" and easily out-bellow the Germans. The Irish journalists begin taking notes.

Then the players wander onto the field for the pre-game warmup, and the noise in the stadium is deafening. The players from both sides kick a ball around. Some do stretching exercises. The two managers stroll about their respective halves of the field, each taking certain players aside for a quiet word. The Irish manager, Mick McCarthy, looks self-conscious, as he always does, carrying the air of someone who is intensely aware that thousands of people are watching his every gesture and he is struggling not to be spooked by it. Then the players troop back to the dressing room. And the Irish supporters begin muttering among themselves. I know what they are saying. It hadn't been mentioned all afternoon at the party. Nobody said anything about what was on their minds; they pushed it back, out of fear, bewilderment and exhaustion at the possibility that the subject would arise again. One man is missing from the team that marched onto the field, kicked the ball around and limbered up. One man is missing from the team that has walked briskly in the cool air back to the dressing room. His absence looms large. He was once the captain, the engine of the team. Some said, in the days that followed his shocking departure, that he had dragged Ireland to the World Cup on the strength of his own fierce willpower and rage. Some said the team, once there, would be lost without him.

The missing man is Roy Keane. Two weeks earlier, at the Irish training camp on the tiny island of Saipan, Keane became upset and begat a drama that tore Ireland asunder. He didn't like the training conditions in Saipan and complained about them in an interview with the *Irish Times*. He also cast aspersions on the commitment of other players. A team meeting was called, and the sound of the resulting argument still echoes throughout the soccer world. Keane called Mick McCarthy some unprintable names and McCarthy fired him from the team. Keane, the captain of Manchester United, has been universally acknowledged as one of the great midfield players on the planet. He's the only world-class player Ireland can claim.

In the absurdly euphemistic language of sports reporting, Keane is usually described as "fiercely combative." The *Irish Times*, a paper with literary leanings, likes to describe him as "unknowable." In other words, a great player and a man aggressively competitive, mischievous, driven and choleric. The shock of his departure was stunning. It has driven some people in Ireland mad with rage and disappointment. In Ireland they've been calling the division of opinion about Roy Keane a civil war. One side says he's a disgrace; he's abandoned his country, his teammates and his manager. The other side says Keane is correct in his complaints about second-rate training facilities and preparations and is justified in his sneering at players who aren't as focused and driven as he was. He should have been accommodated, not dismissed. According to his adherents, he represents excellence, while Mick McCarthy and many of the players represent the old Ireland of the cheerful shambles, all enthusiasm and little discipline. Keane is the Celtic Tiger personified, ruthless and aggressive. He is the twenty-first-century Irishman. He's the present and the future.

The ten thousand Irish fans in Japan don't really want to know. They've traveled far and invested their emotions in the Irish team, with or without Roy Keane. The bickering over him is a wound best ignored, left untreated, an argument for another day. They will swaddle the Irish team with affection and support. This is about Ireland, a small country on the big stage of the World Cup.

In the few minutes before the game begins, the massed Irish supporters start their communal singing. They sing what they always sing when Ireland appears on the world stage in soccer tournaments, a ballad called "The Fields of Athenry." It's a beautiful, simple, powerful statement about the Irish Famine.

It tells the story of a man who was jailed and is being deported to Australia for the crime of stealing corn, "So the young might see the morn." Then it paints a picture of the desolate fields where the famine had devastated the population. It is a song of commemoration and defiance. I hadn't expected this, the unearthly sound of the communal rendition of a sung story about death and desolation. I know all about the great famine of the 1840s and the million dead, Ireland brought to its knees by the devastation. It was a long, long time ago, yet something compels these thousands of Irish people to sing of it, together, in a place far, far from home. I know in my Irish heart what it means. It means the Irish will not and cannot forget that horror and will commemorate it now, with the world paying attention.

The song is profoundly moving when sung together by thousands of people. I'm lost in it. My skin tightens and the hair rises on the back my neck. It's the chorus, sung in low tones, that forces home the message: *Our love was on the wing / We had dreams and songs to sing / It's so lonely round the fields of Athenry.* It captures the sense of loss and devastation with simple, overwhelming eloquence. In the chill air of Ibaraki, it is heart-scalding. The German fans sit quietly, listening in stunned awe. As well they might.

It isn't about them or aimed at them. It's about Ireland's past. The future can wait for a few minutes while the past is asserted. That's part of the complicated meaning of the World Cup. There is an elaborate synergy between the traveling fans and their country's team. A nation projects itself, all its hopes and dreams and tangled histories, onto the team. And the team somehow embodies all the complex characteristics of the nation. The nation's social and political sinews are visible, starkly exposed, at a World Cup, because the tournament transcends a sporting event—it's way, way more than that. The smaller the country, the greater the thrill to be there, and the more intense the involvement in the game, the team and the tournament. Logic lapses, emotion rises and the psychology of a country is dangerously poised between joy and despair. Sometimes, even wars cease to accommodate a World Cup.

For the duration of the tournament, what happens outside of soccer seems inane, not worth the trouble. In Ireland's case in 2002, the new war over Roy Keane is about soccer, but it is also about the society from which he and the team have emerged, a society in the midst of casting off the shackles of the past, yet unwilling to forget. Like a person conflicted over leaving an abusive relationship, Ireland is arguing fiercely with itself.

Ireland, a tiny country of three million people and a bit, has strutted twice before at the World Cup, and twice there has been immense pride in the bedraggled country's success. Every Irish person in Ibaraki knows that. Now, in its third outing, the bedragglement is almost gone. In a decade, Ireland has risen from one of the poorest countries in Europe to something close to riches, sophistication and opulence. Its youth are cocky and cosmopolitan. The young can embrace the old images of leprechauns and priests with a sense of irony. Those signifiers of a rural, backward country, seen all over the park at the afternoon party, are jokey symbols to wear for a World Cup game in a distant country and then discard. While the young wear them, they do it knowingly, with intuitive irony. When Keane was part of the team, he was one of them, impatient with the past and the second-rate. And yet, now that he has walked away from what he despised, few of those who have traveled all the way to Japan can bring themselves to criticize the team he left behind. Anchored down in Ibaraki with a game to attend and a team to support, the Irish draw from something deep in the distant, appalling past to signal defiance, to remind the world that they had suffered, survived, battled and triumphed.

The singing stops just as the players emerge from the tunnel for the game. With every footfall they make, my own and Ireland's step-by-step soccer journey from the past, from that summer Sunday in Longford to this night in Ibaraki, comes back to me, easily and vividly.

"YOU'LL NEVER BEAT THE IRISH"

WHEN I FIRST PLAYED SOCCER in a Carrick schoolyard, I played it fast, like the other boys. We were engaged by the speed of the game and we tested ourselves. It suited us, with all our pent-up energy. We wanted to run like lightning with the ball, and we had to make the ball disappear quickly should a Christian Brother come along. Away from the schoolyard, we tried to play like George Best, the man from Northern Ireland who looked like one of the Beatles and played soccer like a young god. Fleet of foot and able to dance and glide with the ball, he was, the newspapers said, like poetry in motion. We'd only see him on television every now and then, when his team, Manchester United, was on, but we knew what he was and what he meant: soccer was sexy and he was an Irishman. Carrick was near to Northern Ireland, less than an hour away by car, so the place wasn't strange to us. We knew that Georgie Best was an annoyance to the Brothers and some of our parents. He was from Belfast and Protestant, so to some among us he was hardly an Irishman at all. It was an irritating accident of history and geography that the English papers were full of him and talked about his Irish accent. He was a slight figure, almost girlish in his movement and manner. He was distant, glamorous and brilliant, yet to us boys he was somehow closer than the big, strapping men who worked in the shops in Carrick and played for the Leitrim Gaelic football team. George Best was a boy who wasn't from our ordinary world, but he was all ours in our imagination, a force much stronger than earthbound reality in the minds of small-town boys who had glimpsed a bigger world.

When my family moved to Dublin, soccer was my way into the cliquish world of boys at school and on the streets. In Dublin, boys my age were obsessed with English soccer. Their contempt for the Gaelic games was visceral. Their dads might follow Gaelic football or hurling, but for boys of my age, soccer was the glamorous game. In the suburbs, from spring through autumn, it was all we played. It was street against street, gang against gang, and we copied every move we saw on English television. Some boys spent hours on a field attempting to master the overhead kick. Others practiced dribbling the ball past bushes, flowers, anything that could be used to approximate an opposing player. Some ran up and down the street dribbling a tennis ball, having read somewhere that the great English players honed their skills by playing with the small ball in order to make it easier to control the bigger one. At a local shop, my mother put the weekly soccer magazine *Shoot!* on reserve for me, along with her women's magazine and my sister's favorite publication. If I was sent to collect the magazines, the store owner, an elderly woman from the country, would always say it was a pity I was more interested in soccer than hurling because I'd been born in a great county for hurling champions.

• • • • •

HERE IN Ibaraki Stadium, the stage is set. The flags of Germany and Ireland are carried out with reverence. The officials stand at attention. The center circle of the field is covered, waiting to be ceremoniously unveiled as soon as the game begins. Somewhere, I've heard that there's a crude but powerful symbolism to this: the center circle represents the globe and the ball. It is uncovered, flamboyantly, only when the game will begin and the ball is about to go into play, like the world turning. The two sets of

players walk onto the field in single file. The Irish team I can
name with my eyes closed: Given, Finnan, Breen, Staunton,
Harte, Kelly, Holland, Kinsella, Kilbane, Duff and the other
Keane, young Robbie from Dublin. Then the Germans, the
hardy, skilled and intimidating team that has already defeated
Saudi Arabia with a contemptuous self-confidence: Kahn, Linke,
Ramelow, Metzelder, Frings, Schneider, Hamann, Ballack, Ziege,
Klose and the giant Jancker.

During the German national anthem, the German fans sing
lustily and loudly. Then, during the Irish national anthem, sung
in Gaelic, the stadium reverberates with noise. It sounds like the
entire population of Ireland is singing, filling the stadium with
the sound of an ancient language now almost lost in the mists of
time. The TV cameras move down the line of Irish players, and
the images appear on the giant screen in a corner of the stadium.
The players stand stone-faced and hard-eyed. The goalkeeper,
Shay Given, sings. Most don't. Then I look down at the scene
on the field, and there among the substitutes I see the tall, trim
frame of Niall Quinn, his head thrown back and eyes closed,
singing in Gaelic with all his might.

In Quinny, a veteran player, all legs, elbows, enthusiasm and
long years of playing soccer at English clubs and for Ireland, the
past comes to roost. He grew up in Dublin, the son of country
people, and played Gaelic football and hurling and soccer. He
was good at all three. When he was a teenager, a scout for an
English First Division team had seen him and invited him for a
trial. He went, and was rejected. Returning to Dublin, he went
back to playing the three sports. Then he was invited to England
again, to Arsenal, a team with a long, storied history and much
glory. He made the grade, and he stayed. And when he played
for Ireland I knew that my father, the Gaelic nationalist, looked
out for the sight of Quinn belting out the old anthem in the old
language. It soothed my father's unease about the English
game.

The players take to the field now, kicking a ball around, passing the minutes until the referee, a Mr. Nielsen from Denmark,

blows his whistle and they fall into position. I watch them intently, drawn to their professional confidence and skill, the way Robbie Keane draws the ball to his foot and juggles it, a thing he can control with ease, reminding himself and everyone watching of his gifts, his artistry and adroitness. He'll need it all. Up in the stands, there are banners everywhere. The Irish have set out to make the stadium look and feel like one in Dublin, and they've succeeded. They've used the national flag—the tricolor of green, white and orange—on which to write slogans. KERRY GIRLS ON TOUR proclaims one, and behind it stands a group of young women, their arms raised, their voices joining the cacophony of guttural roaring that comes from the sea of Irish supporters. Another flag declares ASHBOURNE SAYS HOWYA. That's a greeting from a town in Ireland, and one of dozens that announce the presence of people from various country villages, Dublin bars and Cork suburbs. One flag remarks solemnly, but with profound grace, IT'S ONLY A GAME.

The referee blows the whistle, the Irish kick the ball and Robbie Keane sprints forward. I'm watching intently, simultaneously absorbed in the game and remembering the days when Ireland's presence at a World Cup, playing Germany, would have seemed an outlandish idea. The Germans move forward, en masse, and Keane is offside. Two minutes later, the ball flies towards Damien Duff on the left side of the field and he takes off with it. Low to the ground and slithery, Duff just keeps going. His shoulders shift as if he's going to shimmy, and two German defenders are twisting and lost. A panicky German, Carsten Ramelow, eventually composes himself and forces Duff off the ball, but he's too late and Duff still manages to send in a cross that Robbie Keane comes close to meeting. This is encouraging to everyone in the stadium. The Irish are intent on scoring. The Germans begin to press forward. In the nineteenth minute, the ball floats into the Irish penalty area, where the tall Klose is waiting to meet it with his head. Steve Staunton, Ireland's captain now that Roy Keane is gone, intervenes. Klose throws himself to the turf in a transparent attempt to convince the referee

he has been fouled. Staunton looks down at him and begins
shouting words that nobody in the crowd can hear. But it is as
plain as a poke in your eye that he is furious with Klose's
play-acting.

• • • • •

WHEN I first began going to see soccer matches, it was years before
I saw a player take a deliberate dive to the ground and feign injury.
The soccer I grew up with in Ireland was a fast, hard-tackling
game. It was never short on drama, and it had moments of balletic
skill, but it was about speed and perseverance.

I became obsessed with soccer in Dublin. Most of the boys I
knew cared little for the Irish league, with its semi-professional
players displaying rough skills. The other boys figured that if these
players were any good, they'd have been spotted by an English
team and would be playing soccer where it mattered, in England.
For me, an outsider from the country who didn't fit in easily with
middle-class kids, playing those pickup games on the street or in
street-league tournaments in the summer just wasn't enough. I
wanted to see soccer played well, and I became addicted to attending games played in places too poky to be called stadiums. I'd be
watching Drumcondra play Shelbourne on a Sunday afternoon, or
Bohemians play Shamrock Rovers on a Wednesday night, among
a crowd of one or two thousand adults, and I'd love it.

I traveled everywhere in Dublin to see games and became an
expert on the bus routes needed to get to the venues. Decades
later, I read Eduardo Galeano's book *Soccer in Sun and Shadow*
and found this sentence in the opening pages: "Years have gone
by and I've finally learned to accept myself for who I am: a beggar
for good soccer. I go about the world, hand outstretched, and in
the stadiums I plead: A pretty move for the love of God." I read
that with the thrilling shock of recognition. At the age of twelve,
I too was a beggar for good soccer, a mendicant weekend drifter
in Dublin pursuing the pleasure of the sweet move, the ball lifted
with elegance and cleverness, the goal that came from a pretty

fluency between players. I only found it now and then, but the
anticipation was always worth it.

• • • • •

ON THE field now, the Germans look cocky, causing some panic
in the Irish defense. Michael Ballack, the handsome midfielder,
floats the ball towards the Irish goalmouth. Gary Breen, the
gangly Irish defender, watches the ball come towards him but
fails to see Klose, who slips by him, meets the ball by the penalty spot and heads it past a surprised Shay Given in the Irish
goal. The Germans have scored. Ireland is a goal down after
twenty minutes. Yet the Irish team is only briefly deflated, and
the Irish supporters only stop singing for a few seconds. They
know what I know: this is how the Irish like it, actually. Backs
to the wall, down a goal and fighting back. It's what they do
best. Something always stirs in the Irish in these moments. The
urge to prove the world wrong, perhaps. Knock the Irish down
and they come back, with a fury of hard work, fueled more by
a spirit of defiance than tactical maneuvers.

• • • • •

BACK WHEN I was a boy, the idea of Ireland playing in a World
Cup was absurd, the dream of a mad few in Dublin bars. One
October night, not long after we moved to Dublin, I went to
see Ireland play Denmark in a qualifying game for the European
championship. My dad took off his Fáinne, the pin that signi-
fied his membership in the Gaelic League, a Gaelic-speaking
organization, and came with me. He was worried about me
going to a game with a big crowd, and I hadn't been able to
persuade any friend to come with me. We stood on the terraces
at dilapidated old Dalymount Park and watched Ireland play a
ragged but determined game against a speedy Danish team.
Denmark scored first, and the half-full stadium went quiet. Then
Ireland's best player, Johnny Giles, scored from a penalty kick
and things livened up slightly, but from the opening moments

a fog had begun enveloping the damp, dank old stadium. As the game went on, it was impossible to see the opposite end of the field. Shortly after the start of the second half, with the game tied 1–1, the referee halted the game. The crowd shuffled off into the Dublin fog. I think my dad was relieved that he'd only been obliged to spend less than an hour at the rundown Dalymount watching soccer, a game that made him fretful. In the years that followed, I began to see that game as symbolic. First, my dad agreed to accompany me, and second, Irish soccer would drift away in a fog of bad luck, ineptitude and low expectations. It would be years and years before the fog lifted, and then it would be thanks to an Englishman.

• • • • •

ALL OF the Irish players on the field below me play their soccer for English clubs, and most play for mid-level clubs, not the star-studded teams in London and Manchester. They're no superstars, with Roy Keane absent, but one or two are truly gifted. Right now, I'm watching every move by Damien Duff, who is beginning to wage a one-man war against the German defense. Duff plays for Blackburn Rovers in England, a once-great team now lacking in dazzle. From my schoolboy days I remember that the Rovers team has a beautiful crest, with a red rose set in a blue circle and the Latin motto *Arte et labore*, which means "By skill and labor." Duff is all that. Time and time again, he moves the ball down the left wing, dodges defenders and readies himself to shoot or pass to the nearest Irish striker. He slips easily past one, then a second opponent, but soon the Germans are sending two or three defenders to stop him.

He's galvanizing to watch, the endless shifting of his hips and shoulders as he feigns moving one way and then the other, leaving the Germans with only one option: they keep pushing him over or throwing their feet wildly at the ball to stop him. He falls, as I watch, and the referee calls for a free kick. Duff stands there, hands on hips, eyeing the German formation, unbothered, unmoved by their attempts to crush him. He's determination personified. He's short—tiny, even—yet oblivious to the size of hulking men trying to take the ball from him. In a mad flurry of play, the ball comes to him again and he races forward. The big German striker Jancker rushes back to tackle Duff. Jancker is six foot, four inches tall, a giant of a man, called Jancker the Tanker by the German fans. Duff skips past him as Jancker lunges and crashes to the ground. Me, I'm on my feet now, all journalistic objectivity gone. Before I know it, I'm roaring, "Go on Duff, go on! Give 'em the Irish style!" The ball flies from Duff's feet towards the German goal and Oliver Kahn, the German goalkeeper, races to punch it away. His fingertips divert the ball. The Irish attack has come to nothing again, but the Germans look shaken. The three reporters seated in front of me have turned and are staring at me. I don't much care; I'm enjoying this. The pretty moves, the skills, are thrilling to me. It's halftime and the Germans look relieved as they leave the field.

• • • • •

MY INTEREST in soccer waned as I became a teenager. I rarely read *Shoot!* magazine and rarely played. I was never a great player anyway, but I was a clever one. It was the ability to predict that made me useful in games. While the other boys focused on their own skills and on running hard, I saw the patterns, the predictability of the opposition. In one game in a street league, I was positioned on the right wing, at the back, as usual. But I liked to wander forward, which irritated the team captain and the coach, if there was one there. In this game, I'd wandered up into the opposing team's half and had my back to the goal as my team took a free kick. I'd watched my teammate take these kicks a dozen times. He hadn't much strength, and the ball always went exactly the same distance. I knew it would land near me. The opposing team wouldn't know that; they'd watch until the ball seemed to drop and then run towards it. As the ball was being struck, I shouted, like a schoolteacher, at one of our strikers, "Move!" and pointed in the direction I wanted him to go. Startled by the tone, he obeyed. As the ball landed at my feet, just as I'd figured, I flicked it sideways, straight to the feet of the striker. The defenders were too slow to react and the striker, with only the goalkeeper to beat, scored easily. The striker walked over to me, delighted with himself, but puzzled. "How the fuck did you know?" he asked. I shrugged, muttered about the pattern I'd seen and said it was just lucky, but I knew it wasn't. Sometimes, soccer is a simple game, made complicated by those who don't see its simplicity.

Just as I became less intensely interested in soccer and more enamored of pop music, girls and poetry, the game itself declined in popularity in Ireland, even in Dublin. The conflict in Northern Ireland intruded on everything and made people unsettled about paying attention to the English game. Gaelic football rose in popularity. At the same time, somewhat bizarrely, Ireland's national soccer team began to improve. A handful of talented young players had succeeded in England, and Ireland made a good run at qualifying for the 1978 World Cup. Liam Brady, a Dublin youth with a name more Irish than mine, was a star in England playing for Arsenal, and he made the Irish team look peculiarly sophisticated. When I was a university student and worked for a summer in England, I went to see him play for Arsenal, but kept my mouth shut on the terraces at Highbury in case my accent invoked any anti-Irish reactions in the crowd around me. I saw Brady orchestrate the game with an innate assuredness. It looked like he could see four moves ahead, and he made every other player look like an amateur. I took that memory with me for years, nurtured it and in my fantasy saw Brady leading Ireland towards a glorious future of beautiful soccer.

• • • • •

THE PLAYERS have returned to the field in Ibaraki. I wonder what Mick McCarthy said to them at the break. A few words would have been enough: "You'll never beat the Irish." From the kickoff they resume their relentless attempt to score and equalize. Most of the play is in German territory. Duff keeps making dazzling runs, moving the entire Irish team forward. The German designated to stop him, Thomas Linke, looks seriously worried and wears a permanent frown. Time and again the Irish try, but every time Duff or Robbie Keane manages a shot, it goes wide or Oliver Kahn stops it. The focus on attacking means the Irish are left exposed at the back. Twice, the Germans almost score. Jancker the Tanker is gifted with a scoring chance, and only his ungainly movements prevent Germany from getting another goal. The Irish fans are singing themselves hoarse now. The sound from the stands is raw, frantic and never-ending.

• • • • •

IN 1900, I left Ireland for Canada. There, soccer became a few paragraphs of news once a week in a newspaper and an occasional game from Italy on an obscure TV channel. I read the scores from England every week, and much was left to my imagination. But some events were clear. English soccer was in decline. There was trouble on the terraces, riots in foreign cities and people killed when the English hooligans went berserk. Margaret Thatcher was disgusted. English teams were banned from European competitions. Even talking about soccer at my university in Toronto was a hopeless cause. To my fellow graduate students, soccer meant hooliganism and madness in distant places. And yet I knew there was a segment of Toronto's population that probably saw soccer as I did. They were Italian or Portuguese men and youths. They sat in smoky bars and social clubs on weekends, discussing the games back home in Europe, waiting for the results to come. I heard about this world, but was unsure how to penetrate it.

Still, sometimes, soccer could sustain me. There were glimpses of it. Once, when I went to get a haircut in Toronto from an Italian barber near where I was living for a while. While sitting in the barber's chair, I saw a photo of the Juventus team taped to the wall. Within minutes I was enjoying a long, meandering conversation about the game. I started talking to the barber about Italian teams I'd seen play on TV in Dublin. I mentioned Liam Brady, who had left England to play for Juventus in Italy. The barber stood back, said, "Ah, Brady!" and blew a kiss into the air. It took him ten minutes to cut my hair; it was an hour before I left the barber shop. And I was glad then that I'd gone to Canada.

• • • • •

THE PACE of the game is now relentless. It's end to end as the Irish attack and the Germans counter-attack. Mick McCarthy makes a double substitution: Niall Quinn and Steven Reid come on while Gary Kelly and Ian Harte go off. This is a telling change, and every Irish fan knows it. Bringing on the tall, aging Quinn is like resorting to calling on your bigger, older brother for help in a fight. Quinn has a back injury, so he can't play full games, but his job is to use his height and cunning to get the ball to Robbie Keane. Immediately, that pattern is played out.

• • • • •

ONE DAY at the library in Toronto, I read in an English newspaper that Jack Charlton had been appointed manager of the Irish national team. This astonished me. Charlton was a legend in English football, the gangly brother to Bobby Charlton of Manchester United and a member of England's team that won the World Cup in 1966. He was English to the core, and part of English soccer royalty. I wondered if anyone in Ireland was as stunned as I was, or if anybody was even paying attention. A year later, while scanning the international soccer results in the Sunday edition of the *Toronto Star*, I was stunned to realize that Ireland had qualified to play at Euro 88, the European tournament that is a mini–World Cup for European countries. I was speechless for a while. My girlfriend asked me something, and I couldn't speak. Something had happened that I couldn't explain to anyone.

• • • • •

TIME IS passing quickly in Ibaraki now. The game is evolving into a bewitching encounter, a classic. The Irish are so determined, never ceasing in their pursuit of a goal. The Germans have found the fluidity of the counter-attack. The stadium is a living, breathing thing, the players are floating on the roar of the crowd, the supporters are rapt, in the ecstatic state that comes from knowing the players are theirs to will towards a victory. Duff is still determined to defeat the German defense on his own. He sends in a ball that misses Quinn and lands close to Robbie Keane. It's between Keane and Oliver Kahn and it's a fifty-fifty chance, but Kahn gets to it first and kicks it far downfield and another German counter-attack begins.

· · · · ·

I **NEVER** got to see Ireland's campaign at Euro 88. But I visited Dublin soon after it ended and bought the T-shirt that half the city seemed to be wearing. It declared, simply, *ireland 1 england 0, stuttgart, june 14 1988*. The Euro 88 tournament had changed everything. The dream of Ireland playing at an international tournament, a dream harbored by a lonely few, had become a reality. It was a surreal enough reality—the man responsible was a tough-talking, garrulous English gent driven by simple ambition. Jack Charlton wanted Ireland to win, to qualify for tournaments and enjoy itself. He'd also done something strange and maddeningly simple in building an Irish team to suit his purposes. He'd trawled through English soccer looking for players with an Irish background, a parent or grandparent who was originally Irish. It had been done before as Irish soccer officials grew desperate for talented players, but Charlton was relentless in his search.

The Irish government had long made it clear that someone whose parents or grandparents had left Ireland was entitled to Irish citizenship. It was a token gesture to the children of the Diaspora, the offspring of the millions who had been forced to leave Ireland in the grimmest days of its history, but Charlton turned it into something extraordinarily tangible. Good players in England who had Irish ancestry were offered the chance to play at the highest international level and make their parents proud. The team he built was both Irish-born and English-born. Men with Irish names and English accents, who'd never been to Ireland, put on the green shirt and somehow it worked. The English press poured scorn on the tactic, declaring that half the team wasn't Irish at all. The Irish public didn't care—everyone had a cousin in London, Manchester or Liverpool. And when Ireland was drawn to play England in its first big tournament, Ireland won. The Irish had beaten them at their own game. In years to come, academics and intellectuals would speculate that the course of Irish history changed on that day. The Irish people looked at the world differently.

• • • • •

THE GERMAN counter-attack is swift and ruthless. Torsten Frings beats Steve Finnan down the right and sends the ball high and accurately towards Miroslav Klose, unmarked in the center of the Irish area. Klose heads it a fraction too high, and the Irish breathe again, start attacking again.

• • • • •

IRELAND QUALIFIED for the World Cup in Italy in 1990. I made sure I was in Dublin just before the opening game, again against England. Some force other than the luck of the draw had arranged this endless series of battles against England—some force that allowed Irish destiny to be played out on foreign fields, against the old oppressor, by men kicking a ball. On the afternoon of the game, to be played that night in Sardinia, I was in the center of Dublin and, hours before the shops and offices closed, I sensed the noise of the city gradually fading. By midafternoon on O'Connell Street, the city's main thoroughfare, it was eerily quiet and it was easy to hear a certain distinct music coming from department stores and music shops. The song echoed through the emptying streets over and over again, the chorus rising with a roar to a mass chant of *"Olé, olé, olé."*

The city was giddy with expectation. Every man, woman and child was going somewhere to watch the game. The chant of

"*Olé, olé, olé* " came from the Irish team's official song and was heard on buses, in bars, wherever people gathered. The game that night was tense and flowed only in fits and starts. It ended in a draw and was celebrated like a stunning victory. The pubs were packed, loud and teeming with smiling people. Every few minutes the chant started again: "*Olé, olé, olé.*"

After the game against England came another draw with Egypt. Ireland and Egypt share nothing except soccer, yet all of Ireland seemed knowledgeable about Egypt's players and tactics. Then another draw with Holland, a team filled with players of awesome skill and reputations like pop stars. Every draw was exuberantly celebrated. On the days when Ireland wasn't playing, people became passionate about Cameroon, a place that no one could find on a map but had the most gleefully talented players anyone had seen. Cameroon was cheered—"*Olé, olé, olé.*" Ireland was now past the first round and set to play Romania under a scorching sun in Genoa. It was tied after regulation time and still scoreless after overtime. That meant the excruciating, drawn-out tension of penalty kicks. At home, my mother fell to her knees in front of a picture of the Sacred Heart and prayed that Packie Bonner, the Irish goalkeeper, would stop a penalty shot. He did. And "*Olé, olé, olé*" drowned out every other sound in the world.

A few days later, Ireland finally lost to Italy in the quarter-finals, but it didn't matter. It was glorious to watch—the crowd of 100,000 people in the stadium in Rome, the mass of Irish fans singing even as the team lost. The joy of the game had gone to everyone's head. Just being part of the World Cup was magical for Ireland. The 1980s had been an utter misery. The economy was a shambles and thirty thousand young people were emigrating every year. The conflict in Northern Ireland had reached a brutal stalemate with the deaths of IRA hunger strikers. In 1986, a referendum to lift a ban on divorce was defeated. There was endless political instability. A reawakening of hardline Catholic beliefs had caused some people to believe that religious statues were speaking to them. The country was economically poor and mocked as backward. Ireland was demoralized, afraid, neurotic and needy. The World Cup adventure was a tonic, a bizarre, uplifting journey from the wilderness to the final stages of the biggest sporting event in the world. It gave people confidence and joy. One of the songs the Irish supporters sang on that journey included the lines *We have Jack to mind us / And the fans behind us.* That, too, was bizarre and uplifting. The Englishman Jack was minding the team, building it, drawing out a spirit of self-possession and optimism that galvanized everyone in Ireland.

Months later, in the middle of winter in Toronto, I was watching a documentary about the sudden end of Communist rule in Romania. There was a scene of mass confusion in Bucharest as word spread that the dictator Nicolae Ceausescu had fled. At first, there was just the sound of excited chatter and noise as thousands of people crowded the streets. Then, from somewhere in the crowd, a chanting started and spread until it seemed that a million people were singing together in a choir of exultant jubilation: "*Olé, olé, olé, olé, olé.*"

• • • • •

IT HASN'T taken the Germans long to figure out that Niall Quinn is there to get the high balls and pass them on to Robbie Keane. Trying to work this motion, Quinn is fouled by Dietmar Hamann on the edge of the German area. Robbie Keane's free kick is taken quickly and skims the outside of the right-hand post in the German goal. Time is running out. I've stopped looking at the clock. There are about ten minutes left, I reckon, but I don't want to know for sure.

• • • • •

IRELAND QUALIFIED for the World Cup again in 1994, just barely. Charlton's team was aging, his tactics now well known. They were simple enough: play the long ball. That meant the ball was always kicked long and hard from the back towards the other team's defense. The Irish chased after it, unsettling the other team and putting them under pressure. It was kick-and-chase soccer, and it wasn't pretty to watch. It was, mind you, extremely effective, and if the Irish players kept running and chasing, they were hard to beat. In 1994, the World Cup was held in the United States, a venue that was resented by many countries because they knew that Americans didn't care much about soccer. It suited Ireland fine. The Irish had a long history in the U.S., and as far as many Irish people are concerned, the Irish helped build American cities and had thrived there. Tens of thousands of supporters could travel there, and it was a friendly place as far as Ireland was concerned. The first game was against Italy, a daunting game to be played at the huge Giants Stadium in New Jersey, not far from Manhattan. Italy, embarrassed at having failed to win the World Cup when it hosted the tournament in 1990, was a confident team, packed with talent.

What happened on that Saturday was the greatest game that Ireland ever played. Unawed, determined, and relying as ever on the long-ball tactic, Ireland scored early and held on to win. The huge stadium was almost entirely filled with raucous Irish supporters. They watched with increasingly manic joy as the great Italian players—Roberto Baggio, Paolo Maldini and Roberto Donadoni—were bewildered, then curbed and defeated by the unrelenting vigor of the Irish. There followed a tense draw with Norway and a loss to Mexico, but Ireland made it to the next round, where it was hopelessly outclassed by Holland. And yet, the defeat barely mattered. Ireland had again qualified for the World Cup and even progressed beyond the first round. Nobody underestimated Ireland anymore.

• • • • •

THE GERMANS are making substitutions now. Klose, the striker, goes off, a defender comes on. Germany is interested in clinging to this one-goal lead and shoring up its defense against the perpetual Irish attack. Quinn has the ball on the edge of the German box, turns and makes a deft pass to Keane. He has taken two seconds too long. Oliver Kahn grabs the ball.

• • • • •

AFTER THE World Cup in the U.S., Jack Charlton's time was coming to an end, but it took a while for anyone to realize it. The team he'd built was getting older. Other countries could anticipate Ireland's style. It was getting harder to win and, after such success, expectations were high. Ireland was becoming more prosperous, and vast armies of fans would travel anywhere to see the team. No matter how obscure the venue in Eastern Europe, thousands of Irish supporters were there. They always behaved so well, and cheerfully, because there was pride in ensuring that the Irish fans were never mistaken for the hated English hooligans. Every traveling supporter had a stake in the team's success, and an opinion. In 1996, Charlton resigned and was replaced by Mick McCarthy, a seemingly ideal transition. McCarthy had been an Irish player and captain of the team in the remarkable Euro 88 and Italia 90 tournaments. He was a tough, calm defender, a hard man to beat and an English-born player with an Irish name who embraced and embodied the side's long-ball style and never-say-die spirit.

• • • • •

THE GERMAN fans are whistling like mad now, mimicking the sound of the referee's whistle they want to hear to end the game. I know the ninety minutes are almost over, but there's no way I'm looking at the clock or my watch. Quinn does it again: he wins a swerving ball with his head and nods it on to Robbie Keane. Kahn smothers the ball frantically. This is unspeakably tense.

• • • • •

IRELAND NARROWLY failed to qualify for the World Cup in France in 1998, and again for the European championship in 2000. Each time, they missed out by a single goal. There were mutterings in Ireland about McCarthy's tactics, his inability to evolve beyond the long-ball game. McCarthy the manager turned

out to be a taciturn character, admired but never loved as Jack
Charlton had been. Expectations were high as the Celtic Tiger
economy blossomed and soccer-obsessed supporters who could
afford to travel everywhere to see the games looked to Ireland
to qualify for big tournaments. The country and the team stayed
in a sort of communal rhythm, every victory a reason to celebrate
a step forward, every defeat a reason to lament the long stretch
of the horizon that loomed over little Ireland's march out of the
past. Money poured into the soccer associations in Ireland thanks
to the country's share of revenues from two World Cups. Young
Irish-born players emerged. Robbie Keane and Damien Duff
were the stars of teenage teams that were feared by the youth
teams of European soccer superpowers. Roy Keane was the midfield boss of Manchester United, the best club in England and
Europe. He'd take us far, people said, and he did.

• • • • •

THE IRISH players are laying siege to the German goal. I can
sense that there are only seconds remaining for a goal to come.
Somewhere behind me, a journalist is shouting into a cell phone
in what sounds like broken English. He's shouting so loudly and
frantically, I can figure out clearly what he's saying: "The Irish
keep coming. The Irish keep coming. Can they do it?"

• • • • •

AT FIRST, it looked unlikely that Ireland could possibly qualify
for the 2002 World Cup. In its European group it had to play
Holland and Portugal, two of the best, most skilled and star-
studded teams. I watched the qualifying games in Toronto bars—
and once in a Portuguese social club. Roy Keane was so obviously
unimpressed by any team he faced as he marshaled Ireland around
him, shouting and waving at players to defend, move forward,
do his bidding. Sometimes the camera would catch him, red-
faced, furious and barking abuse at a player who'd let him down.
Ireland drew with Holland and drew twice with Portugal. At
the social club, I was the only non-Portuguese watching the

game. The young people around me expected their country to cruise past Ireland, and they found the game frustrating to watch as the Irish declined to wilt. A billboard intrigued them. It advertised the betting company owned by a man named Paddy Power. They looked at it and took it to be a reference to paddy power— some Irish declaration of invincibility. I declined the opportunity to correct them. They were already a little afraid of Roy Keane's intensity.

The game that mattered was the second game against Holland, played in Dublin. I watched it in a crowded Irish bar in the Toronto suburbs. Roy Keane was everywhere in the game, launching sliding tackles against the fleet-footed Dutch forwards, controlling the pace and owning the space around him. A win would almost guarantee Ireland's qualification for this World Cup. Ireland won 1–0, playing with a tenacity and confidence that were unnerving to watch at a distance. When the game ended, we looked at each other in that crowded bar and beamed. Two elderly men stood up, embraced and wept. The team had again fulfilled the needs of the country and its vast diaspora.

In Dublin that day, the TV cameras caught Roy Keane's hard, satisfied but unsmiling face as he left the field. Not for him the giddy, lightheaded joy and celebration. For him, it was job done, a victory achieved through hard work, discipline and care. His stern face said it all—luck had nothing to do with Irish success. In the fourteen years since Ireland had first qualified for a major soccer tournament, the country had changed beyond recognition. It had emerged from the fog of joyless self-absorption and found an adult discipline and confidence. Roy Keane carried all that in his head, in his willpower.

By the spring of 2002, the fact that the World Cup was happening half a world away in Japan and Korea was no barrier to the Green Army's march. The country's soccer supporters had money to travel anywhere and could expect the team to win. Besides, the Irish were everywhere. They were working in Australia, in the U.S., in Thailand, Japan and all over the Middle

East. They would descend on Japan in massive numbers. There
was a cockiness about the Irish press's coverage of the team's
strengths. There was an unabashed assuredness among the supporters. When Keane exploded in rage and walked away days
before the tournament began, he had, it seemed, thrust a stake
into the heart of all that confidence and poise. Now, so much
depended on the strength of the team's need to avoid defeat. So
much depended on the team, the country, succeeding without
him.

• • • • •

GOAL! GOAL! GOAL! Steve Finnan heaves a fast and hopeful long
ball towards Quinn, who glances it onward with his head to
Robbie Keane, who meets it and kicks it forward all in one stride
and smashes it over Kahn in the German goalmouth. The ball
hits the post and surges inside, bulging the net. Without pausing,
Keane is still moving, head over heels, dancing cartwheels across
the field, and time appears to stop as the rolling ball and the
revolving Keane seem to hold the universe in thrall.

For a few seconds, no one is sure it has happened. On the
sideline, Mick McCarthy freezes, then thrusts his arms in the
air. It's over now. The Irish are unbeaten. It's 1–1. They have
fought back, and in the end have proved unstoppable in their
driving need to dissent from Roy Keane's withering contempt
for their skills and resolution. The game restarts, but for only
a few seconds, as the German players move slowly, robotically,
waiting for the referee's whistle to end this searing game. The
Irish supporters are singing, dancing, waving flags in unre-
strained jubilation. There's a massive roar as the referee finally
ends the game. The Irish players hug each other, shake hands
with the Germans and drift over to acknowledge the supporters. They are greeted with an increase in the volume of the
chants of "Ireland! Ireland!" And then, as the players eventually walk off the field, there's the briefest pause in the singing
of the Irish supporters before a new mass chant starts: "Are you
watching, Roy Keane? Are you watching, Roy Keane?"

Damien Duff glances back at them and smiles to himself.

Later, as I'm trying to write my game report, I can hear the Irish crowd gathered outside the stadium, unwilling to leave and let the feeling pass. Their singing comes in waves: "*Olé, olé, olé! Olé, olé!*" They're still hanging around in groups singing when I board the bus for the long trip back to Yokohama. On the bus, I can hear four English reporters talking excitedly about the game. Cynics to a man, they still can't stop telling each other how thrilling it was: "It was a classic, wasn't it?" one asks of the other three. "Fuckin' right," another says. "Worth coming here for, anyway, the Irish. Fuck it. Fuckin' amazing team on the night."

Dawn is whitening the streets of the Tokyo suburbs as I ride in a taxi back to my hotel from the Yokohama media center. The driver takes it slowly, even though there's no traffic anywhere. He turns onto a narrow side street. Not a soul is stirring, not a sound can be heard except the hum of the car moving slowly and steadily from one stoplight to the next. I'm lost, tired, back in Ibaraki hours ago and Longford years ago. Then I'm aware of something stirring, shifting on the silent street. I can sense the driver's intense attention on it before I look. On the hood of a sleek saloon car, a woman in a black cocktail dress is spread-eagled, her long, thin legs startlingly white against the dark, shiny surface, as a bulky, grey-suited man thrusts into her. The driver cackles, looks into the rear-view mirror to catch my eye. "Hey! Hey!" he hisses at me. I look away, ignoring him and everything. I've seen more sensuous glory than this.

PART II

MADNESS: SOCCER *in the* TWENTY-FIRST CENTURY

CHAPTER 1

WORLD CUP 2002, KOREA/JAPAN

IT'S A GREY DAY in late May of 2002 when I land at the airport in Seoul, after fifteen hours of travel from Toronto, for my first-ever sportswriting gig. I've never been to Asia, and the scene at the airport is intimidatingly chaotic. For a moment, I have qualms. I look up through the endless glass roof of Incheon International Airport and wonder how the hell I got here. I'm feeling lost, but vaguely reassured by the fact that the material FIFA sent with my press accreditation had advised that there would be greeters to help arriving journalists at the airport. Somebody would guide me, if not in the reporting and writing, then at least on how to get the bus to the hotel, the wonderfully named Hotel Nostalgia.

Sure enough, the arrivals hall seems to be teeming with young women handing out maps and brochures. One approaches me and asks if I speak English. I acknowledge that I do. Then she hands me some papers and begins pointing at something. I look at the material in my hand. It appears to be a bunch of coupons for shopping in Seoul. In fact, looking around, I see that the dozens of young women are handing the same thing to everybody.

Shopping is the last thing I'm concerned about. Eventually, I find another young woman wearing a broad smile and a T-shirt with the World Cup logo and an official-looking badge. She asks me what hotel I'm going to, and I tell her. She takes me to the

door, points at a bus that will drop me there and gives me a
coupon for free travel on the bus. At least that's what she seems
to be saying. She talks so rapidly and excitedly that I'm not at
all sure what's happening. I proceed, regardless. The bus driver
looks a bit puzzled by the coupon, but he smiles, puts my luggage away in the underside of the coach and waves me on. The
airport is miles from Seoul; there's not much to see in the heavy
grey air and I have time to wonder why I'm here. I'm not a sports
reporter.

The Hotel Nostalgia, it turns out, is located in an out-of-the-
way place and at an awkward intersection, so the driver, after
calling me to the front of the bus, and after much pointing and
gesticulating, drops me off around the corner. He points to the
Hotel Nostalgia and twice indicates the problem in driving up
to the front door. I tell him it's okay. I step down from the door
of the bus, expecting the driver to follow me to get my bags,
but the bus immediately takes off, with my luggage.

There I am, in my first hour in Seoul, chasing a bus down
the street and waving frantically. Nobody on the bus looks back.
The driver can't see me. I give up, walk to the hotel and explain
the situation as best I can. A flurry of telephone calls by the
front-desk staff ensues, followed by what appears to be an urgent
meeting of the entire staff. I'm hoping the meeting is about the
luggage. Next thing I know, I'm being hustled into the hotel's
van and, I soon deduce, we are pursuing the bus that holds my
luggage. We find an airport bus after about an hour, but it's the
wrong one. I know it's the wrong bus because the driver isn't
the man who cheerfully made off with the suitcase. Still, the two
hotel employees in the van insist on searching the bus. The driver
opens the luggage compartment, allowing me and the Hotel
Nostalgia staff to peer inside, but I know it's useless. Back at the
hotel, another conference takes place and more phone calls are
made. Again I'm hustled into the van and we take off at high
speed. To where, exactly, I don't know. An hour and a half later,
somewhere in the suburbs, we stop. It turns out we are at the
bus depot. The man from the hotel makes inquiries and we are

directed to a small wooden hut. There in the hut sits my luggage, guarded by two fellows who seem to have been given a message that Korea's competent handling of the World Cup is on the line. There is much joy among the staff at the Nostalgia when we arrive back with the luggage. I thank everyone as best I can. I'm exhausted. I haul the luggage to my room and go straight to bed.

Hours later, I'm in a deep sleep when there is a pounding on the door. I ignore it, but it doesn't stop. I get up and open the door to find, to my surprise, a swaying Swede. Soon I know it is the only other journalist staying at the Nostalgia, a guy from Malmö who says I can call him Bo. A tall, gaunt man in his mid-forties, Bo has discovered that there is another journalist at the Nostalgia and just wants to say hello. Three sheets to the wind, he's also formed the firm impression that I have liquor, and he makes it clear that he'd like some. I bring him in and give him a good measure of duty-free Canadian rye. We talk about the Swedish team, and I'm hoping Bo will soon go back to his room. But no, Bo wants to talk about NHL hockey, specifically about Mats Sundin and Börje Salming. Eventually, Bo tires. He tells me how to get to the media center I'll be heading for the next day and tells me that getting my press pass will be a breeze. "Very, very efficient, Korea!" he says several times. His parting words are a suggestion that we should visit a nearby establishment the following night, a place he describes as "a businessman's club." He tells me that the girls there are nice and the drinks are cheap. He winks at me as he turns to leave my room. I really don't care about girls, drink, Bo or Börje Salming. I care deeply about sleep. I've discovered that this sports-reporting racket is exhausting.

The next morning, I take a taxi to the huge Coex complex in Seoul, where a nervous young woman takes my photo and processes my press credentials. Another nervous young woman shows me to the enormous room where journalists can sit and write, watch the games on countless giant TV screens and buy phone cards for Internet connections and bland cheese sandwiches to eat.

She doesn't say the sandwiches are bland, but she exclaims in a
tortured, anxious manner that there has to be food to suit all these
journalists from all these countries and you couldn't expect everybody to be eating Korean food, even though Korean food is
truly excellent and worth trying. She talks non-stop in an anxious
manner, eager to please and to create a good impression and,
simultaneously, she's obviously a bit terrified. I'm tempted to tell
her the story of my lost luggage and how it was recovered and
how that indicates that Korea is doing a fine job and everything
will be grand. Before I can say a thing, though, she tells me there
is a basement mall with all kinds of fast food restaurants and shows
me where the real restaurant is located, on another floor, the one
that serves excellent Korean meals, and then she's showing me the
notice board where all the daily activities for journalists are posted.
I thank her while she runs away, and then I stare at the notice
board. One item catches my eye. It seems the French team is
holding a press conference and training session that afternoon,
and I have ten minutes to sign up for it. I do. Now, this is getting into the swim of things.

Next, I head for the Korean restaurant. Going up the stairs, I
realize I am surrounded by a large contingent of the French press.
I pause and watch a group of them enter the restaurant, somewhat warily, and quickly retreat. It's lunchtime, and the place is
packed. We all move en masse to the basement food court. Some
of the French stop and peer into a bar with the charming name
Jug Jug Beer, but most seem to follow me into a place that's an
enthusiastic attempt to replicate an American-style Italian pasta-
and-pizza joint. The French press—like the team they're covering, I figure—fear nothing. They are world champions, after all,
and favorites to win the World Cup again. Invading a faux Italian
restaurant at the other end of the world is just another symbolic
declaration that French soccer dominates Europe and the Italians
had better get used to it. The opening game between France and
Senegal will be played the next day. I smile at a French journalist, slide down the bench beside him and ask what he thinks of
the team's hopes. He shrugs. Then he says coyly that he expects

to be in Korea, and later Japan, for the entire tournament, following the French team's progress to the finals. Even with the
god-like playmaker Zinedine Zidane injured and unable to play
the first two games of the tournament, there isn't an iota of
doubt.

After a bus trip to the outskirts of Seoul in a grey, enveloping
drizzle, we are told upon arriving at a former military training
camp that French manager Roger Lemerre and captain Marcel
Desailly will eventually talk to the press. I have already formed
the idea that the French press conference is a bit odd. It is twenty-
four hours to the opening game of the World Cup and most
teams would shut down, ignore the press and concentrate on the
training and tactics for the game.

It is ages before Lemerre and Desailly show up to talk to the
assembled journalists, about three hundred of us. French photographers have kept themselves occupied taking photos of cute
female Korean police officers. Some of the cops look pleased, but
no amount of flattery—and there is lots of it, in French and
English—can actually get them to smile. Still, some actually look
a tad annoyed when the photographers speed off as soon as
Lemerre turns up. It becomes immediately clear that Lemerre is
at peace with himself and his team's prospects. He speaks very,
very slowly. He refuses to answer questions in English, and lis-
tens solemnly to the translation before thinking hard about his
reply. He exudes confidence, and when asked whether he expects
to win the tournament, he shrugs, thinks for a full minute and
says, "I think we'll be there at the end." An English journalist,
obviously amused by the chummy atmosphere, asks if Lemerre
believes that Senegal is in the same league as the world champions. Lemerre shrugs again and talks about respect for the opposition. Then he shrugs again, for good measure.

Marcel Desailly comes along and is very sophisticated, not at
all the inarticulate soccer player spouting clichés. No one is surprised, certainly not the French journalists. Desailly, born in
Ghana and adopted at age three by a French diplomat, is the
epitome of elegance, on the field and off. The captain of the

team, he answers questions in three languages with ease, and declares modestly that he is hoping to see France get beyond the first round. He declares that Senegal plays a "cheerful" sort of soccer. He is an all-around gentleman about the whole thing.

Then we go to watch the training session for a while. Goalkeeper Fabien Barthez lopes onto the field and over to the goal, and one of the training staff gently kicks balls at him. Barthez is less interested in stopping them than in throwing himself around at challenging angles, just to make sure his body is in good shape for some diving saves. He also keeps grabbing his shorts. Then Thierry Henry, the great French striker, runs over for a minute and aims a few balls at Barthez. Mind you, it soon becomes clear that Henry is showboating, deliberately aiming to hit the crossbar and the upright posts, and he often does. Barthez scowls at him and Henry walks away. It is all so easygoing that the French photographers start taking pictures of female Korean cops again. The female cops, on the other hand, are taken with Emmanuel Petit, who strides around the field with his blond ponytail flying behind him. They don't just smile at him, they giggle. It is so relaxed that I half-expect somebody on the French team to invite us over to his place for a glass of wine and a chat.

Then we are all told to leave. While the last of us troop out, I look over at Barthez, who is busy giving all of us a withering look of utter contempt. He glares at the journalists, spits on the ground and makes a great display of adjusting his testicles inside his shorts. And Marcel Desailly had been such a gentleman.

New as I am to this racket, I'm amused by my glimpse of the world champions. From what I can tell, most of the journalists are saying that the French seem very confident and relaxed. Yet there's something about the French attitude that makes me wonder. The players and manager are entitled to be self-assured— they won the World Cup in 1998, but that was in their home country. They won the Euro 2000 tournament with aplomb and fluid, attacking soccer. Yet they haven't actually played a competitive game in two years—as defending champions, they didn't have to qualify for the World Cup. And they didn't look sharp here; they looked soft. Back in the International Media Center, I write and file a story suggesting that the French are too cocky, too smug, and might be in a for a big surprise. It's just a feeling, but I sense that this World Cup will be full of surprises, and not just for me.

The next day, I'm in a taxi with Bo, going to the stadium for the opening game. Even the grey haze that seems to hang permanently over Seoul has lifted for a while in the late afternoon—the sun has shone for a while and the smog seems less dense. Crossing the Hangang River by way of the cheerfully pink Gayang Bridge, with the newly built World Cup stadium shining in the distance, we are more like two excited fans than journalists. Bo is stone-cold sober and says nothing about the proposed visit to the businessman's club. He suggests that the opening ceremonies will be long and tedious, but he is looking forward to seeing Senegal play. He's never seen an African team in action. Still, he expects France to win handily. He has suspected, he says, that Senegal will be overawed by the occasion. A few hours later, along with the watching world, Bo is gazing at a French team that is in disarray and losing 0–1.

Of course, first comes the opening shindig, which is always less about soccer than about national pride and local culture. The overall theme of the ceremonies is the uninspiring "From the East," meant to highlight Korea's traditional culture and contemporary, leading-edge information technology, as well as the cultures of surrounding countries. Long and intricate, the ceremony features more than 2,300 performers and has four themes: welcoming, communication, harmony and sharing. Much of it, however, resembles a bad Broadway extravaganza. Hundreds of dancers in yellow-and-purple robes move in patterns on the field. Sometimes their formations resemble swaying rows of flowers. Flags are waved and drums pounded. Dozens of young women in bustle dresses take to the field and wave. Children are featured prominently. Then a gaggle of creatures that look like Teletubbies arrive and point their monitor-shaped faces at the crowd. That's the part about contemporary technology, everybody assumes.

There are also two spectacularly inept comedians who give instructions to the crowd about how to enjoy the game. This part of the entertainment suggests that, although soccer is alive and well in Korea, it's not the authentically passionate experience it is for followers of the game in Europe and South America. Still, at the end, it seems everybody has enjoyed the spectacle: the few hundred fans from Senegal cheer wildly and non-stop. The French fans only applaud at intervals. Even the thousand or so dignitaries and heads of state and government, including South Korean president Kim Dae-jung and Japanese prime minister Junichiro Koizumi, look pleased with the event. In part, they must feel relieved. Since FIFA announced the co-hosting arrangement in 1996, both countries had vied for primacy. At one point in 2001, the governing body issued a formal reminder to both countries and the world that the official title was "Korea/Japan World Cup 2002." The bulletin had been prompted by the Japanese organizing committee's tendency to promote the event as the "Japan/Korea World Cup." In the months leading up to the opening ceremonies and first game, tensions between the two organizing camps were evident. Brochures and websites from the Japanese made little reference to the games being held in Korea, even though an equal number of games were being played in each country. At one point, the Japanese committee's website bluntly stated, "Unfortunately, we don't know very much about the venues in Korea." All they had to do was look at the Korean committee's comprehensive site.

But it became clear that Korea and Japan shared one quality in their approach to this World Cup: paranoia about playing host to tens of thousands of visiting soccer fans. Japan focused on the threat of soccer hooligans from England, and elaborate displays of measures against them were made to reassure nervous residents of host cities. In Korea, there was a certain nervousness about the visiting Chinese supporters. Being a good host to an old enemy didn't come easy. Korean television had regularly shown footage of Chinese fans rampaging, drinking and smoking at games in China.

The start of the opening game brought a welcome relief. This always happens at tournaments. The host country or countries are wound tight with anticipation, nervousness about the burden of hosting and taking care of countless details. Then, the game begins and the players run freely with the ball and, by proxy, release everyone from the intense worry.

France begins confidently but slowly. The tactic is simple enough: keep possession in midfield and spray the ball forward towards the two strikers, David Trezeguet and Thierry Henry. Senegal's players, all of whom are unknown to most of the world outside Senegal and the French cities where some earn their living playing for the local teams, look impatient with the unwillingness of the French to increase the tempo. They look speedy, defiant and dangerous whenever they get possession. The striker El-Hadji Diouf keeps springing forward, waiting for a pass whenever Senegal has possession. In minutes it is obvious he could beat any French defender for speed. After about fifteen minutes, though, France is probing forward. Henry plays an elegant pass to Trezeguet, who unleashes a curling shot that seems destined for the back of the net but bounces away off the post. Thierry and Trezeguet look pleased with themselves. The French relax.

Then it happens. Diouf takes the ball and moves like a man possessed down the sideline. His long-legged speed is breathtaking. He crosses quickly. Barthez lunges to grab the ball, but fumbles it, and Papa Bouba Diop, who had rushed into the French area, thrusts out a foot to score. As the sudden *ooooh* of surprise is heard in the stadium, Diop runs to the corner flag, pulls off his shirt, places it on the grass and begins dancing round it. Three Senegal players join him. The goal is an example of scintillating soccer—the speed of Diouf, the fumble in the goalmouth, Diop's quick movement and then the dance. The non-French section of the crowd erupts in joy.

At halftime, the locals are already lining up to be photographed with the colorful, singing Senegalese fans dressed in traditional robes. Throughout the second half, France tries to lay siege to the Senegal goal, but nothing comes of it. Shots are scuffed and sprayed wide, and once Henry hits the crossbar with a headed ball. The longer it goes on, the more desperate France become. When Diouf gains possession, the French seem to freeze, terrified of his speed and agility. It ends with Senegal triumphant, thanks to that one goal. It is a stunning upset, and we all know that the game was great, free-flowing soccer, with only two cautions issued to players, one for each team. The underdogs won, and that was the best spectacle of all. Senegal was once a French colony. Most of the players toil in obscurity in French cities, part of the obscure, bohemian undercurrent of French culture made up of those from former colonies, including musicians and DJs from Guinea and Côte d'Ivoire. The game has had that delicious taste that comes when the former servants upstage the masters in skill and shrewdness. The heft of the game was exquisite.

This much I know: on the soccer field, nations and tribes project their arrogance and their antagonisms. Yet it is a conflict of the mind more than it is a battle imbued with authentic, physical malice. There is a set of rules. Outright violence ends in ignominious ejection from the game—and near-certain defeat for your team. There is acting. Players feign injury or exaggerate their umbrage. The referee plays at being in charge when, in fact, he cannot see everything or rely on his assistants to see or explain every foul, every mistake and injury. On the field and throughout the game, everything hangs in the balance. Anything can happen. Pace, ambition, passion, technical prowess and defensive rigor can unfold suddenly while a team is working in perfect rhythm and a collective ambition unfurls.

It is the speed of thought and deed that often wins games. A sense of cunning can have the same effect. The soccer field is a liminal space and the ninety minutes of the game form a twilight time in which limits can be transcended. There is a profound ritual quality involved in a World Cup game—the expectant crowd, the national anthems, the covering and uncovering of the center circle. At times, it's rather like a purification rite, and this is especially true for smaller countries. The indignities and mistakes of the past can be wiped away. In this zone, where everything is in an in-between state, the players can transcend their limitations to become heroes in the purest sense, and muster those acts of glory that they know will survive in the memories of their descendants.

In this instance, the aristocratic smugness of the French was that of colonists arriving to offer a lesson in elegance and sophistication to the coarse enthusiasts they had once governed. The French hauteur was glaringly obvious from the press conference the day before. And it was undone, on the field, by the purity of natural grace and unstoppable ambition.

I know, too, that this victory has a power that's more delicious than Ireland defeating—or even reaching a draw—with England. Ireland and England are geographically side by side, locked in a perpetual fray that is anchored in countless grudges and hurts. Senegal is part of France's past, and forgotten, probably, by the French. The English have learned to be wary of Irish anger and resentment. France was never wary and is now stunned, humbled and discombobulated.

In the press room afterwards, the French journalists are surly. About an hour after the game, when most of the writers have just filed their stories, the restaurant runs out of food. The French take this as a further humiliation, another sign that this crazy adventure in Korea is going off the rails. Some start shouting at the embarrassed Korean staff in the restaurant, telling them, in English, that they are incompetent. The Koreans smile politely, apologize profusely and offer bottles of water for free. The French are not amused. Something strange is going on.

• • • • •

AT THE Seoul airport, very early the next morning, hundreds of reporters descend on the coffee shop. Me too. Some of us are going to Japan to watch games there, and some are going to various cities in Korea. I'm there extra early, anxious about the flight that should get me to Tokyo and allow just enough time to get to the main railway station and aboard a train to Niigata, where Ireland will play its first game, against Cameroon. I get a large coffee and sit near three squat American servicemen. They sure stand out, in their uniforms and caps. And much more so, as the minutes pass. I watch and listen to their responses to the United Nations of soccer reporters gathering around them. I get the feeling that they are used to being the center of attention and authority, but now, in this new Korea of World Cup fever, they're seriously unglued by the situation unfolding around them. I hear them talk about the World Cup, and one says he's not going to watch it unless the United States is doing well. "Soccer is for kids," another says, with a touching finality, and the other two nod in agreement.

When a tall, ponytailed and swaggering Spanish reporter, a watch-me guy, strides into the restaurant in tight jeans, the three U.S. soldiers involuntarily smirk. I'm glued to their reactions, and I know what they are thinking: to them, the flamboyant Spanish reporter represents the unmanly, weirdly foreign dimension of soccer. A few minutes later, their jaws drop. The Brazilian TV contingent has arrived, with a group of seriously glamorous women at the forefront. A pair of Amazons, gorgeous in their designer clothes, high heels and marvelous hair, sit in the middle of the coffee shop. They drink about a gallon of coffee, smoke cigarettes and discuss the French team's performance the night before. They switch languages, from Portuguese to Spanish to English, as other reporters they know gather around them. It is girl talk on a grand scale—astute, sarcastic and true—about the French shortcomings. I wonder if the Americans are immediately rethinking this soccer thing that the rest of the world seems to be so excited about. There are very, very beautiful women involved, and that changes everything.

On the Korean Air flight, I'm sitting next to a producer from Korean TV who tells me, with some delight, that I'm in for a surprise in Japan. He says Korea has been welcoming the world for the World Cup, but Japan is feeling tense. I tell him I have a tight schedule to get to Niigata and he tells me, with an ironic smile, that I'll be lucky if I make it. Two English journalists sitting nearby are all ears and join the conversation. They have the same plan—we are all heading for the Ireland–Cameroon game. We all begin to get nervous. Sure enough, at Narita Airport in Tokyo, the delays begin. The hordes of reporters off the plane are directed to one side, and all of us have our passports and credentials examined, slowly. On the fast train from the airport to the central railway station, I find the two English journalists again, and they both look glum. We rush to the ticket office and produce the coupons we had acquired earlier, by mail. The ticket clerk laughs imperiously at the first one presented to him, then tells all of us waiting in line to take a seat and wait. As the minutes pass, the train to Niigata leaves without us.

Tired and already fed up with Japanese officialdom, I decide to head straight for the media center in Yokohama, not far from my hotel. Things are moving so slowly, I'll be lucky to catch the Ireland–Cameroon game on TV. I take the first train to Yokohama, a suburban service train that is full when it leaves Tokyo and gets even more so as it makes several stops. I find a seat and sit down with my luggage. As soon as I do this, the Japanese woman sitting next to me gets up and moves down the train. Other passengers who are standing alternate between looking at the empty seat and staring at me—and just keep standing. The train stops at a suburban station and a young woman comes rushing through the crowd to the back. First she spots the empty seat, then me. She lets out an *oooooh!* of annoyance and stands there, glaring at me.

At Yokohama Station I find the exit nearest the taxi stand. A few people ahead of me get into taxis that speed off. Then it's my turn. Nothing happens. The nearest driver simply ignores me. I move towards him, and he quickly locks the doors. The four cars behind him do the same. I'm standing there, astonished, as Japanese customers emerge from the station, get into taxis and leave. I am being boycotted. After about ten minutes, a young man approaches me. He's wearing the uniform and white gloves common to Japanese taxi drivers. He bows and asks me if I speak English, and I say that I do. Then he apologizes for the other drivers and asks me to follow him to his cab—at the very back of the line. As we drive to the media center, he explains that the other drivers were all older men and afraid of soccer hooligans. He says that older people in Japan weren't really in favor of this World Cup event—too many foreigners coming. They had seen the English hooligans on TV and were scared. I take this in, simultaneously alarmed and seething. I'd missed a game, been shunned and made to look foolish. Exactly why Japan got involved with the event is a mystery to me.

In the media center, which is almost deserted, I find one of the giant-screen TVs. It is showing raw, pre-game footage from the game between Denmark and Uruguay. I ask one of the staff to change it to coverage of Ireland–Cameroon, which is just starting. He hesitates, obviously uncertain about dickering with the expensive machine. Then I explain, firmly, how I had been delayed getting to the game and need to see it, immediately. He changes the channel. I get some water, take a seat and watch it, utterly alone. Within about two minutes it is clear to me, and the crowd in the stadium in Niigata, that the Irish team, playing without Roy Keane, has acquired a new, visceral determination. Every ball is chased; every tackle is forceful and acts as a warning. Nobody is going to mess with the boys in green. Against the Cameroon team, perhaps the most skillful and mercurial in all of Africa, they are facing tough competition.

But there is a resolve to the Irish that is raw and ragged and guarantees nothing against the team known as the Indomitable Lions of Africa. Eventually, some confusion among the Irish defense leads to a goal for Cameroon. But the Irish don't flag or even seem bothered; they just keep going. And then, in the midst of a fierce, fast attack on the Cameroon goal, the ball flows accidentally to Matt Holland. He unleashes a low, hard kick and scores. Then he runs towards the Irish fans, his arm in the air and a schoolboy's grin on his face. I shout something. I'm on my feet and smiling at the screen. Around me, in the echoing media center, whatever I've said has caused a commotion. Three of the staff surround me, as if I'd soon be tearing the place apart. From the giant TV I can hear the Irish fans chanting. It takes only a second to make out what they're singing: "Are you watching,

Roy Keane? Are you watching, Roy Keene?" I start laughing.
The tensions of the day disappear. Faced with the laughing
Irishman, the hovering media center staff melts away.

It is near midnight when I file my story and set off in search
of my hotel. I have no trouble finding a taxi, but the driver, who
speaks almost no English, seems to be warning me that it is,
actually, a long way away—nearer Tokyo than Yokohama. I ask
him to just take me there and show him a bundle of yen in case
he's thinking I can't afford it. I'd suspected the hotel was probably
out of the way, and I know I'd been lucky to find any accom-
modation near Yokohama, as I'd made my plans rather late. Still,
I have my hotel booking coupons and am looking forward to a
long night's sleep. At the hotel, I go straight to reception. The
young man there is tall, thin and barely into his twenties. He
seems unduly startled to see me arrive. I produce my papers and
he looks at them. Then he laughs. A bizarre argument ensues.
He tells me, in broken English, that he had no knowledge of any
booking and the papers are irrelevant to him. I insist. He laughs.
I get angry. He makes what I suspect are many sarcastic remarks
and gives me a key to a room.

The room, it turns out, is less than tiny, has no windows, and
its sparse furniture is bolted to the floor. It has the look and feel
of a prison cell. I immediately form the view that the room is
reserved for the local drunks, too unsteady to make it any farther
and likely to either knock over the furniture or attempt to steal
it. Still, I go to bed and sleep. But at 7 A.M. I am awake and bolt
upright in bed. The door to the room has been flung open and
a man is shouting at me. I am desperately trying to figure out
what has happened. All I know is that it's very early and a short,
stout man is shouting at me, apparently urging me to leave immediately. I shout back at him. At this point, I am more than a little
weary of Japan. I feel a Roy Keane moment coming on. I leap
out of the bed and stride towards the man in the doorway. I am
wearing underwear and a T-shirt; he is wearing some kind of
uniform and waving a bunch of keys. "Fuck off!" I roar at him.
Several times. I also ask him loudly if he wants his arse kicked

from there to Kinnegad, a town in Galway. I don't know why I
pick Kinnegad. He scurries down the hall. I peer after him. Two
members of the hotel cleaning staff are scurrying away too, legging it down the hall at a rapid pace. It finally occurs to me as
an unassailable truth that it is very difficult to get a good night's
sleep in the sportswriting racket.

I wash and pack my bags, determined to get as far from this
obscure hotel as possible. I figure I'll check out and find another
one, somehow. As I leave the room, I see one of the staff waiting at the far end of the hall and scooting down the stairs as soon
as he sees me. I take the elevator. When the elevator door opens
into the hotel lobby, I am taken aback to see a middle-aged man
in a suit smiling nervously at me and bowing. Several members
of the staff surround him, and they bow too. The man, apparently the manager, gestures that he wants me to accompany him
to the front desk, and I do. There, he places a small wooden
bowl on the counter and begins counting money into it. A fair
amount of yen—about two to three hundred dollars' worth, I
estimate. Then he pushes the bowl towards me and he bows. A
young man then approaches and acts as translator. The manager
apologizes for the events of the night before and the morning.
The night manager had been foolish not to realize I had a reservation, and he had sent me to the wrong room. Of course my
reserved room was waiting for me. The manager would be
obliged if I would accept this money in compensation. I take it,
with pleasure. I then accompany the manager, with some reluctance, to my new room. It is a fine suite, with windows on two
sides and a sizable bathroom. I decide to stay. Then I set off to
see Japan play Belgium.

The young woman at Saitama Stadium who gives me my ticket
for the game is jumping up and down. Literally, she is leaping
on the spot with excitement. I admire the childish enthusiasm,
yet I'm wary. This is Japan's first game. It's a host country and
there's an erratic energy at large, but the Japanese enthusiasm for
soccer and this World Cup is remote and artificial, if it exists at
all. I am quickly learning how soccer and marketing have been

intertwined in Japan. The stern, sculpted face of Hidetoshi
Nataka is everywhere. Giant black-and-white billboard photographs of the Japanese midfielder loom over street corners and
hang in malls. The front man for several big World Cup sponsors, the sheer size of those portraits tells everyone that he's the
face of Japan in the World Cup, carrying the hopes of a host
country on his shoulders. The only world-class player on the
Japanese team, he plays in Italy's Serie A, with Parma, and before
that he played for Roma. The iconography used to sell the
Japanese team, combined with the very real suspicion people have
displayed towards the World Cup, leaves me bewildered.

I watch the Japanese supporters arrive and pour into the stadium. About 90 percent of them are teenagers or in their twenties. Most stop to buy stuff at the countless concession stands,
even though they are already wearing the Japan team shirts,
scarves and headbands. The excitement level is astonishingly adolescent, like the electric mood before a pop concert. As game time
approaches, the atmosphere is childishly ecstatic. The noise level,
with the chants of "Nippon! Nippon!" isn't so much raucous as
it is teenaged shrill and intense. When the Japanese air force flies
three planes in formation over the stadium to open the game,
nobody can hear the noise of the jets. Apart from a small handful
of dignitaries and journalists, there doesn't seem to be anyone
over the age of thirty in the stadium. The Japanese team looks
fabulous—great haircuts and male-model attractive, every one of
them. They make the gangly Belgians look like lumbering goofs.
Masashi Nakayama, who scored Japan's only goal at the World
Cup in 1998, is on the bench and I figure it's because, at thirty-
five years old, he's not even in the target age group for the selling
of soccer in Japan.

The game gets off to an atrocious start as the nervous Japanese
can't settle and the Belgians seem freaked out by the atmosphere.
Nothing much happens in the first half. It takes a goal by Belgian
captain Marc Wilmots, on a splendid overhead kick, early in the
second half to motivate the Japanese. They stop posing as professional soccer players and passion takes over. Nataka stokes the

engine, passing the ball and guiding the play with a sudden urgency. At this point, with grim tenacity setting in, the Japanese players are wonderful to watch, chasing every ball with furious determination and needing—yes, truly, madly, deeply, needing—to score. They do it with a terrific run by Takayuki Suzuki only minutes after the Belgian goal. Eight minutes later, there's another spectacular goal by Junichi Inamoto. Even when Belgium evens the score on Peter Van Der Heyden's goal a few minutes after that, Japan actually keeps going.

The crowd roars, egging them on. All that adolescent energy is focused on moving the team forward. A defeat would be unthinkable. Within mere minutes after the Belgian goal, it seemed that all those youngsters—on the field and in the stands— had suddenly realized that soccer is not about posturing in fashionable European shirts, but about fortitude and freedom. And that's the point I hope some of them have truly absorbed into their hearts.

In the end, soccer is about heartbreak and surviving it by moving onward, because the ball keeps moving. It's about endurance, not nice shirts, fabulous haircuts and fickle fashion. You can't market that essence of it. You have to learn it, and I'm thinking that maybe in Japan they just have. I'm hoping, too, that all those older people who fear the World Cup and the resulting invasion by fans from other countries will learn something.

The game against Belgium ends in a 2–2 draw, and the players and the crowd are obviously relieved. The crowd are all smiles, but they're heading to the concession stands for more shopping. There's no communal singing; in Japan, I'm thinking, improvisations and expressions of personal freedom and pleasure are best hidden, never to be celebrated in public.

On my way back to the hotel, on the short walk from the train station, there are few people about and everything seems to have closed for the night. I'm astonished when a woman waves at me from the open window of a building near the hotel. Instinctively, I wave back. She keeps waving and gestures for me to come towards her. At this point, I hesitate. Nobody in Japan has been friendly to me thus far—what gives? I stop and look. The woman has blonde hair and she's wearing nothing but a brassiere, as far as I can see. I look at the building she waving from. There's a red light over the door. This, I realize, is the local whorehouse. I keep walking, amazed again by Japan. When I enter the hotel grounds, I look back, and the woman starts waving again. There isn't another soul on the streets. Japan has pulled off a draw in its first World Cup game, but there isn't a sign of public celebration.

It's a day later that I go to Ibaraki and the Ireland–Germany game, and by the time I'm back in Yokohama, it's clear that soccer and the World Cup have had a traumatizing impact in Japan. What I experienced—the hostility on the train, at the taxi stand and at the hotel, followed by the profuse apologies and then the abundant hospitality of the local people in Ibaraki, mirrors Japan's complicated feelings about the World Cup. The country is proud to co-host the tournament, but there is a streak of hostility towards foreigners that can morph into a deep need to impress the visitors. As for the game of soccer itself, older Japanese people are frightened of it.

The game is logical, governed by a starkly clear set of laws, but at its core it's about finding freedom within those rules—the dazzling run by a striker, the improvisation of juggling the ball, shifting position and surprising the opposition. It's that spontaneity—the heart-stirring element of soccer—and what it inspires, that scares Japan. Even in its national team there's a reluctance to extemporize, a chronic adherence to method and rules. I've been spooked by Japan, the hostility and hospitality, the waving whore in the middle of the night, the alfresco sex on a car at dawn on a quiet street. I want to get the hell out of here. Back in Korea, I know, the country has been gripped by joy. South Korea won its opening game 2–0, a thrilling victory over Poland. That's where the fun is.

It isn't easy to get out of Japan. I've booked a seat on the fast train from Yokohama Station to Narita Airport and asked the hotel to line up a taxi for me. The manager indicates I'll be at Yokohama Station in about twenty minutes. My taxi driver is about eighty years old and timid both about main roads and driving faster than thirty miles an hour. We mosey along side streets and back roads. I'm getting anxious about the time as the meter goes up and up, registering the cost. Eventually, he has to take the highway to enter Yokohama, and he's both terrified and lost. He can't figure out which exit will take us into the station. We go in circles. I'm pointing to my watch and he grimly ignores me, continuing to circle. I look carefully at where we are and point, emphatically, towards the exit. He hesitates. I shout. He makes it, and then I'm racing into the station knowing I've already missed the train. I buy a ticket for the next one, calculating that it will leave me only fifteen minutes to get to the plane.

At the airport, I race along on foot with my luggage. I'm stopped by a security check. There are about ten people in front of me, patiently waiting to have their luggage and passports examined. I look around and realize the gate for the Korean Air flight is just beside the security check. There's a young Korean Air attendant standing there, clearly looking out for last-minute passengers. I wave my ticket at her, and then my FIFA World Cup press pass. She walks over to me, looks at the ticket and press badge and then, amazingly, grabs me by the wrist and pulls me out of the lineup, barking something at the stunned Japanese security guard as she pulls me past him. She walks me onto the plane and to my seat. In minutes, we are flying to Seoul.

• • • • •

NO SOONER am I back in Seoul than I'm on Korean television, talking about the fate of the French. This is no big deal, actually. The Korean TV stations regularly trawl the World Cup media center, looking for comments from foreign journalists. I see two French reporters decline to talk, shaking their heads wearily as if already exhausted by the topic. And there I am, the nearest reporter, sitting and trying to figure out how to get to Daegu for the United States–Korea game, which is suddenly a hot ticket. I tell the two extremely polite reporters—one of whom is there to ask the questions, the second to translate them—that France has underestimated Senegal and that this might be a World Cup where the underdogs will triumph regularly and surprise the world. For good measure, I say that I expect South Korea to surprise every opponent at the tournament. There follow many exclamations and much smiling from the reporter, which the translator doesn't need to explain to me. And I'm not exaggerating. Since the opening game, France has only managed a 0–0 draw with Uruguay, while Senegal has drawn 1–1 with Denmark. Two games in, France hasn't managed to score a goal, and Senegal looks certain to qualify for the second round.

In the meantime, I have a media ticket for the game between Brazil and China. I'm extremely anxious see Brazil play, but uncertain that I can get to the venue. The game is being played on Jeju-do Island, off the southern tip of Korea in the East China Sea. To get there by train would take many hours and a trip by ferry to the island. I'm told by the extremely helpful—and now a little more confident—young woman on the media desk that there are flights to Jeju-do almost every hour on the day of the game and they're extremely inexpensive. Another young woman prints out the flight schedule for Korean Air and looks me in the eye. With great seriousness, she says: "You have to go there. It is very important that you go there. It's is very important that you see this part of Korea." I call the sports editor in Toronto. "Get a plane," he says. "It's a Brazil game."

My first task, however, is to check out of the Hotel Nostalgia. I'm moving to a hotel much closer to the Coex Center. I'm also hoping that taxi drivers will have heard of the new hotel and that getting there won't require extensive use of Seoul's wonderful but time-consuming translation services. The local authorities have been very shrewd about taking care of their foreign visitors and have set up a team of translators that can be called on easy-to-remember phone numbers. If I'm in a taxi and the driver has no idea what I'm talking about when I ask to go to Hotel Nostalgia, he calls a number on his cell phone, explains the situation, and the phone is then handed to me and I do some explaining in English. After much back-and-forth, it usually works out and everybody's happy, but it takes forever. At the Hotel Nostalgia, I collect my bags and prepare to say goodbye. I haven't seen Bo for ages, but the staff tell me he's expected to return soon. Me, I'm thinking that businessman's club around the corner is an important element in Bo's loyalty to the Nostalgia. Before I leave, I give some small gifts—trinkets, really—to several of the staff members. A friend in Canada had suggested I take some little Canadian items to use as thank-you gifts, and had given me a bag of pencils, key chains and small pieces of fudge with the Maple Leaf and Canada prominently displayed. The two ladies on the front desk are stunned by their gifts. One looks close to tears. When my taxi pulls away, most of the hotel staff and the manager—about twelve people in all—are on the steps, bidding me goodbye.

I'm touched by the sincerity of the people at the Hotel Nostalgia. The sportswriting racket is, I've discovered, a rather lonely gig. Especially if you're from Canada and covering a World Cup. There are few people to communicate with and share stories and experiences. Mind you, solitude is my modus operandi in any case. I'm an observer, a watcher and note-taker. Just as I was a young obsessive, traveling back and forth across Dublin to attend soccer games alone, I'm a solo wandering adult, soaking up the atmosphere in the cities of Japan and South Korea, storing impressions in my notebooks and in my mind. And yet I know that what compels me to wander alone is that I'm not truly cloistered or companionless. I am connected to the crowds, to the supporters of both sides at a game, to everyone who longs for a dazzling move, an improvisation on the field. What I write is the fruit of a collaboration of sorts between me and the cheering, groaning, all-eyes-on-the-game crowds. Still, one reason to look forward to the new hotel is that I've finally run into the only other Canadian reporter in South Korea, Chris Young of the *Toronto Star*, and he's staying there. I check in and make sure the electric fixtures and outlets work. I call the front desk and ask to be put through to Chris Young's room. They tell me he's checked out. He hasn't, I know. He'd gone to another city for a couple of days to see a game, and now he's back. I try to leave a message for him. They tell me he's checked out. Very sorry and all, but he's checked out. No, he hasn't. Yes, he has. Never mind. I have to go see Brazil play China.

• • • • •

I **FLY** out of Gimpo Airport, which handles the domestic routes in Korea. I'm the only Caucasian at the check-in counter, in the airport lounge *and* on the plane. All the flight attendants beam at me and shake hands. I doze off during the hour-long flight, and when I wake up there is a handwritten Post-it note on the back of the seat in front of me. "We are sorry," it says, in an ovular, loping hand. "We offered you a beverage. But you were resting. Please advise us if you would like a beverage." There isn't time. We land soon and I'm anxious to be straight off the plane and into a taxi to get to the stadium. Jeju-do Island is a very pretty place with a certain reputation among Koreans. Depending on who's telling you, Jeju-do is either "the island of flowers and sandy beaches" or "the honeymoon island." If you're not getting the tourism spin, the upshot is that this is the island of wine, women and song. This is definitely the kind of place where you're supposed to enjoy seeing Brazil play.

Seogwipo Stadium, at the southern end of the island, is one of those perfect venues for soccer on a warm summer night. It's a spectacularly beautiful stadium, half-covered by a soaring white canopy that's meant to look like a sail on a boat, and it does. Also, there's a dormant volcano just down the road, Mount Hallasan, and "dormant volcano" just about sums up Brazil's status at the World Cup. The team's first, bruising match, against Turkey, wasn't pretty, but it did show that Brazil, after a torturous qualifying campaign, is here to win. That's as it should be. Put the names together—Ronaldo, Rivaldo, Cafu, Roberto Carlos—and you've got some of the deadliest players in the world, no question.

According to some wire-service reports, there are about 60,000 Chinese supporters in South Korea for the World Cup, but that's an exaggeration, I've learned. Seogwipo Stadium holds 37,000 people, and it is nearly full, but about 20,000 Chinese would be a more accurate estimate. I'd also been told in Seoul that tens of thousands of Chinese were taking part in the second great Chinese invasion of Korea, but that has turned out to be giddy nonsense. Mind you, the ones who are here do their supporting in fine, if ragged, style. They're all dressed in red and they use their sheer numbers to make a point with the opposition. I see a few thousand of them link arms outside the stadium in an impressive display of unity and strength, but it only lasts two minutes before most of them disperse for a bit of shopping before the game actually starts.

The locals in Jeju-do have certainly taken advantage of the games being played here. There are numerous stalls selling knick-knacks and gewgaws, the taxi drivers have increased their prices, and the hotel where I'm obliged to stay later that night—a simple room in an allegedly traditional Korean inn—costs a cool three hundred dollars for the night. That sort of money gets you Ritz-type luxury in Seoul. Once inside the stadium, the first thing I notice is that the island seems to have an inordinate number of dignitaries. The VIP section contains more supposedly important people than had attended the opening game in Seoul ten days earlier. Reporters are pushed out of the way so that a short, very fat dignitary can strut from his car with a police escort. In fact, an entire SWAT team, machine guns and all, springs into action. Amazed by all the fuss and security, I walk up to the guy who seems to be in charge of the SWAT team and ask him why there are so many armed police officers. When he is sure about what I'm asking, he looks at me as if I'm asking the stupidest question he's ever heard. "China! Big game!" he barks at me.

China's supporters would agree with him—as the game begins, anyway. They make an awful lot of noise, and the small knots of Brazilians are dwarfed by the sheer size of the China contingent. A giant red flag floats among the supporters and across the stadium. It's pretty impressive, but the soccer is another matter. I have a good seat, close to the field, and I watch closely when the Brazilians walk out. During China's national anthem, Ronaldo's bucktoothed smirk says, "Really, these guys from China might as well go home now, because there's no hope for them." For about ten minutes, China's players do try hard, but it is obvious their opponents awe them. A Chinese defender has the ball. Ronaldo and Cafu are both running towards him. There is a half-step of hesitation and, well, you just can't do that with Brazil. In that split second of hesitation, the ball is gone and moved rhythmically down the field.

Admittedly, China is without its best defender because of injury. Fan Zhiyi, who has toiled in England and Scotland for Crystal Palace and Dundee United, is on the bench. I reckon that any man who spends a fall and winter playing soccer in Dundee is unlikely to be impressed by the dancing, sunny Brazilians. But he's not playing. China's best man is their twelfth: coach Bora Milutinovic is a wily, mercenary Serb who has coached Mexico, Costa Rica, the United States and Nigeria to the World Cup. The teams don't always win when they get there, but it's his job as a coach to get them qualified, and he does.

China starts sagging as soon as Brazil scores the first goal. Thirteen minutes in, Brazil gets a free kick and Roberto Carlos shoots it home from twenty-five yards. All the life goes out of China's supporters, who are reduced to cheering for a decent save from their goalkeeper. Brazil is on cruise control and glorious to watch—smooth, sexy and fast. For the first time, I can hear the Brazilian supporters' music and singing. Soon, with their team up 3–0, they get bored and go on a walk around the stadium, singing and making music to pass the time. There is a moment towards the end that is stunning. It's only a matter of a gesture, and not everyone sees it. Brazil's Cafu takes the ball far down the right touchline. He beats one of China's midfielders and keeps going at a ferocious pace. He approaches defender Li Weifeng, who stops dead, panicky and unsure of what to do. Cafu slows,

glances at the defender who can't summon the courage or
resources to tackle him, and makes a brisk "come-here" gesture
with his hand. He's telling the defender, "Come on, play. Make
a game of it. Don't be afraid." It's a like an adult instructing a
child. And the child freezes, bewildered. Impatient, Cafu keeps
going down the right wing and crosses to an unmarked Ronaldo,
who is loitering at the back post. With a graceful stroke at the
ball, Ronaldo buries it in the back of the net.

At the game's end, the Chinese supporters leave the stadium
looking defeated and disgusted. In their thousands, they walk off
into the night. They don't stop to party, drown their sorrows or
enjoy the occasion of being at the World Cup and playing against
Brazil. They look like people whose holiday has been ruined, as
if they're engaged in a giant sulk. And ungracious. China has
some enthusiastic, skilled young players with promising skills.
That doesn't matter to the supporters, who bellowed and chanted
until their team was a goal down, then sat morosely, which isn't
the point at all. The point is to enjoy the game, the event, as an
expression of community and permissible, utterly joyous
nationalism.

It turns out that my hotel, the promised traditional Korean
inn, is no such thing. It's a luxury hotel. My room is huge, with
a balcony overlooking expansive, manicured grounds. There's a
bottle of Scotch on the bed, and I am unsure of what to do with
it. No, really, I am. Down at the reception desk, the young man
on duty knows no English and I can't summon the energy to go
back, get the Scotch and try to figure out whether it's a gift or
there to be consumed at some huge mark-up. The young man
figures out that I'm saying something about a bottle of liquor.
He points at the bar, which is closed. Before I can say or do
more, he dashes in, gets a bottle of beer from the fridge there,
opens it and, after wrapping it in a napkin, presents it to me. I
thank him, take it to my room and enjoy it immensely, in bed.

The next morning, the small Jeju-do airport is packed. Most
of China's fans seem to be leaving and have decided to gather,
smoke cigarettes and discuss the game before they board the

planes. I manage to check in, and then suddenly there's chaos. I'm carried along in a stampede of people. I'm not sure where we're all going, but I've got a feeling that the Brazilian players have arrived. Sure enough, there they are. Ronaldo is smiling and waving, shaking hands and not the slightest bit bothered that several thousand people appear intent on touching him. He waves his arm, vaguely, and the crowd moves back en masse. As they move through the airport, all of Brazil's players look oddly fragile, yet unstoppable, fleet-footed and unearthly. Which they are. I miss my flight and spend two hours at the airport watching the busloads of China supporters arrive, smoke, shop and then disappear onto their plane. All the while, the presence of the Brazilians lingers, as if fairy dust has been sprinkled and stays, sensuous, in the air.

· · · · ·

SOME COUNTRIES are writing their own narratives as they progress, steadily and unhurriedly, through the days. They create fresh mythologies as each game comes along. At any World Cup, a constellation of human talents plays hard, accepting a core of agreed ideals. Yet there is also a hierarchy. The reigning champions are favorites to win. The traditional great powers of Europe and South America are expected to play attacking soccer against the lesser powers. But here, far from home, the great powers are finding it difficult to be at ease. They seem vexed, as if haunted by the sights, sounds and smells of their native places. And vexed by the strangeness of where they find themselves. With the exception of Brazil, every one of the top soccer countries looks diminished: France has lost, Italy has been beaten by Croatia, England struggled to a 1–1 draw with Sweden, Germany failed to beat Ireland. Meanwhile, the USA, always patronized and underestimated by European countries, has pulled off a stunning upset, beating Portugal 3–2. For old Europe, the faint, acrid smell of a soccer revolution hangs in the air in Asia.

The Americans are always dismissed, never feared. Soccer is an obscure game in the States, the Europeans know. The players are imagined to be cheerful enthusiasts, all attitude but lacking in skill and, worse, bereft of tradition. This serves the American youngsters well on the world stage. They don't lay claim to nuance, only to fitness and determination. Like all Americans, the players on the national soccer team dislike being figures of fun, and deeply resent being the object of scorn from old Europe. They are thought of as guileless, and they know it. They respond with blistering pace and grit. Against Portugal, in a game I watched while in Japan to see Ireland play Germany, the Americans played with a ruthless precision. Portugal, a team of immensely gifted players known for their flair and swift, passing movement, was never allowed to settle. At halftime of that game, the U.S. was leading 3–0, and it was invigorating to see their swiftness and confidence. Only the hard-hearted could fail to be impressed by their pluck. And only the brutally begrudging could resent the mettle and moxie of the South Koreans who have started the World Cup with such spirit and optimism. Now the Americans will play South Korea in the city of Daegu, in a game loaded with expectation and meaning for both teams. On a sunny Monday morning in Seoul, I manage to get a ticket on the fast train to Daegu.

• • • • •

IMAGINE THE weirdest sound you've ever heard, then turn up the volume on it. It might be something like the sound of sixty thousand people who are confused, dismayed and uncomprehending. It's eerie, somewhere between a desperate, collective whimper and an entire country groaning together. It's made when South Korea misses a penalty kick against the United States and the crowd can't believe it.

I have to sympathize. While I was in Japan, Koreans went collectively mad after their team soundly beat Poland last week. They fully expect the team to keep winning. The mood in Korea is nothing like the nervousness in Japan. In this co-host country, it's not about a pleasant, feel-good feeling for the rest of the World Cup; it's not about making a good showing and avoiding an

embarrassing failure. Suddenly, there is a visceral sense of confidence. The soccer tournament has become woven into the
national fabric. The young, the middle-aged and old are in rapture. There is a simmering sense that South Korea can beat any
team, go far in this tournament and let the world know that this
is a dynamic country, dauntless and self-assured. Just beneath the
surface, there is delirium.

My first real look at the intensity of the Korean soccer pandemonium started at the main railway station in Seoul. Thousands
of young supporters streamed through, getting the trains to
Daegu. Every few minutes, they'd start chanting. In Korean, the
name for the country is Dae Han Min Guk, and it was rhythmically chanted over and over. And they're impressively well organized, these youngsters. They've got their own songs and
mass-movement gestures. There are even distinct signals for the
gestures and songs to start. They're well organized because there
is, in fact, an organization behind them. The Korean Supporters
Club takes its job very seriously. The leaders, who have had much
media exposure, are almost as famous here as the players on the
national team, and they're taking the meaning of "loud and
proud" to an entirely new level.

On the train, I find an English-speaking Korean journalist.
He explains that the leaders of the Korean Supporters Club are
heroes to other youngsters and are held up as model citizens by
their elders. This past week, politicians tried to get in on the act
and use the leaders of the Supporters Club to get young people
interested in politics. Local elections will be held in a few days,
and the government is worried that potential voters will be distracted by the World Cup. They've asked the leaders and stewards
to include a reminder about the elections in their written program for the game against the United States and on their website.
It's caused a big controversy: the government expected the
youngsters to comply, and they refused. My fellow journalist,
who uses "we" when he talks about the Supporters Club, tells
me, "Our feeling is that the South Korean team has made the
Korean people proud. Politics has not done that for South Korea.

Anyway, everybody is supposed to vote."

The Supporters Club began preparing in earnest in January. But the fanatics had been getting ready for years, studying the actions and movements of the supporters of teams all over the world. They'd seen how the really big clubs in Italy, Spain and France have highly orchestrated supporters, chants, movements and, most important, conductors—or capos—who increase the volume and choreograph the support in the stands. The word went out at the friendly games prior to the World Cup as well as on the Internet. Volunteers were needed to lead, conduct, train the masses in how to sing, move, beat the drums and, possibly, terrify opposing teams with the intensity of their support. And it happened. Young men who called themselves the Red Devils, volunteers all of them, spontaneously sprang from the group of ardent followers of the team. Like the capos who boss the hardcore supporters of the big teams in Europe, they spend every game with their backs turned to the action on the field, imploring the supporters to sing, chant and move in unison. They choreograph, organize and encourage. At the warmup games, they taught the supporters the movements, organized crowds for outdoor big-screen broadcasts of the games and taught the off-stadium supporters the same movements. They've become famous conductors, waving batons and controlling choirs of tens of thousands.

In the stadium in Daegu, the Red Devils have arranged an astonishing mass demonstration of support. To describe the scene as a sea of red would be an understatement. It is a display of blinding, monochromatic support. The fans have a routine where they wave their right hands downward, bow down slightly, then throw their heads back to shout, *"Dae Han Min Guk!"* and a mass of drums pounds in response. Imagine about sixty thousand people doing this in unison; it's an awesome spectacle. To top it off, the Red Devils have organized sections of the crowd to carry white banners. On a signal, these are raised and you see *Dae Han Min Guk* spelled out in Korean script. Watching from the media area, I realize something is different here. A vast number of the

Korean supporters, and some of the leaders, are young women. It's the young women, some of them teenagers and some in their twenties, who are the most vocal and who are completely unself-conscious about the vigor of the chants and movements. They look confident and cool, empowered by the occasion and their role. They're more intense than any group of male soccer fans I've ever seen.

This was going to be an important game even before both South Korea and the United States won their opening matches, and each is certain of making it to the second round if they win here. There are almost forty thousand American soldiers stationed in South Korea, and young Koreans are increasingly resentful of their presence. And then there's the sour note from the Winter Olympics in Salt Lake City a few months ago. South Korean speed skater Kim Dong-Sung finished first, but was disqualified for allegedly blocking American Apolo Anton Ohno. Koreans felt the fix was in. So, on this day, they want very badly to beat the United States.

There are a couple of thousand Americans in the Daegu stadium, gamely dressed in wigs, wearing face paint and chanting something that is probably "USA." I find them by using a pair of binoculars offered by another journalist. They can be seen on the TV monitors in the press area as the cameras pan over the crowd, but you can't hear them. They're not only being drowned out by the Koreans in the stadium; there are thousands of people sitting on the hillside overlooking the stadium and singing like mad. With the binoculars, I can see that some are perched in the trees for a better look—they're probably singing too. I have the eerie feeling that I'm part of a mass event I cannot really comprehend—it seems the attention of all forty-eight million people in this country is focused on this place.

It's a fine game, full of high drama, played in the heat and humidity of Daegu. First, there is a massive gasp as South Korean player Hwang Sun-hong is cut over his right eye during a clash of heads with an American and blood pours from the wound. Young women shriek in horror. Hwang is soon back, playing with a huge bandage on his head. Then the Americans score. John O'Brien makes a lightning dash down the middle and chips the ball to Clint Mathis, who has plenty of space because all the Korean defenders have begun to move upfield. Mathis, a youngster with a Mohican hairdo, rams the ball past Lee Woon-Jae with his left foot and the crowd is stunned into silence. But unlike the Chinese supporters in the game against Brazil, the Koreans don't give up. The cheering and chanting stop for a split second, but then get much louder.

Mere minutes later comes the penalty. It's an early, automatic chance to even the score—you know that's what the supporters feel. But it is badly taken and U.S. keeper Brad Friedel stops it succinctly. There is mass mental confusion among the crowd. How could a penalty be missed? South Korea has lost the rhythm, but the crowd soon has it again as the Red Devils exhort more singing, more chanting. In the second half, they get the reward of better play. The South Korean players fight back with endlessly thrilling, incessant pressure. There is endless running by both sides. South Korean coach Guus Hiddink makes as many substitutions as allowed. The young women in the crowd take their shrieking to another level when Ahn Jung-Hwan appears on the field. The handsome, long-haired Ahn is the poster boy for the South Korean team, a rock star—like a god to young women here. Someone in the media section tells me his nickname is the Electric Eel.

Everyone knows that if anyone can score, it is Ahn. And indeed he does, with a beautifully taken, glancing header that sends the supporters into orgasmic ecstasy. These people—men and women alike—are having hot sex with their star player. You can feel it in the charged air. After the goal, to rub it in, Ahn dashes to the corner flag and does what will be called, in the next day's press reports, "the Ohno gesture." He mimics the American skating to a gold medal he didn't deserve. The crowd knows it and loves him for it.

A draw is a fair result for two teams playing with passion and flair. Both are underdogs at the World Cup, and both keep their hopes alive for progressing to the next stage. Outside the stadium afterwards, I see a young woman, about eighteen or nineteen years old, standing and sobbing. She has the South Korean flag painted on each cheek and a soccer ball painted on her nose. Her body is shaking, as if with delirium tremens. Her friends, all young women of the same age, step away from her, then enfold her in a group hug. I can see they're all weeping. But they aren't crying with disappointment; they are exhausted beyond endurance and emotionally wrecked. Their bodies have been through an incredible emotional wringer and weeping is all that they can do.

I keep that picture of the crying, hugging women in my mind as I ride the fast train back to Seoul. Onboard the train, the staff are grinning, giddy. I ask for a beer from the man with the food and drink cart. When I reach for my wallet, he laughs. My beer is on the house. In fact, all the beer is on the house. And the entire compartment starts laughing. It's infectious. No neutral could want South Korea to lose a game now. The sound of the collective dismay and confusion over the missed penalty was weird enough. The sound of their despair would be unbearable.

It's pouring rain when I arrive back in Seoul and head for the media room at the Coex Center. I see the phalanxes of riot police standing under the canopy of the convention center, on the alert for trouble with fans returning from the game or just going crazy in the streets. There have been huge crowds watching the game on giant screens all over the city. It is hours after the game now, but in the distance I can hear the mass chants of "*Dae Han Min Guk!*" The sound gets closer, and in the pouring rain a group of hundreds of teenagers is moving down the street, past the Coex Center, chanting. Some are dancing, leaping in the air. I stop to watch.

The dozens of policemen, mostly teenage boys, sheltering in the awning, are as giddy as the youngsters marching down the street. The youngsters, seeing the cops, stop and chant for them. One teenage girl at the front jumps in the air, and her little Korean flag falls from her knapsack to the ground. I watch as a young police officer, egged on by his grinning colleagues, emerges from under the awning, picks up the flag and hands it to the young woman. Her wet hair is plastered to her head, and when she smiles at the police officer, it is a smile of indescribable delight. Then, with great solemnity, she hands the little flag back to the young police officer, and he, with equal gravity, places it in his flak jacket. It flies from his back as the police march off a minute later in the wind and rain. It's one of those achingly sentimental moments that you would think was staged if you were to see it on TV, but it's real and breathtakingly sweet. All of Korea is in ecstasy. People here have been freed by the tournament, by the national team's success. They're relaxed, friendly and more confident, and they smile constantly.

• • • • •

THE NEXT day, I experience real evidence of Korea's transformation. I arrive late for the media bus to the game between France and Denmark in Incheon, so I consult the young men and women at the information desk about getting there by subway or bus. A cheerful young lady pores over a subway map with me and explains the various changes I'd have to make. I ask her how long it would take and, after mulling it over for a few seconds, I ask her how much it might cost to take a taxi to the stadium.

At first, she's dismayed, telling me it would cost a lot. I explain I have to be there early, or my media ticket will be given to someone else. She grabs a notebook and pencil and says, "Come with me." I follow her out of the building and down the steps to the sidewalk. When I hesitate and begin to ask what she plans, she laughs, slaps my shoulder bag with a flying hand and says, "Don't worry, mister, don't worry." Then she literally skips, like a child, down the rest of the steps. She hails a taxi and begins a rapid-fire negotiation with the driver. She writes a sum on her notebook. The driver takes the pencil and writes another sum. Then they both nod to each other.

The young woman explains to me that she's negotiated a price. The driver will take me to Incheon. He will let the meter run until it reaches a certain amount, then he'll turn it off and I will pay him a lump sum, on top of the meter price, when we get to the stadium. I do a quick calculation and reckon it's a bargain. As I get into the cab, the young woman gives me another friendly slap on the shoulder. "Don't worry, mister," she says again. "We take good care of you." When the cab takes off, the young woman stands on the sidewalk, waving at me. For obvious reasons, I keep thinking about my few days in Japan. And about my first day at the media center in Seoul, when the young people taking care of the reporters had that terrified, anxious look about them. For all Koreans, that nagging insecurity has evaporated. They are fearless now, soccer shaping the way a society sees itself.

In Incheon, France bows out of the World Cup without even scoring a goal. It is a sad thing to watch. Unless you're a Dane, in which case it's brilliant. But watching a great team implode, frustrated and bitter, is not a pretty sight. In the hours leading to the game, all the focus was on Zinedine Zidane. He would save them, was the consensus. The French were going to use "Plan Z," score the four goals needed to progress to the next round and get back on track. All the weight was on Zidane—a man with a monk's tonsure, shy smile and magic feet. He's the embodiment of the best of French soccer and the sport itself. He's gifted, smart on the field and sincere.

I find Zidane an entrancing figure. He's a nice man, by all accounts, an enigma known affectionately as Zizou. The best-paid soccer player in the world, he's a fella who lets his wife make the business decisions and keeps to himself when he's not doing his job for Real Madrid or the French national team. He's iconic because he's a very, very good player and because he embodies a kind of plain goodness that professional athletes usually leave behind when they stop being ordinary people. In France, during the spring elections, when the anti-immigrant right-wing politician Jean-Marie Le Pen had a strong showing in the first round of the presidential poll, Zidane made a unique foray into the spotlight outside sport.

He spoke out against Le Pen and did it with a quiet, heartfelt loathing for the right winger that was eloquent in its pith. Encouraging French voters to reject Le Pen, Zidane refused to even refer to him by name, calling him "the other." The son of Algerian emigrants to France, Zidane was obviously enraged. He wasn't speaking out as a star of the French team, with its many non-white players. He was speaking as a man deeply offended by the mere existence of Le Pen and his ideas. Le Pen responded by calling Zidane "nothing" and "no more important than any other voter." That was a mistake. Some people in France said that Le Pen lost all of France that day.

So much depends on Zidane in Incheon. He's been injured in a warmup game, and in France's first two games of the tournament, his absence was glaring. If he comes back, the French feel, their luck will return too. Before the game, I walk among the supporters to find someone to talk to me about Zidane in plain terms. The French fans are discreet. They don't dress in outlandish costumes and make a lot of noise before the game. They wear their blue shirts, occasionally a blue hat, and walk around confidently. The Danes, on the other hand, have gone all out for color and comic relief. Many are in fuzzy versions of Viking helmets with horns. They sing as they gather en masse. They stand out, whereas the French are just there. David and Emilie, an elderly French couple in matching number 10 Zidane shirts, talk to me for a minute about the man. "He's important because he's so good that the other players want to be as good," David tells me. "Today, even if he's not fit for the game, he will play. That is the man."

When Zidane arrives on the field, you can tell he isn't fully fit. His thigh heavily bandaged, he looks like a diminished, wounded warrior, more hopeful than happily game-ready. Still, the French and the Koreans chant his name. During the national anthems, even *La Marseillaise* is interrupted when his face appears on the big screen in the stadium. Everybody roars. For a while, he shows flashes of his brilliance. There is a back-heel pass to David Trezeguet that comes to nothing. There is his shot on goal that comes from nowhere and fails. He tries to take a pass in the penalty box and falls, clutching his thigh. The first goal for the Danes puts France even deeper in the hole. All hope is fading. A humiliation beyond imagining is in the offing. At halftime, I walk among the French VIPs—easy to do, because they've all strode outside, smoking cigarettes and staring glumly. "Too slow, too slow," a woman says to me, without prompting. She could only mean him—Zizou.

The French players come out for the second half with pep and zip, but Zidane can't carry it off. Nobody could. The lowest point comes when Sylvain Wiltord stretches to take a soaring ball in the Danish penalty box and falls over. The supporters of Denmark laugh.

At the end, having won 2–0, the Danes walk over to their ecstatic supporters, applaud them and throw shirts to them. The French walk to their supporters and applaud too, but then withdraw quickly—except for Zidane. As he leaves the field, he walks slowly to each part of the stadium and looks up at the people in the stands. It isn't a phony gesture—the typical salute of a defeated, bitter team is the token of hands applauding in the air and eyes on the ground. When Zidane walks to where the reporters sit, I can see his eyes, wide and challenging, looking all of us in the face. It is the gesture of an honest man, one who knows he has failed. It is not the farewell that anyone expected, not even me, with all my self-proclaimed power to see the flaws in the French force arrayed here. Zidane never got a chance to play at his best, and luck was never with the French as soon as they began with such hubris.

It is a more exciting World Cup with the dismissal of the French. It's a startling, large-scale realignment of the reality of the tournament. But Zizou's self-esteem is on a smaller scale. Not everyone can carry the weight of the world.

• • • • •

AFTER ATTENDING the Denmark–France game in Incheon, I race back into Seoul to watch Ireland play Saudi Arabia in Yokohama on television at O'Kim's. I've been told that O'Kim's is South Korea's only Irish bar. It turns out that it isn't really a bar at all; it's a pretty fancy restaurant in the sleek basement mall of the Sheraton Hotel. It's a steak-and-fries sort of place. I soon form the impression it's the kind of place where visiting business-men take their South Korean "girlfriends" and make like the international men of business they've seen on TV. There is enough green baize and replicas of old Guinness mirrors and posters to make it Irishy, but it is an upmarket Irishy kitsch. Entering, I'm asked if I have a reservation because, you know, reservations are recommended. I don't, of course, and for a minute wonder if it has been worth the race from Incheon.

Still, I'm at O'Kim's and I stick to it. The game is on TV, after all. A pint of Guinness costs about sixteen dollars, so I stay away from that. Oddly, the place is full of Germans watching the Germany–Cameroon game. I sit beside one of them, a guy in a business suit who could obviously afford the pints and who tells me he's keeping an eye on the Ireland game because he wants to see Ireland beaten. He was furious when Germany let Ireland score in the dying seconds to tie that game. The only guy in the entire place making an attempt at being part of Ireland's Green Army is a solitary figure in a green shirt, Dennis. He is nervous about the game, he tells me, because you never know with the Irish team. "You can't beat them," he says, "but they don't know how to have a solid win. I wish they had Roy Keane now. They need someone to intimidate the opposition." He's one of those people still bitter about the Keane fiasco. "Mick McCarthy organized a kangaroo court to get rid of Roy. No manager should do that." I leave Dennis alone to worry about the game.

Watching the game in a bar in another country seemed the right thing to do. I could have watched it at the media center and seen the TV feed in several languages, including English, but there's something special about watching international soccer in a bar or club somewhere far from the venue and the home countries of the teams. The World Cup qualifying games are almost never on regular TV, and you have to find out where you can see them on closed-circuit satellite and pay money to enter. If you do, you're part of a special worldwide fraternity.

It is my last night in Seoul. the *Globe and Mail*'s main sports columnist, Stephen Brunt, has arrived in Japan, and my time as a sports reporter is coming to an end. Being at O'Kim's makes sense, because I started the journey to the World Cup almost two years ago, as a fan, in the backroom of a bar on Yonge Street in Toronto. Ireland was playing the Netherlands in Rotterdam, there were about fifteen of us there to watch, and the consensus was that the Irish had only a slim hope of making it to Korea/Japan in 2002.

A few minutes into that game, it was clear that the Irish team hadn't heard they had only a slim chance. Jason McAteer, who usually sat on the bench for Blackburn Rovers, went tearing down the right flank like a man provoked. The Dutch defenders were stunned by the audacity and failed to react. McAteer made a perfect cross to Robbie Keane, who had raced down the middle. He met the cross with a perfect header and scored. Some of us looked at each other and knew it was suddenly all right to be optimistic about the long and winding road to the World Cup. There were many weekday afternoons or Saturday mornings in bars after that. There was that memorable Saturday morning at a Portuguese club. And there was the magic morning at the Galway Arms in Toronto's west end, watching Ireland beat the Dutch 1–0 and seeing old men cry, overcome.

There are no such scenes at O'Kim's. We all watch quietly as, in the pouring rain of Yokohama, Ireland soundly beats Saudi Arabia 3–0. There is the sweet sight of Robbie Keane doing cartwheels across the field after scoring a goal. There is Gary Breen's schoolboy glee after scoring, like a kid hollering "Wheeeee!" and Damien Duff blowing kisses to the sodden supporters in the stands. There is some cheering from the small handful of Ireland supporters at O'Kim's, but no passionate display. Still, I'm glad to be here. It's a treat to attend World Cup games and it's a privilege to travel with the media pack, getting good seats and seeing the best players in the world. But in O'Kim's, with the one drink I could afford, I'm thinking of all the obsessives around the world who turn up in bars and restaurants every few months to watch, hope and sometimes celebrate. In countries where there's no hoopla about soccer between World Cup tournaments, there's a madness and a nobility in it.

· · · · ·

WHEN I land in Vancouver to catch a connecting flight to Toronto, the customs and immigration officer asks me where I'm coming from and the reason for my travel. I tell him I've been covering the World Cup in Korea and Japan. He stares at me. "But it's still going on!" he barks. I explain that another reporter is taking over from me and I'm on my way home. "But it's still going on!" he says again, as if he's talking to an idiot. I spend several hours hanging around the airport in Vancouver, but the customs officer seems to be the only one there who knows about the World Cup. It's the umpteenth airport I've passed through in the past two and a half weeks, and I find it dismayingly subdued. It seems bizarre to me that there aren't giant TV screens everywhere, showing soccer games, and that dozens of people aren't crowded around the screens, cheering, groaning in unison or simply transfixed.

After the long flight home to Toronto, I sleep for two days. When I resurface, it turns out that South Korea has beaten Portugal, Belgium has beaten Russia and Japan has defeated Tunisia. Early on a Sunday morning, still groggy, I watch Ireland play Spain in the sudden-death second round. Ireland plays well, keeping possession and controlling the play. But Spain scores first on a fast move. Ireland is awarded a penalty and Ian Harte fails to score. In the dying seconds, Ireland gets another penalty and Robbie Keane scores emphatically. In extra time, both teams look exhausted. Nobody scores. It ends in a penalty shootout and

Ireland loses 2–3. I fall asleep after that, and dream of airports, missed planes and penalty kicks.

On Tuesday morning, shortly after dawn, I set out for an Italian bar in Toronto's Little Italy. A friend, Mary, has invited me to see Italy play South Korea there. Still jet-lagged and dizzy, I'm wide awake, excited about seeing a game in a crowded bar. The place is full when we get there and is soon completely packed with loud young Italian men drinking coffee and shouting. They expect Italy to win, and win handily. It's Italy, after all. As soon as the TV signal starts, with the sounds and sights of the stadium in Korea, I know with certainty that Italy will lose. I just know. I remember the noise in Daegu, the sea of red coloring the stands and the ferocity of the noise. There is no possibility that the Italian team is prepared for this. Italy's manager, Giovanni Trapattoni, has picked a team based on size and strength, the better to intimidate the slighter Korean players. This is much discussed in the bar on College Street, and someone lowers the volume of the TV and the eardrum-bursting chants coming from the Koreans in the stadium. I keep my mouth shut about the outcome I'm expecting.

Italy scores first. Francesco Totti whips in a ball from the corner and Christian Vieri outmuscles several Korean defenders to power a headed ball into the net. Then Vieri makes a foolish mistake: he looks at the crowd and puts a finger to his lips. He's telling the Korea supporters to hush. Around me, Italian men cheer and shout, but I know what I can't say: that Vieri has insulted all of Korea, and the payback will be immense. The noise level in the stadium rises and rises. Thousands of miles away, through a TV speaker, I can hear the rage in it—the raw, ceaseless anger. The Korean players feel it, and so does the referee. The direction of the game is now beyond the Italian team, for all their skill and force and patience. The Koreans never seem to tire, even as the Italian players go into full time-wasting mode.

It's late in the game when Korea equalizes, sending the game to extra time. The Italian players and the people around me in Toronto are equally furious. A 1–0 victory, with Italy keeping possession, slowing the game down, had seemed probable and just. Then Totti is ejected from the game for time-wasting. A goal by Italy is disallowed. In the bar, the focus is on the referee, who is deemed incompetent by those around me.

Korea wins by a goal in the final minutes of extra time. It's Ahn again. I knew it would be, and every Korean knew it too. What's happened is easy to grasp if you're not Italian and stunned, stung, by the humiliation. The Koreans never stopped running, never stopped trying to score. They outran and outplayed the Italian superstars. The Korean supporters expected nothing less— nobody tells them to hush. By the time I leave the bar, a TV crew is already there, interviewing angry Italians who rant about the referee. I walk home, delighted for Korea.

• • • • •

THE FINAL game is between Brazil and Germany. Brazil wins handily against a German team that has had more luck than skill over the weeks of the tournament. The better game is the one for third place, between South Korea and Turkey. The Koreans want desperately to win, to cap their co-hosting of the World Cup with a finish in the top three. Turkey has quietly, efficiently moved through game after game with determination and panache. It's the first time since 1954 that Turkey has even qualified, and the country's success is as remarkable as that of South Korea. This World Cup, the first played in Asia, has changed the long-standing hierarchy of soccer. Remarkably, it has happened in a tournament at which the elite countries all qualified; for the first time, all of the previous champions—Argentina, Brazil, England, France, Germany, Italy and Uruguay—were present. And the standard of play was high. But the old idea of a tight circle of European and South American countries dominating the tournament has been shattered. When the quarter-final stage unfolded, countries from Europe, North America, South America, Africa and Asia were all still playing.

The third-place game, played in Daegu, is scintillating. Turkey scores after ten seconds, thanks to a mistake by the Korean defense. This is a signal that perhaps, finally, the Korean players have succumbed to fatigue and simply don't have the energy for another always-running, always-attacking game. And yet, for a long period, they do muster another fabulous onslaught. After eight minutes, the score is level at 1–1. Two minutes later, Turkey scores again and it's 2–1. The fans in Daegu, the TV commentators and everyone watching around the world is charged, delighted by the drama and the furious pace. Ahn is inspired, improvising ball-control tricks and jinking this way and that, surrounded by bewildered Turkish defenders who have discovered why the locals call him the Electric Eel. He's savoring every second of his last World Cup game. It's virtuoso soccer he's playing, and anyone watching can tell it's a display that will probably never be repeated. He saunters with the ball, a boulevardier, relaxed and making others looking clumsy and inelegant. He scores, but the goal is disallowed because he's a fraction offside. He looks disgusted with the referee but starts all over again, running, dancing and several times making fools of Turkish defenders.

I can hear the crowd squeal. The Turks' star player, Hakan Sukur, is also playing the game of his life. Largely ineffective in earlier matches, he seems a man released from shackles. The game goes on and on delightfully, all speed and skill. The Turks score again—it's 3–1—and then, in the first of three minutes of extra time, Korea scores on a long, hopeful shot from midfielder Song Jung-Hyun.

The whole, watching world is hoping for a late, dramatic equalizer to make this glorious game last longer, but it doesn't come. Turkey wins 3–2 and most of the Korean players, exhausted beyond imagining, fall to their knees. Then a remarkable thing happens: some Turkish players begin pulling the Koreans to their feet, embracing them and tugging them into acknowledging the supporters in the stands alongside them. Both teams link arms together in one long line of players, from two countries, and bow to the crowd. Hakan Sukur, Turkey's greatest living player, walks from the field waving a Korean flag. The generosity of spirit is electrifying, and the spontaneity of the gesture makes it movingly authentic. There is no enmity, only empathy and goodwill. Both Turkey and South Korea know that they are the true champions of this World Cup. Watching this scene, I'm taken back to that pre-game party in Ibaraki, where that joyous lunacy seemed to be unleashed among the German and Irish fans.

• • • • •

IT IS said that national cultures are defined by national pastimes, and that national games in turn prescribe the way nations perceive themselves. This is often true, and particularly so of the great American sports of baseball and NFL football. Baseball, with its languorous pace and deep associations with summertime and childhood, encapsulates the idyllic New Eden that Americans believe is their country at its best. NFL football represents rigor and toughness, brawn and calculation. It is the American male defined. It is also true that, in Canada, hockey has a depth of meaning in the collective soul. It is a rough, dangerous, but still elegant game played on the ice, often by night, by men wearing layers of protection. Thus, it has a primordial significance for Canadians—it's about the need to defeat the ice, the cold and the darkness. It's about the need to play, to gambol in the face of the elements that could defeat Canadians if they allowed themselves to be conquered. It's about surviving. Hockey has no such significance in other countries and is only played seriously in a handful of places, just as baseball and American football are only played earnestly in a tiny number of other countries.

Soccer has long since become the international game, played in different styles and with slightly varying tactics, but played the same, really, all over the world. It defines internationalism, not a single nation. With this World Cup being played in Korea and Japan, two countries that had not traditionally been much associated with the sport, there was much talk of soccer as a herald of globalization—a cultural equivalent to economic globalization, that dismaying attempt to integrate countries and economies, diminishing the uniqueness of each. This would suggest that the international popularity of soccer has become associated with Third World sweatshops and the appearance of McDonald's outlets in countries all over the globe. But the game of soccer has actually never been part of this phenomenon. Its spread around the world began as an offshoot of imperialism at the end of the nineteenth century, a period marked by a surge in international trade between powerful European countries and their colonies or former colonies. Technology, especially television, has spread the appeal of soccer in the twenty-first century, facilitating the flow of information about games and tournaments, highlighting the sport's simplicity and grace. Just as television itself transcended cultural barriers and kicked open the shutters in closed societies, soccer has acted as a way for smaller, remote countries to engage with the rest of the world. At the level of club soccer, with players being transferred from one country to another for millions of dollars and the international sales of club shirts and other gewgaws financing such deals, soccer comes close to acting as part of contemporary economic globalization. But at the international level, at the level of the World Cup, soccer has had a benevolent, transforming power. On the evidence of the World Cup in Korea and Japan, soccer is not a force for negative nationalism. It is not war by proxy. It is, rather, the enabler for liberal, creative and constructive tensions between countries—and, best of all, those tensions can end in generosity and empathy.

CHAPTER 2

EURO 2004, PORTUGAL

IT WAS A TWO-HOUR train trip that defined a tournament. On a Monday morning, I was on the crowded platform of the shiny new glass-and-steel railway terminal in Lisbon. I was running late, and was relieved to find the train to Porto just pulling in. The wake-up call at the hotel hadn't come, I'd left the hotel in a panic and, midway between there and the station, in the taxi, I realized I'd left my cell-phone recharger plugged into the wall of my room. It was too late to turn back and retrieve it; I was counting myself lucky just to make my train.

There was bedlam when the train pulled into the platform to take on passengers. People wandered from one carriage to another, as nobody except the locals seemed to understand the complicated seating system. English, Danish and Italian fans shuffled about groggily, quickly gave up trying to figure out the system and sat anywhere they could. A group of elderly nuns, on their way to the holy shrine of Fatima, were having none of it. They had tickets with assigned seats, and those seats were occupied by young men and women from several countries, who were not going to Fatima and not holy at all, and many of those young people were already asleep.

The nuns stood and waited for an official to sort it out. As the train moved off, they swayed this way and that, so obviously in a huff. The sight of sulking nuns in the morning is a bracing one, believe me. They looked absurd, all in black, clutching handrails, trying hard to stay upright as the train gathered speed. Finally, an official arrived and looked at the tickets the nuns were clutching. He moved briskly through the carriage, ordered some Italian fans out of the seats they had claimed at random, and the nuns sat down with obvious satisfaction. I was watching, enjoying it. A nun shot me a full-on, dead-eyed stare. "No riff-raff," the look said. The Italians, all men, hung around long enough to mutter about their exasperation and give the nuns long, studious glares, rich with old enmity, before moving on.

The English fans went to sleep, all of them. Two were asleep near me, both of them wearing sunglasses. A young Portuguese woman discovered the English lads in her seat and the one next to it. She peered at their sleeping bodies. Eventually, she nudged one of them, gingerly. No response. Then she shouted, "Excuse me! Is this your seat?" The one she'd poked now awoke slowly, lowered his glasses and, after a pause, drawled, "I dunno, darling. Is it yours?" Then the pair of them moved to the nearest empty seats and promptly went back to sleep. The nuns looked out the window.

Many of the Danes, all men, invaded the restaurant car and decided to drink it dry of beer before anyone else got a chance. It was about 9 A.M. They grew sentimental and loquacious as they drank and drank and the garbage bin filled to overflowing with empty beer cans. They flirted outrageously with the petite woman struggling to run the bar. When I arrived, for coffee, I had to wait a while to get her attention. I knew from the way she giggled and twirled her hair that she was enjoying the Danes immensely. After a while, a group of Italians came in and began downing espressos. They ignored the Danes at first, but after a few beery salutations from the well-oiled fellas, everybody ended up shaking hands. The Italians smiled indulgently at the tipsy Danes. The woman in charge of the bar looked vaguely irritated that the Italians had arrived to distract the attention of the Danes from her and her terrific, long, dark hair.

When the nuns got off the train at Fatima, several Italians made a point of standing and staring at them from the windows.

Some had a whale of a time making subtly rude gestures. They giggled and nudged each other, willing the nuns to look at them. The nuns did, and appeared even more disgusted than when they'd had to stand and wait for somebody to shift the Italians out of their seats. I wandered back down the train. The English still slept.

A group of teenage schoolgirls had gotten on at Fatima. They were ecstatic to discover hundreds of male soccer fans with little to do but admire them. A small group made forays up and down the long train, buying drinks and candy they didn't need, enjoying much attention from the tipsy Danes, but they couldn't be persuaded to stay in the bar and drink beer. They were too young to drink beer, they said. So were many of the Danes, actually. The schoolgirls giggled a lot. A languid sort of giddiness hung in the air—everyone on holiday, obliged to be friendly and sweet because the thing that mattered, the football, *futbol, futebal, calcio* or soccer, had cast a spell. The train moved through green fields, past farms, and slowed as it reached the curve of the bay south of Porto. We all looked at the ocean waves as the Atlantic was glimpsed for a minute. A middle-aged Italian man stood at the open half-door between the carriages, sipped coffee and smoked a cigarette with great contentment. Still, the English slept.

At the Porto station, there was further bedlam. Some of the English had missed their stop at Coimbra, where England was going to play Switzerland in two days. They descended on the ticket office, trying to get back. After an agitated official tried to get them to form an orderly line and have their tickets changed, many decided to simply return to the platform, board the next train back towards Coimbra, and take their chances. The street outside the station entrance was suddenly crowded with arriving passengers. The half-dozen cab drivers beamed; they'd be busy for hours. Soon there were no taxis at all. Some drivers made gestures to let the Italians know they'd be back to collect them. The Italians, sensing they'd have a long wait, headed for the nearest restaurant.

Then the Danes started singing. There were hundreds of them

in their team's red shirts. They stood together facing the street and just began singing. The robust sound of mass male singing filled the air, and all activity in the streets ceased as the local people stopped to look, listen and admire. Cars stopped and the drivers gazed in wonder at the Danes. People emerged from stores to look and listen. Windows opened and faces peered out. The entire neighborhood was an audience awed by the Danish singing. It seemed that several parts of Europe, in one ragtag, motley army on a train, had arrived in Porto from Lisbon and announced its presence with mass singing to no purpose but to say hello, and it was magical.

• • • • •

I'D ARRIVED in Lisbon via London. This made sense, not just for ease of travel, but because England is expected to be the story of the tournament. Not the team, but the fans. England's presence at the World Cup in 2002 had been trouble-free. No hooligans, no fighting, no trashed bars or terrified locals. But that was in Japan, and few English fans could even afford to travel there. Portugal is on England's doorstep, a place the English have been going on holiday for years.

Before I went to Portugal, I spent an inordinate amount of time explaining why I was going. I said that Euro 2004 is, after the World Cup and the Summer Olympics, the largest sporting event in the world. But the title seemed bland and the event unimportant to those outside the soccer world. What they were unaware of is that, for three weeks, Portugal would be the center of that soccer world, and for that matter all of Europe. After a torturous two-year campaign, sixteen European countries had qualified for a tournament that will bring a million and a half fans to Portugal and be seen by billions around the world on television.

For some soccer fans, the Euro tournament is preferable to the World Cup. It's shorter, the play and rivalries more intense, and there are fewer no-hope teams to distract from the main attractions. This tournament is dominated by the top teams from

FIFA's rankings of the world's soccer countries. It features the cream of European soccer, playing at the highest possible level. There has been a Euro tournament for decades, but it came into its own in 1996. After the collapse of the Soviet Union and the arrival of many new countries eager to compete at the highest level, the qualifying for Euro 96 was fiercely competitive. The old favorites had a tough time getting through the qualifying rounds, making them better teams.

Euro 2000, held in the Netherlands and Belgium, was considered a classic. The French, coming off a host-country victory at the World Cup in 1998, were the favorites, but the Dutch were also flying high and enjoyed the bonus of home support. The final games were thrillers, with France defeating vibrant, enormously talented Portugal in the semifinal and Italy in the final. Both games were won by goals scored in sudden-death overtime, cranking up the excitement level. The level of skill was high and the entertainment level was higher still. The world's imagination was captured.

This tournament in Portugal promises exquisite games. I'm certain of it. For a start, there's certain to be tremendous pressure on Portugal, as the host country, to at last fulfill its promise and land a major trophy. The Portuguese team has been thrilling fans for a decade. The core of the 2004 side has been drawn from what is called the Golden Generation of players that won several world and European youth tournaments a decade ago. At the senior level, they have yet to live up to the expectations set at those tournaments. For some of the top players—Luís Figo and Rui Costa—this may be their final opportunity to play together on the national team. At the same time, Portugal has a stunning new talent in teenager Cristiano Ronaldo, who has emerged in one season playing for Manchester United as a startlingly gifted winger and playmaker.

For France, too, the pressure is high: they limped out of the World Cup in a kind of numb disgrace. The blame was put on the team's manager rather than the star players. Now, however, another controversy surrounds the current manager, Jacques

Santini, who became highly regarded for compelling his players to transcend the disaster of the World Cup and breeze through qualifying for Euro 2004. However, just before the tournament, he announced that, as soon as it's over, he'll leave the national program to take over as manager of Tottenham Hotspur in the English Premier League. That announcement bespeaks a problem behind the scenes. It remains to be seen whether the performance of the two best players in the world—France's Zinedine Zidane and Thierry Henry—will be affected.

The Dutch, the other favorites to go far, if not win the tournament, turn out be in disarray, too. As so often happens with a talented Dutch side, the team is racked by infighting. There are factions and cliques that don't get along, and it is rumored that stars Ruud van Nistelrooy and Patrick Kluivert—two essential components to the Dutch attack—are barely able to tolerate each other's presence in the same room. In the final Dutch warmup game, a 1–0 defeat to Ireland played in Amsterdam, the Dutch team was booed off the field.

In these circumstances, an unlikely team might take advantage of the disharmony in superior opponents. The English might do well, but theirs seems to be a team built more on hope and hype than brilliant talent. Yes, they have David Beckham, but he rarely shines in big, high-pressure games. The two strikers who will be needed to score goals against tough opposition, Michael Owen of Liverpool and Wayne Rooney of Everton, are mercurial talents who might either be masterful or outclassed—nobody knows. The team from Spain has a reputation for failing when it comes to big competitions. This time, expectations are lower, so the Spaniards could surprise many by going all the way to the semifinals and beyond. Much depends on Real Madrid's Raul, who hasn't had a strong season with the club, but there are other exceptional talents in Juan Carlos Valeron, Xabi Alonso and Fernando Torres. Italy faces its ancient problem—the constant controversy about the selection of aging stalwarts over younger, fresher talent. Christian Vieri will be there, along with talismanic Francesco Totti, but there's a feeling in Italy that aging Alessandro

Del Piero has been called up to the national team only for sentimental reasons or to please a team sponsor. Exactly what manager Giovanni Trapattoni is doing has been difficult to decipher. Italy is still feeling stung by their exit from the World Cup in a bizarre defeat to South Korea—a game that lives in infamy among Italian supporters—and there is much pride to be restored.

In the midst of these glamour teams, though, I think the surprise highlight could well be supplied by the Czech Republic. The team always performs well on the international stage, and in Pavel Nedved it has a genuinely fast, gifted player who seems to be in his prime. The Czechs have been placed in a group that also contains Germany, the Dutch and Latvia. While Latvia is expected to exit early, the Czechs, Dutch and Germans will battle it out. Germany is at a low ebb, but has brought in many young talents who played well at the under-21 level. Maybe those youths can surprise everyone.

What I don't know is that what is about to unfold is something no one could have predicted. The pecking order of European soccer will temporarily be turned on its head.

• • • • •

AT HEATHROW, I eyed the English passengers with grave interest. It was two days before Euro 2004 was to open, but some on my plane were probably going to Lisbon to get an early start. The plane was half-full, and there were no obvious hooligans on board. The only talk about soccer came from a group of six young men who were casually but expensively dressed. They sat together, drank coffee together and then, oddly, went to the newsstand together and bought magazines to read on the plane— GQ, Esquire, Maxim, and the like. The kind of magazines that informed young, well-off Englishmen how to dress, drink, drive and disrobe young women. Each of them bought two. When the flight landed in Lisbon, I saw that they had left them all behind. For some reason, I looked at the cover of each and noted the price. In my head, I totted up the total cost of the twelve magazines—almost as much as my ticket from London to Lisbon. This was England in 2004: cocky, extravagant, glossy and Beckham-esque in everything. I really couldn't see these guys getting drunk on cheap lager and leading a violent charge on Portugal's sleepy towns.

As soon as he determined I was a journalist, the immigration official at the airport was anxious to canvass my opinion of the possible looming hordes of English hooligans. I told him, truthfully, that the problem seemed to have been solved by the police in England and that Portugal was not likely to suffer much more than drunkenness. "But there are so many of them!" he exclaimed. "Many, many hooligans." I suggested that he shouldn't worry. He straightened up and looked me in the eye. "If they come, we are ready!" he said. Then he welcomed me to Portugal. There was no point in explaining to this nice man that if any English hooligans did show up, they could probably be distracted by the police distributing glossy magazines about shoes, suits and the disrobing of women.

• • • • •

AT SOME point over the next twenty-four hours, I fell in love. With Lisbon. A city of stone that is obsessed with soccer; a city of cafés and conviviality; of early-morning mist over the yawning mouth of the River Tagus; of luscious pastries and ambrosial port wine; of breathtaking light at noon and bewitching laughter at night; of broad avenues and tiny cobblestone streets; of ancient trams gliding ever upward into the steep hills that surround the downtown; of churches and fado bars; of sweet and pleasant people. I stayed at the Sheraton for the Friday night when I arrived. It would be my only night in such a hotel. The next day, the price of my room would triple.

At the media center, it was all hustle and bustle, the climax of six years of preparing for thousands of journalists and more than a million soccer fans to descend on the country. I'd be up and down to Porto for the next two and a half weeks, and there would be one night when I had no hotel reservation—an arrangement that was dealt with in minutes, as were those for the media pass, the game tickets and all else that I would need. I was cheery and delighted with my second major assignment to cover a soccer tournament. Best of all, I wouldn't be alone this time. I'd only spent twenty minutes with Chris Young of the *Toronto Star* in Korea, but I'd be sharing an apartment with him in Porto for a while. I write about this in a "Postcard from Portugal," a series of brief *Globe* pieces designed to add color to the soccer coverage. I announce that we'll be shacked up, like the Mole Sisters. An editor deletes the reference to the Mole Sisters.

• • • • •

ON SATURDAY morning I take the train to Porto, where the opening game between Portugal and Greece is to take place. But only a handful of Greek fans are on board, and nobody from Lisbon. In Lisbon, going to Porto for any purpose is considered an outlandish thing to do. My hotel turns out to be in the Villa Nova de Gaia district, south of the city center and on the other side of the River Douro. It's an ancient part of Porto, and it's where the "lodges," or storage areas, for port are located. My hotel, though, is very new, just opened, and the cab driver at the station has to confer about its location with at least four colleagues before we set off.

• • • • •

THE STADIUM in Porto is new, too, and the next day, when I ask to be taken to Dragão Stadium, the driver is bewildered. "Football!" I said, figuring that, as Euro 2004 is due to open in three hours, the destination will be clear. I am informed, with much merriment, that the stadium is home to FC Porto and must always, always, be referred to as Porto Stadium.

By either name, the facility is magnificent. First come the opening ceremonies. A galleon of sorts occupies the middle of the field, and people representing fishes dart around it. For about an hour, the glorious history of Portugal's past as a seafaring and conquering nation is enacted. Then the soccer starts. It would

be a grievous error to suggest that Portugal expects to win—it
has been *ordained* that the home team will prevail and then, holding focus, win the tournament outright. But Portugal loses,
beaten 2–1 by Greece. This is trouble. Greece! Along with Latvia,
Greece is considered the weakest team in the tournament. The
Greeks appeared at the World Cup in 1994, but failed to score a
single goal or earn a single point. They failed to qualify for the
World Cups in 1998 and 2002. Of the players, only the stocky
little Giorgos Karagounis is well known, because he plays for
Inter Milan.

Portugal's players, each one a great talent, play like nervous,
underrehearsed actors on opening night. They fuss and flub
passes They look amazed that the Greeks have four men playing in defense. They seem to take umbrage at the rigor and discipline of the Greeks. Under a German manager, Otto Rehhagel,
the Greeks haven't a worry in the world as long they keep playing their rigid formation and maintain possession of the ball.
They attack twice and score two goals. Portugal constantly tries
to attack, but can't penetrate a team prepared to defend forever.
From the kickoff, Portugal looks rattled against a side that is
splendidly organized, concise and predatory. After mere minutes,
Karagounis takes the ball in midfield, sees a Portuguese defense
hesitating and unleashes a shot. It's 1–0. Portugal coach Felipe
"Big Phil" Scolari, a man who coached Brazil to victory at the
World Cup two years earlier, looks on, puzzled and then furious. At halftime he makes substitutions, bringing on youngsters
Deco and Cristiano Ronaldo. It is Ronaldo, fabulously gifted in
ball control, who emerges the fool and fouls Giourkas Seitaridis
in the penalty area. Even the referee, the great Pierluigi Collina
of Italy, a man whose authority is emphasized by his grim
demeanor, looks slightly amused by events.

Greece's performance is far from pretty. They cannot echo the
elegance of Figo, the pirouettes of Ronaldo or the deft feints of
Costa. They keep things plain and frighteningly, coolly effective.
In the last, dying moments, with the stadium silent except for the
few hundred delirious Greek fans in the corner, Greece lets

Ronaldo reach the ball from a Figo corner and heads home a goal that is well earned but redundant. It is the ninety-fourth minute. The Greece coach, Rehhagel, is instantly declared a genius. He has taken ordinary players and molded them into a disciplined group who can beat the fast, albeit nervous, Portuguese. Much has been made of his experience in Germany, but this is no made-in-Germany tactical victory; it comes from a playbook that countless national teams have studied—when faced with faster, more talented and attack-minded teams, the policy is keep possession, hold the ball, play the ground. Never let the ball free unless you're certain it'll reach a team member. Claim the ground you hold, never yield, and if goals must come, they will come from what the opposition awards you—free kicks, corner kicks, penalties. The other team can't score if they don't have the ball.

It is, to some, ugly soccer, but to a tactician it is a beautiful example of how the soccer field is a venue where small men can beat larger men and small countries can drain the force from a larger one's ambition. Do nothing erratic. Don't be awed. A goal here, a 0–0 draw there, and at a tournament, a disciplined team of small talent can go far—and give succor to the underdogs, the unglamorous and unpopular. This type of game is what it is: a route to glory by dint of restraint and resolve.

● ● ● ● ●

VERY EARLY the next morning, I head back to Lisbon. The cab driver tells me I don't need to go to the main station in Porto— all trains stop at the old station in Gaia. I hope he is right as we cruise slowly through the cobblestone streets, past the port lodges with the whitewashed signs declaring they belong to Taylor's, Croft or Sandeman. At the crest of a hill, the car pauses in the silent streets and I suddenly see the wide expanse of the mouth of the River Duoro, the morning mist still lingering over the water. It takes my breath away.

The Gaia station is a dilapidated, near-deserted old building. Three men are hanging around outside; the station's doors are still locked. Eventually, the stationmaster comes grumpily on duty a few minutes before the train arrives. He's testy and he looks hungover and angry. He's in no mood for chatter after the previous night's defeat of Portugal. When he examines my ticket, I offer up a *"Força Portugal!"* He grimaces and walks away, muttering a mantra I know translates as "disaster, disaster."

The train is crowded, mostly with Greek fans returning in fine spirits from a glorious victory. The middle-aged businessmen, prosperous-looking and obviously heading to Lisbon for the sort of meeting that requires a good suit, gaze at their laptops as the Greeks move to and from the restaurant car.

In Lisbon, the old central station is full of police officers watching the English fans. There's wariness in the air. And on the taxi ride to my hotel, I see what makes the Portuguese wary: in one of the city's old squares, English fans have gathered, thousands of them. They've staked out their territory on a traffic island, as cars and buses snake around them. They are sullenly isolated there, with their flags and their beer, staring out at the locals, who avert their eyes. Many stand bare-chested, with beer bellies. The cab driver glances at them and snaps, in English: "Trouble, trouble. Beer, beer." I don't argue, but the English look more absurd than menacing. The song "Clocks" by Coldplay is on the radio as we sweep past the massed English army of fans, and in my mind the English look more like stoned rock music fans than hooligans.

For all the pasty white flesh, beer bellies and angry looks, English soccer has long since been gentrified. The poisonous rage that had once been part of the culture has withered away. In Thatcher's England, the thugs were located and isolated. In Blair's England, the game has become entertainment again—a commodity, a "Cool Britannia" cornucopia of pop-star players, pay-TV hyperbole and fashionable shirts, shoes and men's perfumes.

There is something faintly ridiculous about it all, the manic insistence on the superiority of English club teams filled with players from France, Holland, Spain, Italy and every corner of Europe. The English national team cruises along on a mad optimism fueled by tabloid-press attention and the mind-boggling assumption that, because the English players have the coolest, sexiest wives and girlfriends, they have the world beaten already. I suspect that some among the beer-bellied hordes hugging the center of a patch of a grass in Lisbon know more about the shopping habits of David Beckham's wife than they know about the tactics the English defenders might use against France later this evening.

• • • • •

IT IS a grand game. But first there is the getting there. I take the subway to the Estádio da Luz, and almost every other person on the train is an English supporter. They're very cheerful, all smiles, and there's no hint of aggression. In fact, most are teenage boys and young women and they seem very preppy, not the least bit interested in brawling. Outside the stadium, their sheer numbers are apparent. The stadium holds sixty-five thousand people and about forty thousand English are here. The Lisbon police are clearly nervous, but pragmatic. When it looks like some hundreds of the English are getting fed up waiting in line to go through security, more entrances are opened and all the swearing and complaining stops.

In the press room, I spot Tom Humphries of the *Irish Times*. A writer of some genius, one who can be as effectively whimsical as he can be passionate, Humphries is a man I admire enormously. He's also a key figure in recent Irish history—it was his interview with Roy Keane that precipitated the bitter arguments that led to Keane's absence from the Irish team in Korea/Japan. I approach Tom as a kid would approach a famous player. I gush, telling him I always read his column and have also read his book. Tom, a bear of a man, finds this terrifically amusing. He smiles, looks down at me and says, in his Dublin accent, "You've too much time on your hands, young man."

Minutes later, Tom and I are trying to get into the press area of the stadium. But the doors are locked. The police tell us we can't go to another entrance. We need to go through special

security because we have laptops and other equipment. It's about
fifteen minutes before the game begins. Tom introduces me to
some other Irish reporters. I am a figure of great curiosity to
them—Irish-born, living in Canada, the TV critic for a national
newspaper and on assignment covering major soccer tournaments. We decide that telling some official about the potential
headline—"Irish reporters barred from England game"—might
get the doors open.

Eventually, we're in. Chris Young and I are seated together,
with an excellent view of the field and the WAGs—wives and
girlfriends—corralled next to us. It's comical, really. A small
army of women who all look rather alike: blonde, thin and
bosomy, surrounded by their pals, press agents, bodyguards and
God knows whom. The one none of us can see, because even
in this crowd she's tiny, is Beckham's wife, Victoria. She's surrounded by handlers whose job it is to make sure nobody can
see and photograph her until she's ready. This is a source of
much snide comment from the journalists around us, who are
French, German, Swiss and Italian. Some make mocking hi-
how-are-you waves at the WAGs and, in several languages,
announce that they're all ugly. The handlers and some of the
WAGs wave back, oblivious to the foreign-language insults.
When some journalists begin to laugh hysterically, there are
mystified stares, and then glares. When the England team walks
onto the field, the photographers focus on Beckham, then twirl
and aim their cameras where Victoria is sitting. At this moment,
outright farce ensues. Her handlers move out of the way and
we all get a brief glimpse of Mrs. Beckham, wearing giant sunglasses and waving wanly at something in the distance.

At every England game, at home or abroad, the WAGs sit corralled like this in an exclusive area, with a fine view of the field.
It occurs to me that there's something familiar about the scene,
something that harks back to descriptions I've read, and depic-
tions I've seen in movies, of Victorian England at the height of
the old Empire, at war in some far-flung locale such as Crimea.
It's uncanny how those gathered women—pampered, tanned and

privileged—resemble the wives, fiancées and mistresses of English generals gathered for a picnic and fine view of the battles. The fans may no longer be hooligans, but the English national team is still going to war.

Tom Humphries has long taken the view that at major tournaments, the England team is the fat man who falls on the banana peel in an old-fashioned slapstick comedy routine. It always happens. There's such hyperbole and grandiosity surrounding the England team that, when the overrated players inevitably lose a game and exit the tournament, it's because of some appalling, awful mistake, a rogue referee or some other villain. There was Beckham's childish kick at an Argentine during a game at the World Cup in France in 1998 that got him ejected and reduced a rattled English side to ten men. There was the long, long ball from Ronaldinho of Brazil during the 2002 World Cup, a ball that caught goalkeeper David Seaman by surprise, way off his line and obviously stunned that that the ball was coming from such an incredible distance. He failed to stop it, and England lost. There was the feeling in England that that was a freak goal, a once-in-a-lifetime shot that hit the net. It's always, always, something freakish or foolish that is the cause of England's downfall. The atmosphere that surrounds the team is a complicated mixture of arrogance and farce. The fans, the media and even the players cannot make up their minds whether England approaches a tournament with cocky superiority or the nervous energy of the plucky underdog.

On paper, the English team looks far less glamorous than the star-studded French side. It looks as if they will rely on luck and the bulldog spirit to force an unlikely victory; those realists who are present hope for a draw. But on this night, you can't ask for more in an international soccer game. It unfolds as a thriller that the English seem destined to win, but they fall to defeat in the dying seconds. There are two superb goals, a missed penalty and a well-taken penalty in a last-second climax. As in many classic operas, there is tragedy and farce.

For the first thirty minutes, the French show the sort of flair and poise on the ball that make them deadly opponents—they're the sort of team that makes everybody else look a little slow. To the massive number of English fans, it's a matter of urging on their underdogs. They sing and sing, cheer and whistle. They even try to drown out the French national anthem at the start, a serious breach of etiquette at international tournaments. The French team doesn't mind. They begin and play havoc with the English defense, with Robert Pirès making countless blazing runs down the right side. Within minutes, the English goal is under siege, and goalkeeper David James is reminding his defenders to keep calm.

For half an hour, this continues English strikers Owen and Rooney make occasional forays towards the French goal, but the entire English team is being outrun. Then, England gets a free kick and Beckham, the free-kick specialist, takes it. It lands perfectly for Frank Lampard to head a glorious goal that leaves French keeper Fabien Barthez wondering what has happened. Suddenly, the second act is under way. Convinced they can score and win, the English pick up the pace. The entire stadium is enthralled by the skill and pace of the game. Thousands of English fans begin whistling a tune together. The enjoyment level is wildly high.

Chris Young turns to me and says, "This is a fucking brilliant game." And it is. Even as the second half starts and the French midfield keeps trying to send pinpoint passes to Thierry Henry, the English hold firm and never panic. Wayne Rooney begins to match the French for pace and uses his tanklike body to harass defenders.

The French still aim for poise and flow, but Zinedine Zidane seems to be floundering. His passes simply can't connect. I'm watching him as he walks slowly to the touchline, well behind the play, and vomits onto the grass. He's dehydrated and exhausted—he seems spent. By this stage, the English fans are roaring. They sing "God Save the Queen" and "Rule Britannia" several times. They sense a famous victory is minutes away. Then, a tragicomic moment turns the operatic game towards its third and final act.

Rooney springs forward, heading towards the goal with only French defender Mikaël Silvestre to beat. Silvestre brings him down. The referee points to the penalty spot; the English supporters are ecstatic. Beckham takes the penalty shot and misses. Barthez, Beckham's old colleague from his Manchester United days, saves it with aplomb. Now, the French are rejuvenated. Even Zidane moves up into another gear, and when the opportunity comes, he takes it.

The English players are deflated, in shock, after the penalty miss. Emile Heskey commits a panicky foul. The resulting free kick is just outside the English penalty area and Zidane unleashes a blistering shot that goes straight into the English net. It is now the ninetieth minute. The English fans are stunned into silence; the players look even more bewildered, but worse is to come.

A minute after Zidane's goal, as the clock ticks on injury time, David James is all nerves as he tries to stop Henry in the penalty area. Henry is manhandled to the ground. The referee has no option: it's penalty time again. Zidane takes the kick and scores. Seconds later, the final whistle comes. The game has turned and twisted like a perverse narrative about hope and spirit being crushed by fate, haste and the horror of time running out. The French supporters dance and sing in the stands as the English sit, some weeping openly. Chris heads off to try to get into the post-game press conference. I go looking for the English fans to see if I can score a quote, an authentic reaction. One man knows what I need before I can even ask. He stares at me and puts out his arms in the gesture of defeat. "After all of that . . ." he says, and pauses. He tries again. "After all of that!" Then he has to gulp for air. "After all of that, we fucking lost! I don't believe it."

There's no point telling him that European operas are often like that. Two games into the tournament, and both Portugal and England have lost.

• • • • •

THE NEXT morning, I take that memorable train ride back to
Porto. I'm learning fast. In Korea and Japan, the smaller number
of supporters from other countries made it an anomaly of a tournament. Part of the vigor and charm of Euro 2004 can be ascribed
to the sixteen traveling armies of fans who move around Portugal,
from game to game, city to city, supporting their country. There
are only a few hundred Greeks, apparently, but forty thousand
English and as many Dutch fans. About twenty thousand Swedes
are expected. It's a surreal and captivating ambience. The traveling fans are everywhere, and the locals must cope. They knew
it was coming. Leave town for an afternoon and you return to
find that twenty thousand people, all wearing the same color of
shirts, have taken over the downtown bars, restaurants and
cafés.

From Porto, I immediately board a bus to the ancient town
of Guimarães, where Italy will play Denmark in the afternoon
sun. It's about 95°F and the reporters are beginning to wilt, but
only slightly. A woman journalist from Denmark makes a fuss
about having to wait in the sun to go through a lengthy security
check. The Italian contingent, nattily dressed and seething with
contempt for everything Portuguese, take this as a sign to launch
an assault on the security check. In the midst of much annoyance
and angrily expressed grievances, they all suddenly shut up.
Arsène Wenger, the French manager of the English team Arsenal,
is ushered through. He's doing some TV punditry. The female
Danish journalist is now behind me and tells me, in excellent
English, that the word Arsenal is pretty darn funny if you think
about it. She really should consider wearing a hat in full, 95-
degree sun, but there's no point in telling her.

As it happens, the game is hardly worth the fuss.

• • • • •

IT IS a watchword within the insular Italian soccer culture that
the national team always starts slowly at an international tournament. And sure, it's true that the Italian team has gradually

sputtered to life at a World Cup or two, but what happens in Guimarães is a bit much. The immensely talented Italian front line, featuring Serie A superstars Alessandro Del Piero, Francesco Totti and bull-like Christian Vieri, manage a 0–0 draw with Denmark, and it is more than the lethargic Italians deserve. The Danes are the highlight, playing a crisp, disciplined game, always moving forward and looking for scoring chances. The final score doesn't do them justice.

In truth, little happens. At the end, an English reporter sitting near me asks, "What the hell do I write about?"

Well, I have my own ideas.

First, there is Vieri strolling the field, occasionally seeming to lose interest in the contest and pausing to gaze down at his hideous lime-green boots. Maybe he was marveling at the amount of money he is being paid by some athletic shoe company to wear such ugly things on his talented feet. And then there's Totti, of whom so much is always expected. He loped around for a good while in the first half and, on occasion, stopped to scratch his ass. These are the things you don't see in the televised version—you have to be there. Perhaps what he was wondering about was why the Danes took the game so very seriously indeed.

Ignoring what was clearly hot air from the Italian propaganda machine—suggestions that there would be a scoring feast and Denmark would have to defend hard—the Danes raced and pushed forward constantly, partly on the strength of the roars and singing of their marvelously vocal supporters, but mostly because they actually wanted to win the game. Yes, it was a hot afternoon in Guimarães, and the town itself is a tad sleepy, but there was no excuse for Italy's mediocrity. What energy the Italians spent was channeled into complaining. There were more divas on the Italian team than you would find at the annual Milan fashion show. Del Piero dove, Vieri grumbled at the referee often and Totti looked on with apparent uninterest.

They looked like self-satisfied fops. For the first thirty minutes, Danish winger Martin Jørgensen did a merry dance around the Italian defense, and with the entire Danish team capable of moving forward, goalkeeper Gianluigi Buffon was the busiest man on the Italian side. In contrast, Danish keeper Thomas Sørensen was relatively idle.

It was the sort of game that English TV soccer commentators call "an absorbing encounter." That means the observer is supposed to appreciate the nuance of tactical formations and the shifts therein. In reality, there was nothing absorbing about it. I don't know what they call this sort of game in Italy, but I hope it is something approaching "a disgrace." And I take the view that Vieri really should give up the lime-green boots, no matter how much he's being paid. Given his performance, they're clearly a distraction for the player wearing them.

The thousands of cheering Danish supporters who came all the way to Portugal seemed to enjoy themselves. I've no idea what the English reporter filed for his paper, but that's the gist of what I write.

· · · · ·

BACK IN Porto that night, three things become clear. First, my laptop isn't working properly. It's supposed to be wired for high-speed Internet access, but it declines to cooperate. I've had to use dial-up connections over regular phone lines, using phone cards, a practice that is time-consuming and fraught with tension. Already, I've absconded from the stadium in Guimarães on the last bus out of town for Porto without filing my story. There is no working phone at the apartment I'm about to begin sharing with Chris Young. Second, by pure coincidence, most of the phone system in Porto has collapsed. Parts of the city have no landline service at all. Third, the Dutch have arrived, for the next day's game against Germany. The streets of old Porto are a sea of orange, the color of the shirts worn by thousands of Dutch fans.

I cab it to my hotel in search of a working phone line. A nice young man tells me that the phones aren't working but he can get me into a nearby hotel where, he's been told, the phones work. It's not such a nice hotel, he warns me, but if I want a room he can get me in. I accept. Fifteen minutes later, I arrive at the new hotel. The first thing I notice is that there seems to be a waterfall in the lobby. It turns out some pipes have burst and water is pouring through the ceiling. Staff with buckets and mops are working frantically. At the front desk, I ask if the phones are working. The young woman gives me a sad look. They stopped working ten minutes ago. Do I still want the room? Yes, I have no choice. In a tiny room without running water—the water's now been turned off—I try to file my story using a cell phone connected to the laptop. Can't make it work.

I call the *Globe* in Toronto and explain. There's silence from the guy on the sports desk. Someone will call me back. Thus, at 2 A.M., I end up dictating, over a crackling cell phone connection, the story about Italy playing Denmark. When I get to the bit about Totti scratching his ass, both the editor, in Toronto, and I, in Porto, start laughing.

The story appears the next day, but that isn't end of it. In the *Globe*'s daily internal memo assessing the day's paper, a senior editor points out that my use of the word *disinterest* was incorrect. He uses my story to lecture staff about the difference between *un*interested and *dis*interested. I am cited as an example of poor writing. The man is obviously unaware of the nineteen-hour working day I had. I decide to let him know. And then head off to see Holland play Germany before there's a reply.

At lunchtime on the Avenida dos Aliados, the wide main drag in Porto, there's an ocean of orange shirts. The Dutch fans have taken over, lending a dash of bold color to a street of imposing, but grey, nineteenth-century buildings. The Dutch are also here to have fun. They are expecting to win. I see a large group of them on their march to the Porto stadium for the game. They are led by an eccentric fellow dressed as a cowboy, but head to toe in orange—orange Stetson, shirt, jeans and cowboy boots. He even has an orange holster—without, of course, an orange gun. Coming in the opposite direction is a group of German fans, and they are all in white. They stop, bemused by the wacky Dutch group. The orange cowboy, a genuine wit, throws his arms in the air and declares to the Germans, *"Vive la France!"* The Germans burst into laughter. It's a light moment that precedes a tense, entertaining game.

The Dutch may fully expect a win, but they are just kept afloat in the tournament by a goal from Ruud van Nistelrooy in the eighty-first minute. Along the way, a youthful German team tears the Dutch defense to shreds. The Dutch start lively enough, but lack imagination. Soon, the Germans sense that the Dutch are playing a predictable pattern and begin sending balls forward through Michael Ballack and Dietmar Hamann, who is playing better here than he's ever played for his club team, Liverpool. Ballack owns the midfield and makes his opponent, the famously arrogant Edgar Davids, look ineffectual. The Germans run riot, and Dutch captain Phillip Cocu can be seen lambasting his colleagues for their sloppiness. It ends 1–1, and it is more out of relief than joy that those in orange shirts are singing at the end. I think of the orange-clad Dutch cowboy— he had his wits about him, but his team didn't.

• • • • •

THE NEXT morning, Chris and I are eating a hearty breakfast in a tiny café next to the apartment. We sit at the counter and, in a mixture of pidgin Portuguese and English, chat with Maria, the woman in charge. It is mid-morning, and after our meal we make sarcastic remarks about editors at various publications. Prominent political and lifestyle columnists are also eviscerated— us being at a safe distance in Porto and all, and it being unlikely that our remarks will be overheard and reported back.

While we gossip and gripe, the café fills with construction workers on their lunch break. Most drink draft beer with a shot of whiskey poured into it. Maria sees us looking and offers us a beer and a shot, on the house, but we just drink more coffee. We encourage her, the construction workers, and all of Portugal to be hopeful about the country's chances. Maria, in her apron with a Luís Figo shirt beneath, wags her finger and tells us we are flattering the Portuguese team, those guys who couldn't even beat Greece. At least we *figure* that's what she is saying.

The construction workers drink their beer and shake their heads in despair. Portugal has disgraced itself. A man from a local store comes by for his morning coffee and is delighted to use his English to translate for us. Yes, he confirms, the whole country is depressed. Then we journalists chat amongst ourselves, admiring the compact café. I remark to Chris that the clock on the wall—a souvenir of the World Cup in France in 1998, with a soccer field on its face and little soccer balls in place of the numbers—is a beauty, a classic novelty piece that represents the local obsession with soccer.

A few minutes later, as we are about to pay and leave, Maria shyly hands me a plastic bag. Unsure what is happening, I just smile and look inside. There is the clock. I am speechless. Thankyous in English and Portuguese are inadequate. We stay and have lunch. We stay for ages. We have beer, but not with the shots of whiskey. We are all friends. It's the way it is.

· · · · ·

TWO THINGS are happening on this day. The entire country is on tenterhooks about Portugal's game against Russia in Lisbon. At the same time, there is a keen, nervous interest in the Greece–Spain encounter in Porto. We want to see if the remarkable Greeks can carry off another upset. For Portugal, the question is this: Will the dreaded neighbors next door crush Greece and take control of their group in the tournament, setting up a titanic, and possibly disastrous, encounter between Portugal and Spain in a few days?

By game time, you can cut the tension with a knife. The air around the Bessa stadium is filled with the sound of Spanish fans pounding their drums when we arrive. You can hear it for miles. There is an unnerving quality to that sound—it's triumphant and emphatic even before the game has started. Inside the small stadium—Bessa is home to the Boavista team, the working-class heroes of this part of Porto—the Spanish fan presence is extraordinary. They get a rhythm going, and it is glorious. After the drums come the mass clapping, the jumping and shouting of

"*Viva España*"—and then, for good measure, a few "*Olé, olé, olé*" chants.

The Greek fans, vastly outnumbered, could not care less. Their team has beaten Portugal; anything can happen. And it does. In the end, you could say that the Greeks beat Spain by drawing 1–1. The Greeks, playing the sort of spirited but disciplined soccer that served them so well against Portugal, hold off wave after wave of relentless, attacking Spanish play and then manage to equalize after Spain finally scores. The Greek midfield is astonishing throughout, with Theodoros Zagorakis and Panagiotis Fyssas battling endlessly to stop every Spanish attack. And there is wave after wave of elegantly fast Spanish play in an effort to finish off the Greeks. Like Portugal a few days earlier, the Spaniards discover that the Greeks are riding a wave and it's impossible to resist. The small, hardy band of Greek supporters are the happiest group in Porto by early evening.

• • • • •

THERE'S A melancholy feeling central to the Portuguese spirit. It's called *saudade*, as far as I can gather, and its core expression is the eerily sorrowful music called *fado*. The music, drenched in regret, is not so much the equivalent of the blues as it is a stubborn, languid refusal to be optimistic. It's all about the greatness of the past, the problems of the present and a delicate hope for the future, but a fragile hope that's sure to be crushed. That melancholy feeling pervades Portugal for days. The population collectively throws up its hands and expects the worst. The country goes into a massive mope that is inexplicable unless you understand that *saudade* feeling.

The big mope ends a few hours after the Greeks draw with Spain and Portugal beats Russia 2–0. The two Canadian reporters watch it on TV, in the bar of the Sheraton hotel. We had no end of trouble getting in, as the bar was closed to riff-raff such as us and was full of well-dressed business types. Only the prominent display of our press badges, and the promise that we'd only stay for a few minutes, got us in.

A hotel-manager type eyes us throughout, even as the game plays out on TV, and I don't blame him. We are dressed casually for the setting. I'm in jeans, a polo shirt and nylon jacket. On my head is a baseball cap that announces I'm from Canada. Still, we are eventually forgotten and allowed to watch the game to the end. Then we walk back to the apartment, write down our expenses for the day, have tea and biscuits, call friends and family in Canada, and sleep. Every time I write about the tea and biscuits and living like the Mole Sisters, an editor takes it out.

• • • • •

IN COIMBRA the next day, England thrashes Switzerland 3–0. The town of Coimbra is pretty. It's got an ancient university that dates back to the thirteenth century. It is home to only about 130,000 citizens, who live in a certain splendor amid old buildings that mark that this town was once, centuries ago, the capital of Portugal. On the day when English and Swiss soccer fans invade the town, there is a kind of all-consuming chaos of stopped traffic, frazzled police and long lines of excited people waiting in line at endless security checks that seem to start about 6.25 miles from the town. And yet, the only ugly event is the game itself.

England faces a decidedly determined group of players who are obviously out to ensure that the superstars never keep the ball in possession long enough to set up flowing play. In return, some oddly crude, nervous actions by the English defense end with several Swiss free kicks that show they might score. That isn't supposed to happen. It is ages before the game settles and England begins to dominate.

After the game, the English soccer fans are very cheerful, as well they might be. I hear one fan say to another, "Well, we beat them, but they were shit." He's right. The victory keeps England's hopes in the tournament alive, but really, this was a trouncing of a mediocre Swiss side that played with ten men for the latter portion of the game. A better team than England would have made it a five- or six-goal feast. The Swiss are doomed to failure after defender Bernt Haas receives a second yellow card and auto-

matic dismissal sixty minutes into the game. The English fans
sing "Cheerio, cheerio" as Haas leaves the field. Even some of
the Swiss players smile at that. And down to ten men, the Swiss
know no one would blame them if England hit them hard with
more goals.

On this day, I am deeply interested in the Swiss team, actually. It was Switzerland that proved to be Ireland's undoing in a
fraught and fractious campaign to qualify for Euro 2004. After
the epic events of Ireland's appearance at the 2002 World Cup,
things fell apart. Ireland lost—and lost badly—to Russia in its
first qualifying game for Euro 2004. Then, on an October night
in Dublin, Ireland lost to Switzerland, no less. It was a game the
battling, never-say-die Irish could expect to win with ease, but
the team looked tired and deeply unsure. A tactical mistake engi-
neered by Mick McCarthy from the sideline gave Switzerland
certain victory with its second goal in a 2–0 win.

I watched it on TV at McVeigh's in Toronto. Heard the chilly
silence in the Dublin stadium following the second goal. Then
saw McCarthy's face harden, horribly, and age a decade as the
crowd began chanting, "Keano! Keano!" It was an unmerciful
taunt, a brutal reminder that, no matter what had happened in
Korea and Japan, the upshot was that McCarthy had sent Ireland's
best player into exile. The crowd was unforgiving. McCarthy
was unrepentant. Soon after, he was no longer Ireland's manager.
Another heart grown brutal from the fray.

His replacement, Brian Kerr, was a mild-mannered man who
had been in charge of the Republic of Ireland youth teams, which
had won both the under-16 and under-18 European championships. No other Irish teams had actually won a trophy before.
Kerr's appointment was greeted with enormous optimism in
Ireland. It was viewed as a breath of fresh air after the McCarthy–
Keane saga. And yet, a year after McCarthy departed, Ireland
was trounced by Switzerland again, thus failing to qualify for the
drama in Portugal. The Swiss had proved hard to beat. The easy
win by England over a mediocre Swiss team only emphasized
how low Ireland had sunk.

On this warm summer day in Coimbra, England doesn't look too sharp, either. Those allegedly great players—Beckham, Steven Gerrard and Michael Owen—seem so ordinary, laboring to overcome the Swiss. It's the English supporters who are exceptional. They're so unfailingly cheerful, even as the police and security officials, and Portugal itself, seem to loathe and fear them. They wait in line for hours, they sing and whistle in unison; they seem to have an unfailing, intoxicatingly sunny disposition. They're on trial, they know. One hint of hooliganism and the summer adventure in Portugal will end immediately.

By late evening, Chris and I are back in Porto, eating in a *churrasco* restaurant, a large, crowded, cheerful place. We're sitting at the counter, glad to find seats, glad to taste the tall glasses of cold beer, and we're looking at the menus. Around us, we know, there are dozens of English supporters. They're eating, drinking, watching the TV screens that replay the day's events at Euro 2004. Out of nowhere, a young man appears beside me. He introduces himself with a terribly sincere politeness and says he can recommend a few items on the menu. He's English and he's happy. And he's trying hard to dispel any notion that the English fans should be feared. It's an achingly honest gesture, this appeal to two journalists to acknowledge that the English are earnest, peaceful people—charming, even. When we leave more than an hour later, he's still there and he nudges his friends to say hello and salute us.

On the street, waiting for a taxi, we fall into conversation with two English couples. They are in their twenties, and both guys look like Jamie Oliver. They sound like him, too. Their girlfriends have the slatternly look that young English women seem to cultivate in Portugal. They wear low-cut tops that expose loads of white but reddening skin.

Around us on the street, there are Italian and Swedish fans teeming, looking for late drinks, laughing and relaxed. The two countries will play in Porto the next day. I realize the English look less chic, less sophisticated. They carry an air of gauche optimism. But they're knowledgeable and deeply thoughtful about the team, the games they've seen. While we're talking about the victory over Switzerland, one of the young women offers an analysis of how Steve Gerrard should operate in midfield in tandem with Wayne Rooney in front, in a tactical formation that ignores Michael Owen. It is an unerringly accurate dissection of England's faults and the possible solutions. We could talk all night. The English are a complicated group. Feared, unconsciously steeped in war imagery, yet cheery and optimistic, there are times when it seems they don't fit in Europe at all.

• • • • •

THE ITALIANS are in a huff following the three-game ban imposed on Francesco Totti for spitting at a Danish player in their game a few days before. Few saw it happen, but the Danes complained and had video evidence of the persistent spitting. UEFA, the governing body of soccer in Europe and the organizer of the tournament, moved swiftly to suspend Totti. The three games are no more than he deserved. The entire Italian team played with a sullen, disgraceful lack of interest against Denmark. And the Swedes are hot, having put five goals in against Bulgaria. They could crush Italy today. This is not supposed to happen, but the tournament is turning into a meltdown for some renowned national teams and elite players. The great are underperforming, while the unheralded—the Greeks—are obstinately proving impossible to beat.

It is a vastly different Italian team that takes the field, different in outlook and style, but still a team that can't buy a win. The game ends in a 1–1 draw, which does Italy little favor. Italy looks unlikely to progress beyond the first round. The team now has only two points from its two games. The Italians are a bitterly disappointed team. Their fans are disillusioned, too. The heat wave has ended in this part of Portugal, leaving the city of Porto cool, overcast and grey. The weather suits the mood of the Italian fans. They were fearful before the game, disappointed in Totti and unable to excuse his behavior. Totti is iconic in Italian soccer, a representative of the working-class spirit. In his public persona, he's a bit thick—there are two best-selling joke books that celebrate his cheerful dumbness. But he's adored. There is something plain weird about not having him aboard now.

The Swedish fans, by contrast, are as sunny as the weather was a few days ago. Having trounced Bulgaria 5–0, they're looking forward to more goals from Henrik Larsson and Zlatan Ibrahimovic. The surprise is that the Italians begin with an exuberance and determination that had been entirely missing against Denmark. The Totti controversy seems to have united and rejuvenated them. Even as the national anthems are being played, the Italians are ostentatiously linked arm in arm, a sign they are raring to go. In what is a stunningly good first half of soccer, the Italians play with fast-paced flair, passing confidently and always looking to get the ball to Vieri or Antonio Cassano, who's replacing Totti on the attack, and it is Cassano who scores first. The Swedes are their equals. Brimming with confidence, the two strikers, Larsson and Ibrahimovic, dart in and around the Italian defense. Larsson in particular seems to be in exceptional form, sprinting forward constantly, unnerving the Italians with elegant flicks.

It's beautiful, end-to-end soccer as the two teams match each other in pace. The Italian team comes out early for the start of the second half, another indication of its determination. There is a spate of fouls and yellow cards as both teams struggle to take control. From the Italian tackling and back-passing, there are suggestions that they might be happy with a 1–0 win. This is a terrible mistake.

After a lull, the Swedes roar back to life and, to all but the Italians, a Swedish goal looks inevitable. The equalizing goal, which comes after eighty-four minutes, shows that the Swedes can easily match the Italians for flair. An innate defensiveness had kicked in when Italy felt comfortably ahead, 1–0. On the sideline, wily old Giovanni Trapattoni waves frantically for his players to hold the ball and move back. It's the same mistake Trapattoni made against South Korea two years

before—gambling on slowing the game, wasting time and
clinging to a fragile lead.

· · · · ·

THE ITALIAN media are restless after the game. Anyone can tell
they're looking for an angle, an excuse. I'm in the press area for
hours because the laptop still isn't working and I'm obliged to
rely on help from the teenage technicians who are on duty.
They're sympathetic to my plight. They see it as a challenge,
making sure my copy goes off to Canada through a complicated
system of dial-up connections and phone cards. By the end of
the evening, though, even they're annoyed. They're volunteers,
obliged to wear lime-green shirts, and they have other interests.
They are mostly young men, and among the other young staff
in the media center there's a tall, willowy young woman in tight
jeans. The lads want time with her, and the Canadian with the
low-rent laptop is holding them back.

Around me, the Italian reporters are focused on calculating
the odds of Italy progressing on the basis of two drawn games.
They realize everything might hinge on the outcome of the
coming game between Sweden and Denmark. Two Scandinavian
countries. Neighbors. The Danes are already deeply insulted by
Totti's spitting. The Italian reporters are seeing a potential conspiracy. It's already on the news wires.

As darkness falls on Porto, I notice that there are an awful lot
of people wearing the Greek colors. At the opening game
against Portugal, there were perhaps a thousand Greeks in evidence; now there are many, many more. They're coming here
now with a reason to believe. And that belief is being ignored
by everyone else.

· · · · ·

THE NEXT day, a Saturday, Chris Young and I leave Porto for
Lisbon. It's a quiet train ride—the games are happening somewhere else. Lisbon looks glorious, as it always does, all light and
air and blue sky. Old trams rattling along small streets, church

bells ringing. My hotel is part of a chain, and the cab driver has never heard of it. He deposits me at a large and gleaming new Sana hotel where, he explains, somebody can tell me where to find this place I'm supposed to be staying.

In the lobby, inquire. A young woman tottering along on high heels, in a tight hotel uniform, helps out. In fact, she leads me to the back of the hotel and down an alleyway. She points to a small building down the street. "That is your hotel, I'm afraid," she says. It is indeed, and seconds after checking in, I'm afraid too. The answer to every question is "No!" At more than two hundred dollars a night, the hotel promised "alarm, radio, laundry and dry-cleaning services," but provides none. Some serious price-gouging is going on, and everybody knows it. But at least I have a tiny balcony, overlooking a pleasant backstreet, and from there I can hear church bells and the chants of fans from multiple nations as they come and go from one of the main subway stations.

I write and file a brief story about the bizarre little hotel I've landed in, and as soon as the story appears, a travel agent in Toronto offers to move me to much better lodging for the same price. I decide to stay put. Fatigue is setting in, the sort that comes after ten days of endless travel, late nights, deadlines and an unreliable laptop. Besides, Portugal's playing Spain the next day in Lisbon, and that's a game that all of Portugal is waiting for, and wondering.

• • • • •

I TAKE the subway to the game, curious to see the fans from both countries as they trek to the gorgeously colorful Estádio José Alvalade. It's a couple of hours yet before the game, and there are few Portuguese fans traveling; most of the people on the subway are deliriously cheerful, partying young Spaniards. I'm kept busy with requests to take pictures of them hugging each other. A threesome comprising a boyfriend and girlfriend and the girl's brother wrap themselves in a giant Spanish flag and have me take their photo as they try to stay upright.

Outside the stadium, the Spaniards dance and sing and try to get the watching Portuguese crowd to join them in a big, madcap dance of friendship. The Portuguese want nothing to do with it. They don't glare or become rude. They just prefer to stand around and look gloomy. Portugal's relationship with Spain is tricky. Spain tends to ignore Portugal and pretend it doesn't exist, even in soccer; Portugal resents Spain's size, strength and arrogance. It's a very male thing. A few hours later, none of this matters in the slightest. Portugal triumphs 1–0. The game begins with a weird, surreal liveliness that indicates both the weight of the occasion and the nerves of the Portuguese team. They play gloriously skillful, thrusting soccer, yet can't get in a position to score. Luís Figo is in fine form, endlessly prowling the midfield, taking the ball down the wing—left or right, he seems to be everywhere—and young Ronaldo is clearly out to show off his every trick.

The only problem for the Portuguese is that it's all flow and no show. For the second half, coach Scolari introduces the veteran Nuno Gomes. That's the needed touch. Twelve minutes into the half, Figo's sweet move finds Gomes just outside the Spanish penalty area, and the veteran turns, twists and shoots the unstoppable ball into the Spanish net. It is a goal of startling beauty and speed. All of Portugal is roaring, cheering, ecstatic and ignited by its flamboyance.

As we write our stories afterwards, the reporters can hear Lisbon rocking, the sound of a city now gone mad. A huge knot of tension has been undone, a triumph over Spain achieved. Lisbon is lost in joy and an enormous party is under way—though to call it a mere party would be an understatement. It's a challenge now to convey the epic scope and delirium. The population of the Lisbon area is about two and a half million, but it is swollen by tens of thousands of soccer fans from all over Europe. England will play Croatia here the next day, and there might be forty thousand English and ten thousand Croats in the city. In two days, Germany will play the Czech Republic, and there are about twenty thousand Germans here, while the Czechs keep pouring in. The celebrations are not just about Portugal; they belong to everybody.

Around Estádio Alvalade, mayhem prevails. Chris and I wander, looking for a way into the subway, a tram stop or a place where a taxi might be found. Nothing. The subway has stopped running. The trams have stopped moving. There are no taxis because all the streets are clogged with the dancing, singing, chanting masses. Children roam the streets where no cars can pass. We walk for ages and eventually commandeer a taxi whose driver has given up trying to get past the stadium. He agrees to take us on a circuitous journey towards downtown, but warns us he has no idea how close he'll get. Eventually, somewhere, he stops and drops us off. The next street is closed off, jammed with partying locals. Chris calls his friends, a young couple who own the apartment in Porto. He asks for advice on where we are and how we might get back to our hotels. They tell us to stay where we are and they'll come and get us soon.

We stand on a street corner, waiting and watching. There's no point trying to get a drink in a nearby café—it's overflowing and chaotic. We watch a teenage boy shimmy up a lamppost and sing the Portuguese national anthem from his perch. A group of teenage girls, drinks in their hands, cheer him on and applaud from the ground. It's a fine anthem, with a rousing chorus of "Port-u-gal! Port-u-gal!" in the middle. That's where he falters a bit, and it could be that he's transfixed by the view, from fifteen feet up, of a great deal of cleavage. He eventually starts singing again anyway. It's a mostly residential neighborhood and several dogs are barking too. In the distance, car horns honk endlessly. On balconies, people stand around, banging on anything to hand.

We two reporters look absurd, we know, with our laptop bags, jackets and caps, notebooks and all the other stuff we cart around. People are dancing and swaying to disco music, holding drinks, toasting each other, toasting every cheer that goes up from anywhere. And we stand there, drinking bottled water, watching.

Soon a taxi pulls up, carrying Chris's friends, and we squeeze

in. I'm in the front, next to the driver. And we're off on a journey through tiny backstreets and alleys, climbing hills. For a few
minutes I'm terrified as the driver goes relentlessly on, dodging
groups of revelers, breaking fast around tight corners and only
slowing slightly when we hit cobblestones. He's following orders
being barked from the back seat—left . . . next right . . . left
again. It's a heck of a journey. Somehow, we end up in the Bairro
Alto, the old warren of narrow cobblestone streets and bars that
overlooks the downtown. Then we're in a tiny *fado* bar.

Like many bars in the area, it's so small it only seats about ten
people. Twice that number are squeezed in. Miraculously, some
people leave as we arrive and we get seats by the wall. The noise
is intense, but the cold beer tastes fabulous. The entire bar, the
entire city, is drunk and singing or shouting. After a few beers
and several toasts to Portugal, I leave, hoping to get back to the
hotel.

I'm not sure where I am or what direction to follow, so I
wander around the Bairro Alto for a while, watching the crowds,
listening to the sound of endless laughter. Outside a bar, a young
woman in Portugal's team shirt and shorts is having her picture
taken with all the male customers as they leave. Apparently, she's
the waitress, now off-duty. The thing is, she wants each guy to
lift her up and hold her, lengthwise, in the air for the photo.
Several oblige. She sees me watching and invites me to lift her
for the photo. I decline, politely. Soon afterwards, I regret my
decision—I could have gotten a copy of the picture, me holding
aloft a tipsy waitress dressed in Portugal's team colors. A memento
for friends, or something to share with the sports desk back in
Toronto. The caption would be "Hard at work covering Euro
2004."

Around 3 A.M. I'm in line for a taxi with about fifty others.
We are all immensely tired, but the Portuguese youths in the
lineup keep singing. There are also three bulky Croatians, all
wearing baggy pajamas in the red and white colors of their country, standing in line with the solemn air of men who have drunk
so much they are inert. Eventually, one of the Croatians moves,

gravely and slowly, asking everyone for a cigarette. He gets one, lights it and inhales deeply. Then he throws back his head and, to the traffic and the singing throng around him, he roars out one word over and over: "Port-u-gal! Port-u-gal! Port-u-gal!" Drunk as he is, he achieves perfect pitch. And, for the night we're all having, perfect pith.

I'm back at the hotel at about 5 A.M. I pull a chair out onto the tiny balcony and, as I indulge in a glass of duty-free brandy, listen to Lisbon as dawn arrives. I can hear laughter and, somewhere, somebody is singing the national anthem. A man walking his dog stops and watches as a truck drops off copies of the day's papers at the newspaper kiosk. From five floors up I can see the photos of the game on the front pages. It is a mystery to me how anybody could have put a paper together and delivered it. And it occurs to me that this experience is a helluva lot more interesting than being the television critic for my newspaper.

• • • • •

LATE THE next afternoon, on the subway to the Estádio da Luz, we are packed in like sardines—some amazed elderly women with their shopping, a large group of English fans, lots of Croatians, and me. There are silly hats, painted faces and many young men and women wearing their countries' flags as cloaks. It is very jolly, all things considered. Some hesitant back-and-forth chanting starts. The Croatians lustily sing a traditional song and rattle the subway car with the strength of their voices and the stamping of their feet. Some of the English—gentlemen and determined to prove it—applaud. Then the English sing "Rule Britannia." The elderly women look a little nervous, but most are agog. This isn't the Euro 2004 they'd been watching on TV at home, where it is all about Portugal. The Croatians respond to "Rule Britannia" by chanting "Dado Prso," the name of their star striker. To this, the English response is "Rooney," except it is sung as "Rooooooooooo-ney!"

Cometh the hour, cometh the man, and in this Euro 2004

campaign, the man for England is Wayne Rooney. To the world outside English soccer, that's a surprise. The beauty that is David Beckham's face is on the cover of *Vanity Fair* magazine. Indeed, Beckham is the face of English soccer to the world. But Rooney is the heart, soul and, well, the bollocks. He's eighteen years old, and he's not what you'd call handsome. Before Euro 2004, the *Guardian* had assessed him coolly along these lines: "He looks like a bouncer, a guy whose hobbies are stalking women and breeding attack-dogs." It's cruel, but true. He looks ordinary, working class and slightly dangerous.

And now anyone watching England's dazzling 4–2 triumph over Croatia knows exactly who Wayne Rooney is. The boy isn't beautiful, but what he does on the field is wondrous to behold. He scores two great goals and sets up another one. He looks as if he could score a dozen more. It doesn't start that way, though. The Croatian team brims with confidence. They'd drawn 2–2 with France a few days ago. They have shown compact, often terrifically elegant play. Prso is a standout. The Croatian players and their raucous fans are buoyant—they know they can beat England and knock them out of the tournament.

And for a few minutes, it looks as if that will happen. The English defense, always shaky when defending free kicks or corners, makes an atrocious mess of a Croatian corner after five minutes. Croatia scores first. There follows a period of much inelegant industry on the part of the English. Paul Scholes bustles about the midfield, passing quickly and looking for chances. Steven Gerrard is his equal and then his better, getting the idea that unleashing Rooney is the best plan. The crowd senses it too. Every time Rooney touches the ball, the mood in the stadium changes to mass anticipation. Rooney is still a kid, and he plays like one—like a boy who thinks the point of playing soccer is to score goals, and the more the better. On a counter-attack in the final minute of the half, Scholes sends Rooney clear and, from just outside the penalty box, he fires a shot straight into the corner of the net. It is an awesome, confident and deadly strike.

The Croatians try toughness. After sixty-eight minutes, Rooney does it again, in style. The English fans are ecstatic. The stadium throbs to Rooney's beat, sways to his rhythm. The fans have long since stopped singing "Rule Britannia," as they did in the games against France and Switzerland. It is an immensely cheerful throng that sings "Here we go, here we go again" every time Rooney rushes forward with the ball. When Rooney is substituted by manager Sven-Göran Eriksson, the fans hate to see him go. It is Rooney's night, an invigorating display of skill and cunning.

Back at the start of the game I noticed that, as the teams came out, the photographers had cameras pointed at David Beckham again, and his wife in the stands, because Beckham is, well, a megastar. He is, but in this game, he's a paltry player compared to Rooney, the plain-faced boy who looks more like a bouncer than a pop star. It's goals that count, and Rooney is now rocking the tournament.

• • • • •

TWO SMALL problems have arisen. England will play Portugal in Lisbon in a quarter-final game in a couple of days and, after that, I'm scheduled to leave. Nobody back in Toronto has said anything about staying on. Interest in Euro 2004 is high in Canada—there are large Greek, Portuguese and Italian populations in every Canadian city, and the success of Greece and Portugal, combined with Italy's travails, has made the tournament a phenomenon. But nobody seems willing to commit to ensuring that I stay through the end. Instead there is, I'm told, wild interest in the theory that Italy will be robbed of glory by conspiring Scandinavians. You couldn't make that up and have it believed by anyone except an Italian conspiracy theorist: if Denmark and Sweden conclude their game with a 2–2 draw, then Italy is out of Euro 2004, no matter how Italy performs against Bulgaria in a game being played simultaneously. I'm in Lisbon, the Denmark–Sweden game is in Porto and Italy–Bulgaria is in Guimarães, but I'm told to watch the games in a public place and report back on the plausibility of the conspiracy theory.

Watching the Sweden–Denmark game in a café in Lisbon is a memorable experience. There's no better place than Lisbon for conspiracy theories. Once the venue for a terrible Inquisition and, during the Second World War, home to half the spies in Europe, the city thrives on the drama of big rumors. Also, everyone here is a soccer connoisseur. In the crowded café, there is much amusement about Italy's suspicions—except, that is, among the Spaniards. Although Spain is now out of the tournament, thousands of young supporters have stayed on, enjoying a holiday. The ones in the café are teenage couples and they behave, I've noticed, the way all Spanish teenagers do away from home: they kiss, grope and fondle each other with abandon. A young couple by the TV screen is a distracting presence for a while. The young man's tongue appears to be halfway down the young lady's throat and she keeps trying to sit on his lap. When they finally unlock and the young woman sips her beer, his hand strokes her posterior constantly. They're oblivious to anyone or anything else. An English journalist takes his eyes off the Spaniards long enough to tell me that an Italian TV channel wanted to put eight extra cameras at the Denmark–Sweden game, expecting to catch evidence of collusion. Permission was granted for two additional cameras.

Both the Swedes and the Danes have already denied that any prearranged 2–2 result is in the cards. At a press conference, Lars Lagerbäck, one of Sweden's coaches, said, "Machiavelli might have been Italian, and Italians might like to think in a Machiavellian way, but it would not be possible to play for a 2–2 draw against Denmark, and I don't think it will end 2–2—that is a very unusual result." On the big TV screen, just before the game starts, the cameras find a banner in the crowd. It reads, "2–2 and the spaghettis are out." The entire café laughs.

In truth, Denmark and Sweden are fierce rivals, and the idea of them colluding seems implausible. The Danes start strong and after twenty-eight minutes are ahead 1–0. At halftime, the café manager switches the channel to the Italy–Bulgaria game. The score on the screen draws gasps: Bulgaria is ahead 1–0. To add to the high drama, the start of the second half in both games brings goals. And in the end, there it is: the magic scoreline the Italian conspiracy theorists had predicted: Denmark 2, Sweden 2.

Unaware of the dreaded result in Porto, the Italians keep pressing and, in extra time, Antonio Cassano scores the winner. At the end of both games, thankfully, Italian coach Giovanni Trapattoni is unwilling to suggest that the Scandinavian teams had deliberately played for a draw. "I have no argument with the result, and the federation will not protest against it, absolutely not," he says. Of course, as unlikely as it may seem that twenty-two players, two coaches and a referee would act in cahoots, many Italian fans will always believe there was a fix.

• • • • •

IT'S QUARTER-FINAL time and, on my last scheduled day in Portugal, I'm officially asked if I can stay on. It turns out to be impossible, given the extra costs of game tickets, new hotel bookings and another trip to Porto. So, it's decided I should go back to Toronto and write about the key remaining games from the Toronto neighborhoods where the interest is fanatical. There is the feeling that Euro 2004 will end with an "all-Toronto" final. But first, England plays Portugal in Lisbon. The publisher of the Globe, an Englishman, asks for my prediction, via email. I reply that England will start fast and score early, and spend a long time defending the slim lead. Portugal will probably be nervous, equalize late and the game will go to penalties—England has a habit of losing on penalty kicks at the quarter-final stage of competitions.

And that's essentially the way it plays out.

It is a night of sublime drama. Games such as this, thrillers with the galvanizing ebb and flow of great narrative sinew, only happen every two years—at the World Cup or at the European championship. And this is a game for the ages. England starts vigorously, and after only three minutes, Michael Owen springs on the loose ball near Portugal's goalmouth. With the defenders unsure, he wallops it into the net. The English fans roar and roar. At the start of the game, they'd had the unusual experience of being outsung by the opposition fans. Having beaten Spain and feeling their team was now destined to win the tournament, Portugal's supporters were ready to rock the stadium. It isn't easy to drown out thirty thousand English supporters, but it happened.

Watching the game unfold, I can see the magnificence of Luís Figo, a tireless general of the midfield, constantly clashing with Beckham but leaving the golden boy looking slow-witted. For a while, the momentum swings back and forth as England tries to spring Rooney loose. The English supporters are understandably uneasy half an hour into the game, when Rooney leaves the field with what looks like an ankle injury. The Portuguese equalizer comes seven minutes from the end of regulation time.

Extra time—and not of the sudden-death variety—is inevitable. Portugal scores, then England equalizes. Thus the fans are subjected to the agony of shootout kicks from the penalty spot. Beckham, going first, misses. The Portuguese keep scoring, but then Rui Costa, by now twice the country's savior, misses. After the first series of five pairs of kicks, the game is still not settled. Now it's sudden death—they'll keep going until one side misses and the other side scores. The Portuguese goalkeeper, Ricardo, a man with an astute sense of the occasion, takes off his gloves when Darius Vassell steps up to take England's next kick. It's a dare, a taunt and a gamble. He tosses the gloves aside, a gesture that declares that he will stop the ball with his bare hands, no matter how hard and fast it flies. The gambit works: Ricardo dives superbly to stop Vassell's shot. What takes place next is the sort of thing you couldn't put in a child's story about sporting glory and have it believed by an adult: it is Ricardo, the goalkeeper, who steps forward and scores the penalty-kick goal that puts Portugal into the semifinals and sends England home.

Around midnight, near my hotel, I watch an old lady on a balcony banging a pot with the flat of her hand, using as much energy as she can muster, to add to the sound of Lisbon going berserk again. Then, looking down at English fans traipsing from the subway station, she also manages to summon some words in English. "Goodbye," she says cheerfully. "See you next time." The English ignore her. Their hearts have been broken again. England is out, and Portugal's team continues its bizarrely dramatic journey through Euro 2004.

The people of Portugal are entitled to bang their pots and party on. And for the second time in five days, Lisbon goes crazy. This time, Chris and I are able to make it to the subway before the city shuts down. We meet up in a tiny bar near my hotel at about 2 A.M. It is my last night in the city and I'm savoring every minute. The bar has a dozen or so customers, all guys, all of whom are way beyond euphoric. They are also penniless—they've been drinking for hours. They realize we're reporters and begin chatting with us. They're tickled that we've come all the way from Canada. After a couple of rounds of beer, on us, I buy them shots of Canadian Club whisky. We toast Portugal, Canada, Pierre Trudeau and lord knows what. Then everybody walks home—giddy, joyful, tipsy and terrifically pleased.

• • • • •

IN TORONTO, that most multicultural of cities, only the Greek community fully understands what's going on. By the time Greece plays the Czech Republic in a semifinal game, the country's team has already achieved an astonishing result—it has beaten the host country, Portugal, and the reigning European champions, France. Only Greek fans grasp that the team is now unstoppable. To everyone else—the still-surly Italians, the no-longer-melancholy Portuguese, the cocky Czechs—Greece has a team of limited talent that has been getting by on a combination of luck and pluck and can easily be beaten. Only the Greeks understand that the national team—unheralded, unglamorous—is now motivated by something that transcends even the roar of the crowd: the hopes of a country. Greece is on an arc leading to ultimate glory, moving with a steady rhythm towards an inevitable conclusion. For all its lack of magnetism and prestige, Greece is gliding on the transformative and recreative power of imagination, of storytelling. Stories that come true.

I'm not in Portugal or even on the Danforth, the Greek area in Toronto. A man I run into at the Prague Deli, around the corner from my house, recommends that I watch the semifinal game between Greece and the Czech Republic at the Chopin Restaurant on Roncesvalles Avenue, long the home of Toronto's Eastern European community. The Chopin is full, but not packed. It's Polish-owned, but it has served as a haunt for Czechs in Toronto during Euro 2004. They are there in numbers, all confident that the fast, gifted Czech team can cruise to a victory over the gutsy Greeks.

The Czech players start with the same attitude. But after twenty minutes or so, they begin to realize what Portugal, Spain and France had already discovered: the Greeks are resilient and organized and they never give up. The Greeks soak up the pressure and look for little opportunities. Their discipline and resolve are something to behold. After an initial quivering, they settle down and get on with the game. They pass efficiently and maintain possession with aplomb. The are unhurried, patient. The Czechs throw caution to the wind and simply flow forward. Histrionics ensue. There are many hard tackles and referee Collina, in charge of his last international game, casts a cold eye on the Czechs-turned-thespians as every tackle by a Greek defender brings loud and near-hysterical complaints. The Czechs looked frustrated; they're still arrogant, but they are tiring. The Greeks know it. Late in the game, Traianos Dellas bundles in the ball from the corner, off his head and shoulder, and it is in the Czech net. It's over for the Czechs. You could hear a pin drop in the Chopin. The mood is one of ugly disappointment. The neutrals in the bar whisper about the goal—ugly, but deserved, they say. Meanwhile, the Czechs sit, stone-faced, not believing what has happened. No one dares say a word. That's how it's been at Euro 2004 whenever Greece plays: every team has thought it could stop them when, in reality, nobody could.

• • • • •

THEN, AMAZINGLY, Euro 2004 ends as it began, with a game
between Portugal and Greece.

It's been three weeks since I sat in the stadium in Porto, as
stunned as everyone else, watching Greece beat Portugal 2–1.
Before that game, nobody would have predicted that the tournament's final would feature the same two teams. Now I'm in
Tivoli Billiards in Kensington Market in Toronto. I choose to
watch the game not in the neighborhood now known as Little
Portugal, but in a place that was once the heart of the Portuguese
community. Many of the first Portuguese businesses in Canada
were started in Kensington, just as Jewish, Italian, Hungarian
and Ukrainian arrivals had all settled here before, one after the
other. And Tivoli Billiards was, not so long ago, an informal
hiring hall for newly arrived Portuguese men. In the 1960s they'd
sit here, drink coffee and hope to be hired for the day on the
sites where downtown Toronto's business towers and apartment
buildings were being built. It's now a place for hard-working
older guys and retired men to gather, talk work and soccer, and
be in the company of other men who have labored hard to build
Toronto.

They are confident. Portugal will play attacking soccer,
finally put Greece in its place and win the tournament it is
hosting. To the men around me, Luís Figo is some kind of god.
He is also, I can feel, one of them. The Portuguese captain is
a laborer, an organizer and a man of great responsibility. There
have been times when he carried the weight of Portugal's hopes
on his broad shoulders, just as they had borne the burden of
family, work and advancement in Canada. He's solid, manly and
proud. He's a grown-up, while the younger, flashier players on
the team must seem to these men like their teenage kids. They
understand Figo's work ethic. Not for them the rush to drive
cars through the city, honking horns and shouting "Portugal!
Portugal!" before and after games. In the hour before this final
game, some hug each other; others shake hands and just beam

with delight. The TV screens show the field in Lisbon, with a giant, golden soccer ball at its center. The ball busts open and thousands of balloons in Portugal's colors ascend to the sky. The singer Nelly Furtado, a Canadian of Portuguese parents, walks onto the field to sing "Força," the official song of the tournament. The men around me stop chatting and watch intently. She could be their daughter. They know she is the daughter of one of them. For me, the experience is not like being in Lisbon for the game and those formal celebrations, the color and noise of the event. It is better.

But fairy tales can come true, even when the world's game is being played at its highest level. The outstanding, cannily cool Greeks manage a huge upset and become champions of Europe, beating Portugal 1–0. In truth, the Greeks deserve to win. They do it with the same tactical cunning and calm dedication they have brought to every game. Portugal is favored to win, with all that star-power flair and home-country support. The Greeks keep possession, harry the opposition and sneak in a goal when the opponents briefly become disorganized and undisciplined.

What the Greeks do is determine the tempo of the game from the beginning. Portugal goes on the attack early, but after trying moves down the left, the right and through the middle, they find no route to the Greek goal. The speedy Ronaldo and determined Figo begin to look desperate. The crowd in Lisbon seems to wear a collective frown of worry.

The goal that wins it is typical of the Greek success story. It comes from a corner after fifty-eight minutes and the corner came from a rare Greek counter-attack that transpired after Portugal attacked frantically but got nowhere.

The game has five minutes left when a man runs onto the field waving the flag of Barcelona, a team to which Figo once belonged and then left amid bitterness. The man taunts Figo and then throws himself into the Portuguese goal. It looks like a mad act, but there's something macabre about it, and it signals that some force beyond the game is pushing Portugal to a defeat. The Greeks hold firm for a famous and fabulous victory for the underdogs. The TV pictures show Cristiano Ronaldo crying. The prime minister of Greece cries, too, but with joy, not frustration.

At Tivoli Billiards, there are downcast eyes and sighs. An awful melancholy descends as chairs scrape the floor and men walk outside to smoke cigarettes and look at the gleaming towers of downtown Toronto, a city they had helped build with hard labor. On the other side of the city, they know, the Greeks are pouring into the streets and celebrating madly.

My heart goes out to them. I'd spent weeks in Portugal and fallen hard for the country. I know the sense of pessimism and disappointment that lingers under the surface. The anguish that comes with a glorious but long-distant past and an inadequate present.

At the end, just before the Estádio da Luz erupts in colorful, spectacular fireworks displays, the TV commentator reminds viewers that the Greek coach, Otto Rehhagel, is German and Portugal's coach, Luiz Felipe Scolari, is Brazilian. The point is to tell us that, even at this intensely competitive, nationalistic level, soccer transcends borders and nationality. And then the Greeks collect their medals and the trophy that is the most highly prized in soccer after the World Cup. No, the Greeks didn't always play in the fashion that people have in mind when they call soccer "the beautiful game." But they have played it well and cannily, and they've thrust themselves forward in a drama rich and vivid in its intensity and surprise. Anyone in the world can see that.

I walk home through the quiet streets, west of downtown Toronto. Somewhere else in the city, the Greek population is noisily rejoicing. Here, the streets are stunned into silence, as the soccer world is, really. Greece has achieved one of the great possibilities of soccer—the ability to deny the world a predicted victory—and in doing so has also given assent and hope to all small nations, everywhere. When the ball rolls across green grass, wherever grass grows, anything can happen.

WORLD CUP 2006, GERMANY

"WHO YOU GONNA CLAP your hands for, boss?" The question comes from a man running a store in Kensington Market in Toronto. It is a week before the opening of the World Cup, and I'm standing on Augusta Avenue, gazing at the vast array of international soccer shirts he has put on display. This is my little world: the ever-evolving narrow streets, alleys and nooks of multicultural downtown Toronto. This is an everywhere. Up the street, the space where Tivoli Billiards once sat is now occupied by some kind of Latin nightclub venue called, with cute ironic purpose, Super Market. The steps outside remain unchanged, and I reckon that if I were to pass by late at night I might see the ghosts of anxious Portuguese men there, pacing and waiting and hoping for work. I don't tell anyone that, mind you, but I do tell the man with the racks and racks of soccer shirts that I'm a neutral for the World Cup. He gives me an indulgent look. "No such thing, boss. Everybody is gonna clap their hands for somebody. It's the World Cup!"

So I ask him if he has shirts for all thirty-two countries taking part in the tournament. "No, maybe twenty-five right now," he says. "I wish I had them all." I ask which shirts are selling well. "Brazil, Portugal, England. Everybody loves Brazil."

Indeed they do, and at this point, the Brazilians are the favorites to win it, as usual. But that's just sports talk, and probably inaccurate. Or so I inform *Globe and Mail* readers in a pre–World Cup feature. I also tell them that Brazil is the favorite to win any World Cup, and with good reason, but the real magic of the World Cup is found in the opening rounds, when every country can pull off an upset, defeat a superior team and achieve the sort of worldwide glory that only Cinderella teams achieve.

Already on this day in Kensington Market, shirts are selling briskly, flags are being readied and the various bars and restaurants are preparing for a month of soccer-watching customers. And it's happening around the world—in countries that haven't qualified this time, and in countries that have never, ever qualified nor can even hope to make it. I explain to readers that it's never going to be about the thirty-two countries battling away in Germany; it's about the world being entranced by the tournament, the games, the players and atmosphere that emanates from TV coverage in countless languages. FIFA estimates that eight out of every ten people on the planet will watch at least part of the World Cup. That's an audience in the billions and, as I loftily tell readers, other major events—the World Series, the Summer Olympics, the Super Bowl—are comparative pipsqueaks in the popularity stakes.

I tell stories in the paper. I ramble on about how the feeling of a global village started with the 1970 World Cup in Mexico. For the first time, most of the games were broadcast everywhere, and much of the world was mesmerized from the moment it started. Back then, I was a schoolboy in Dublin, and the time difference with Mexico meant the games were aired late at night, but we were all allowed to stay up and watch. On the BBC we could see live games from exotic places named Guadalajara and Puebla-Toluca. We were cheering for England, God help us. What played out in the blazing sun of Mexico's cities changed forever the perspectives and thoughts and dreams of every small boy watching in England and Ireland. The World Cup was a stage, the grandest, most international and most thrilling stage ever created. By the end of it, we had forgotten England's dogged soccer style and inglorious defeat. It was the speedy, grinning Brazilians we fell in love with. That World Cup was our window on the world, one that gave us a picture of a sunny, glorious future. We were too young to lend gravitas to it. We just knew we'd seen magic and wanted more.

By the 1978 World Cup in Argentina, I was a university student studying for my final exams. Late at night on a tiny, barely functioning black-and-white TV, I watched the free-flowing Dutch, the driven Peruvians, the unlucky Scots and lucky Argentines. In a semifinal, Argentina needed to beat Peru by four goals to get to the final. They beat them by six, an unheard-of feat. The morning after that game, I was in the cafeteria and the cashier, an elderly woman near retirement, gave me the wrong change. I stared groggily at the money and she stared at me in the same fashion. "Sorry, son," she said. "I was up all night watching the soccer." I told her I'd done the same. "Wasn't it brilliant?" she said, her eyes shining with delight. I'll never forget the light in those old eyes that day.

I also point out to readers that, when the 1994 World Cup was played in the United States, that country was mystified by the great wave of supporters who landed for the tournament. They didn't really get it, the U.S. media. Late-night talk show hosts mocked the visiting soccer fans, failing to grasp that the World Cup empowers people to lose their inhibitions and act like excited kids. It's all in fun, and every soccer follower knows it. I tell readers about the Germans, dressed in their traditional lederhosen, playing a madcap, friendly game of soccer with Irish guys dressed as leprechauns in Ibaraki in 2002. I hope somebody understands.

I explain, too, that the man selling shirts in Kensington Market is correct, in a way: there are no authentic neutrals. The World Cup is everybody's tournament and party. Nobody can be neutral about the joy and pleasure it brings. Everybody's gonna clap their hands for that. And then I pack my bags and fly to Munich.

• • • • •

THE REASON why Germany is hosting the eighteenth World Cup is understood to be murky. Nobody had expected the country's bid to win, and conspiracy theories abound about the reason why a single vote cast by a FIFA official rewarded the Germans. The only thing certain is that Germany was very, very determined to hold the World Cup in 2006 and equally insistent that it would be a well-run, joyous tournament. A reunified Germany is on display, and a new Europe too—the Europe of the single-currency euro, a Europe that's prosperous and generous. Certainly, the German hosts are generous to the journalists. We have all been given a pass to ride the trains for free for a month.

But in the frenzied anticipation before this World Cup opens, the soccer talk is not about Germany. It's about South America, Africa and Eastern Europe.

Almost two hundred countries had participated in the long qualifying campaign, and thirty-one had made it. Only Germany, as host country, had an automatic berth. Brazil, the title holders, had a qualifying battle and, as the World Cup draws near, the team's attacking resources look outrageously overstocked. Brazil's team includes the magical Ronaldinho, two-time World Player of the Year, plus Ronaldo and the young, tantalizingly raw talent Robinho. On paper, the team is unparalleled. Argentina has qualified with a strong run of victories and was actually the top team in the South American group, beating Brazil on goal differential.

Things have changed in Africa. The two traditional powers, Cameroon and Nigeria, have failed to make it. Instead, Angola, Côte d'Ivoire, Ghana and tiny Togo have qualified. Côte d'Ivoire has Didier Drogba, one the best strikers in the word, as their lead man. Togo has Emmanuel Adebayor, who has lit up many games as a goal scorer for Arsenal in England. From Eastern Europe, Ukraine has breezed to the World Cup, qualifying quickly, losing only one game along the way. In Milan-based Andriy Shevchenko, they have a man considered the most deft and gifted forward in Europe. Serbia and Montenegro has qualified with the best defensive record in Europe, very rarely allowing the opposition to score and, obviously, the team will be tough to beat.

Trinidad and Tobago is the sentimental favorite, an underdog team for many people. The Caribbean country is the smallest, in terms of population, to qualify, and everyone expects its exuberant fans to dance and make music no matter what happens.

Me, I've followed the Republic of Ireland's qualifying games with ever-increasing skepticism. For all of Brian Kerr's talents with youngsters, it seemed he could exact neither passion nor skill from the team he managed. Ireland was drawn in a competitive group that also included France, Switzerland, Israel, Cyprus and the Faroe Islands. Kerr's tactics were conservative: win at home in Dublin and force a draw away in other countries. After a 3–0 home win over Cyprus in Dublin, Ireland managed three tied games. It was Switzerland again that proved Ireland's undoing, and then Israel. In June of 2005, the Irish team surrendered a 2–0 lead and allowed the visiting Israelis to leave Dublin with a draw. A loss to France and then a lethargic, scoreless draw at home with the Swiss meant that Ireland ended up far from close to qualifying. I had been in Dublin for the game against the Faroe Islands, a team of amateur players who defended with determination, essentially parking ten players in front of their goal, and Ireland struggled to beat them. Afterwards, at the press conference, Kerr was introduced with glee as "the man of the hour." He looked abashed. As well he might have been. There was something delusional about the celebrations in Dublin that night. Only the tiny handful of supporters from the Faroe Islands, who had danced away the night on the terraces at Lansdowne Road stadium, seemed to grasp that the game was a gift to Ireland. And then Brian Kerr seemed to disintegrate under the pressure, withdrawing from the press and resenting the expectations. The glory days were gone. Perhaps prosperity had damped Ireland's urge for sporting greatness. No matter. Ireland was not the only tiny country capable of grit, determination and

stunning upsets. Other countries were poorer now, and more
desperate for the grandeur of World Cup glory. This might be
their tournament: anything could happen in Germany.

• • • • •

I'M A bit amazed when I arrive in Munich. Germany seems
spectacularly welcoming on this morning. There is some delay
in retrieving my luggage, but when I do, I follow the signs
towards the exit. A few minutes later, as I'm standing outside,
contemplating a line of taxis in the sunny, mild Bavarian morning, I'm puzzled. I haven't passed through customs or immigration control. Maybe there's been a mistake; maybe I've taken the
wrong turn. But I'm here, and free to roam. To tell the truth,
I'm a bit disappointed there was no conversation with an immigration official about the threat of English hooligans. I'd been
looking forward to that.

The taxi into downtown Munich passes under a giant
U-shaped sign that features German goalkeeper Oliver Kahn
diving spectacularly to stop a ball. I try to talk about this with
the driver, but he isn't interested. The thing is, Kahn is a cultural
icon here; but he is also a very divisive figure. Me, I feel I know
him well. I can recall the long and thrilling assault by Ireland on
the German goal that night six years ago in Ibaraki. It was Kahn
who kept Germany in the game as Duff and Robbie Keane tried
tirelessly to score. Kahn was formidable, intimidating and stunningly fast and agile. His fingertips and fast reaction kept Germany
in the lead until the final seconds. He is a man to be respected.

Before Michael Ballack recently ascended to captain the
German team, Kahn was the dominant player, a man notorious
for his temper, for his animal-like roars at fellow players and for
leaving his pregnant wife for his young girlfriend, a waitress. For
many German men, especially male soccer followers, Kahn is a
natural leader, a traditional, hard man and the very opposite of
the polite Ballack, a guy born in the old East Germany. For those
German men who fetishize beer-drinking and boorishness,
Ballack is too aloof, too pretty, and there is too much of the

metrosexual about him. He lacks the right stuff to represent the country. If he leads the team to a World Cup championship, at home, all might be forgiven. But that's no certainty. The team is now made up of kids, led by the enigmatic East German. It's all very German and very complicated, because in the last few weeks it has become clear that Kahn is no longer even the first-choice German goalkeeper. Team manager Jürgen Klinsmann announced he would prefer Kahn's longtime rival, Jens Lehmann, to guard the German goal. This is a seismic shift in Germany, a rejection of the aging warrior. Well known for his rage, Kahn had been sullen, even acrimonious, about the matter in pre-tournament interviews.

I'm fiercely interested in the symbolism. The new Germany. The German goalmouth now in the care of a stranger. The captain now a man born in the old East Germany. My driver, who has excellent English, doesn't want to touch the topic. So I shut up and wait for a glimpse of the new Allianz Arena, where the World Cup will open and where Germany will play Costa Rica the next day, a Friday. The stadium is hard to miss. It's in the countryside, seemingly miles from the city, and sits there like a big, soft, white pillow tossed into the green fields. The driver points to it. "Beautiful, yes?" It is spectacularly beautiful, as a matter of fact.

My hotel, chosen and booked rapidly on the Internet, is called Roma something-or-other. It isn't beautiful at all—it's cheap, clean and very, very small. My room is tiny and the bed resembles a narrow coffin. I'm here two nights, one of them short, and, well, it will do. Mustn't grumble—I'm here for the World Cup. Immediately after I check in and drop my bags, I get to work. I need to get back to the stadium to get my accreditation badge and all the other things that FIFA requires. I've only slept a little on the overnight flight from Toronto and I should be tired, but I'm jazzed, walking at a brisk pace towards the Hauptbahnhof, the main train station, just down the street. The first thing I notice is that most of the businesses on the street are bars. And they are named Candy Bar, Love Bar, Dolly Bar and

Sexyland. They're all strip clubs. And they all appear to be offering special deals for the World Cup. It's mid-morning and all the
bars are closed, but two Costa Rican supporters are standing
outside Candy Bar giving the World Cup Special sign a close
reading.

At the train station, I waste fifteen minutes trying to figure
out how to take the underground U-Bahn to the Allianz Arena.
German efficiency? Don't get me started. It's less than twenty-
four hours before the elaborate opening ceremonies, and some
guys are just now putting up the posters and signposts telling
passengers where and how to get the train to the stadium. I
abandon the station, go outside and take a taxi. The driver spends
the journey explaining to me, in English, that, really, I can just
take the U-Bahn—it's right there, in the station. Yes, it is. I
should just take the time to find it. Honestly. He wouldn't joke
about it. I'm smiling all the way. It's an unexpected pleasure to
find that Germany is a bit laid back and harum-scarum about
the World Cup.

I really get the picture outside the stadium while waiting in
line to enter the media center. There, several workmen are toiling away, equipped with shovels and a pickaxe. They're trying
to finish work on a parking area for some of the sixty thousand
spectators—the fans, VIPs and media—who will flock to the
stadium the next day. You don't get much precision engineering
with a shovel and a pickaxe, and the two workers are sending
waves of dust and bits of gravel flying towards the long line of
journalists who are waiting to get their press badges and tickets
for the opening game. There are hundreds of us standing in line
in the midday heat, most of us unsure whether we're in the correct line and some of us displeased to find dust and gravel raining down. An Italian fellow asks the workers, in fractured
German, what the heck they're doing. They don't stop to answer.
The pickaxe makes an awful racket as it hits hard stone. Eventually,
we all enter a flimsy-looking tent to get our passes and tickets.
Pickaxes, shovels and tents. It all seems a bit lackadaisical and
last-minute.

Then there are the regulations. Germany is famous for its regulations about this and that. Regulations underpin the order and efficiency, right? At the approach to the stadium are numerous signs warning people that it's a non-smoking area. Some journalists making the long march to the media center inside the stadium are smoking. They are told to put out the cigarettes, and they do. Then somebody notices that people driving into the stadium in cars are smoking but not told to stop. This is true. We all stand and look at the cars and trucks and, indeed, inside the cars there's a fierce amount of cigar and cigarette smoking going on. In fact, just outside the stadium, some young people are practicing the flag-waving moves for Friday's opening ceremonies, and the man overseeing them is smoking a cigar as he waves a stick at them. An American reporter points this out to a young policeman who smiles, shrugs and tells us to "enjoy the match." He's not being sarcastic. He's just deeply unbothered by whatever is going on. Inside, there are two—count 'em, two—small elevators to take the hundreds of journalists up to the media center, several floors up. Apart from an elderly English writer, nobody is particularly put out. The Englishman snarls a complaint at a teenage security guard, who blushes. The rest of us tut-tut among ourselves. Silly old English guy. Quit complaining. We're getting the vibe: relax. The World Cup is about to start, and we're here. Secretly, I think, we're all as skittish as children.

As a mass of us waits for an elevator, a rumor goes around that somebody tried to take the stairs earlier in the morning and hasn't been seen since. Much tittering. It's no use complaining, as the Englishman has discovered. He demanded to see somebody in charge. He's been told that the senior staff in charge of running the media center are in a meeting. It's probably a joke, but he doesn't get it. I write a report about Munich on the day before the opening of the World Cup—the last-minute preparations, the strung-out feel to it, the Costa Ricans contemplating the closed strip clubs, the skittish journalists. The news that Michael Ballack is injured and might not play the next day. The piece appears briefly on the *Globe* website a few hours later, but not in the paper itself. It's not what anybody wants to hear, I guess. But it's all true. There is a surreal atmosphere in Munich, a slowness and an aching, nagging suspense.

The mood shifts as the sun sets on this Thursday. Throughout the old downtown, I can hear the chanting of groups of German fans and the more exuberant "*Olé, olé, olé*" of the Costa Ricans. If the two groups meet, it is all handshakes and smiles. Groups of opposing fans pose for photos together. The Germans, more flush with cash and already somewhat liquored up, are buying the Costa Ricans beers in the cafés. Visitors from other countries, suddenly finding the World Cup atmosphere they'd been looking for, are taking photos of everybody with a team shirt or a flag. I walk the streets, eat a steak dinner, drink a single beer and then sleep early and long. The following day, the entire world will begin to shift inexorably towards joyous insanity. My life will be games, trains, planes, hotels and bus trips. I'm the traveling man here. My colleague Stephen Brunt, the one who is, actually, a distinguished sportswriter, is based in Frankfurt and will cover key games there and in nearby cities. I'll be based on and off in Berlin, but mostly I'll traipse back and forth across Germany. On this night, I don't care. I'm going to be at the opening game of the World Cup, again.

• • • • •

EARLY FRIDAY morning, I have coffee with three lads from Costa Rica. With a ballet of gestures and bits of broken English they tell me that, in truth, they have little hope for their team. The players are either too old or too young. Legendary forward Paulo Wanchope is a fine fellow, they indicate, but past it. When I ask, "Who is the truly great player on the Costa Rica team of the moment?" they all pause and argue among themselves for a minute. Finally, one says, "Ten. Ten men." The others nod sagely in agreement. I ask them what that means. And one guy says, "It's ten men plus the goalkeeper. No stars. Costa Rica can only do well if ten men work together like one man." Mother o' God, it has started already—the poetry of it. Their slim hopes juxta-posed with their geniality. Their determination to think them-selves lucky to be here. They also feel that their main hope lies in the mediocrity of the German team. A draw or even a win against the second-rate German squad is possible. Then, anything might happen against the other teams in their group, Poland and Ecuador.

Things don't work out that way. At the end of the day, the Germans win, and in outstanding fashion. Everyone in Munich, apart from the Costa Ricans, breathes a huge sigh of relief. It would be bad for the atmosphere if Germany didn't start in high gear. But the prospect of four weeks of Teutonic despair has diminished. And more than a billion television viewers around the world savor it, too. Germany wins 4–2, and an opening game with six goals is a sign of a potentially fabulous tournament to come. Officially, and as far as many Germans are concerned, playing host to the World Cup came two years too soon. The players aren't tough enough yet. The youngsters aren't clever enough yet. But the plausibility of those accusations of lack of guile or callowness is not on display at the Allianz Arena. After only six minutes, midfielder Philipp Lahm finds space and unleashes a fine, gloriously curling shot that, although it now stands as the first goal of the tournament, could yet be one of its finest. Costa Rican goalkeeper José Porras tried, but few keepers on the planet could have reached and stopped such a shot.

Within minutes, Costa Rica replies, and delightfully, using the tactic that is, clearly, its one and only method. Forward Paulo Wanchope slips past the German defense with a lovely bit of speed and a feinting run and scores a delightfully sly goal. As the game progresses, it is obvious that Wanchope, whose long, lithe limbs and sprinting ability have made him a great poacher of almost-offside goals, is Costa Rica's single weapon. He loiters up front and waits for the floating ball to come to him. Sometimes it does, but the Germans can see the obviousness of this approach. The Costa Rican rally lasts only three minutes, as Miroslav Klose, on his birthday, scores a goal that is good, but not brilliant, compared with Lahm's earlier classic. So three goals in seventeen minutes make the score 2–1 for Germany, and every time Lahm or Klose has the ball, the crowd seethes with excitement. They sense a rout. For much of the second half, German goalkeeper Lehmann could use his hands to knit himself a sweater. He sure isn't using them to stop shots from Costa Rica. In fact, by the end, Germany manages twenty-one shots, to just four for Costa Rica. Still, for a neutral observer, the statistics tend to lie. Costa Rica tries, and succeeds, in making a contest of it, and no one can dismiss this game as a meeting of giants and minnows. It is fast, flowing and vastly entertaining soccer.

During the earnest but entertaining opening ceremonies, I'd been watching the VIP section of the crowd where the legendary Pelé, a World Cup winner for Brazil in 1958, 1962 and 1970, stood. He had carried the World Cup trophy onto the field as part of the ceremonies. There was a parade of World Cup–winning players, which was rather sweet—old and middle-aged men walking proudly, the ancient deeds honored here. Children in lederhosen carried the flags of thirty-two countries onto the field. The German singer Herbert Grönemeyer, with Amadou and Mariam, two blind musicians from Mali and his musical co-conspirators, performed "Celebrate the Day," the official song of this World Cup. And it was terrific. The German sang something earnest and the African musicians took it away, somewhere into Africa. The whole stadium was standing, applauding, swaying to the hip-swinging rhythm of it. Pelé just smiled. I sat with Cathal Kelly from the *Toronto Star*. Cathal is at his first tournament, and he's excellent company, a man with an eye for the telling detail. He was the one who spotted Oliver Kahn making a show of arriving on the German bench, waving to the crowd, hogging the limelight. With the other sixty thousand people there, we watched Kahn soak it up. Cathal started writing. I started writing. Pelé was still smiling. Now mostly an ambassador for soccer, he could only have been delighted with the game that unfolded. A solid win and an entertaining game certainly changed the mood in Munich. The question now is this: How good will Germany become in the following games, when Ballack comes back from injury? The Germans will meet more determined opposition than Costa Rica, but they've found a free-flowing rhythm and a spirit that will surely take them far.

When I walk the street hours later, past the cafés and strip clubs, there is noise everywhere. The Germans have hope now, and they're drinking mightily. There's singing in the bars, on the sidewalks and from the roofs of buildings. I'm passing Dolly Bar when a man comes tumbling out of it—literally, tumbling. He's been ejected, and he lands in a heap on the ground. He's also laughing his head off, not hurting at all. He's got the Costa Rican flag tied around his neck. Immediately, two of his friends emerge to check on him. One of them is a man I talked to early that morning. "Hey, Canada," he says. "Good match Paulo Wanchope! Good goal, Canada." He's right. It was a good goal. The fact that Costa Rica lost doesn't seem to matter.

Five hours later, at dawn, I'm back on the street, dragging my luggage to the train station to get to the airport for an early flight to Berlin. The Dolly Bar is still open, music blaring out. As I walk down the street, I discover that all the bars and cafés are still open. There are people drinking beer and singing in every single establishment. The sun has just come up. This World Cup is under way.

• • • • •

THE EXPRESS bus from the station to the airport has a single passenger: me. The driver is singing to himself as we speed along. As I'm the only passenger, he offers to drop me right at the Lufthansa entrance for my flight. He's a real gent about it. Inside, I line up to check in and, tired, decide not to try to use my pidgin German when I get to the Lufthansa desk. "May I speak English?" I ask of the young woman who takes my passport and examines it. She pauses a beat, pouts, looks at me thoughtfully, puts a hand on her hip and says with a sigh, "Oh, all right, John Doyle. But just this once, okay?" I can hardly believe it. She's joshing with me. It's an unholy hour of the morning and this woman is giggling, handing me the boarding pass as she says,

"It's much nicer here. Come back to München soon. Okay, John Doyle?"

On the plane to Berlin, I'm seated with several journalists: a man from Austria; a Dutch woman; two Italian guys. Three FIFA officials, two men and a woman, distinctive in their tight grey suits and self-important attitude, breeze on board and take their seats. The Austrian looks at me, nods in the direction of the FIFA officers and makes a sarcastic remark I don't quite grasp. The other journalists start laughing. In Berlin, on the way from the tiny Tegel Airport to my hotel, the cab driver offers vital information. Berlin is nice, he tells me, very welcoming. Berliners like everybody. Except the Russians. The Russian are scum, he suggests. Even the Berlin whores dislike the Russians. But nobody will think I'm a Russian. Then he asks if I've ever played golf in Banff, Alberta. I haven't. He has. He liked Alberta a lot. The presence of very few Russians in Banff might be one reason, I suspect. The hotel I'd chosen—on the Internet, in a panic—is gorgeous. I'd picked it because it was reasonably priced, situated in what was East Berlin and near to a train station. It's a beautiful creation, artfully constructed from a nineteenth century industrial building. "Welcome to our house," the woman says when I check in. I'm looking around, taken aback. There is exposed brick and carefully placed bits of industrial machinery to catch the eye. A splendid exhibition of photographs of East Berlin in the 1960s graces the walls. My room is large, comfortable and has original art on the walls. The Internet connection works instantly. I can sleep easy.

Awake a few hours later, I realize that there's hardly anybody else staying at the hotel. I watch the game between England and Paraguay in the hotel bar, in the company of the bartender, three Dutch guys and several members of the hotel staff. It is a dull, plodding game, and everyone watching in the bar has taken the view that England is merely lucky. And it's true. A few minutes into the game a free kick from David Beckham goes dipping and bending into the penalty area. A Paraguayuan defender tries to kick it clear, but the ball goes the other way, past his goalkeeper.

England wins 1–0 thanks to that lucky own goal. The camera cuts to the English supporters, who, late in the game, are delirious. The bartender scoffs. The Dutch guys laugh. They are intrigued by Beckham, certainly, but for England they have nothing but contempt. England has come to this World Cup on a wave of hype, as usual. The team has asserted that it can win the tournament. The idea of England winning it in Germany adds a certain frisson to the suggestion, but it's all merely notional. Every fatal flaw of English football is on display: the lack of sophisticated tactics, the reliance on dogged effort and the absurdity of the trepidation that fills the faces of the English defenders as the opposing players move the ball in short, quick passes, as if they'd never seen such play. And then there is the WAG factor. They're back and, much photographed, they're all over the German papers. This is England's opening game, and already there is WAG-fatigue in Germany.

• • • • •

EARLY THE next morning, I take the two-hour train journey to Leipzig to see Holland play Serbia and Montenegro. The new central station, Berlin Hauptbahnhof, is a stunning spectacle of glass and steel and is strangely quiet at the hour I arrive. I had expected to encounter the Oranje Army here, the boundless battalions dressed in orange on their way to Leipzig. There are indeed hundreds of them, some gathered and doing their "Hup! Hup!" chant as they board the train. It turns out, though, that these are mere stragglers. The Oranje Army has been camped in Leipzig for days. The historic city of Bach and Goethe, and the only one from the old East Germany to act as a host city for this World Cup, is temporary home to about sixty thousand people from the Netherlands, and they're in excellent form.

Leipzig's central station doubles as a shopping mall, and in the vast lower levels where the supermarkets are, the Dutch are buying their beer and wine. I stand on the main level looking down at the sea of orange. Outside, under a blazing sun, it becomes clear that the Dutch dominate Leipzig as emphatically as an invading army. As I was in Portugal, I am awed and amused by the sheer size and enormous good cheer of the Oranje Army on the march. The Dutch fans don't just wear orange shirts to support the Netherlands, they also wear orange hats, shorts or pants, socks and shoes. The female Dutch fans sometimes wear orange grass skirts and wigs. Watches, jewelry and sunglasses are orange. These Dutch fans will throw orange-colored confetti on the field just before the Netherlands plays a game.

I'm taking shelter in the shade outside the station when a chaotic musical racket starts somewhere to my left. Soon there appears a division of the Oranje Army setting off for the Fan Festival site, led by a brass band—that is, a bunch of burly musicians dressed in orange, playing orange trumpets and orange French horns and one giant orange tuba. Photographers race after them to capture the madcap scene. TV crews follow them up the old cobblestone streets, desperate to get footage. I'm watching with some amusement from the shadows as the cameras frantically follow the monochrome parade. An English journalist joins me and asks if we're in the correct spot to get the bus to the stadium. He tells me that he's been in Leipzig all weekend and, nearby, there's a large campsite where tens of thousands of Dutch supporters have made themselves a temporary home, waiting for today's game. He says the site has become an attraction for the locals, with a constant stream of adults and kids going out to gaze on the huge, orange-clad crowd. The Dutch sleep in orange tents and sit in orange deck chairs. Some have orange-painted barbecues and orange-colored plates, cups, glasses and utensils.

Eventually, the media bus arrives and begins the journey around Leipzig to the stadium. It passes the campground where the Dutch are staying. There's a traffic jam. Some of the Dutch are trying to leave and get to the game, while locals are turning up just to look at and take photos of this great swath of orange among the green fields. Some Dutch fans are singing, dancing and banging orange tamborines, while German parents point out the incredible sight to their children.

Most groups of traveling soccer fans at a big tournament

intuitively see the occasion, and the mass gathering, as a vehicle
of identity—and it tends to be a unified, single identity. It's a
simplified form of nationalism, usually. It can be delivered with
a sense of irony, or just good humor about national stereotypes,
but it tends to be uniform. The Dutch throng, however, allows
for difference and is more motley than it first appears. Men dress
as women—in fact, the first Dutch fan I see as I arrive at the
stadium is a tall, thin young man dressed only in a woman's
bikini and an orange wig. He's camp as hell. Throughout the
Dutch horde there are others, some with fake breasts swaying
away under their orange shirts, as well as women posing as very
masculine, butch figures—construction workers with orange
hard hats, for instance. It occurs to me that the Oranje Army
not only offers an expressive support for the Dutch team, but it
acts an affirmation of collective Dutch identity—of the
Netherlands as a tolerant, easygoing country where all manner
of quirks and personal identities can exist together under the
huge umbrella of the idea of the Netherlands. Mind you, almost
every single member of the Oranje Army is white, while the
national team is not all-white at all.

The Dutch are different in their attitude to the game too.
Holland revolutionized soccer in the 1970s—first, in club soccer,
as Ajax and Feyenoord emerged from nowhere to dominate the
European Cup competition. Then, at the 1974 and 1978 World
Cups, Holland easily breezed through the early rounds—trouncing both Brazil and Argentina in 1974—and reached the final.
Each time, Holland deserved to win, but lost. In the process, it
certainly gained the attention of the world. Holland played the
most fluid, elegant and attacking soccer ever seen. For a time,
Holland made Brazil look predictable, almost pedestrian. The
Dutch game was all about fluidity and the creative use of space
on the field. Formations, in particular the 4–4–2 system favored
in most of Europe, mattered little. Players moved endlessly out
of position, and when one did, a teammate took over that empty
space. Some called it "total football" because it involved the total
use of the team and the field, but in truth it was much more

mercurial and defied easy definition. Led by the sublimely gifted and supremely confident Johan Cruyff, the Dutch style essentially emphasized the beauty of play, not the brawn of battle. It was sexy and scintillating to watch, especially the élan of the tall, rail-thin Cruyff. He seemed to embody an enlightened new approach to soccer. The Dutch players were known to bicker among themselves, were thought to lack discipline, but the team and country didn't seem to care. The Dutch had this odd idea: it is more important to play beautifully than to win. It was a sixties ideal suddenly and presumptuously applied to soccer. It made sweet, fuddled sense.

On this afternoon in Leipzig, Holland plays well, though not beautifully, and wins 1–0. One man bosses the game, and the Oranje Army follows only one leader: Arjen Robben. Few games have been so much about one man's gifts and skills. It isn't just the winning goal he scores; it's that it is a killer goal, breathtaking in its beauty and precision. Robben is released with a flowing flick-on from Robin van Persie. He runs forward, pacing himself perfectly, and deftly slides the ball under Serbia and Montenegro goalkeeper Dragoslav Jevric—child's play. He runs on the left for ages and then, when defenders crowd him in panic, he coolly moves to the right and continues. He makes a mockery of Serbia and Montenegro's reputation as the best defensive team in the world. It's a reputation well earned—hardly anyone scored against the team in qualifying—but that reputation is now in tatters thanks to the pumped and primed Robben. Serbia and Montenegro has simply never encountered the arrogance of a team led by a man having a beautiful day.

In a desperate measure, late in the game, Serbia and Montenegro brings on six-foot, eight-inch Nikola Zigic. It is a fact of soccer that a small man can beat a big man with ease. Maybe the news didn't reach Serbia and Montenegro. In the stands, the Dutch fans chortle and taunt the gangly Zigic. Arjen Robben grins. There are a few hundred fans from Serbia and Montenegro, their voices lost in the stadium. Their team is demolished, and they look demoralized. At the end of the game I wander into the area where the Dutch had congregated. At the back of the section, I find the man I'd seen earlier that day, the one dressed only in a woman's bikini. He sits there, looking at the deserted field, watching as the stadium empties. He's calmly smoking a joint, a can of beer at his feet. "Good game," I say to him. "Beautiful," he says, and takes a long pull on the joint, crosses his legs, exhales and sighs, lost in thought.

• • • • •

ON THE train from Berlin to Hanover the next morning, to see Italy play Ghana, a small group of Italian guys commandeer the restaurant car. They seem determined to get very seriously drunk. It's only a two-hour trip, so that isn't going to happen, but an effort is made. One tipsy Italian guy approaches me. "Who are you?" he demands. "I'm a journalist," I say, cool as you like. "Ah, a photographer," he says, strangely satisfied with his conclusion. It turns out that, like all tipsy Italian guys from Toronto to Turin, he has strong opinions about the Italian side and wants them known. "Lippi is shit," he says, referring to the Italian manager, Marcello Lippi. I have no response, which he takes as explicit encouragement to continue. Next comes a pithy prediction about the evening's game and Lippi's tactics: "Tonight, he will play 4–3–3, with Totti, Toni and Gilardino up front. This is shit. Ghana will score first and Italy will eventually win 3–1, but Lippi is shit." I smile and nod, as if well pleased to receive this sage advice. The tipsy Italian is wrong. It turns out that Marcello Lippi has done something important for the national Italian side: put goal-scoring first and encouraged the display of attacking skill. It works beautifully on this night in Hanover; Italian artistry is on full display. And, even better, it looks as though Italy could even take things a notch higher.

Italy has a history of slow starts in tournaments. There's arrogance to that. You know the Italians are thinking that they are great artists sizing up the artisans playing for the opposition, and they're not inclined to take matters seriously until it counts. A 1–0 lead will do, goes the thinking, after which the team will just see it out with a bolted-tight door of defense. But here, Italy has something to prove. There's that record of failing early at Euro 2004 and losing to South Korea at the previous World Cup. And there's the whiff of scandal—allegations of fixed games, referees in disgrace and booze, hookers and big betting—wafting over Italian soccer. An Italian journalist I chatted with in the stadium said this tournament and Italy's performance would be "a psychodrama" for the country. There was a feeling in Italy that it was time for a good, ethical shake-up. If the Italian team did well, the housecleaning would be postponed, as usual, but if the team failed badly, there would be an "earthquake" in Italian soccer. This guy is taking to me because all that talk about the scandal in Italy has made even the Italian press a bit nervous and voluble. Most Italian journalists aren't the least collegial. They keep to themselves and look on the sportswriters from other countries as ignorant hacks. I suspect they think we're all badly dressed, too.

There's a narrative plausibility to the journalist's theory. After all, thirteen of the twenty-three players on the Italian squad play for the four Serie A teams being investigated. They might want, individually, to show that they win with style, skill and verve, not through backroom shenanigans. And yes, those Italians do carry it off with such guile, style and utter ruthlessness. Italy wins 2–0 against a battling but bewildered Ghanaian team more fascinated by the World Cup than focused upon it. Some neutrals love the traditional Italian style of careful build-up and tightly organized play, but most don't—the Italians are hard to love. In fact, throughout this solid, deserved win over Ghana, one can feel the sharp disappointment of many in the crowd who really, really want the underdogs from Africa to beat Italy—to do so would mean attaining a special level of glory. And yet there's justice in the Italian win. The consummate superiority of Italian skill is on full, breathtaking display.

Hanover is very different from Leipzig. There's no shyness here. It's a grand, ancient city with an old town center full of picturesque alleys, broad avenues and expansive gardens that tell you it was once an important, imperial place. There are a few hundred Ghana supporters around the town in the late afternoon, and they're so noisy and colorful they seem a much larger group. Actually, the handful who sing and dance and bang drums will become world famous: for weeks, even months and years afterward, the same group of Ghanaian fans will be featured on every YouTube video of this World Cup.

Italy's players are sublimely focused and intent in scoring from the start. It isn't just the delightful trickery of Luca Toni or Francesco Totti's casual dynamism. It is their mastery of tactics. They could anticipate most moves by Ghana and, in a half-second, prevent them. At the game's core is Andrea Pirlo, who opens the scoring with a blistering long-range drive in the first half. The goal comes after a long period of Italian dominance. For a time, Ghanaian goalkeeper Richard Kingston looks a shaken man. The ball flies at him from every direction, and Ghana is lucky to escape from a flurry of Italian misses and corner kicks. But it is not merely Pirlo's goal that matters. He orchestrates from the middle, delivering deft passes here and there, always skillfully slicing open Ghana's defense. When he supplies a superb pass to substitute Vincenzo Iaquinta for a second goal, he is finishing the inevitable.

And Ghana? Not to be underestimated, was the buzz before the game. Tough, tricky and disciplined. This is Ghana's first World Cup, but the country has a deserved reputation for one of the best youth systems in Africa and has done very well in international youth competitions. It has several players playing for top teams in Europe, including a few in Serie A in Italy. In Berlin, a Ghanaian journalist told me that, back home, they kind of sneer at the African teams with big World Cup reputations, Nigeria and Cameroon. "All style," he said. "Not tough, like us." Well, there's tough and then there's ruthless. Apart from a fine period between the fiftieth and sixty-fifth minutes, Ghana looks like an underdog team fueled by hope rather than sharp skills. The Italians cheer with delight at the end; everyone else looks a little disappointed after wishing and hoping for an upset victory by

Ghana. It's not just about supporting the underdog; it's about envy, too. This Italian team looks so composed, so skillful, so cold-blooded in its confidence.

In the same group, the Czech Republic has just trounced the USA 3–0. The European powers are rising. Meanwhile, over in Kaiserslautern, Australia has beaten Japan 3–1. This is excellent news. The loud and happy Australian fans are adding an extra dose of merry, cosmopolitan glamour to this World Cup.

• • • • •

THE NEXT day, happily for me, my game to cover is in Berlin. No trains, no planes to another city. The hotel is still largely empty, and after breakfast I wander into the lobby. There, sitting in a chair, reading the English tabloid the *Sun*, is one of the Gallagher brothers from the band Oasis. I'm not sure if it's Noel or Liam Gallagher, but I know one of them is famously argumentative, so there's no way I'm going to strike up a conversation. I just watch him reading the World Cup coverage in the *Sun*.

Later, I'm in my room, writing a feature about the referees at the World Cup. Yes, the referees, the ones who are invisible until they screw up. "Are you blind? Where's your guide dog?" That's the sort of printable insult I heard during Germany's triumph over Costa Rica. German Philipp Lahm was pulled to the ground in the penalty area by a Costa Rican defender. From my position, I could clearly see the wild grab at his shirt and the player literally tossed to the ground. It was a penalty, and tens of thousands of German fans saw it, too. Referee Horacio Elizondo of Argentina saw it differently. He indicated that Lahm had dived, and he waved the play forward. If Germany hadn't had the lead, there would have been rage over Elizondo's mistake.

Insulting the referee and riffing on the theme of his eyesight, or worse, is part of the game. As an impressionable child in Dublin, I loved hearing the insults shouted in the stands. "Go home to your mammy, you tosser. Tell her you're a tosser." That's one I remember, probably because I was at an age when being sent home to mommy was a thing to worry about.

The insults are more vicious now. And the refereeing situation
is the potential fault line in this World Cup. Referees in important games are under bizarre pressure. FIFA insists on appointing
officials from all parts of the world; the reasonable point is made
by critics that refs from countries where soccer isn't as intensely
played or watched are overawed and spooked by their duties at
these, the biggest, most important games. To ward off controversy, FIFA has announced that referees who perform poorly will
be sent home. Nice try, but that's too late for some aggrieved
teams that might be on the losing end of an incompetent ref's
decisions. Since the previous World Cup, the top two refs in the
world have retired or quit. The legendary Italian Pierluigi Collina,
famous for his glare, retired when he reached the age limit.
Anders Frisk, a Swede generally considered Collina's successor as
the world's best, quit after he handled the explosive Champions
League clash between Chelsea and Barcelona. Fueled by fulmi-
nations in English tabloids, one of which was being read by one
of the Gallagher brothers down in the lobby, threats were made
against Frisk's family. He decided he'd had enough.

Referees are also, increasingly, the targets of suspicion. The
current scandal in Italian soccer involves the alleged picking of
referees who are partial to certain teams. It has been alleged that
some top teams bribed referees with booze and prostitutes. There's
an increasing feeling, worldwide, that the caliber of officiating
is not what it should be. FIFA is aware of this, but is reluctant
to admit that major problems exist. Blind as bats to bad decisions,
are the FIFA suits.

Right now, the man considered the best is Markus Merk, a
German who handled the game between the Netherlands and
Serbia and Montenegro in Leipzig. Vastly experienced, he handled the Euro 2004 final between Greece and Portugal and the
crazy Champions League clash between Inter Milan and AC
Milan, a game he called off when it looked as if outright war
was taking place between fans in the stands. A dentist by trade,
Merk is famous for his calmness and adherence to both the rules
and a sense of fair play. Here in Germany, he caused a fuss off

the field when he publicly challenged a German government plan to charge a fee to patients visiting doctors and dentists.

It's calmness and a shrewd sense of fairness that make for the best refs. Players and fans alike hate a stickler who calls minor fouls in an effort to impose himself on the game. It bespeaks insecurity. Mexican Benito Archundia, who will take charge of tonight's game between Brazil and Croatia, has a reputation for being precise and tough. A lawyer, he speaks several languages, including Japanese, and he's handled big games in Asia. One of his two assistants working the game is Canadian—Hector Vergara of Winnipeg.

I take breaks from writing and wander the neighborhood. Mostly, I traipse up and down the Karl-Marx-Allee, a few blocks away. A grand boulevard built by the communists in the 1950s, it was once the most important street in East Berlin—indeed, it was originally named the Stalinallee. This is where the big May Day parades were held, and the wide street is lined with massive apartment buildings built in the style of socialist classicism, rooted in the Soviet Union's esthetic of plainness embellished with forthright flourishes of gilt. I know from reading about the area that the street was also the focus of an aborted worker uprising in 1953, as construction workers demonstrated against their government, and that more than a hundred people died when the uprising was crushed with the arrival of Soviet tanks and troops. On this sunny day it's possible to admire the dated, distinctive Stalin-era architecture and, even better, to appreciate how much has changed.

In the handful of chic little bars and coffeehouses on this section of the street, there are German flags, of course, but on this day the flag of Brazil hangs too. There's samba music playing over the sound systems. Groups of Brazil fans are moseying around and, as always, there's a posse of very fetching young Brazilian ladies wearing tight clothes and big smiles. They are the most photographed of fans at a World Cup, and they know it. Many are willing to preen for any camera, over and over again. In fact, as I finally figure out, for some female Brazil fans the main purpose of being here is to be caught on TV cameras or photographed. They want their image beamed all over the world and printed in as many newspapers as possible. And every press photographer here knows it. On the Karl-Marx-Allee, it's an unexpected exotic sight—photographers following those tall, leggy, beautiful figures, as if the exotic birds of Brazil had landed in this place where stern socialism was once anchored. It's a hot, sunny afternoon and there's an air of languid lust hanging in the air. What was East Berlin is, on this day, romantic, sensual and even voluptuous. It's the coming game that has done it—for some people, the World Cup doesn't really start until Brazil plays, and for an hour or two in the afternoon it feels like Brazil has kissed Berlin.

• • • • •

WITH ALL this idling and wandering, I'm late leaving for the Olympiastadion to see Brazil play Croatia. And I have to be there early, because I don't actually have a ticket yet. This is the only World Cup game for which I'm on a waiting list, tickets to be distributed two hours before the game to the lucky few. I take the subway to the Berlin Hauptbahnhof, where a media bus to the stadium leaves at regular intervals. The station is in the middle of nowhere, surrounded by acres of sand and gravel. I'm crossing this ground in 91°F temperatures, carrying equipment, and I'm legging it hard, huffing and puffing. I can see the bus sitting there, seemingly miles away. Halfway across, my cell phone rings. "Ye-hes," I answer, trying to keep moving. It's a guy named Dave from some radio station in Canada, and he wants me on the phone to take part in a discussion on the question, "Why doesn't Canada field a team for the World Cup?" I stop in the middle of this Berlin mini-desert, breathless and speechless. I can see where Dave is going with this. He figures Canada could just get a bunch of guys together and send them off to the World Cup. Maybe they could even play Brazil or England and, after planting a lucky loonie in the center circle, Canada would probably do okay. "It doesn't work like that," I bark at Dave. "Countries have to qualify.

Compete. You can't just decide to join in."

Dave is unconvinced. "But Canada fielded a team before," he counters. "Yes," I snap. "Canada qualified in 1986." Dave has issues with this. "No," he says confidently. "I think it was more recently. It was 1996." The absurdity of this discussion is beginning to expand alarmingly. "The World Cup is every four years," I shout. "Count backwards. There was no World Cup in 1996. I have to go now."

At least the bus is still there. But to my horror, it's empty. That means I've missed the one I needed to catch to get to the stadium in time to claim my ticket. This is obviously the next bus. The driver is loitering on the other side of the vehicle, in the shade. For some reason, he is grinning from ear to ear. "Hello, good day," he says, full of the joys of life.

"What time do you leave?" I ask. He looks at his watch and, beaming, says, "Thirty-five minutes." I ask how long it takes to get to the stadium. "Thirty-five minutes," he says, still smiling. I swear and leg it back across the scorching desert towards the taxi stand.

My driver, a Turkish chap, immediately informs me that Turkey should be at the World Cup, not Switzerland. I am fully aware that Turkey and Switzerland played an ugly brawl of a qualifying game a few months ago. A lot of people ended up in jail or in hospital. "Definitely," I say. "Switzerland is terrible." He drives off at breakneck speed. This lasts maybe three minutes, because there is heavy traffic heading to the stadium for the big game. Near the Olympiastadion, it is traffic chaos. Streets are closed. Everything has stopped. The taxi next to us is stopped, too. The driver of that cab gets out to talk to a police officer. As he does, his door makes a slight impact with the side of my driver's taxi. The Turkish zealot leaps out and shouts at the other driver, who shouts back. The police officer walks away. I know what is happening—I've been around. Remarks about slutty mothers, masturbation and sex with farm animals are being enthusiastically exchanged, is my guess. In the back of the cab, it occurs to me that there should be a World Cup for swearing taxi drivers. Canada could field a team for that. I make a mental note to mention the idea to Dave for one of his panel discussions.

I get out of the cab and walk the rest of the way to the stadium. There are several hundred journalists on the waiting list. I know that some of those who begin pleading for a ticket are only there to take pictures of Brazilian women. I glare and swear, taxi-driver style—but silently—at them. In particular, I aim my venom at a short, heavy-set man from Peru who whines continually about his need to get a ticket and tries to push me aside by shifting his ample arse, an arse encased in trousers with numerous pockets, each of which contains a piece of sharp-edged photo equipment. For a minute, I think I'm falling to the ground with broken ribs, but I manage to stay on my feet. Somehow, I end up with a ticket by saying two words over and over to the FIFA official: "National newspaper."

• • • • •

THE OLYMPIASTADION is imposing, and it has an unnerving history. Two stadia have existed on the site, the first built for the 1916 Summer Olympics (which never actually happened) and the second for the 1936 Summer Olympics, Hitler's showpiece games. The stadium is set in a sprawling park, and most of the surrounding buildings were untouched by bombs during the Second World War. After the war, the British military occupation used some of the buildings as headquarters. The main stadium is also home to the local soccer team, Hertha Berlin. Evidence of the club's history is everywhere. Sections of the 1916 and 1936 structures can be seen all around the grounds and there is graffiti celebrating Hertha Berlin. Traipsing into the building, I stare at everything. The Brazilian press corps, on the other hand, are oblivious. Many of them wear yellow Brazil shirts, like some traveling fan club— they do the media thing differently in Brazil, obviously. They're talking about how many goals Brazil will score.

What happens is that Brazil wins 1–0, yes, but something more significant takes place: the hype about this Brazil team is finally deflated. What will be remembered and noted by every team opposing Brazil here is how Croatia restricted Brazil and how vulnerable Brazil looked for long periods. This is a very slender victory. The Brazilians, with all their outstanding talents, look uncoordinated, lazy and unable to play together. Ronaldo, the star of the 2002 World Cup, plays like a twerp, loitering on the field with a sulky look and a distinct lack of interest in doing anything except waiting for the ball. The star of this game is Croatian Dado Prso, whose name was sung so lustily in Lisbon, a relentlessly moving, probing, driving striker. He is all determination and skill, doing little back-heel flicks that leave defenders looking like lost children searching for the ball.

For the first few minutes, Brazil does the expected, moving forward with ease and attempting to glide, with sublime ball-control skills, through the Croatian defense. It looks good, but gets them nowhere. Croatia doesn't just keep Brazil at bay, it rattles the lazily organized Brazilian defense. They succeed for forty-four minutes before falling behind, thanks to one gorgeous move by Brazil. In midfield, Emerson sizes up the scene and sprints forward with the ball. He feeds it sweetly to Cafu, who moves it quickly to Kaká. After a fast switch from one foot to another, Kaká aims at the gap in the Croatian defense and scores.

Still, for the second half, it is a fifty-fifty game, with Croatia enjoying equal possession. And for long periods, Croatia has Brazil pinned back. Anyone watching can only admire Croatia's grim determination and flashes of flair. The Croatian fans are out in force, and they're loud. With their checkered shirts, flags and singing, they seem to have an indomitable spirit. Unimpressed by the media buzz that they were facing what could be the best Brazilian team of all time, the Croatian players and their supporters respond with élan. Bursting the bubble around Brazil's alleged brilliance has taken some doing, and now, it's been done. Near the end of the game, an addled Croatian fan runs onto the field and tries to kiss Prso's feet, and everyone in the stadium— not to mention the tens of millions of viewers watching on

TV—needs no explanation. Brazil has come to Europe riding a wave of hype and presumptions, but it has been deflated by European-style doggedness. Brazil doesn't deserve this 1–0 victory—even their supporters in the crowd of seventy thousand must know that.

Later, on the bus leaving the stadium I'm surrounded by reporters from Brazil. They're deeply unconcerned about their team's performance. They are, in fact, showing each other photos of topless women on their cell phones.

• • • • •

LEIPZIG AGAIN the next day. Ukraine is playing Spain. I'm in the city early, watching the supporters from Ukraine move slowly through the town. They're the most subdued fans I've seen, a fact that surprises me. This is Ukraine's first World Cup, a massive occasion for the country. And the team has qualified easily. It has some excellent players, including, in Andriy Shevchenko, one of the best goal-scorers on the planet. The Spanish fans are out in force, gloriously colorful, confident and cheerful, but the supporters of Ukraine don't chant or sing. They wear their team shirts and some have flags draped around their shoulders, but they look unsure of how to behave. Most walk around quietly, and I reckon they're just absorbing what it feels like to be at a World Cup and carry your country's colors. At the exit from the train station I see a father with his young son, both dressed neatly in Ukraine shirts, the boy with a little cap. Dad smiles a little nervously as they emerge into the sunshine from the station. And then it happens: they meet the massed supporters of Spain. The boy, age ten or so, clings tight with fright to his father's hand and shrinks into his father's side. Eyes wide and bright as silver dollars, he takes it all in, the sights and sounds of the Spanish on the march, ready to make their famous presence felt by making one hell of a racket.

The boy looks at the enormous throng of people in red and yellow shirts, and then he hears it as it starts, that thunderous pounding of the Spanish drums and the rhythmic clapping. He sees the young women dressed in faux flamenco dresses with flowers in their hair. He sees young men dressed as matadors. He sees the mass of them crouch in unison and leap in the air, the drummer pounding and urging them on with the roar—"*Olé! Olé, olé, olé.*" The sheer Latin swagger of it, the confidence they show, the joy that emanates from them. This is Spain's twelfth World Cup, and they know how to enjoy it. They aren't afraid to be ridiculous because they know that's what the World Cup means: being empowered to celebrate every cliché about your country and do it with style.

The boy is spooked, but I'm guessing he will remember this forever and eventually know instinctively that this is what the World Cup really means. He will know that no one should hesitate to celebrate being here, that this is a mass carousal beyond imagining. It is about players on the field, but so much more. It is about the freedom to sing and dance in the streets.

All day, the boy's fright and wonder sticks in my mind because the entire Ukraine team behaves like that—afraid and awed. It's uncanny. Ukraine has come here for the first time, swaddled in dreams and expectations. Furious in the pace of its qualifying run, Ukraine left Turkey, Denmark and European champion Greece in the dust as they glided into automatic qualification. And yet this turns out to be a welcome-to-the-big-time game. Spain wins 4–0, easily and smoothly; Ukraine's dream turns into a nightmare. Thrashed and utterly outclassed, it is a stunning collapse. From the opening minutes, Ukraine looks terrified as Spain goes straight at the World Cup debutante, sending a clear message that this isn't a time for cagey play and sizing up the opposition. Ukraine's defense clearly does not know what has hit them, with Luis García, Fernando Torres and David Villa running rampant. In the Ukraine goal, Olexandr Shovkovskiy looks lost.

The game is thirty-two minutes old before Ukraine has a shot on goal, an extraordinary occurrence for a team that has been toasted as the next great European scoring machine. Soon enough, the Spanish players reduce the game to a walking pace, then occasionally stir themselves enough to offer Ukraine a master class in skills, tactics and formation. With mere minutes left, Torres scores a wonderful goal that results from one of those sublime passing moves that Spain can so easily pull together against a spooked opposition. Ukraine is very afraid, like that little boy with his dad.

Around the world, it's a boy's dream to play at a World Cup, or to be at a World Cup when your country plays. It's what millions strive for and dream about. Once there, every kid knows, you play the game of your life, enjoy yourself, dig in and stay proud. The World Cup is an invitation to the players and the fans to come and do their best. Big countries and small, old powers and newly freed nations, play on the same field. While listening to the sound of the Spanish drums in Leipzig in the evening, I reckon that somebody had better explain the World Cup to Ukraine, and fast.

• • • • •

THE NEXT day, I set out on a cross-country journey. This is an exhausting prospect, in reality, but it's the best part of being at a World Cup: being part of a vast, living and endlessly moving phenomenon. First stop is Nuremberg to see England play Trinidad and Tobago. It's an early, sleepy start for a five-hour trip, but by the time I have to change trains in Kaiser-Wilhelm, I'm wide awake. When the connecting train arrives, there are thousands of English supporters on the platform waiting for it. I watch them pile into the train in their white replica shirts. Most have ROONEY or OWEN emblazoned on the back. Then, for a second, I think I'm imagining things. In my sleep-deprived state, I think I see, among the English, a shirt that proclaims GRETZKY 99. I search the train for the shirt and its wearer, and I find him. The guy wearing it is Eric, a businessman from Toronto and a fanatic for England. He attended all of England's qualifying games and got the necessary points needed for the World Cup tickets. He is only part-English, he says, and although a supporter, he despaired of some English fans. "They love their home teams and know the players well," he tells me, "but they don't know anything about tactics, as Italian or French supporters do. They follow personalities, not strategies." Still, Eric and all the thousands of English fans are pretty sure that England will trounce little T&T.

Any neutral looking for a Cinderella team to support is drawn to Trinidad and Tobago. The team, known as the Soca Warriors, represents a country with a population of just 1.3 million people. Trinidad and Tobago is the smallest country to qualify for the World Cup, and is led by one of the great playboy-characters of soccer, one Dwight Eversley Yorke. In Leo Beenhakker, the team also has one of the wiliest coaches in international soccer. Nobody is giving Trinidad and Tobago much chance of winning a game, let alone progressing beyond the opening round, but the team is in Group B with England (overrated), Sweden (already held to a 0–0 draw by T&T a few days earlier) and Paraguay (unimpressive against the overrated English), so you never know what might happen for the tiny nation.

It was when Beenhakker, the veteran Dutch coach, took over that T&T somehow turned into World Cup qualifiers. At sixty-three, Beenhakker embodies old-school soccer. A cigar-chomping, no-nonsense boss, his long career has included spells at the helms of the Dutch national team and Real Madrid. In this instance, with T&T, he has somehow coaxed outstanding performances from a motley crew of mostly journeyman players and guided them, or goaded them, to the World Cup.

At the team's center is the maddening, thirty-three-year-old Yorke, the only T&T player to have an illustrious top-level career. Even his start in professional soccer is remarkable. He was playing as a semi-professional for a local team in Trinidad when England's Aston Villa played there on a pre-season tour of the West Indies in 1989. Someone spotted Yorke's talent, and a year later he was a highly paid professional for Villa, playing in the Premier League. By 1998, he was one of the top players in England, and Manchester United pounced, obtaining him for an

$18 million transfer fee. There, Yorke was part of the legendary team that won the Premier League, the FA Cup and the European Champions League in 1999. He also gained a reputation as a charmer, a ladies' man and devotee of busty models. He had a long, torrid and tabloid-frenzied relationship with a woman known in the English media only as Jordan—a model whose entire "celebrity" career was based on her ever-expanding bosom. She is, bizarrely, one of the most famous people in Britain. For all his success with the ladies, Yorke had trouble at work. He fell out with Manchester United manager Sir Alex Ferguson when he failed to return promptly after playing an international game for T&T. In early 2005, he went to Australia to play for Sydney FC. However, since T&T qualified, he's spent months back in Manchester, training to prepare for the World Cup. Yorke is a gifted player and, clearly, an exasperating man. The English writer Hunter Davies, who ghostwrote Yorke's biography, began referring to him, in columns he wrote, by the ironic title "Dwighty Baby."

Beyond Yorke, T&T are genuine minnows at this World Cup. The other players toil weekly for such unglamorous Scottish and English clubs as Falkirk, Port Vale and Wrexham. The gloriously named Stern John, who is usually in the forward line with Yorke, plays for Coventry. These Soca Warriors have nothing to prove—they got here. But they also have nothing to lose, and this is probably their single chance to earn immortality in their home country.

For England, the past is its burden in this tournament. Forty years after the at-home victory in the 1966 World Cup, the cult of '66 has grown to extraordinary proportions. The English players wear replicas of the shirts worn by that storied team. When the shirts were unveiled, several players, including David Beckham, talked enthusiastically about emulating the '66 heroes and marking the fortieth anniversary by winning another World Cup. This sentiment is dangerously delusional, but widely accepted as fact in England. Yes, this is a talented English team, perhaps the best in years, but that focus on the past makes the

English blind to the reality of the present. The reality is that Italy, Brazil, Argentina and Holland can easily match England's talents—and trump England in creativity and drive. And here, on this night in Nuremberg, England struggles to beat the smallest country at the World Cup.

The city of Nuremberg is an unsettling place. Famous as the site of the Nazi rallies and then the post-war trials, it was bombed heavily in 1945, after which much of it was restored. It's two cities, really—one within the old medieval walls and the newer city that sprawls in all directions. The soccer stadium is next door to the grounds where the Nazi rallies were held. On the walk into the stadium, I see England's team bus arriving. "One nation, one trophy, eleven lions," it says in big letters on the side. Later, the team that leaves the stadium on the bus must know the lie in that slogan.

Lions? England plays more like confused and meandering kittens for much of its flattering victory over Trinidad and Tobago. It is a grim display. Awkward and unimaginative for much of the game, England's superstar players are easily held in check by superbly disciplined opponents. The attacking duo of Peter Crouch and Michael Owen labor through the first half. Owen appears to be unfit, and Crouch seems nervous. It is Crouch who finally scores in the eighty-third minute after having long, high balls sent his way for ages. The relief for the English team and its fans is profound. One minute into extra time, Steven Gerrard fires a bullet shot to score and settle the game, but anyone watching can see that the team's banality is blatant. With this sort of performance, England would be torn apart by several of the top teams at this tournament.

There are about sixty thousand English supporters in Nuremberg for the game. Only a fraction of them have tickets; the rest watch the game on giant screens in an official "fan park" on a fairground alongside the stadium. There is a wonderful atmosphere after the game. Many of the supporters of Trinidad and Tobago have come to Germany from England,

and there isn't a hint of animosity or anger. There is, however, a ferocious amount of beer-drinking going on. Because of the number of English fans who've descended on Nuremberg, the only hotel I was able to reserve is an hour outside the city. The journey involves a slow trip on a suburban train route, followed by a taxi. I'm accompanied by Trevor and Jack, two English guys I meet on the train platform. It turns out that Trevor and Jack are the most boring men in England. An attempt to engage them in conversation about the game ends abruptly. "We're just getting started, roight?" Trevor says. "No worries about England." Trevor and Jack then carry on a long conversation about the merits of Jack making a play for a woman named Julie. Jack is pretty sure she was flirting with him earlier. Trevor raises the topic of Julie's breasts, which are, apparently, quite ample. Jack hushes him, then begins a long description of the journey from his house to Julie's place, which apparently takes five minutes on the bus. I'm pretty sure that if David Beckham got on the train at one of the many deserted suburban stops, Trevor and Jack would ignore him and continue to talk about the flighty but bosomy Julie. They're still talking about her when the taxi we share arrives at the hotel. Me, I make a very cranky call to the sports desk in Toronto, a call filled with complaints about trains, hotels and Englishmen. It's 2 A.M. and I'm tired, but I know that if I mention Julie I'll be summoned home.

At this point, I've hit the wall. After eight days of exhausting travel and writing, I don't care much about Cinderella teams, the pagan festival that is the World Cup for the fans—but not the journalists—the scandal in Italian soccer or the team spirit in Germany. As luck would have it, the next day is a travel day only. All I have to do is get to Frankfurt. I drink the two beers in the mini-bar and start laughing to myself. I have conjured up a mental image of Trevor and Jack, in twin beds, still discussing the likelihood of Jack scoring with Julie. In six hours, I'm supposed to be on a train to Frankfurt.

• • • • •

ON THE train, I fall into conversation with a woman, aged about sixty, I estimate, who is drinking beer, chain-smoking and has lots to say about the German club team, Werder Bremen. I am informed that Bremen is the business: a good team with loyal players, astute management and an excellent bar in the stadium. The conversation starts because, having learned that I'm Canadian and knowing that the Canadian player Paul Stalteri has played for Bremen, the woman figures I should know everything about her favorite team. I'm obliged to her and, although she is tipsy, she has better stories than Trevor and Jack. She explains that European club soccer thrives because it exists on two levels. There are the glamorous teams that bring the non-addicts to the game, such as Chelsea, Real Madrid and, in Germany, Bayern Munich. The latter is called "Hollywood" in Germany, apparently. Bayern has tons of money and acquires highly paid players with ease. The other level is where teams such as Werder Bremen function. In Bremen, she says, it's important that the team is part of the local culture. Nobody is "Hollywood." It's vital that the local people, the season-ticket holders, see the players, manager and bosses in the shops and restaurants. That breeds loyalty from the supporters. Non-Hollywood players perform better for the national team, she says, pointing out that Miroslav Klose is a Bremen player. I mention that I'll be going to the game between Portugal and Iran the next day. She tells me emphatically that Iran should not be allowed to participate in the World Cup. "They don't allow women to attend the games there," she says. "This is what you call bullshit." It's a fair point, I think. As the train nears Frankfurt, she orders more beer and tells me that Frankfurt is a pain-in-the-ass city and I won't like it there.

This proves to be true at first. My hotel is near the Frankfurt airport, and I leave the train at the stop for the airport. I'm relying on the website promise that the hotel operates a shuttle bus from the airport. An hour and a half later, I take a cab. The

driver is delighted because, actually, the hotel isn't near the airport at all—it's miles away, surrounded by several other hotels
which, I'm sure, also claim to be "airport" hotels. An attempt
via email to meet up with three other Canadian reporters in
Frankfurt falls through. Instead, I write an opinion piece arguing that FIFA should have barred Iran from this World Cup. See,
women are barred from attending soccer games in Iran. Any
country that promulgates a system of sex apartheid in soccer
should not be allowed to be here. It's that simple. In Iran, women
work in many areas of business and government. They work with
men in offices and other places. There are women in Iran who
are customs and immigration officers, police officers and taxi
drivers. They run businesses. But if the national team of Iran is
playing in its own country, women cannot attend. Also, in Iran,
apparently, women can play soccer, but must do so covered. Men
cannot watch women playing soccer, and no male coach is
allowed to advise and train a women's team. If a male coach is
needed, he provides information by mobile phone or some other
ludicrous system.

Excuse me, I argue, but soccer is the world's game, not the
men's game. There are many women working for FIFA. There
are hundreds of female journalists covering this World Cup.
There are tens of thousand of women attending the games. As I
see it, FIFA is insulting every woman involved in this World Cup
by tacitly endorsing Iran's policy of barring women from attending games. The Iranian authorities would change their rules darn
fast if FIFA were to eliminate the country from taking part in
international tournaments unless it allowed everyone to attend
games. The woman on the train was correct. After I file the
story, I'm informed by the sports desk that a great many people
are angered by my meager assessment of England in the report
on the game against Trinidad and Tobago. This is good, actually: angry Englishmen can call the paper to complain until
they're blue in the face. At least in England, Julie can attend any
football game she chooses.

• • • • •

THE HOTEL bar is packed with the staff from various airlines,
so I join them to watch Argentina play Serbia and Montenegro
on the big-screen TV. It is a game of unnatural beauty—a 6–0
demolition by Argentina, but to watch it is to witness the performance of an exquisite, incendiary dance. Gods toy with
mere mortals. Early on, it is obvious that this is Argentina's
day. Argentina moves the ball with an intuitive understanding
of the sensual proportions of the game. They delight in
caressing and passing the ball. The first goal is a peach. Juan
Pablo Sorín's back heels the ball unexpectedly, opening up
Serbia and Montenegro's defense as a deft hand might find the
erogenous zone of a lover. Javier Saviola cuts inside and eases—
he doesn't kick or strike, but *eases*—a perfect pass to
Maxi Rodríguez, who stabs a shot past the goalkeeper and into
the net.

It is what happens next that hushes the Russian, Korean and
Swedish flight crews in the hotel bar. Argentina gives a master
class in balletic passing to score again. There are twenty-one
passes between players before Juan Román Riquelme, on the
edge of the penalty area, feeds the ball to Saviola, who then
directs the ball to Esteban Cambiasso. Cambiasso then unerringly slides the ball to Hernán Crespo and keeps loping ahead.
Crespo nonchalantly back heels a return pass to Cambiasso, who
hits the ball hard and straight as a shaft and scores. The room
I'm in goes quiet. The German commentator on TV is beside
himself. He has seen, as we all have, a sublime, rippling movement of seduction and penetration. There is a vain attempt by
Serbia and Montenegro to fend off this graceful plunder and
violation, but there is already an air of resignation among the
players. It persists until six goals are scored. At the game, in
the stadium, is Diego Maradona, the greatest of all Argentinian
players. The camera shows him as he jumps, shouts, punches
his fists in the air. He looks a little absurd, this short, now
doughy man, with his declarative gestures, but nobody laughs.

What is unsaid is clear: Argentina, in full flow and possession, has taken the ball, the game and possibly the tournament, beyond the reach of anyone else.

• • • • •

FRANKFURT'S STADIUM is all new and shiny—a little antiseptic. Around it on a Saturday afternoon, supporters of Portugal and Iran are getting to know each other—shyly, at first. Kids have their faces painted. Parents watch, smiling. A Portuguese man who wears on his head a plastic replica of a wine casket, with numerous corks hanging from it, looks at the Iranian father beside him. Both their kids are having their faces painted in their country's colors. The Portuguese man extends his hand and introduces himself to the Iranian. Cautiously, the Iranian man shakes his hand and they have a conversation in a combination of English, German and much miming. They eventually walk away together with their kids. I'm hanging around, watching. I like Portugal and its people. I've written in the paper that Iran shouldn't even be here. Still, on this lazy Saturday afternoon, I cannot begrudge the Iranian fans their place here. They're an odd assortment. There are many young people, expensively dressed, who ooze money and attitude. But there are hundreds of older people too. Women in headscarves scurry about, taking care of children. The men stand in groups, smoke cigarettes and cheer loudly whenever the flag of Iran appears in the gathering crowd.

I follow the two men who just met. The man from Portugal meets up with his wife, a petite brunette in a very short skirt and a tight, revealing Portuguese team shirt. It says FIGO on the back. The father produces a camera and calls on the Iranian man to bring his family together for a group photo. There's a moment's hesitation but, I can tell, he figures this is all about the kids. His wife, as small as the Portuguese woman, joins him and calls the kids over. She's in a long, ankle-length skirt and a white cardigan. My God, she must be feeling the 86°F heat. The kids come, big-eyed, giggling. I watch as the two families—four parents and four kids—crowd together for a photo. The kids are priceless, all with smiles on their painted faces. After a passerby has taken the photo, she hands the camera back. The man slips it quickly into his pocket and hugs the Iranian dad. Then he hugs the Iranian man's wife. The Iranians look a little startled, but for a minute they're all hugging, the kids and the parents. The Iranian man is bewildered. His wife is laughing in a protective way, as if it this was a crazy, laughable thing to have happen—sheer madness. But it wasn't. Nobody has paid the slightest attention but me. Everyone is here to see and encourage the gods of soccer to do their battle on the field. And everyone here is the same, really: rambling people of pleasure, cordiality and kindness.

• • • • •

THE GAME is a slog. Portugal wins 2–0, but Iran's resistance is admirable. This is a tough team, with three players who turn out every week for clubs in the German Bundesliga. Ali Karimi, their best player, plays for Bayern Munich now. But a handful of top players do not make a great team. Still, the first goal was Portugal's only indication of true quality. It came in the sixty-third minute, thanks to a beautiful, crafty move by Luís Figo on the left. He changes direction with the ball and offers it to a perfectly placed Deco. The resulting shot is a beauty of a goal. The second goal comes from a penalty. Again, it is Figo moving relentlessly into Iran's end before being brought down by a clumsy tackle. A penalty kick is inevitable. Cristiano Ronaldo takes it and scores, making a great show of the moment.

Ronaldo spends much of the game showboating. An immensely talented player, he continually overdoes the step-overs and dancing-feet movements to the point of redundancy. An English newspaper has described his style rather cruelly, but with some accuracy, as "Michael Flatley with rickets." Ronaldo clearly believes he is lord of the dance, but his audience is often less impressed. As ever, Portugal struggles to find a rhythm until the dedicated, determined Figo bosses the game. He is inexorably driven, and while others flounder or pout, he goes on, endlessly toiling. Firm, fixed forever as stalwart. I can picture the scene in the bars and Portuguese social clubs in Toronto, the young men and women urging Ronaldo on while the old men watch Figo do the real work. Portugal has had it relatively easy here, placed in a group with Mexico, Iran and Angola. And after this victory, its progress to the next round is assured.

• • • • •

I TAKE a bus to the Frankfurt airport after the game, it being the easiest route to the alleged airport hotel. The airport, a travel hub, is crowded with passengers going this way and that. I end up sitting with my laptop in a place called The Irish Pub. These faux-Irish bars have spread like weeds throughout Europe. I'm having a beer and a breather after the game, waiting for results from other games and trying to assess who is in and who is out of this World Cup. The Czech Republic–Ghana game is on the big-screen TV and the place is crowded with people watching it, some probably missing planes to see it. A sign over the door reads CÉAD MÍLE FÁILTE—Gaelic for "a hundred thousand wel-comes"—as do the menus and beer mats. Those earnest men who fought, killed and died for an independent, Gaelic Ireland could not have dreamed that, less than a hundred years later, bits of the Gaelic language would be used to sell a concept of Irish convivi-ality and fun in every corner of the world. Their pictures hang in many of these places—men, like Michael Collins, who were once called insurgents or terrorists. There's a rich irony right there, I know. And inevitably there are pictures of the great Irish writers, too. Just over my head is a framed photocopy of a page from James Joyce's *Ulysses* with a sketch of Joyce beside it. I wonder what "Sunny Jim" Joyce would make of this phony Irish bar, and of the World Cup being watched and enjoyed here? He'd be okay with it, would Joyce. An internationalist to the core, he wrote passionately about the need to escape the confining traps of nationalism. He'd love this great convergence of a multitude of streams from different cultures. He'd love the Esperanto of soccer language.

• • • • •

IN THE morning, I'm to take the train to Munich to see Brazil play Australia and I arrive at the Frankfurt station way too early. I'm sitting in a station bar, drinking espresso and orange juice as the space around me fills with all of humanity. This is the tenth day of the World Cup, and six countries are playing today: Brazil, Australia, Japan, Croatia, France and South Korea. The station is a mass of people from these countries, heading hither and thither to the games. The Croats are here, men in the heat of the morning wearing little but underwear in their country's colors. There are hundreds of Japanese too. As I make my way to the platform, I pass through them. Most are dressed so neatly in Japan's blue team uniform—families in blue, gangs of teenage girls in blue, faces painted with the rising sun. I must look friendly, because I'm asked to take photos. For thirty minutes I act as photographer for the Japanese fans. There are middle-aged women in kimonos. There are teenage boys, all fastidiously cool in their torn jeans, sneakers and team shirts. They are so incredibly polite. I get thank-yous and bows. I tell none of them that I was in Japan for the World Cup four years ago and people tried to throw me out of my hotel and refused to take me in taxis because I was a foreigner. I'm as polite as they are. It is required. A small bow to the sweetness of the day, to the tournament.

There are thousands of Australians. According to the newspapers, thirty-five thousand have come to Germany for these games. Their team, the Socceroos, is an underdog that fears no one. These Australians are not merely happy to be here, they are hungry for success. The last time Australia qualified for a World Cup, in 1974, several members of the national team were semi-professionals who held day jobs. Some had problems getting time off work to play at the tournament—such was the depth of Australia's skepticism about it. In fact, according to a story in Sunday's *Observer*, from London, many Australians in those days referred to soccer with the racist insult "wogball." As far as most were concerned, soccer was a game for immigrants—and, really,

these peculiar people would eventually take up Aussie-rules football and cricket, wouldn't they? Perhaps some did, but soccer
slowly grew. Today, Australia struts. The fans expect success, and
that's not unreasonable. This isn't a plucky team hoping for the
best. Far from it.

The Australians, most of them young, swarm the station now.
Many carry plastic inflatable kangaroos. It would look absurd
in any other context, but here it makes perfect sense. Young
men and women, most of them tipsy or stoned, clutching plastic
kangaroos, on their way to Munich to watch their country play
Brazil. I'm on the platform when the train to Munich pulls in,
coming from some other city. I can hear it before I see it. Not
the roar of the engine or the tooting horn, mind you: it's the
music. All the way down the train, windows are open and people
are leaning out, waving, dancing. The samba music is pounding
inside from boom boxes. The Brazilians are coming. As the train
slides into the station, I can see a young woman leaning out the
first window, waving the flag of Brazil. She's young and lovely
and her long, brown hair streams behind her as she holds out
the flag, defiantly, but grinning all the time. She's shouting
something I can't hear. The noise of the train and the samba
music combine to drown her out. I hope someone is taking a
photograph of this. The moving train, the young Brazilian
woman leaning out, brandishing the flag, the Australians salut-
ing her with a roar. She looks like the woman personifying
Liberty in Delacroix's painting, *Liberty Leading the People.*

The journey to Munich is a speed-train party. The Brazilians
drink and dance. The Australians drink and dance. A Brazilian
woman, busty and buttocky, her hips throbbing to the beat,
grabs a plastic kangaroo and dances with it lasciviously. The
German conductor moves along slowly, checking tickets half-
heartedly. He has the look of a man pleased to have been given
the Sunday morning shift. The train is crowded, noisy and surreal. But the atmosphere provides only a taste of what's happening in Munich, where a jolly mayhem has descended. Every
bar is packed. The police are trying to limit the people taking

the U–Bahn to the Allianz Arena (now clearly marked) to those with game tickets. A group of sozzled Australians tries to get around the police by crawling on the ground. Most can barely get to their feet when the ruse fails. There's a band playing, marching up and down the street outside the station. Apparently, the band came all the way from Australia to keep the spirits up. It's playing "Waltzing Matilda," and hundreds of Australians start singing the song. Brazilians who have run out of money are demonstrating dances and asking for donations in return. Tourists take pictures. Photographers from the German papers encourage some Brazilian ladies to dance topless, but there's nothing doing. At least while I'm watching, anyway.

I squeeze onto the media bus to the stadium and stand all the way. When we reach our destination, I haul off my luggage and bag containing my laptop and equipment—and wait. There's no point in lining up to get through security yet; I'll wait until the crowd from the bus are through. The noise around the stadium is deafening, a cacophony of samba music, Australians singing and the police making announcements about how to get into the stadium. Then I hear a voice: "Carry your bags, Mr. Doyle?" It's Chris Young, and it's the first time we've met up during the tournament. He helps me with the bags and I show him how to get into the press area. We agree to meet later after we've both done some writing. An hour later, we're on a balcony, looking down at the Brazilian and Australian fans still streaming in. "Are you tired or are you happy?" Chris asks. "Happy," I say, "but sometimes I wish I could get as drunk as these people. " I tell Chris I was at the Portugal–Iran game the day before. We talk about Figo and those games in Portugal where we saw him drag Portugal to the final of Euro 2004. The Australians sing "Waltzing Matilda." We can barely hear each other speak. This is the life.

• • • • •

BRAZIL BEATS Australia by two goals and advances to the knockout second round. But it's clear that all isn't well with the wonder boys from Brazil. This is still a shaky-looking team. There is no poetry. Australia creates numerous chances, with Marco Bresciano, Mark Viduka and Harry Kewell all coming very close. In fact, in the Brazil goal, keeper Dida has a rough night. I wonder what she thinks about the chaotic defense playing in front of him. Australia lacks its opponent's bag of magic tricks, but Brazil could learn a great deal from the linked and sometimes lovely play of an underdog team. For Australia, the game is about charging forward in a coordinated attack and shifting back to defend with the same smooth decisiveness. Adriano gets the first goal in the forty-ninth minute, and Ronaldo is marginally better than he was against Croatia. Still, he is substituted again in the second half. The second goal, a tap-in, comes from substitute Fred in the ninetieth minute, while Australia is busy pushing hard for an equalizing goal. The loss is tough on Australia, which has played an excellent game. But other results mean that Australia takes its rightful place in the next round.

After two games, this is still not the Brazil team the world was promised. This is a collection of marquee names and divas. Brazil needs to figure out were the poetry went. I decide that the team is not going to win this World Cup. But its supporters don't seem to care much; they're here to party. Me, I need a night's sleep and I'm actually relieved that my cheap hotel near the stadium doesn't seem to house any Brazilians or Australians. Early the next morning, I'll be flying from Munich to Hamburg to see Ukraine play Saudi Arabia.

• • • • •

THE SUBURBS of Hamburg are leafy and pleasant. I know, because I get a good look at them from a suburban train. I'm utterly lost: I took the wrong train, not the one going to the stadium. Miles from downtown, I get off and take another train back to the city center. I pass the time by looking at the German newspapers. There are as many photos of pretty young female fans as there are of the players from various countries. Obviously, in Munich the previous day, a Brazilian woman had been persuaded to pose topless. I can only hope she was paid a good fee. Such photos are selling a lot of papers here.

Ukraine hammers Saudi Arabia 4–0 in what is a bizarre reversal of the game between Ukraine and Spain. This time, it's the Saudis who look nervous and timid, in particular goalkeeper Mabrouk Zaid. Ukraine is not slow to take advantage: within five minutes, Ukraine is ahead 1–0 and keeps going. Andriy Shevchenko looks more like the striker he is, a man worth $65 million for his services.

There are Saudi fans here, all men and all bellicose. At the last World Cup, the Saudis were eviscerated, beaten 8–0 by Germany, swept aside by Cameroon and Ireland. It is being present here that's most important, I think. After that is achieved, the players don't care. In fact, I've started to loathe them. I saw the games in Korea and Japan, the piteous performances by the Saudis. Sad bastards, the English would call them. I want to shout at them, these players so hostile to the event. I've no idea why they wilt. It's a mild, lovely night in Hamburg. I've come a long, long way to see this. And I'm sitting here, head in hands, the smell of Munich on Sunday in my head—the smell of beer, flesh and sex. Not this. So I leave. Two beers in the Hamburg night, and back to Berlin in the morning.

• • • • •

A NEW hotel, a Best Western bossed by a woman who has a low opinion of journalists and the World Cup. I raise her suspicions by checking in and then, after going to my other hotel, returning with more luggage—and then, a short time later, asking for the front desk to call a taxi for me. I have to get to the Olympiastadion to see Germany play Ecuador. I'm waiting outside for the taxi when the boss lady bustles out. "Are you leaving?" she asks, accusingly. Unsure, I say "No." She looks at the taxi, now pulling up, and raises her eyebrows. "I'm going to the match," I say. "I'm a journalist." She gives me a long, warning stare. "I know," she says, in a tone best described as dark. Already she has my credit-card details and a photocopy of my passport,

so I give her my business card. It says, TELEVISION CRITIC, THE
GLOBE AND MAIL. That'll confuse her. I wave at her from the taxi.
I have met the only person in Germany who isn't in the World
Cup groove. Maybe she thinks I'm actually a Russian.

This is the cusp of the second round and, if Germany wants
to avoid meeting England in a few days, it needs a multi-goal
win. And Germany beats Ecuador 3–0. It's an emphatic victory,
of the sort that is necessary to keep German spirits high. In the
next round, Germany will meet sterner competition. Tellingly,
coach Jürgen Klinsmann uses his substitutions to give Miroslav
Klose, Torsten Frings and Bernd Schneider a rest before the battles ahead. Berlin goes a bit mad, and even in this sprawling city
it isn't hard to tell what's happening. It isn't a carnival or a raucous party—no, it's a sort of spreading bliss. Berlin isn't Germany;
it's separate, coquettish, sophisticated, not easily impressed. And
now it's happy—except for the boss lady at the hotel, who has
probably run my name through Interpol by now.

It's Tuesday, and on Saturday the next round will begin. Half
of the thirty-two countries here will have been eliminated.
Spain, Italy and Argentina look to be the strongest contenders
to reach the final. Only one African team, Ghana, will
progress.

• • • • •

OVER THE next forty-eight hours I make a lightning return to
Hamburg to see Italy play the Czech Republic. Italy wins 2–0
and appears to be ready to do even better. The Czech display is
a shambles. The team has lost point man Jan Koller to injury,
and in this game one of its players is sent off near the end of the
first half. Back in Berlin, I see Ukraine again, this time against
Tunisia. It's an accident of geography and travel that I keep seeing
Ukraine play, but I feel like I'm on a study mission.

The morning of the game, I cross Berlin and go to Checkpoint
Charlie, the legendary crossing point between the western sector
of Berlin and the East German part. A replica of the checkpoint
hut—the place used so often as a setting in John le Carré novels

and movies about the Cold War—stands there, and around the corner there's a long stretch of what remains of the Berlin Wall. All of it encapsulates what was once the great division in Europe, and the world, between the West and the Soviet Union.

The stretch of the wall is an unsettling, puzzling sight—this mundane, inanimate thing, now being allowed to crumble, once embodied the rift that separated the world for so long. Near Checkpoint Charlie, a group of Ukraine supporters, distinctive in their yellow and blue shirts, are doing their sightseeing. For them, citizens of a new country that could only attain independence once the wall fell, this was a day to see iconic elements of the past and consider Ukraine today, as well as its future. They are here in Berlin because Ukraine has been an independent country for fifteen years now and is entitled to play on the greatest stage in the world, the World Cup—to win or lose on the strength of its team. Gone are the Cold War days when Ukrainians played for the Soviet Union. Russia didn't qualify this time, but Ukraine did. There must have been exquisite satisfaction in knowing that, as the fans gaze on Checkpoint Charlie and the old wall.

Both Ukraine and Tunisia deserve to be at this World Cup. For Ukraine, it means so very much to transcend the Soviet past. For Tunisia, it's about national pride too. Anyone watching can admire the grit being displayed. The game is ill-tempered, inelegant. Tunisia's bustling forward Ziad Jaziri tries hard, but turns thespian looking for fouls and free kicks. Then he turns into a thug, first swinging a hand at the face of Anatoliy Tymoschuk, then lunging for a feet-first tackle. The referee produces a yellow card; two yellows means a red, and Jaziri is gone. Down to ten men, Tunisia has its back to the wall. Eight men are lined up like statues in front of the Tunisian goal to protect it. All pride and pugnacity, Tunisia regains its composure and surges forward again and again. This is about stubborn resistance and guts. It takes a penalty, and a dubious one at that, to break the Tunisians down, and Ukraine wins 1–0.

I'd been looking forward to seeing Tunisia play. I'd been alerted to this team and its merits ages ago, by my father. He knows his stuff, but he's not usually so knowledgeable about international soccer. He gained his knowledge through his friendship with a chap named Safieddine, who works in his local bar. Safieddine had been educating my dad about the tough Tunisia team, and he was intrigued.

Time was, back around the time of the Cold War, that contact between an Irish person and a Tunisian could only occur if the former took an expensive and exotic holiday in northern Africa. Now, as Ireland, Europe and the world change, a Tunisian is part and parcel of an Irish bar.

• • • • •

ON SATURDAY, the first day of the knockout stage, I'm headed for Leipzig again, for Argentina against Mexico. At this point, I think I've seen all there is to gawp at during a World Cup, but the morning arrival at the Berlin Hauptbahnhof opens my eyes again. There are, I'd guess, about fifteen thousand Mexican fans there already. They are all in green, the country's color, and almost every one of them is wearing a sombrero. Standing in line to get the usual—espresso and orange juice—I'm the only one among hundreds in the coffee shop who isn't in green and a sombrero. They are an immensely cheerful crowd, the Mexicans, carrying laughter and optimism with them everywhere. There seem to be as many women as men in the traveling crowd, and many families, with elderly men and women being graciously helped along by youngsters. There are an estimated forty-two thousand Mexicans in Germany for the World Cup, a fan army ranking in size only behind the English and the Dutch.

Mexico considers itself a soccer power. It has qualified for numerous World Cups and hosted it twice. It has made it to the quarter-finals twice. In recent years, in regional competition and at last year's Confederations Cup, Mexico has beaten Argentina twice. Defeating Argentina or Brazil is always something to strive for. It's a necessary thing. There's resentment about not being taken seriously. Mexico means business, and that's why there is an enormous traveling army of support behind it.

The game is an astonishing spectacle. Argentina, overflowing with talent, stormed through the first round, slowing only to play a sort of leisurely waltz with Holland. And they even did that with a kind of bemused aplomb. The team became everybody's favorite to roll on to the final—there is so much skill and trickery within the team, with Juan Román Riquelme, Carlos Tévez, the teenage Lionel Messi and about six others. And yet, one knew that if anybody was going to call a halt to Argentina's gallop here, it would be Mexico.

And Mexico scores first. Team captain Rafael Márquez catches the Argentine defense lazily ignoring him. The loud Mexican supporters are delirious. In minutes the score is level, though—a corner lands in a melee in the Mexican penalty area, and as Mexican striker Jared Borgetti lunges to clear it out of danger, he falls and sends it into his own net. Argentina's Hernán Crespo goes on a triumphant run as if the goal is his, but it isn't. As Crespo runs away in triumph, Mexican goalie Oswaldo Sánchez walks out from the goalmouth to stare at the replay on the big screen. He wants to know what the heck has happened. Mexico is briefly deflated, and what transpires for the rest of the game is a gripping, thrilling game of attack and counter-attack. For long periods, Mexico matches Argentina in skill, strength and determination.

For any neutral watching the game, this is soccer at the highest level, with both sides equally determined to engage in scoring. There are few fouls, few acts of operatic, time-wasting drama. It is all pace and a pleasure to watch, right up until the end of normal time.

Messi is introduced late for Argentina and has an immediate impact, dazzling the tired Mexicans. He's lightning on feet, this nineteen-year-old, and the fact that he could be left on the bench for most of the game only underlines Argentina's strength and confidence here. But it is too late for Messi to turn the game's direction and avoid extra time. In extra time, it takes a wonder goal to do it, but Argentina finally beats this admirable Mexican team. The goal comes from Maxi Rodríguez, who calmly chests down a cross, takes aim and unleashes a curling left-footed shot

that is just out of reach of Sanchez. It is one of the best goals of
the tournament.

Mexico has come close to delivering the biggest upset of this
World Cup, but it is Argentina that will go on to meet Germany
in the quarter-finals, in a mouth-watering match this Friday in
Berlin. I will miss Mexico and the sight of those hordes in their
giant sombreros. It is about 4 A.M. by the time we all arrive
back in Berlin from Leipzig, off the standing-room-only trains.
I wait for a taxi at a street corner with two young Mexican
women, both of them hauling enormous suitcases. I ask if they
are heading home to Mexico right now. "Oh no," one says.
"We're going to a party now." They deserve it.

● ● ● ● ●

BACK TO Nuremberg again. This time, I take a cheap Lufthansa
flight, avoiding hours on the train and gaining five hours' sleep
instead of two. I check out of the hotel, park my luggage, ensure
there's a room reserved for a few days hence, and ask for a taxi
to the airport. All good. Then Boss Lady arrives. It's déjà-vu
time. "Are you leaving?" she asks. I acknowledge that I am, but
say I have a reservation for a few days later. "You are going to
the airport?" she asks, eyebrows raised. It occurs to me that Boss
Lady hasn't noticed that the Berlin Wall has fallen and, yes,
people can go this way and that without permission. My gambit
is to raise the issue of the minibar. "There are supposed to be
two beers in it," I tell her. "And last night there was one. Just
one." "There is a coffee machine," she counters.

At this point, other guests are gawking through the windows
of the ground-floor restaurant, wondering why Boss Lady is
having a tense conversation with the guy who always has his
laptop, looks like he's had two hours' sleep and often wears a cap
that says CANADA. For some reason, I'm put in mind of a certain
situation in Portugal. I offer my hand to Boss Lady for a handshake. She shakes it, but with obvious reservations. "*Vive la
France!*" I tell her, loudly. She backs off, a little.

The game I attend will become notorious as the Battle of

Nuremberg. Portugal plays Holland and wins, 1–0. But it's not
the result that registers around the world. A total of sixteen players are given yellow cards, while four are given red cards and are
dismissed. Both teams end the game with nine men on the field.
It's a splenetic, stopping-starting game. On TV, I'll learn later,
the game was denounced as a disgrace, a terrible example of top-
class soccer. Well, it was thrilling to be there. Close to the field,
I can see and hear the madness play out. The referee—from
Russia, no less—loses control early. Instead of awarding a free
kick and warning a player, he begins waving the yellow card.

Portugal starts the troubles, for sure. Determined to quell
Holland's Arjen Robben, they have three men surround and
harass him. Twenty-three minutes in, Portugal gets a fine goal
from Maniche, on a swift counter-attack. Then, bizarrely,
Portugal goes into time-wasting mode. As the first half ends,
there is a portent of things to come. Portugal's Costinha is sent
off after his second yellow card, forcing his team to start the
second half with ten men. It seems that Holland will surely gain
an advantage from this development before long. Instead, the
game's rhythm disintegrates. Luís Figo gets into a disagreement
with Mark Van Bommel and promptly head-butts him. The referee issues a yellow card when a red is deserved, and all the players stand around, gesturing and swearing. The entire Portuguese
bench is on its feet and roaring. The Dutch bench is also standing and shouting. The referee is panicky now, and Figo knows
it. He delivers a dramatic, scenery-chewing performance in reaction to a push from Khalid Boulahrouz, and it is Boulahrouz
who is sent off. The atmosphere on the field and in the stadium
is poisonous. At one point, as another complicated and incom-
prehensible fracas is unfolding on the field, I notice the sort of
thing you don't see on TV: a young man in a wheelchair, a few
feet away from me, is staring at the group of players arguing on
the field and bellowing so lustily his lungs must hurt. "Figo!
Figo! Figo!" he shouts. But Figo has already left the field, substituted. It is hard to keep track of what's happening.

I stay at a hotel near the old downtown, where I'm embedded

with the Oranje Army, drowning its sorrows. The Dutch, being the Dutch, believe they played the better game. The consensus theory is that the Dutch team loses games when it doesn't wear its orange team shirts. Tonight, the team opted to wear white. I don't know if it's plausible, but all the drunken Dutch fans in the hotel bar accept it.

· · · · ·

COLOGNE NEXT, for Ukraine playing Switzerland. It is the worst game of the tournament.

Mind you, I have a sneaking admiration for the Swiss fans. Many of them look like young professionals. Neatly dressed young men and women, in their red shirts, they have their faces ever-so-neatly painted. They look confident, cool and prosperous. But that's only a portion of the Swiss fan base. The rest, the charming ones, are a mad crowd. They bring along their cowbells and ring them incessantly. And they wear the wackiest gear on their heads. Portly men who one imagines toil as sensible bankers will take to the streets of foreign cities when Switzerland qualifies for a tournament, wearing plastic cow's udders on their heads or giant plastic triangles of Swiss cheese. They couldn't give a damn how ridiculous they look. When I emerge from Cologne's main station, the first thing I see are about five thousand such Swiss guys, lounging on the steps of Cologne Cathedral. A legion of portly, middle-aged men, plastic cow's udders on their heads, banging on cowbells. They're just weirdly lovable. The team bus bears the slogan "2006, it's Swiss o'clock." Hilarious. Nothing about warriors and lions for them.

The game is a dire, defensive nightmare, 0–0 at full-time and still scoreless after extra time. Then it turns out the Swiss can't take penalty kicks. They look as though this aspect of the game were a novelty suddenly invented to fool the naive Swiss. Ukraine wins the penalty shootout. This is the fourth time I've seen Ukraine play, and I am thoroughly sick of them. They're due to meet Italy in a quarter-final game. That'll finish them.

• • • • •

HANOVER NEXT, for Spain versus France, the most delicious of
the second-round games. France surges to life at last, winning
3–1. It is a great game, marked by artistry and quickness. It is
also Zinedine Zidane's game. Age has not withered him, only
added to his calm, guile and finesse. The second round of this
World Cup was in sore need of style, magic and knock-'em-dead
soccer, and the man whom many had written off as past it, an
old warhorse, emerges to propel France to its best performance
since the 1998 World Cup. He even provides an exquisitely exe-
cuted goal in the final minute.

The last few days have been a poor exhibition of the wonders
of World Cup soccer. The bizarre yellow-card bonanza of
Holland–Portugal, a plodding but lucky England winning over
Ecuador (a game I declined to watch on TV on the afternoon
of the Portugal–Holland game) and the momentous tedium of
Ukraine's win over the Swiss. If any game was going to give
this round that pleasure-shot of artistry, it was this one—the
Latin swagger of the thrilling Spanish team against the cool élan
of the French. The game lives up to advance billing, and it is
the mercurial French who triumph over a skilled but immature
Spanish side. There will be greatness in the future for the
Spanish, but here, their zest is no match for the finely honed
French combo of age and youth, cunning and determination.
Spain oozes confidence, but Patrick Vieira and Zidane com-
mand the field, coolly intimidating the strikers who face them.
Eventually, the Spanish players begin to look like enthusiastic
boys playing against deeply experienced, wise men.

Spain tries its neat passing game in an attempt to unlock the
French defense through nimbleness, but nothing works. France
looks entirely comfortable. Zidane is an electrifying figure, commanding the midfield, spraying balls forward with exquisite precision, cajoling his teammates. *Move back. Move forward. Stop there.
Wait till I tell you to move.* It's imperious, and the thing is, he
knows exactly what he's doing. The extraordinary revival of this

French team is even more emphatically obvious when France is
leading 2–1. With mere minutes left, the players still push forward. In injury time, Zidane springs forward to collect a pass,
keeps his cool and calmly moves the ball around the keeper for
a goal that is the perfect coup de grâce. For several years, Zidane
hasn't looked anything like the player who became an icon at
France '98. He's thirty-four now and will retire after this World
Cup. In the qualifying games and in the early games here, he
has looked as if he'd opted for one World Cup too many.
Whatever happened to inspire him again seems to light up the
entire French team. Spain is unbeaten in twenty-five games—its
last defeat was against Portugal at Euro 2004—but it has never
met a side as gloriously adept at commanding the field as this
French one. The French have this knack for cunning, surprise
and for eventually exerting their superiority. Zidane embodies
all of that again. Now, France will meet Brazil in a quarter-final
game that will be a rematch of the World Cup 1998 final that
made Zidane a legend.

• • • • •

AGAIN, IT'S a train. It's well after midnight, and I'm on a rattling two-hour trip from Hanover to Berlin. There's a moment
in this journey when it becomes clear to me that this is the representative World Cup adventure, the encounter that will linger
long afterwards and, years later, play out in my mind in glorious
detail. It's the unexpected event that explains the reason for
everything—the long hours of work, writing and travel, the endless deadlines, the rushing for planes, trains or buses to get to
the next city, the next game. It's the reason why I exist for weeks
in this state of hope, exhaustion and exhilaration. It's where the
mental exuberance and manic joy erupt. It is the transcendent
moment when I know why being present at a World Cup tournament is a ludicrously happy experience. And the reason is a
young woman named Christine.

The train is carrying hundreds of people who have attended
the France–Spain game. Tucked into my seat, I find I'm

surrounded by French fans. They chat for a while, and then they all fall asleep. This strikes me as odd: I've been on post-game trains in Japan, Korea, Portugal and Germany, and I've never seen the supporters of the winning side simply doze off, contented with the win. That's the French supporters, though. Me, I'm supposed to be writing on my laptop, and here are dozens of sleeping French people I don't dare disturb. So I ease out of my seat and set off for the bar car, which is packed and noisy. Spanish fans are drowning their sorrows, some enthusiastic German drinkers are sympathizing, and a few journalists are on the beer, swapping stories, consoling each other about deadlines and barking about mad editors back at the office. Everybody is having a ball, actually, even the handful of French supporters huddled in the corner—three middle-aged couples, smiling, keeping to themselves.

Christine is running the bar, and she has foolishly told some Spanish guys her name. There are constant cries of "Christine, may I have a beer?" or "Christine, do you have vodka?" Christine keeps her cool. Twenty-something, tall, blonde, lovely and struggling to keep an unruly mass of curly hair in check, she can handle the braying crowd. She is in charge, strong and astute in assessing the men around her. I wait in line and stand at the counter. The Spanish guy parked beside me needs to cling to the bar counter to keep upright. Every time the train swerves round a bend, his fingers clutch at something—sometimes me. After a few minutes of drunken, stoic passivity, he lurches forward in slow motion and lets his cap slide off his head to fall on the floor of Christine's tiny workspace. He may be lacquered, but he's got ideas stirring in his tired head. The idea, obviously, is to get a glance down the front of Christine's shirt as she dives to retrieve it. Christine reads the game well and immediately lifts the guy's cap with her shoe. It's a deft movement, a flick of a perfectly positioned foot, the instep flexing and the cap landing where she wants it to land: on the counter, right beside the Spanish guy's elbow. I watch this in stone-cold sober astonishment. Christine is skilled with her feet. Christine is a soccer player. And she is very, very good. The Spanish guy just stares at the cap beside him like a man who has seen Fernando Torres send a swirling ball towards the goal, and he focuses his bleary eyes on the player in front of him, then says, very quietly, "*Olé*, Christine."

I order coffee, because I still have to write when I get back to Berlin. When Christine gives me the coffee, I catch her eye and say to her, "I think you and I are the only sober people here." She pauses to do the mental translation and says, with unerring German gravity, "I think you are correct, sir." A journalist from Yemen buttonholes me and, in heavily accented French peppered with BBC-accented English phrases, proceeds to tell me a great deal about how the people of Yemen feel about Zinedine Zidane. I don't understand all of it, but the upshot is that, in Yemen, Zidane is worshipped as a deity because he has the deep-set eyes of a god. I think that's it, anyway. I tell him that in Canada, people feel much the same. It's only natural—those eyes. A Spanish chap, with a matador's hat that's only slightly askew on his head, elbows in between us. Previously, he had devoted his efforts to appearing very sober and to saying, "Christine, may I have a kiss?" but he's been listening to my conversation with the man from Yemen. He tells me he is delighted to meet someone from Canada. What luck, he seems to be saying. It turns out that he has two dreams: for Spain to win the World Cup and to visit Toronto. Or so he says, anyway. It becomes clear that he thinks Toronto is next door to where the Rocky Mountains are situated, but I don't correct him. He is also deeply interested in how many soccer fans there might be in Toronto. It's a fair question. And as I answer, somewhere in the back of my mind I'm thinking that this is a rare and lovely scene of utter woozy madness, but exquisitely so. In a moment of reverie I decide that a phrase used by FIFA to market the World Cup is the absolute, incontrovertible truth: "One world. One game."

There's a commotion at the bar now. The guy who'd let his hat fall to the floor has done it again. And Christine has kicked it deftly back to him again. There's a larger audience this time, though—word has spread, the spectators are primed. A call goes up for the guy to do it a third time and for Christine to catch the cap as it falls and to kick it back onto the counter. She's game. We're all agog. Even the French supporters. The three women among them shout out encouragement to Christine, and she politely acknowledges their solidarity. The cap slides off the Spanish drunk's head and, with a swift kick, Christine sends it flying back. It lands where it should. The car erupts. "*Olé, olé, olé!*"

With that, the train slows and we all sway and stagger as it enters Berlin. Christine lowers the metal grille over the bar counter and announces that it's closed. A man waves a camera and calls out, "Christine, please, can I take your picture?" Christine says "*Nein!*" briskly and busies herself tidying her work area. But from where I'm standing, I can see the delighted smile on her face as she turns away from the crowd. It's a message she sends: no photos, just remember this. When the train pulls into the station platform and the doors open, the goodbyes to Christine are many and passionate and are expressed in several languages. Two Spanish guys stand on the platform and blow kisses at her. She waves. The three French couples all giggle as they watch this, then they wave at Christine, who has finally removed her work apron and, as if freed by this action, flashes a peace sign at the Spanish boys. In the enormous glass atrium of the station, a cry goes up and echoes: "*Olé, Christine.*"

Now, me, I probably look like a bit of a idiot for a few minutes—I'm writing things down in my notebook, walking, stopping, writing, walking, writing: *Christine closing the bar as the swaying train pulled into Berlin late at night. The cheers and the kisses blown at her. She used her feet with dexterity. She didn't dive. She used her head. She kept the ball going. And that, after all, is the true essence of the beautiful game.*

I tell the taxi driver to drop me off when I'm about a mile from the hotel, so that I can walk awhile in the still of the warm Berlin night. The signs of mid-tournament madness are everywhere. The flags of a dozen countries can be seen hanging in

windows, from balconies, on cars and tied to lampposts. Hundreds
of thousands of people have been watching the day's games on
giant screens around the city. The air feels full of the peace of
pleasurable exhaustion. As I turn onto the street for the hotel, I
notice the profound silence and then just stop and stare. There,
on the ground in front of me, is a sleeping young couple—teenage Germans, the boy blond, the girl with flaming red hair.
They're sleeping peacefully, curled up on the sidewalk, spooning.
Like most of the local teenagers, they have the punk-like look
of Berlin bohemians: spiked hair, carefully torn shirts and cropped
jeans with boots. Their blanket on the street is the German flag.
The girl clutches a corner of the flag to her chest and the boy's
hand grasps hers. All I can do is absorb this extraordinary scene
and tiptoe quietly away, leaving them to their peaceful sleep.
There is such equanimity, such tranquility and trust embodied
in the sleeping couple. This is what the World Cup has bestowed
on Berlin. This is what Christine meant when she flashed the
peace sign: just remember this.

• • • • •

IT'S A sublime night, and I never actually get to bed at the end
of it. A few hours after arriving in Berlin, I flee the World Cup
for thirty-six hours and go to Dublin. My book *A Great Feast of
Light* will soon be published in Ireland, and people want to talk
to me about it. Mainly, though, I want to see my mother and
father, enjoy a home-cooked meal and sleep in a bed that isn't
in a German hotel. I arrive in Dublin, not having slept for more
than twenty-four hours. This doesn't quite register with my dad,
who is anxious for me to come to the pub and meet Safieddine,
his friend from Tunisia. Soon enough, sleepless but drinking
Guinness, I'm listening to Safieddine tell me where Tunisia went
wrong. He's heartbroken, I can tell. Ireland didn't qualify for the
World Cup, but Tunisia did. If only they'd got that one goal
needed to get past the first round, he'd have been so happy, a
lord of the pub, a man from a country that mattered.

I need sleep. A nap seems destined, but back at my parents'

home, there's been an urgent call from the *Globe and Mail* that must be returned. It turns out that I've won an internal *Globe* award for writing, or something. And I know this is prestigious. I've no idea if it has anything to do with my World Cup coverage. My colleague, Stephen Brunt, has been covering the glamour games, and I seem to have been traipsing around Germany for weeks following Ukraine. I'm put on hold while someone gets the editor-in-chief to talk to me. I sit there waiting, thinking about that young German couple sleeping on a Berlin street, hours earlier. The things I've seen. When the editor-in-chief comes on the line he's blustery, and I suspect he's utterly mystified as to why some committee of editors and writers has bestowed an honor upon me. He begins listing off the names of previous recipients. The point, I think, is to make me feel humbled. I am, but the main thing on my mind is an unassailable truth I discovered in Korea and Japan four years earlier: it is very, very difficult to get a good sleep in the sportswriting racket.

• • • • •

BACK IN Berlin on a Friday morning, it turns out I still have a room at my hotel—the luggage hasn't been sent to the authorities. I'm off to the Olympiastadion to see Germany play Argentina in the quarter-final game. The sober German press has begun to call this "the reality-check game." You see, a German newspaper called this World Cup "a four-week vacation from reality," referring to the sudden outpouring of patriotism and support for the German team that began after Germany defeated Costa Rica in the opening game. Frankly, most Germans were surprised that their team was so good. Before the tournament there had been much doubt, just as there are doubts about Germany, the country, today. The "reality" being forgotten for a few weeks is the economic drag of the cost of reunification. Citizens of the old West Germany are not accustomed to the higher taxes and higher unemployment rates that came with the cost of accommodating East Germany, connecting it to the West and absorbing all those need-a-job new citizens. Part of "reality," too, is the suspicion that exists about some of those people who were born and grew up under Communist rule in the old East. Those Easterners are greedy and grasping, mutter some people who have paid higher taxes so that the East can get new roads, a rail system and be as high-tech as the West. That was the cruel reality to escape for a while with flag-waving and support for what might be a weak but lucky team.

Well, in soccer terms, a game against Argentina is indeed a reality check for Germany, the team. It has won games, but the Argentinians will truly test the team's mettle. If the surprising success of the first round had seemed a dream, then harsh reality would come courtesy of the tough, technically brilliant Argentina. And the test is passed. In the context of German history—both soccer history and the evolution of the country—this game, won by Germany on penalty kicks, is a triumph. It is 120 minutes of two evenly matched teams trying to unlock the other's defenses. It has theater, histrionics and tension. Argentina's tactic is to be tough and provocative. There are niggling fouls and absurd over-reactions every time an Argentina player is touched. If goals are going to come—and one is sorely needed to open up the game— it will come from a set piece. And thus, four minutes into the second half, Roberto Ayala scores for Argentina with a diving header from a corner kick. Exactly how it crosses the packed German goal line is unclear, but it stokes the game to fervent life. Then it is all Germany for a while. Next, true theater. Argentine goalkeeper Roberto Abbondanzieri is injured colliding with Miroslav Klose during some jostling on a corner kick. The German fans react with scorn, but the keeper is truly injured and has to be replaced. Germany is given new hope. Minutes later, Michael Ballack supplies a superb ball, it's nodded on by Tim Borowski and Klose heads home his fifth goal of the tournament. The game is tied.

In extra time, the dynamic is with Germany, but it's all tired legs on the field and terrified gasps from the crowd when Argentina mounts a swift counter-attack. Ballack, the fulcrum, seems to falter; an injury from an earlier game has returned, and

the captain paces a small area in the center of the field, unable
to do much more. Finally, he hobbles to the sideline for treat-
ment. The allowed substitutions already made, Germany is essentially down to ten men. Ballack hobbles back, but looks barely
able to move. Then to the agony of penalty kicks. The German
team huddles and seems to pray. Oliver Neuville takes the first
for Germany and scores. Ballack takes Germany's second, and
scores.

Then Jens Lehmann saves twice and Argentina strikes no
more. This is no vacation: Germany is one game away from playing in the World Cup final, right here in Berlin.

I'm reluctant to leave Berlin while the city is in ecstasy. But
I have to leave for Gelsenkirchen, hours away, early next morning for the England–Portugal quarter-final.

· · · · ·

"I WANT to be a Scot," an English fan tells me ruefully after the
game. "At least I wouldn't keep believing that England was going
to win the World Cup. We always screw it up. I want to be a
Scot. It was horrible in there. We can't even take penalties. What
kind of a bloody useless team is that?"

England leaves this World Cup, a mere quarter-finalist, in
another heroic failure. It always happens: an English team is
praised as a world-beater and then fails, miserably, near the end,
and with elements of farce and self-destructive behavior. As usual,
the team is revealed to be commonplace, banal and bereft of
creativity.

All the elements of tragicomic drama fall into place. David
Beckham leaves the field injured, his face knotted in pain and
disappointment. Some see tears on that famous face. Soon, Wayne
Rooney is sent off after a tantrum. Ironically, after being reduced
to ten men and losing their captain, England's players perform
with the sort of determination, flair and verve that they had so
obviously lacked in earlier games. There is tenacity. There is
vitality. Some, such as Owen Hargreaves and Peter Crouch, play
the game of their lives.

But England seems to live in absurd fear of penalty shootouts. They are an integral and expected part of the game at a World Cup and other tournaments. Other teams take them seriously. England, it seems, merely cringes and collapses in failure.

The game begins as expected: England plays a cautious first half against a cagey but cunning Portugal, which, missing several key players, is, in truth, far from its best and eminently beatable. But England manager Sven-Göran Eriksson goes the conformist route, using a 4–5–1 formation, with an increasingly frustrated Rooney isolated at the front. Portugal packs the midfield, too, so England's tactics are glaringly designed for stalemate, not scoring success. In the 86°F heat of Gelsenkirchen, and in an enclosed stadium, it is an excruciating, tense match. Minutes into the second half, with Portugal, especially Figo and Tiago Mendes, causing regular panic in the English defense, Beckham hobbles to the sideline. He's replaced by Aaron Lennon, who immediately shows how Portugal can be beaten. But his dazzling runs never connect, and Rooney looks taken aback by Lennon's speed and lack of caution. Then events evolve into farce. Trying to beat two defenders, Rooney becomes entangled with both. Ricardo Carvalho is on the ground, Rooney seems to aim a foot at him. Whether it is a deliberate act or merely a player trying to steady himself doesn't matter. As Cristiano Ronaldo harangues the referee, Rooney turns on his Manchester United teammate and pushes him. Out comes the red card and Rooney is gone. Beckham stands on the sideline, bleating, pointing a finger at the referee.

From there, the English players engage in magnificent backs-to-the-wall soccer. Hargreaves, the Canadian-born midfielder, morphs into a one-man attacking machine. The tens of thousands of English fans, far outnumbering the Portuguese, egg the team on, sensing a heroic ten-man victory. It never comes. As in Lisbon two years earlier, Portuguese goalkeeper Ricardo transcends the tension and stops England's penalty shots. He knows England is rattled by penalty kicks. He only has to keep his cool, and he does so with ease. Most of the English shots are sad efforts. The last, decisive Portuguese penalty is taken, as the narrative demands, by Ronaldo. He scores and, in his self-confident way, briefly taunts England's supporters. He has every right. At this level, soccer is a game of skill, tenacity and raw cunning. Portugal displays them all and reveals England to be the sorry mess of a conformist, banal team it has always been in this tournament. In Ronaldo, whom the television cameras caught winking at the Portuguese bench after the Rooney red card, and in the referee who sent off Rooney, the English press has its villains. There will be phony outrage.

There is nothing phony about the reaction of the English fans. I spend seven hours with them on the long, endlessly delayed train trip back to Berlin. These are the working-class stiffs who support England with admirable passion. They have shaken off their image as hooligans. They are decent people supporting the lame efforts of highly paid superstars, and they know it. They are tired, hurt and angry, but they don't blame the referee or Ronaldo. I sit with three of them on the train— Dave, Barry and Danny. "England is shit," Barry tells me. His friends tell him not to swear and say that to a reporter. The young man sighs and gathers his thoughts. "England is poo," he says. "England is wank." Word spreads that France has just beaten Brazil in the other quarter-final game. There are groans. There is little conversation on the train to Berlin. But I learn that the trio have come to Germany for this game only. They hadn't tickets for the first-round games and, in a fever to join the party, they took a cheap flight to Hamburg, the train to Berlin and started looking for tickets from scalpers. They claim they'd bought two pairs and resold the fourth for enough of a profit to cover the cost of the other three. Now, once in Berlin, they have no plan but to head to the airport and look for a cheap flight to London. There is no bar on the train, no food or drink for sale. The train is old, uncomfortable and slow. The English fans understand. They are being carted like cattle out of Gelsenkirchen—and Germany, just in case.

It is a bleary, grumpy bunch who line up for taxis early on Sunday morning in Berlin. The English fan beside me is a tall, strapping lad wearing a Beckham shirt. Out of nowhere, along come three very drunk German youths. One walks directly to the English guy beside me, arranges his face into a sneer and sings, *England's going home again / England's going home.* I brace for trouble. But the English guy calmly takes in the sneering face and beery breath and says, with aplomb: "All right, Otto. Having fun, are we? Nighty-night now." He stares down the German with a grim smile. The disappointed German youth reels away. Then the English guy looks at me and rolls his eyes. It's a victory, a very English one.

• • • • •

ON MONDAY morning I fly to Frankfurt and then home to Toronto. There is an inevitable flapdoodle at the hotel. Boss Lady says I'm supposed to stay one more night. Various pieces of paper, all poorly printed, are pored over. I assert that I'm due to check out that day. She sulks, declining to admit that the paperwork supports me. The staff stand around, on tenterhooks. "Now, I'm leaving," I tell her. "And the coffee machine stopped working last night." She's red-faced, on the brink of fury when I begin shaking hands with the staff and wishing Germany well in the semifinal game. A tall young woman, the one bossed by Boss Lady at breakfast to take the names and room numbers of the diners, tells me she's from Ukraine and doesn't care if Germany wins or loses. She also has a cousin in Manitoba. Boss Lady glares. Only the young lady from Ukraine waves goodbye.

I make the plane for Toronto with minutes to spare. For reasons I don't question, I'm suddenly flying business class. As soon as I enter the plane, I'm handed a glass of champagne. I've nothing to toast but the tournament. Me, I'm thinner and probably crazier than when I arrived weeks earlier. It's been a great World Cup. The late assertion of European supremacy was a surprise, but Germany, France and Italy have played thrilling soccer and reached the last stages aided by cunning and resilience. Germany was a wonderfully welcoming country, laid-back and utterly calm about hosting it. With the exception of Boss Lady at the Berlin

hotel, I didn't meet a cranky person. There was negligible violence and no tension, a remarkable achievement given the millions who poured into Germany and went from city to city
floating on beer, mostly. The tranquility was astounding. It was
exactly what the World Cup promises: one world, one game,
one big celebration.

• • • • •

AT HOME in the days that follow, as France and Italy win their
semifinal games to set up an all-European final, I find that in
explaining the allure of the World Cup, I tend to sentimentalize
and idealize. Then the World Cup final unfolds, and within it is
the most-watched act of violence, ever. When Zinedine Zidane
head-butts Marco Materazzi on the field in Berlin, a strange sort
of rage is unleashed with startling clarity. I'm watching at home
on TV, taking notes for an online piece I'll have to write as soon
as it ends. I can't explain to the friends watching with me in my
home what's happened. I understand it but can't explain it.

It's a good game too, France ahead on an early penalty that
allows Zidane to score with the sort of emphasis that makes
people worship him. Italy equalizes soon after. The two teams
are evenly matched, with plenty of scoring chances. France has
gained the momentum in extra time when it happens—the incident. It happens off screen, and everyone in the largest TV audience ever to view a sporting event is, at first, puzzled. Then we
all see it: Zidane turns quickly on Materazzi and head-butts the
Italian with enough power to send him to the ground. The red
card comes out of the referee's pocket and Zidane walks away,
past the World Cup trophy itself. Italy wins the penalty shootout
and the tournament.

There is much hand-wringing about Zidane's action. So many
claim to be stunned by it. (I am in Newfoundland weeks later,
and people are still talking about the incident. I hear it memo-
rably described by a local as "Buddy buttin' Buddy in the soccer.")
I'm not. It was foreshadowed in Tim Parks's book *A Season with
Verona*, in which he describes a game Zidane played in 2000 for

Juventus of Italy: "Zidane in particular has a crazy, bullish anger about him, a head-down tension and animal violence that no doubt goes far beyond football, reaches back into some profound personal quarrel this man has with the world, his days as a poor immigrant's son in the white man's France, perhaps." But perhaps not. I remember Zidane's honest gaze on the people in the stands in Incheon when France left the World Cup without even scoring a goal. Zidane is, I think, partly the poor immigrant's son whose anger at the world rises from something in his youth, but he is also part artist, aware of his own skills and of how sublime soccer can be. He has an artist's cold, intense loathing for those who refuse to play soccer with the elegance and calm grace that he brings to it. When Materazzi taunted him and impeded him with niggling fouls, Zidane, playing his final game, reacted with rage not just against Materazzi but against every player who had sullied the game, who had diminished the game by refusing to play it beautifully. It was a great artist's unapologetic rage against mediocrity.

A few days after the final, I'm in Kensington Market, where the man who was selling soccer shirts and flags has a new T-shirt for sale and prominently displayed. It shows Zidane's head-butt and Materazzi falling. The T-shirt declares, "Don't fuck with Zizou." I ask if the shirt is selling well. "Selling very well, boss. Not a problem there." I ask him what he thought of the incident. He looks to the heavens and then laughs. "You don't fuck with a man like that. Not him. Not that man."

CHAPTER 4

EURO 2008,
AUSTRIA/SWITZERLAND

IT HAPPENS IN SALZBURG, on a bus. Salzburg, city of music, of Mozart, as well as cemeteries, a great cathedral and two castles. An ancient, lovely city devoted to culture. A World Heritage Site, a wee city of 150,000, and stunningly beautiful. Mozart is the main business—everything from music festivals to little chocolate thingies he is alleged to have favored. It's here that the surreal, magnificent madness of it all is revealed.

Greece is playing Sweden. Before the game, I stand for a time on the bank of the Salzach River, watching as groups of Greek supporters gather on one bridge over the river and, with gusto and good cheer, chant and sing at a far larger group of Swedes gathered on another bridge a short distance away. The display is colorful and vastly entertaining.

As I stand there, a Greek fan comes and stands beside me, chortling away at the sight. He steals a look at my press badge and says, "Canada!" He asks me if I'm from Toronto and I admit that I am. "You know Danforth?" he says. Indeed I do, I reply, and mention that there had been wild celebrations on that street when Greece won Euro 2004. "That was historic," he says. Then we both return to watching the mass singing competition, the sound echoing out all over the extraordinary vista of the old town. The mass of yellow shirts belonging to the Swedes and the blue and white of the Greeks lend a vivid pageantry to the spectacle. The young man beside me says, "I think today is a historic day for Salzburg," then walks away smiling.

He's right, of course. The color, sound and atmosphere have transformed this ancient place. Euro 2008 has poured ebullient, joyful people into Salzburg. Not that everyone is as happy, mind you. In the late afternoon, all the buses from the old downtown are taking the Swedes, Greeks and anyone who cares to the stadium. I'm watching the throng, the movement of it all, when I see a young man—in his late teens, perhaps—walking along the street with a grave sense of purpose. He stands out because he's one of the few people not wearing the colors of either Sweden or Greece. He's dressed in jeans, a sweatshirt and a grey jacket, and he's carrying a violin case. He arrives at a bus stop and waits. And waits. Wherever he's going, he's not going to get there soon. He has a solemn, annoyed look on his face. He's determined to ignore everything around him—the color, the singing, the chanting, the laughter and the beauty of it all. He cannot, will not, look at the handsome Greek men, the blonde Swedish girls in the summer sunshine. Mozart must be rolling in his grave, I think, if he sees this young man, a devotee of music, ignoring the splendor of the occasion.

Sweden beats Greece 2–0. It's just after midnight and I leg it out of the stadium. Salzburg might be cultured, but it is also small, tricky and complicated to navigate. I figure I'll leave the stadium quickly, with the fans, and try to get my hotel, wherever it is. I jump onto a crowded bus, purportedly heading for the main train station, the focal point of transport. I'll surely get a taxi there. The bus is packed tight with happy Swedes. I'm squeezed in among the smiling faces and swaying bodies as the bus—a long one with an elastic bit in the middle—pulls away. Soon a Swedish guy, a short, burly fella with grey-blond hair, shouts something in Swedish, then the entire crowd at the back of the bus starts singing, in English. To the tune of the Pet Shop Boys' "Go West" (always played at the games), they sing with great gusto their special song for the Greek team and supporters: *Go home to your hairy wives / Go home to your hairy wives / Go hooooome!*

It is mercilessly rude and silly but delivered with a childish, gleeful delight. As usual, the Swedish supporters include many families, and I can see a middle-aged mom and dad, with their son and daughter, aged about fourteen and twelve, belting out the song with relish. Next, the entire back-of-the bus population collapses in laughter as the bus takes a sharp turn and we all tilt to one side. Then I see a small group of Greek guys in the middle of the bus, draped in Greek flags, staring at the singing Swedes. One of them stands up, which is difficult with the crowd and the swaying, and sings out, "*Champione! Champione! Olé, olé, olé!*" It's a pithy reminder that, no matter how juvenile the Swedes might be, Greece is still, at this point, holder of the European Championship. He spots me—easily done, as I'm the only person at the back of the bus not wearing a yellow Swedish team shirt—and rolls his eyes. Then he bows to the Swedes, who promptly applaud him.

Minutes later, we're still cruising and swaying through outer Salzburg. A Swede spots the sign for an IKEA outlet. Thunderous and prolonged cheers ensue. "Hurray for IKEA!" is the gist. Soon the bus stops at a red light and we all peer out at a corner café where many people are on the patio drinking beer. More lusty cheering and singing starts. "Hurray for beer!" is the gist. I'm pretty sure a twelve-year-old Swedish girl is bellowing, "Hurray for beer!" We are into Salzburg now, and the bus stops in traffic, where a large group of police officers—the *Polizei*—are standing. The Swedes all wave. The short, burly one calls out the window, "Hello, *Polizei! Guten abend, Polizei.*" And a cop, trying to be waggish, makes a great show of looking at his watch and calls back, "It's *guten morgen now.*" Hundreds of Swedes on the bus giggle. The Greeks guys are in stitches. Then the Swedes start singing again. "Hurray for the police!" is the gist.

The bus finally stops somewhere. We're not at the train station, but the driver is shouting something in German that indicates the bus doesn't go any farther—too much traffic. When the back doors open, the short and burly Swedish guy who has been the ringleader for the childish mayhem puts an arm around me.

"We go for beers, yeah?" he says. I hesitate, but I figure there's time for one beer anyway. He's delighted, yells at his friends to get the Greek guys, and we're all off in search of a bar. The nearest possibility is an imposing hotel, but the two security guards at the front door are having none of it. They wave us away. The ringleader announces that there's another place nearby—he's sure of it. The small posse moves on, with three Greeks now bringing up the rear, and everyone can tell they're just a little enchanted by two very pretty young Swedish women who are taking turns leaping into the air to no purpose. We turn a corner and march down a street. There isn't a bar or restaurant in sight. At the end of the residential street the ringleader announces that he's pretty sure the bar was here, right here in this spot. We are, in fact, standing at the end of someone's front garden.

The front door of the house bursts opens, and an elderly man emerges and shouts at us to go away. We scatter like children caught misbehaving. Giggling. Up the street we regroup. The two leaping young women indicate that they'd rather eat than drink beer. Must be all that leaping. The Swedish ringleader agrees that food would be a good idea, as do the three Greek guys. There's a stall down the street selling sausages. Everybody can smell the food and veers in that direction.

I bow out, as I have to finish writing and send the copy to Toronto. I shake hands with everyone and start looking for the train station. Just as I see it in the distance, I can see the chaos at the taxi stand. A lot of people are gathered there, and some are running into the street to scoop a taxi as soon as one appears. My heart sinks. It might take hours to get out of here and reach the hotel, which is just on the outskirts of the old city—I think. Just then, a van pulls up beside me, and it's a taxi. The driver orders me to hop in, and I do. He tells me he'll take a complicated route to the hotel. It'll take longer, he says, but he wants to chat with me anyway. Some time later, we seem to be passing through open country. He could be giving me a nighttime tour of *The Sound of Music* landmarks, for all I know.

We are in the midst of a good discussion about the skills and managerial merits of Giovanni Trapatonni, the coach of Italy at the 2002 World Cup and Euro 2004. Trapatonni has spent the last few years managing the local team, Red Bull Salzburg, with great success. Recently, though, he's been appointed manager of the Republic of Ireland team, and I'm deeply interested in the elderly Italian. My driver tells me that Trapatonni is a great manager and can make any team a winner. Mostly, though, he's distracted by the chatter from the dispatcher that's coming through on the radio. He's chortling away to himself, then he starts translating for me. What the dispatcher said is this: "Six Swedish guys want a taxi to take them to meet nice local girls, not hookers. They're very drunk."

As we near the hotel, the driver obviously remembers what he really wanted to chat about. He pulls over for a minute, gives me a long stare and asks if I'd be interested in buying some dope. He's not saying he's selling, but if I were interested he could make the deal happen. I decline the offer, telling him I'm really looking forward to a cold beer in the hotel room. That'll do me nicely, thanks. No problem, he tells me; he figures he will find some Swedes who are interested. "The Swedes are very happy and very drunk and this is good," are his parting words.

I'm just into the hotel room when the cell phone rings. It's the sports desk back in Toronto. What am I writing about and when is it coming? That's the gist. I tell the editor that it's just about the game. Sweden beat Greece 2–0. There is no possible way to explain and describe in the newspaper these long, mad nights when there's magic in the moonlight, or those dreamy, delightful days that bracket the games. I can't yet chronicle this mad, magnificent world I inhabit, this vaudeville, this place that the gods of pleasure and play have blessed.

• • • • •

EURO 2008 has been anticipated as a great tournament, and it is—mainly because it's truly European. England failed to qualify, as did Scotland, Wales, Northern Ireland and the Republic of Ireland. The absence of England has made Euro 2008 a better tournament. And not just because England's squad is truly mediocre and its dull, plodding play would have lowered the tone. Without England, we've all been spared the tsunami of coverage about David Beckham's foot or Michael Owen's groin. Because the English media are so large and relentless in their coverage, if England is at a tournament, a lot of the twaddle enters the mainstream English-language media around the world, making England seem more important than it is. Most players for England's national team are overrated, overpaid and over the moon about themselves. Most lack discipline and skill. Tellingly, few ever succeed when playing for European club teams. They are simply afraid of the rigors of playing in Spain or Italy.

This is what I tell the readers, anyway. It doesn't go over well. But no matter, because Euro 2008 will be a tournament more dramatic and more testing than the World Cup for the sixteen teams involved. Nobody except Austria can be ruled out of a potential long run towards the semifinals or the final itself. There are few obvious contenders. If you want a safe bet, there'd be only a single potential one: Germany might make the final. But you never can tell. Four years before, in Portugal, the Greek team went from a shocking opening-game victory over Portugal to a shocking final-game victory and became champions of Europe. Back then, Trapattoni famously observed that Greece won the tournament "with three free kicks and a corner." Greece is back for Euro 2008, but the likelihood of a second stunning victory seems remote. Yet every team ought to be wary of Greece, and every unheralded team will be energized by Greece coming from the background to win a European championship.

On the surface, there are four strong contenders. Italy, the reigning World Cup champion, was tipped to win it until captain and defender Fabio Cannavaro was injured and ruled out of the entire tournament. And Italy's tendency to do a slow-burn start to tournaments will prove to be a weakness, because Euro 2008 doesn't afford them that luxury. France, the World Cup finalists, have gifted strikers and a dodgy defense. Holland is full of pep and drive but, like France, suffers from a leaky defense.

There are several second-string teams who might emerge for a
long run into the semifinals. Portugal has Cristiano Ronaldo,
the best player in the world, and is under much less pressure than
when it hosted Euro 2004. Croatia seems the most dangerous
team in the tournament. It ensured that England didn't qualify,
for a start. An injury to the goal-scoring machine Eduardo da
Silva has dented the potency of Croatia's attack, but this is a team
with tremendous resolve and spirit. Spain looks good, but usually fails—that is the cliché about a team brimming with talent,
speed and grace. But at past tournaments, almost every team
member played his club soccer at home in Spain. Now, several
key players are in the English Premier League, an experience
likely to toughen them. Toughness is what Spain needs. Well,
that's what I write in the paper. Very wise, I am. I know in my
soul that sometimes great soccer tournaments evolve with a
dream logic that resembles a fable, not a narrative with a sche-
matic beginning, middle and end.

And then: Euro 2008 turns out to be Spain's tournament. And
Holland's too. The Dutch play sublime soccer in game after game
until, well, they seem happy to have proved a point and they go
home. Yet it's Russia's tournament too. In one game, Russia
elevates itself to a status that inspires fear and awe. Mind you,
when it comes to emotion, it is mainly Turkey's tournament.
What Turkey achieves matters more—far, far more—than goals.
The Turks have a complicated, resentful relationship with the
Swiss, and it's much the same with Austria. There are scores to
settle, on both the sporting and sociological levels. It matters that
Turkey performs well, but it matters even more that it happens
in the host cities of Euro 2008. There has been a Turkish community in Switzerland since the 1960s. Most Turks arrived in
the 1960s and '70s as migrant workers. Their jobs are in the
industrial, catering and textile sectors. They do the dirty work.
Patronized and often facing discrimination, they resent their
menial status. Even as they integrate—two of Switzerland's
greatest players, Hakan Yakin and his brother Murat, are of
Turkish descent—they face problems. Second-generation Turks

in Switzerland and Austria feel the sting of discrimination and
condescension. So, in every game Turkey plays in Switzerland
and Austria, every goal scored transcends the game.

• • • • •

A COLD coming I have of it. For a start, my bosses have reminded
me, as they must, being bosses, that I'm the Television Critic,
not the Soccer Critic. I've been briefly, and with exasperated
sighs, released to cover international soccer again. This assignment is partly on my time and my dime. Some of my vacation
and some of my own money. That's okay, boss, and worth it.
When I change planes at Frankfurt at 6 A.M., en route to Vienna,
I'm amazed that I've made it. A celebratory beer seems reasonable. In the rush of getting ready, I don't think I've slept for three
days. I did my day job up until an hour before I left. And then,
as I'm drinking the beer, I see a small group of people, Croatian
fans, in the airport lounge, and they're laughing, lightheaded,
adding charm and color to the grey morning and the grim airport setting in their distinctive red-and-white-checked shirts. I
know this is where I should be: on the road, watching and
observing, absorbing the gleeful tumult and writing to the
rhythm of it.

• • • • •

I LAND in Vienna on an overcast Saturday morning. The tournament will open in Switzerland tonight—in Basel, with the
Swiss playing the Czech Republic, and in Geneva, where
Portugal plays Turkey. The paper's other man covering the
tournament, Stephen Brunt, is there and covering the Swiss
side. Each day, Euro 2008 will switch between the two countries. Vienna seems subdued on the eve of the first big game
here, between Austria and Croatia. There are a few Austrian
flags at the airport, but emotions are not exactly running at a
fever pitch. On the train into town, I notice the flag of Turkey
everywhere on the balconies of apartment buildings where the
working class live.

My hotel is called the Palace, which it isn't, but there's a bed, and the expensive Internet connection works. I'm taken aback by the subdued atmosphere in Vienna. In fact, it's beyond subdued and bordering on ill-tempered. The national team of Austria is certainly an underdog; the whole world knows it. A year before the tournament, there was an infamous campaign by local soccer fans to have the national team withdraw from Euro 2008 because, they argued, it's a rubbish team. The campaign wasn't ironic; it was dead serious. One always hopes that an underrated host country will do well, because it increases the feel-good quotient. The situation in Austria is downright bizarre, though. The consensus seems to be that there had been some sort of mistake.

Never mind Austria's disdain for its own team. For a while, I'm thinking the country might as well put up a No Riff-Raff sign. At the Vienna airport I see a booth decorated with the Euro 2008 logo and "Welcome!" Advice and greetings—or so I think. I mosey over to find about the express train into the center of Vienna. Too tired to try out my wobbly German, I ask, in the polite Canadian way, "May I speak English?" The previously smiling young woman narrows her eyes and glares. "Yes, I speak English," she snaps. "And German!" I leave with a map of Vienna, incorrect information about the cost of the express ticket, and a disconcerting first impression.

I really shouldn't be surprised. For months I have despaired of finding soccer fans in Austria. In advance of coming here, I tried to contact local fans to tell me about soccer in Austria. I trawled the Internet and found supporter groups online, but I didn't get a single reply to numerous emails. Well, there was one, from a young man named Max, who said he didn't really want to talk about it.

According to surveys, half the Austrian population just doesn't care about Euro 2008, and about a quarter of the population outright dislikes the idea of the tournament, fearing disruption to routine and criminals coming in among all those foreigners. What do Austrians care about? Well, according to those same surveys, in sport they care about skiing; otherwise, they like the opera for entertainment. It seems the country was asleep when somebody put its name forward to co-host Euro 2008. Or, possibly, at a long opera, or up in the mountains skiing.

The Palace hotel staff is polite but distracted and obviously nervous about the Croatian supporters—a few middle-aged men and women in Croatia team shirts—sitting at the lobby bar, drinking, laughing and enjoying themselves, as people do on the eve of a big international soccer game. Arriving at the media center, at a building clearly marked accreditation center, I get my credentials but I'm told, amidst much tut-tutting, that I really should have gone to the other building marked accreditation center, the one where I'd get my "kit." After a hike, I find it—and my kit, which turns out to be a knapsack with some promotional stuff from McDonald's and the Austrian post office—not a free stamp, but a sticker with a soccer ball on it.

Everybody seems wary. I took a taxi to the media center and then asked a man at a stand marked "info" about the nearest subway stop, but he put up his hands and declared, "Please don't ask me!" It turned out there was a problem with the connection between his computer and the printer. So he was all busy with that. Or, possibly, thinking about skiing.

It takes a while to understand Vienna, but eventually I do, and I like it. It's evolving, and in its own way—waltzing with the past and crashing into the future. A city of ornate opera houses and *kaffeehausen* serving cake with splendid formality, it's a city inextricably linked to its imperial past. We think of Vienna as a German city in tone and attitude, but as the center of the Hapsburg Empire it was always different, self-important. Although I begin by thinking of it as a small, sleepy, self-absorbed Western European capital, its natural hinterland lies to the east. You can be in Slovakia in less than an hour on the train. And since the collapse of the Soviet Union, the city is full of arrivals—artists and students, especially—from the Czech Republic, Ukraine and Croatia.

It's a languid, lovely city, eternally a city of duality. It is joked that the Viennese are in bed by 10 P.M., or when the opera ends,

whichever comes first. But another aspect of the city comes alive at night—the bohemian Vienna of nightclubs, sidewalk bars and secret parties. It's a city that celebrates the stark, raw eroticism of the work of Egon Schiele, the doomed young artist whose expressionist paintings got him jailed. And, simultaneously, it celebrates the lavishness of the work of Schiele's mentor, Gustav Klimt. Eventually, on a day when I'm sitting at a sidewalk café, watching the Viennese shopping, chatting, consuming cake and indulging in all manner of pleasures in clothes, wine, sunshine and those thin, pink, sugary wafers that everybody seems to eat all the time, it dawns on me that Vienna is a very, very sexy city. It's a city that really loves a spectacle—anything that is grand, spectacular, showy and vivid. That's why, eventually, Vienna embraces the chromatic, gaudy, operatic spectacle that is Euro 2008.

• • • • •

ON THIS Saturday, though, the focus is on Switzerland. The Czech Republic beats Switzerland 1–0, which means it is unlikely that the Swiss are in this drama for much longer. Portugal beats Turkey 2–0, but doesn't really look emphatically superior, while Turkey seems a tad unlucky. I watch these games from my hotel room, trying to stay alert on strong coffee. I'm also sending comments to the online edition of the paper via a BlackBerry. This will be the first tournament that is truly multi-platform. I'm supposed to write two pieces a day, one for the print edition, one online—and blog and send regular comments to add to what Stephen Brunt is writing in Switzerland. It's a frantic way to work, but decidedly connected—I can see the stream of comments from readers all over Canada, watching the games on a summer Saturday afternoon, and they're fabulously opinionated. The street outside is silent, but when I turn off the TV I can hear music coming faintly from the open window of an apartment across the street. Verdi, it sounds like. Something from *Aida*.

• • • • •

ON SUNDAY, it's clear the Croatians supporters and press are here
in force. They're downright cocky, with reason. The Croatian
fans are the ones creating the color and noise on the streets.
There's not much sign of Austria fever, but Vienna seems much
more friendly after a decent night's sleep. On the subway to the
stadium, the Austrian fans are a little shy. They're mostly teenagers and older people, and they look on the raucous Croatians
with a kind of envy and amusement. There is much mingling,
flirting, hand-shaking and embracing outside the stadium.

Then the game begins. Croatia is lucky to get a 1–0 start,
thanks to an early penalty. The game grows tense as Austria
finds its confidence and an astonishing vigor. For long periods
the Croatian team is limited to last-ditch defending against a
country ranked ninety-second in the world, below Oman, Qatar
and Guatemala. This Austrian team is not exactly filled with
star players, but what it has is a desperate sort of pride. Its performance cheers up the Austrian supporters immensely. Croatia
looks like a team that merely believes its own hype. After the
game there's a rainstorm, and water pours through part of the
roof of the media center. The German reporters watching the
Germany–Poland game decline to move until forced by the staff.
Germany looks tough but slow in that game.

• • • • •

MONDAY STARTS with a brisk three-hour walking tour of Vienna.
The people from the city's tourism board are wonderfully accommodating and provide me with a guide, an English woman who
has lived here for decades. She takes me everywhere on foot. We
stroll through the stalls of the open-air Naschmarkt, stop at Café
Drechsler, Café Sperl—an untouched classic of the *kaffeehaus* tradition, glorious in its shabby luxury—Loos American Bar, the
Leopold Museum, the Kunsthalle, plus many palaces, libraries
and shops selling pastries. I'm stunned to find the fan zone for

Euro 2008 set into a park in the middle of the old Habsburg
palaces and surrounded on all sides by some of the most spectacular architecture in Europe. I write a feature story about the
history of the European championship tournament and, as I usually do, predict France's early exit. Happily for me, somewhere
over in Switzerland, France plays to a dreary 0–0 draw with
Romania.

• • • • •

BUT IN Bern, mind you, something altogether more exquisite
unfolds. Holland takes a grip on Euro 2008 by beating Italy 3–0
in a sizzling end-to-end game. I know people are saying that the
tournament has got off to a low-key start, and this game sets it
on fire as the Dutch play a stunning counter-attacking style and
Italy exhibits brilliance, despite ending up well beaten. There is
a lightness of touch to the Dutch style that is exquisite. They're
back, the Dutch, and of course there are about seventy thousand
Dutch fans in orange swarming the small cities of Switzerland.

• • • • •

I SPEND some time at the media center at the stadium in Vienna
and get a reminder of the peculiarities of the press gang at tournaments. I've already had an introduction to the weirdness if it.
A few minutes into Sunday's game between Austria and Croatia,
I was sitting in the press area and was gripped by that penalty
call against Austria, like all the reporters around me. Except, not
exactly like all the reporters around me. When Luka Modric
scored from the penalty spot for Croatia, the reporter to my left
just leapt into the air and did a little dance, fists thrusting up and
out towards the Croatia supporters' section. He was united with
them. He was one of them. Of course, these things shouldn't be
done. The reporter should have been embarrassed by the display
of partisanship, but he wasn't. And he wasn't alone in his disre-
gard for the traditional etiquette. I was reminded of the reporters
from Brazil wearing Brazil team shirts, the ones who cheered
every Brazilian move, at the World Cup in Germany. Many in

the press pack from Argentina did the same. I saw a guy from an Argentinian newspaper throw his arms around a player and hug him, instead of interviewing him. I remember I lost my composure in Ibaraki, six years ago, but I wasn't wearing an Ireland team shirt.

The Italians are more subtle, but often guilty of being cheerleaders. There's the immediate search for injustice: it's the referee; it's the staff at the team hotel; it's a plot against Italy. And, as is true of the German press gang, the Italians' media passes often make for interesting reading. About half of them appear to be called Professor, while the Germans are big on being Doctor. I've always assumed this has to do with the official title a person with a BA or MA is entitled to receive in Italy or Germany. Me, I've got two university degrees, but I wouldn't even mention that unless there was a point, and I'd be mortified if anybody called me "Professor." I just write for the paper. But the most fury-inducing writer is the one who talks everybody through the game. He's the one doing rapid-fire play-by-pay, except he's doing it for himself and his cronies, not TV or radio. No matter what the language, I can tell what's going on—"Pass it to the right—to the right, I said! Can't you see your teammate there, in space? Are you blind? Oh my God, you really are blind and giving me a heart attack." Some guys keep this up for the full ninety minutes. It's a wonder there haven't been assassinations in the press area.

In Austria, the German reporters strut around like they own the place. Which they did, once. It's their language spoken here, which probably emboldens them, along with the fact that Germany is favored to win the tournament. Already, I've seen them stake out vast areas of the small, cramped media area for themselves. They spread newspapers all over, like teenagers trying to save a space for the ones coming later.

The English press gang is here, but resentfully. England didn't qualify, so there's not that much to get excited about—except, perhaps, keeping an eye on European players rumored to be playing for English club teams soon.

There is also great interest in the possible existence of German and Polish hooligans. On Sunday afternoon I watched as a young English reporter studied the news on Austrian TV in the media center and called his paper every time there was an update on some drunken scuffle or another. It went like this: "Hello, Mike . . . yeah, earlier I said four people were arrested. Now the TV here is saying seven arrested. I'll keep you up-to-date, right?"

In that instance, I assumed the angle for the story was that hooliganism is a European problem. It used to be an English problem, but now it's not—it's Europe's shame, or something. The English reporters also have a weird fondness for telling jokes about their wives. There's one woman somewhere in England whose fake tan is the subject of much jollity in Vienna. And then there's the drinking—or lack of it. There is always beer for sale— Carlsberg only, as it's a big sponsor—in the media center café. But one of the bizarre rules enforced by UEFA is that the beer can't be sold before or during the game. Large signs make this clear everywhere. It's bizarre because the stone-cold-sober journalists are surrounded by tens of thousands of fans who drink copiously before and during a game. A beer would sometimes help in surviving the hurly-burly and the irritating counterparts from other countries. Mind you, I've no idea what they say about us Canadians. Probably that we grumble too much about the no-beer rule.

• • • • •

NEXT DAY, I'm off to Salzburg for Greece versus Sweden. Three hours and a bit on the train with many Swedes aboard, and one large group stands out. Far as I can tell, they mostly doze on the journey towards the Alps, drink apple juice in great quantities, and one guy stays awake to guard the huge stock of beer—crates and crates of cans of it—to be consumed later. Admirable organization skills evident there. I'll have my adventures in Salzburg that night, but the game, too, is thrilling to experience, as the defensive-minded Greeks meet a mercurial Swedish team that has, in Zlatan Ibrahimovic, one of the world's most lethal strikers.

The Greeks, European champions and all, can't hold it together, in the end. They stick to the formula that has won them so many games by a single goal here and there. It holds them in good stead for an hour, but in Sweden, Greece finally faces a team that doesn't underestimate them and understands their tactics. Then, twenty-two minutes into the second half, Ibrahimovic produces a bit of magical play and a stunning twenty-five-yard strike to give Sweden the 1–0 edge. Ibrahimovic, the Inter Milan forward, hasn't scored for his country in three years, and never is a goal so golden. After an exquisitely played give-and-go with veteran Henrik Larsson, his strike puts the Greeks behind and forces them to do what they clearly cannot: play passionate, attacking soccer and score. They never even look capable. Six minutes later, sensing panic, Sweden pours towards the Greek goal and, in a mad scramble, Petter Hansson manages to hustle the ball into the net for a second goal. That ends Greece's resistance.

A portion of this tournament is now coming into sharp focus: Spain is in the pole position to qualify for the next round, having demolished Russia; Greece faces a Russian team anxious to wipe out the humiliation, while Sweden will face Spain with considerable confidence. The likelihood of Greece retaining the European trophy it won in Lisbon four years ago is very remote. Neutrals watching the tournament will be relieved.

• • • • •

BACK IN Vienna, it's Austria against Poland. I wake up to find the Palace packed with Poles, all jolly and optimistic that they will give Austria a thrashing. If nothing else, they'll be jazzed on coffee. There's much to-do in the restaurant when the espresso machine fails and a party of three blonde Polish ladies are very anxious that it work again—now! Before the game, I go to one of the main train stations to make reservations for trips in Switzerland, where I will be the next day. No success. A mysterious business, this co-hosting between countries. The Austrian Federal Railways are of the attitude that the Swiss are being difficult, about everything. There are many Polish fans in the station, too, and a heavy police presence, but there's nothing more than singing and hip-hip-hooraying going on. There had been some scuffles in Klagenfurt when Poland played Germany a few days earlier. But nothing happens at the station apart from singing.

I've noticed that Vienna is full of florists, and there's one right in the station. And I see two Poles buying bouquets of flowers—I assume for their wives or girlfriends, who are with them. Later, on the subway to the stadium, I see more Polish men carrying flowers. Outside the stadium, all becomes clear: a handful of Polish guys, smiling self-consciously, are handing out flowers to Austrian supporters. The Austrians are taken aback. They're not rude about it, just perplexed. This makes the Polish guy I'm watching even more painfully self-conscious. He is shouting *"Polska!"* loudly and handing out lovely red carnations.

I feel for him, this large, gruff-looking man, trying so hard to be gracious. His face is beet red with embarrassment, or drinking, or something. Yet I'm pretty sure he's not drunk. He is as awkward as a kid bestowing his first Valentine card. And I admire him immensely. This is not his thing, this flower-giving before the game. Something—the unwelcome police presence, the stories in the papers about drunken Poles throwing beer at Germans—has inspired him to transcend that, to forsake his instinctive urge to bellow and shout and frighten others, and to just join the party, to make it clear that the Polish supporters are at one with the enchantment, the spirit of tenderness and chivalry that characterizes these tournaments.

I think of the Ukrainian supporters in Leipzig two years ago, the ones who were flummoxed by the atmosphere, the vibe of joy and affability. They never quite grasped the mood, the pulse of the tournament, the temple of delight that is the stadium, the need to relax and kiss the fleeting joy as it passes, as fast and soaring as the ball itself. Handing out flowers, though—my, that takes courage. And it's good; it's tenderness itself. Watching it confirms my feeling that the mood of the tournaments, the over-riding tremor of affection and ecstasy, is deeply sensual, and touches the erotic in all of us.

• • • • •

THE GAME is a 1–1 tie, and a bizarre game of frantic racing, missed chances and dogged craft between two mediocre teams battling for integrity and pride. For Austria, all the problems are laid bare. Like other the host countries, Austria has found that the journey to the big tournament is maddeningly easy. As hosts, they automatically qualify. No eighteen-month campaign of travel and games against tricky opposition teams; only friendly games that are designed as preparation, but are meaningless. It's easy, but maddening, because when the tournament begins, there is only pride to fuel the team. In reply to the naysayers in Austria, there hasn't been a rough-and-tumble, battle-hardening campaign on which to build. Switzerland has already discovered that. Now Austria is left with just a technical possibility of reaching the second round of Euro 2008.

And Austria has itself to blame. This game begins with them going full tilt in search of a goal, and failing miserably. Three times in ten minutes, a goal looks inevitable. Pouring forward, the Austrians cause panic in Poland's defense. Twice, Martin Harnik has only keeper Artur Boruc to beat, and twice he fails to score. As time goes on, even the Austrian supporters lose count of the missed chances. There is something cruel about it—some cruel god deciding Austria shall not score, even when gifted with golden chances. Poland responds with tough tackling to slow the tempo. It works. After thirty minutes, the Poles make a rare foray towards the Austria goal and score. The scorer is offside, but the referee fails to see that. The goal diminishes Austria's confidence. Heads are bent in disbelief.

Austria revives, but it doesn't last. Poland sucks the life from the game. The defenders play the Greek tactic of endlessly passing to each other. More frustration for Austria. A minute into added time, referee Howard Webb, from England, awards a penalty. The Poles are furious, incandescent, but Webb is correct this time. Austrian veteran Ivica Vastic, thirty-eight years old, takes the penalty well and scores.

It's a game that will be forgotten in a tournament that has seen outstanding attacking skills from Holland and Spain. The disappointing results for both Austria and Switzerland will cause some of the excitement here to evaporate. But there is still a lot of great soccer to come. The neutrals, but not the locals, can rejoice.

• • • • •

THE NEXT morning, a 7 A.M. flight to Geneva, then two hours on the train to Bern. It is bewildering to travel, on four hours' sleep, from Vienna, which is German-speaking, to Geneva, which is French-speaking, and on to Bern, which is German-speaking again. The early-morning flight is full and 95 percent male. And it's a "them" and "us" scenario, "them" being the besuited businessmen with nice briefcases, "us" being the journalists, distinctive with our dangling press badges, all of us looking like zombies, hauling bags with laptops, electrical adapters and reams of paper from UEFA. I suspect that, mentally, we're all in another time zone and we look as though we're living off the fare from stadium vending machines. In Geneva, the tiny hotel is near the train station, as promised. My room's not ready, though. Several expensive espressos are consumed at nearby sidewalk cafés. Then the train to Bern. Mountains, lakes, trees, fields, cows, Switzerland.

I'm here for Holland against France. Bern is, by mid-afternoon, all orange. In fact, it is impossible to convey the scope of the orange that envelops Bern. No, really, I mean that. This Oranje Army is bigger than that at Leipzig. Maybe it's because France is the opponent; maybe because Holland has emerged here as the team of the exquisite game, the sweet touch, the effortless goals. Maybe they're all here—eighty thousand, or more, the authorities are losing count—because they know, they just know, this is where it matters to be Dutch for a while. The streets of Bern are rivers of orange. There's a large statue on a pedestal in the center of town, and the figure, whoever it is, is way the heck up in the air. Now he's draped in an orange banner and he's wearing an orange traffic cone on his head. I wander the streets and see some of the few hundred France supporters here. They look vaguely amused. I feel sorry for them, dryly ironic in their French team shirts, berets and big plastic baguettes. They're cute, and rather sweetly self-deprecating, but they are lost in the vast sea of orange.

The game is sublime, as Holland bests France 4–1. The Dutch offer a master class in dazzle, the sort of freewheeling, always-in-search-of-a-goal soccer that they suddenly epitomize again. It is one lightning counter-attack after another—the sort of speed and ball control that destroyed Italy in their first group game. Holland scores after ten minutes—an inelegant goal from a corner kick, but one that forces France to start attacking. The Dutch take this with aplomb, clearing easily, sending the ball forward towards the French goal at dizzying speed and working it with stunning confidence.

The stadium in Bern is small, tiny even, and I'm seated a couple of rows behind the Dutch bench. Every now and then, during a stop in play, coach Marco van Basten summons a player to the sideline and crisply gives orders and direction. This is done with few words, some gestures and smiles. The Dutch are enjoying this, as well they might. Goal after goal is breathtaking to see, the skill and enthusiasm magnificent. Van Basten has learned how to mesh individual skills and shifted to an unusual 4–2–3–1 formation—it means using two holding midfielders, usually Giovanni van Bronckhorst and Demy de Zeeuw, while Wesley Sneijder acts as a sort of fulcrum in front of them, spreading the ball to two wingers and forward to the lone upfront man, Ruud van Nistelrooy. The ceaseless fluidity confounds the French, whose coach, Raymond Domenech, looks shell-shocked by the time the game ends. At this tournament, Holland has now defeated both the World Cup champions, Italy, and the runners-up, France, with stunning ease. It has qualified for the next round with a game to spare.

There are wild scenes at Bern's railway station later. I've missed a train back to Geneva and have an hour to wait, so I witness it all—the great mass of orange-clad people trooping through the station, the occasional chants of "*Hup! Hup!*" as some celebrate and reluctantly leave the scene of victory. In Bern, the police have just discovered a small potential problem: the police tape—the stuff used to mark off a crime scene or a no-go area for the public—is orange colored. So are the traffic cones. Somehow, great swaths of the orange tape have been liberated and used to create a giant canopy over the entrance to the station. The Dutch own the town, and they know it.

In a station café, I stand between groups of Dutch and French fans. The Dutch sing, the French smile. A Dutch guy says, in English, "Why are you smiling? We humiliated you." A French guy laughs. "It's okay," he says, "Now we make Domenech go away. It will be fine." When the Dutch guy leaves for his train, he approaches the Frenchman and puts out his hand. Tipsy, he musters some sobriety, as well as some French. Taking a deep breath, he says, "*Merci beaucoup pour la victoire. Vive la France.*" The French guy says, solemnly, "*Merci, monsieur,*" and shakes his head as the Dutch walk away.

As I wait on the platform for my train to Geneva, a special overnight train to Amsterdam loads up with Dutch fans. When it pulls out of the station, orange-clad people can be seen at almost every window, leaning out, singing and waving. The cops wave back—many have whipped out cameras and are taking photos. They may want to forget Switzerland's poor showing in the tournament, but they'll want to remember this. It's what they'll recall on long, dull winter nights: the summer of the Oranje Army on the move, resplendent in vibrant color and alive with joy.

· · · · ·

GENEVA LOOKS pretty enough on a Saturday, though I don't see much of it. Friday-into-Saturday had been a twenty-one-hour ordeal. I sleep and dream of home, of Canada, and when I awake I feel very, very far from home. There's an email from Stephen Brunt, who is in Austria to see Spain beat Sweden. Take the day off, he suggests. Nobody in Toronto is responding to phone calls or emails. We're adrift in Europe. Enjoy it. I could use a good meal and beer, but I'm frightened of the prices in Geneva. A chocolate bar costs about twenty dollars, it seems; God only knows how much a steak dinner and beer would be. After an hour of walking, I land in a Turkish restaurant where the patrons are watching Russia defeat Greece. Because Russia wins, Spain has qualified for the quarter-finals as group winners. Russia now needs a win against Sweden to reach the round of eight. The Turks—in the restaurant, all men—are impressed by Russia. But, mainly, they're looking forward to Sunday, when Turkey plays the Czech Republic here in Geneva. That's my game too.

* * * * *

BY MID-MORNING on Sunday, I've seen enough of Geneva. I walk to the Lake Geneva shoreline and see Czech supporters eating and drinking there, making their own racket. One chap calmly opens a large can of beer and begins draining it while he's having his face painted. I pass about fifty Czech couples holding hands, strolling along, looking at the swans in the water. Even as the party builds up at the outdoor bars and restaurants, the local Swiss, God love them, merely run by—jogging, no less—in their preppy gear, with iPods on, ignoring the spectacle. Some sit in the coffeehouses, intent on their laptops, while the happy Czech and Turk fans surround them.

Here's the deal on Czech Republic–Turkey: each team has played two games, won one, lost one, scored twice and conceded three goals. Thus, according to the rules, if Turkey and the Czech Republic reach a draw, a penalty shootout will decide who makes the quarter-finals. While I'm on the hotel room balcony, there's a bit of a commotion. Turkish TV has arrived at Kebab Istanbul, an establishment I can see from the balcony, for the necessary "color" piece about Turkish fans getting ready for the big game. By the time I walk by, the TV crew has stopped working and the reporter, easily spotted in his sleek suit, is in the middle of the crowded kebab joint, consuming vast amounts of coffee and smoking up a storm, which means he fits in nicely, except for the suit.

What happens at the stadium is a game for the ages, an epic,

come-from-behind victory. It ends Czech Republic 2, Turkey 3.
A full hour after the game, most of the thousands of Turkish fans
are still inside the stadium, celebrating. They can hardly believe
it, and on that score they're not alone. The Czechs are ahead 2–0
at one point and look to be cruising to an emphatic victory. But
Turkey, driven by something beyond the game, beyond logic,
keeps going. You can feel it in the air, even as the game looks like
a hopeless cause. The Turks in the stands—men, women and children, the old and the young—are seething. This is Switzerland,
this is where they sweep the streets and carry the garbage, wash
the soiled linens and turn their faces away from the insults and
the condescension. This is where they have something to prove.
This is where their resilience triumphs.

Turkey scores in the seventy-fifth minute and that means a
tense, thrilling final fifteen minutes in search of an equalizer that
might send the game to penalties. As the Turkish pressure
increases and the fanaticism of the crowd becomes overwhelming, Czech goalkeeper Petr Cech, considered one of the best in
the world, makes a fatal mistake: he fumbles a ball. Nihat Kahveci
for Turkey pounces. It's 2–2 in the eighty-seventh minute. Two
minutes later, driven by something no person can capture or
explain, Nihat does it again. It is 3–2 for Turkey.

Four minutes of extra time are added by the referee, and no
sooner have they begun than Turkish keeper Volkan Demirel is
red-carded for elbowing Jan Koller, who is leading a desperate
Czech charge for an equalizer. Turkey has used all its substitutes.
Reduced to ten men and without a goalkeeper, Turkey survives
the dying minutes of a game that will long be considered a classic. To the joyous fans, it must feel like more than that. It must
feel like the revenge of generations.

• • • • •

IT'S A long, long journey back from the stadium to the hotel in
Geneva. It's raining steadily, but I don't care. This is why I travel,
this is the addiction: cities after dark, the sounds of tens of thousands of voices, in triumph and despair, echoing in my ears. By

the time I've written my report and sent it, the wide suburban streets around the stadium, still blocked to traffic, are empty. It's past midnight, and even here, in the rain and the broad, barren streets, I can hear it from somewhere—"Turk-iye! Turk-iye!"

After a lengthy march in the rain, I find I've missed a train by four minutes. The attendant makes that clear—not a few minutes, not five, but four. There won't be another for an hour. There's a German reporter there too. "I fucking hate Switzerland," he says, and we march off, over hills and dales, to get a tram. I'm back at my hotel near 2 A.M. And up at 5 A.M. for a 7:15 flight back to Vienna. I'm a little numb by then, but the lack of sleep and journey back to a city I've begun to like brings a calm lucidity. Everything is heightened.

• • • • •

MY FIRST task this morning is to change hotels in Vienna. The Palace was fine, but full this week. I go there first to retrieve my luggage. The manager, a thirtysomething woman whose main interest is her hair, emerges to greet me. "Oh, Mr. Doyle, you have come back to us." I understand the Viennese now. The narcissism, the hint of coldness only lasts until they know you slightly. Then they are all charm, the faint suggestion of flirtation from the women, an open, masculine friendship offered by the men. They have the assuredness of Dubliners and the assessing eyes of Montrealers. This is Vienna. There is no city like it in the world. Their welcome, once given, is a great compliment. The manager is distressed to hear I must move to another hotel. I even believe her. She pouts, and offers me apples to take to my new hotel. Apples, yes. Some Germans, lounging in the lobby, smoking cigarettes, cigars and pipes, watch with solemn interest. I resist the temptation to ask if they know a certain hotel in Berlin, the one with a certain boss lady in charge.

And then I'm in a Best Western, clearly one for tourists, not zombie-like journalists or sleek business types. It takes me an hour to rearrange the furniture to figure out a way to sit and type at the laptop. A query about lunch or a late breakfast brings a long and very complicated answer. So I mosey out. Cobblestone streets, trams, coffeehouses filled with people who look like they sit, drink coffee and smoke for a living. I walk into a hole-in-the-wall bar/restaurant steps from the Best Western, order a bite to eat, take in the surroundings. The walls have 1970s-era framed pictures of topless models. Two very elderly ladies sit at a table, with enormous glasses of beer (this is noonish, now) in front of them, smoking and chatting. Boney M is playing on the stereo. I could be in the Dublin of my childhood, except for the topless models on the wall. A reminder that Vienna is unique, neither this nor that. Talk, drink, music and a languid pace matter here. An omelet, salad, glass of beer and a coffee cost me ten euros. You wouldn't be allowed a look at a cup of coffee for that amount in Geneva.

• • • • •

GERMANY PLAYS Austria tonight. The game is the last hurrah for the host country. It's Germany 1, Austria 0 at the end. It seems that almost every Austrian fan in the stadium sticks around to honor the team. In truth, Austria never looks capable of taking a game away from Germany. And it is a dreadful game. Germany is focused on defensive play from the start. Plenty of enthusiasm comes from the Austrian players, but poor passing and a confused front line—they often get in each other's way—let them down. I'm deeply puzzled by Austria now. A year before, at the Under-20 World Cup in Canada, a skilled and fearless team had gone far. The youngsters looked tough and keen. I'd admired their main attacking force, one Erwin Hoffer, and this is the first time I've seen him play for any length with the senior team. He's good, but he can't defeat Germany alone.

Germany is lackluster but wins on a beauty of a free kick from Michael Ballack. A sour atmosphere pervades the game. German coach Joachim Löw and his counterpart, Josef Hickersberger, argue bitterly with each other and a UEFA official on the sideline. The referee dispatches both into the stands. Löw immediately goes to sit with German chancellor Angela Merkel, who is at the game. They're not far away from me. It's a surreal show. Merkel is agitated, gesturing at German inefficiency on the field. Löw explains things to her. The crowd, mostly Austrian, watches in sullen amusement—then boos and hisses the pair of them. I begin to hope that Portugal can take Germany apart in the quarter-final in a few days.

• • • • •

GERMAN FANS party late into the night, but for themselves and themselves alone. It's very quiet in Vienna the next morning, following Austria's exit from Euro 2008. That is hardly unexpected—and Vienna is a sleepy, self-involved place most of the time. Today, the action switches over to Switzerland, with Italy playing France in Zurich and Holland playing Romania in Bern. As ever, there are suggestions of murky doings emanating from the Italian press. A draw in Zurich and then Holland conspiring to go easy on Romania means that the two titans playing in Zurich would both be out of the tournament. Here we go again: Italy the victim of elaborate intrigue and connivance.

I read the English papers, an often hilarious exercise. This, in the *Times*: "Some excellent football is being played at Euro 2008, of a standard to which John Terry and company can only aspire. Frankly, for the moment at least, matching it is beyond their capabilities. England failed to qualify for this tournament, and now we are reminded why. So many other teams are better." And this in the *Guardian*: "The footballers of this country simply cannot play at a level that requires more than honest toil." England outclassed by the continental style and panache of Johnny Foreigner.

I write, for the online paper, a jokey series of complaints about conditions for the press. The media center sandwiches are woeful and yet, in certain circumstances, you seriously contemplate consuming one. I did once—consume one, that is. I remember it well. Then there's the cost. In Geneva it's cheaper to buy a new polo shirt than have a soiled one laundered at the hotel. In Vienna, it's the same, but you could get two shirts for the price of a single one in Geneva. In Austria and Switzerland, they use different plugs—one's a two-pronger and one's a three-pronger. At the stadiums, they're all the same—two-pronged—but there are the hotels to worry about. We get free high-speed or Wi-Fi connections at the stadium media centers, but once you're in the stands, in your seat, it's no certainty. As almost everybody blogs or does live updates now, so we need to be in touch through every minute. That requires an expensive thingy that's plugged into the laptop to get a signal in an emergency.

Tom Humphries of the *Irish Times* wrote a story about covering the World Cup in Germany that, funny though it was, caused nightmares for some of us. In Munich, he took a taxi to the stadium and the driver placed the reporter's array of bags in the trunk. Humphries retrieved them at the stadium, but later opened his bag of adapters and connectors to find it was actually an identical bag containing the taxi driver's lunch. Fortunately, he had a receipt for the taxi—an essential for a journalist—and the driver was found and the bag was recovered hours later.

I give thanks for the fine breakfast buffets provided in hotels. Excellent if you might not eat again until after the late evening game. I point out that my current hotel in Vienna offers a real kick-start to the day. There's a bottle of sparkling wine on ice beside the fruit juice, for those who want extra fuel.

For Euro 2008, the Austrian and Swiss railways didn't release their special tournament timetable until April. A huge mistake. I needed to know many months ago if I'd be able to travel back to Vienna after writing about a game in Salzburg that ended close to 11 P.M. Would there be a train at midnight, or later? Did I need a hotel to stay over, or should I plan on stretching out on the street? If I did, could I stay in touch with the office by Wi-Fi? Still, we are lucky little Canadians, being allowed in and all.

• • • • •

I WRITE an opinion piece suggesting that Germany is overrated. An opening win against Poland seemed to advance the idea of a great German team tearing through the tournament to the final, but it was a false dawn. Only the sheer luck of being drawn to play Poland and Austria has ensured that Germany has made it past the first round and avoided humiliation. That, and a towering display from a single player, Michael Ballack. It will require more than Ballack to beat Portugal in the quarter-final game.

I also write that I'm fed up with puffed-up, pompous, pipe-smoking German reporters.

• • • • •

OVER IN Switzerland, Italy beats France and Holland beats Romania, both by scores of 2–0. Italy needed desperately to win and has upped its game. The Dutch cruise by Romania using much of their B-team. The Dutch will now play either Russia or Sweden in the last eight. Italy will play Spain, here in Vienna— a mouthwatering game. I'm sure some Italians will say the past week has only been Italy's traditional slow start in a tournament. But tonight they got a break—a penalty and the chance to play against a ten-man team that seems to be at war with the coach.

Meanwhile, back at the office in Toronto, a colleague replacing me as the television columnist has had enough. Not of the TV column part; she's had it with the phone calls. I'm in Austria and Switzerland, but people want to react to pieces I've written by giving me an earful. So they call the *Globe and Mail* and rant. Apparently, they do this about four times an hour. My colleague, who has considerable experience as the theater and art critic, has never experienced anything like it. She's at the end of her tether. Englishmen call and swear a blue streak about my disdain for England. Turks call and explain the injustice of a penalty call. Germans complain. Portuguese argue.

The scale of interest in Euro 2008 is a great mystery to my colleagues. But I'm not surprised. It is followed daily and intensely by a vast portion of the population in Canada. It matters deeply to them. However, there's still a commotion back at the office. I think my phone has been disconnected. Certainly, the outgoing message has been changed. A new message tells people to call the sports editor. It's very, very late in Vienna now, but my heart sinks. The sports editor is a nice, tolerant man, undeserving of a daily barrage of calls arguing with Doyle's assessment of this or that.

I'm thousands of miles from the office, it's the middle of the night and I'm busy smoothing ruffled feathers, trying to explain that, next to the World Cup, this tournament is the biggest event on the planet. The callers are not cranks, or crazy. They care. This Euro 2008 coverage matters more than anything else in the paper.

• • • • •

TO SALZBURG and back in an afternoon and night. The fun of the first time can't be replicated. I go to see Spain play Greece. There's something about the day, the tempo of the tournament, that tells me this is when it becomes driven by dream logic. Pundits watching from somewhere else will be surprised. They can't feel the cadence of it. This game in Salzburg has an unreal quality. Spain has already qualified for the quarter-finals. Greece is out of the tournament, no matter what happens, but it's a team looking to restore self-worth, so it plays a tenacious, stop-start game. Spain grinds out a 2–1 win. What's notable is the determination shown, the need to win when it isn't necessary.

In the other game, in Innsbruck, there's more at stake: Russia needs to beat Sweden to advance to the quarter-finals. Sweden can qualify with a draw. For Russia, though, the much-talked-about Andrei Arshavin is available after serving a two-match suspension, and he's probably the best player on the team. Russia plays a stunning game of attacking soccer. Sweden isn't easy to beat, but Arshavin scores twice, displaying a level of trickery and ball control that's thrilling. Russia dominates utterly, and could easily score three more. Suddenly, the world of soccer is head over heels for Russia. The tournament is now askew: Holland, Russia and Spain are playing spectacularly well. France has trundled home. The host countries are no longer involved. The nagging dream of this tournament taking flight, and climaxing in great flourishes of elegant European soccer, is realized.

• • • • •

CROATIA AND Turkey in the quarter-final in Vienna, then. Vienna is a city of 1.5 million people. Twenty thousand Croatians live here, and there are thirty thousand fans from Croatia descending on the city for this game. Vienna is also home to seventy thousand people who are Turkish or of Turk ancestry. A few thousand have traveled from Turkey, but what matters is the number of Turks here, along with those who have come from Switzerland and Germany. For both Turkey and Croatia, the feeling is that this is their transcendent hour. A win and they're one game from the final, the championship of Europe within reach.

From what I'm been told, the song that is most popular with Croatia's fans can be translated as *We're not many, but it doesn't matter / We're capable of destroying anybody's dreams.* Indeed. Croatia is the smallest country at Euro 2008, yet it has breezed into the quarter-finals with three wins, including an evisceration of Germany. This is extraordinary for a country of four million people, one that is only seventeen years independent. Yet in soccer it is feared, admired and sometimes loathed. Yes, loathed.

Undoubtedly, part of the fuel that drives the Croatian team to extraordinary heights is the fierce, intense nationalism of a young country. Even mediocre players are better when they know that they can become legends by scoring against one of the world's great soccer powers. At the same time, that nationalism has caused problems for Croatia. The fans have a history of chanting racist slogans, and the apex of distaste for Croatia's brand of nationalism came when fans formed into the shape of a swastika during a friendly game against Italy in August 2006. FIFA was appalled, and made noises about banning Croatia from international play if the action was repeated.

Here at Euro 2008, Croatian fans are being watched closely, and UEFA has reportedly warned the team that it will be expelled from the tournament immediately if there is any evidence of racist chants or banners. Slaven Bilic, the Croatian coach, has dodged the issue in press interviews. Bilic himself is a charismatic, mercurial figure. A former player—he was on the Croatian team that amazed observers at Euro 96—he is charming and expert at deflecting attention away from any problems associated with Croatia's fans. After retiring from soccer he qualified as a lawyer and is also an enthusiastic musician. He plays regularly in a rock band. For all the charm, Bilic is a man in charge of a powder keg. One display of racism or Nazi sympathy from the thousands who follow Croatia, and the team is on its way home.

It's because of what it does on the field that Croatia is able to endear itself to soccer fans. It believes that the best form of defense is attack, and it plays fast, galvanizing soccer that results in goals, not stalemates. Like other teams from the Balkans, Croatia builds its formation around a midfield playmaker, someone who sprays the ball towards two wingers and two strikers. It has been said that Balkan countries make a fetish of the midfield playmaker and overemphasize the tactic. But it has worked for Croatia. In fact, Bilic's innovation is to have not one, but two of the so-called playmakers. Usually, that means Niko Kovac is rooted in the center circle while the more forward-moving Luka Modric is directly in front of him. Lacking the goal-scoring machine Eduardo, who is injured, the system has resulted in an extraordinary amount of ball possession for Croatia. The team is not going to score a lot of goals here, but it is certainly going to prevent opponents from scoring.

Croatia faces a Turkish team that is hurting—good players are injured and it's without suspended keeper Volkan Demirel. Yet this is a Turkish side that has shown an astonishing resilience, coming from behind to beat Switzerland and achieve that amazing victory over the Czech Republic. The problem, apart from suspensions and injuries, is that Turkey has only played aggressively attacking soccer after falling behind. Mind you, Croatia has a habit of scoring early, and, if that happens, Turkey will need to get the engine going a lot sooner. In its current incarnation, Turkey reminds me of Ireland—the backs-to-the-wall bravery, the energy that arises from being on the brink of humiliation, the fervent need to avenge a thousand hurts and insults.

• • • • •

IT IS a game to shred nerves. For the first time here, the huge stadium in Vienna is pulsatingly alive, throbbing with human noise, and there is a surreal magnificence to it. The players, the fans and even the press are one mass of emotional energy. If you're here, in this cauldron, you know, you just know it in your blood, that strange, stunning events will unfold. This is a fable now. There will be screams and tears; nightmares will become bliss; exultation will evaporate. The rhythm of it will never settle until it ends.

The Croatian players and supporters are cocky, to begin. Croatia is supposed to be the small power destined to end up in the top four. It has the talent, the skills, the commitment and extraordinary confidence, especially the blithe, smiling impudence of coach Bilic. The Turks are battered; the team has the air of a bruised boxer getting back into the ring, riding on unearthly confidence that defeat doesn't have to happen, that something can be summoned from the depths of some human need to ensure survival. Turkey's fans know it too. There's a giddiness about their singing and chanting that masks fear. I look and listen to them and know that, across Europe, there are street sweepers and chambermaids sharing this experience. People used to servitude are tense but alive with the scent of possible triumph.

The game is 0–0 at the end of normal time. Croatia has missed chances and there's a magical aura about Turkey's aged replacement keeper, Rustu. He's thirty-five years old and past his prime. He even looks older than his years, a man from another era with his ponytail, bald patch and mustache. But he's an electrifying figure in action—all too human in his small mistakes and large enthusiasm. He saves the day. He scrambles to make up for an error. He's gangly, nervous and majestic all at the same time.

When the game goes to extra time, Turkey's players seem oddly revitalized. As if, somehow, they are relieved to escape the long stalemate of 0–0 and are now pumped for a real game, one with dynamism and goals. Croatia senses this and pushes forward. The

Croatian supporters are now in a state beyond game-watching; they begin to chant and sing in unison. They stamp their feet. Flares go off in their section of the stand, the red smoke lending a menacing but ravishingly beautiful quality to the scene. Then their noise reaches an amazing unity of purpose. The level rises. The entire stadium pulses and trembles. It's like the sound of a vast, bellowing army on the march, intent on total plunder.

In the press section and among the Turks, everybody watches, awed, and many reach for cameras, hoping to capture this extraordinary scene. But they can't. It's the noise, the vibrations that you feel in every fibre of your body. No picture will do it justice. The police and stewards on the sidelines move towards the tens of thousands of Croatians who are the source of this noise, this intimidating spectacle. There is no trouble, no violence, but the bewilderment is visible on the faces of the cops and the stewards. This is mayhem, tightly wound but never unleashed. It's the Croatians asserting their unity and stature, and the noise is there to spur the team to victory with the force and vigor of its impact.

The players on both teams know the field is a dream-place now. Both sides attack, back and forth, back and forth. In the dying seconds, a frantic Rustu makes a terrible error of judgment. He abandons logic and races out of his goal to tackle Luka Modric, who simply crosses the ball over him and Ivan Klasnic heads it into the net.

Croatia's celebrations are beyond wild. Coach Bilic is a bundle of ecstatic, running, jumping joy. There can only be a single minute left to play. Croatia has won it. In the anarchy, Croatian goalkeeper Stipe Pletikosa sprints out of his goal and sets off on a run, leaping over the advertising hoardings, passing the stewards and police, joining the Croatian fans in celebrating a last-ditch victory. The din from that section is ear-splitting. Seconds later, Turkey's Semih Senturk is looking at those same Croatians, putting his finger to his lips, signaling for them to shut up. He's just scored. It isn't over.

Fittingly, it is the volatile, often awkward-looking Rustu who is the architect. To take a free kick, just as the referee is looking at his watch, he strides way out of his area and sends the ball downfield with furious power and unerring accuracy into the Croatian penalty area. In a flurry of legs, Semih turns and smashes the ball into the top corner of the net. It is 1–1 with mere seconds left. From the Turkish fans there is the sound of sudden, stunned jubilation. They knew this would happen. It was destined. The Turks never, ever stop trying. It is an electrifying end to an astounding game.

Now must come the penalty kicks, but the Croatian players are in shock. Moments ago, they could taste victory; now it has been snatched from them. They've collapsed mentally. They can't do it. Their shoulders sag, their concentration is gone. As soon as the first penalty is poorly taken and misses, everyone in the stadium knows it is Turkey's night. The Turks score convincingly in penalties, and Rustu—of course, of course—saves one. The victory is emphatic, ecstatic.

• • • • •

WHEN I emerge from the subway a few hours later, I can tell that old Vienna is awash in sensations it can't have felt in years. There is noise coming from all directions.

It's nearly 2 A.M., and I stand and watch as a group of Turkish mothers in headscarves dance with their little children. They whoop and holler. They hold hands and dance in a circle, singing something that includes "Turk-i-ye!" every few seconds. The warmth of their joy, on the old cobbled street, in the cool of the night, is exquisitely pure. Farther down the street, the Turkish boys and men are bolder. I see a group decide to take their party from the sidewalk to the middle of the road. Full of mischief, they dare the traffic to stop, which it does. And in achieving that, they know they've won something more than the game—the city in which they and their ancestors have toiled is theirs for a while. It feels like some authoritarian power has just been overthrown.

And farther down again is evidence of the way a host city changes during a tournament. A group of people at an outdoor café are watching the Turks celebrate. It is soon pretty clear what I'm seeing: while I was at the game, the Spanish arrived. Two cars parked in front of a café have been covered completely with the flag of Spain. The young men and women in the café are in their team shirts and thoroughly enjoying what they are seeing. As a group of Turks move and dance down the cobblestones, halting traffic, the Spaniards cheer them. As soon as there is a pause in the Turks' singing, the Spaniards start their own, and for a minute, the street is filled with the chaotic sound of some thing about *Turk-i-ye!* all mixed up with *Viva España*. I wait to see if there is an embrace or even a kiss. There isn't, but there is enough enchantment in the moonlight to give me a memory of Vienna more vivid than any other.

· · · · ·

THERE IS a day of pause before Spain plays Italy in the next quarter-final in Vienna. I look at the emails, the reactions from home. Except they're not only from home. Some coverage has gone viral. The *Wall Street Journal*, *ESPN* and the *Guardian* have picked up *Globe and Mail* material, and it seems that half the world is on to us. There is a stream of invective about cautious remarks I'd made about Turkey's chances. A Turkish man—writing from Tokyo, of all places—has sent a pithy, blistering reply to something I've written.

Croats are angry. Croats are melancholy. They write from California and Canada.

A well-connected German in New York City writes to inform me that he's seen my negative remarks about Germany, written earlier, and has faxed the article to the German team's hotel in Austria. He knows the number, he knows certain people. He also knows that my ignorant comments will inspire the German team to greater efforts and victory. He may well be right. Germany beat Portugal 3–2 in one of the other quarter-final games.

In the hole-in-the-wall bar near the hotel, I watch Russia

destroy Holland 3–1 in a game of spellbinding artistry. Andrei Arshavin is again the magician for Russia. The Dutch have played so beautifully here that it seemed unlikely they could be so easily defeated, and yet they are. There's a bittersweet irony in this. Russia's Dutch-born manager, Gus Hiddink, the brilliant mercenary, has done it again. Just as he managed South Korea in 2002, applying Dutch soccer style and practices in Korea, he has succeeded again with Russia. Holland is essentially defeated by one of its own geniuses.

Distant from the game, watching it on TV, I suspect a touch of hubris has infected the Dutch. Well satisfied with their elegance and goals, they are unprepared for Arshavin, who is on some personal quest to exhibit his outrageous skill to the world. He torments them. He looks like an apple-cheeked, easy-smiling youth, but he is twenty-seven years old. Clearly, he is adroit, brilliant, but so casual about the fact that he only rouses himself to certain challenges.

The Dutch, so good for so many games, present a fine challenge. Arshavin is masterly with the ball, dodging tackles, sending in crosses with perfect precision. He is a surprise to the Dutch and to the world, and he likes it. In the bar, the crowd watches, utterly absorbed, enjoying the brilliance of the Russians. People squeal at Arshavin's jaunty dexterity. And then, it seems, they remember: it's Russia—Russia! Who knew? Viennese wariness stops short of escalating to the loathing that some Berliners feel for Russia. But history counts here. The people in the bar share the view, I think, that the tournament has taken a crazy course. It has, like a ball kicked high and swerving in the tossing breeze.

• • • • •

ON A gloriously sunny Sunday in Vienna, Spain's hour has arrived. The truth about this Spanish team will emerge. Are the midfielders too slight? Are the gifted, fast-passing forwards capable of squeezing out a cagey 1–0 win? Or are they going to collapse when the Italian defense is shut like a bolted door? The inescapable fact is that the last time Spain beat Italy in a competitive game was eighty-eight years ago. The news of Italy's triumph over France the other night was, apparently, greeted with despair in Spain. It was all, "Oh no, not Italy!" There is angst, nothing but angst, in the Spanish media. While Italy might relish every game here and fear no one, Spaniards have a deep and abiding fear and loathing of the Italian style. They believe that Spanish players engage in a "pure" form of the game, one anchored in ball skills, speed and hunger for goals to please the crowd. They see the Italian style as cynical—more about brutality of mind and body, about rough, tough canniness and guile, than beautiful athleticism.

Spain's fear of Italy encapsulates the clash of soccer esthetics. In a way, the psychology is simple: the bright, talented kid is afraid of the snarling, experienced veteran. It's a case of beauty and the beast, the Spanish feel.

There's something peculiar about Spanish soccer, and it's not just the distaste for the Italian game. Spain's soccer culture is self-involved to the point of being seriously neurotic. La Liga is one the top leagues in the world. Spanish club teams routinely reach the final stages of the Champions League. In Real Madrid and Barcelona, Spain has two of the most storied teams in the soccer world, both supported and admired around the world. But part of the problem is that the outside world doesn't matter—Spanish soccer is all about Spain. It's about the bitter, complicated rivalry between and Real and Barca, with all the attached layers of politics and regional rivalries.

On numerous occasions, Spain has qualified for a tournament, universally admired for the skills of its players, their goal-scoring instinct and slick passing game. And then Spain promptly collapsed against less talented, but tougher, teams. Around the world, the belief is that the Spanish players always look like they want to go home, where there is less melodrama, less cheating and fewer bone-rattling tackles. It is definitely supposed to be different this time. Spain's coach, Luis Aragonés, an eccentric, choleric man, declined to pick the veteran Raul for Euro 2008, pointing out acidly that Raul had never won anything for his country.

As usual, Spain opened strongly, destroying Russia 4–1 with an attractive style of slick passing and forward movement. David Villa scored the first hat trick of Euro 2008 in that game, and his partnership with Fernando Torres looked sublimely productive. Authentic hopes about Spain, though, were really raised in the game against Sweden. A tough team to beat, and physically strong, Sweden called a halt to the passing game that Spain loves to play. It was when the game was tied 1–1, and Sweden looked physically dominant, that Spain's mettle emerged. The quick passing went out the window. It was kick-and-run soccer, and no shoulders sagged on the Spanish side. Villa scored a last-gasp goal to get the win and, with that, opinion about Spain's toughness shifted from skepticism to belief. Then Spain soaked up the dour tactics of Greece and won.

Now it's Italy that emerges as the true test for Spain. Italy's traditional strength is a combination of skill, ferocity of spirit and pragmatism. When skills won't win the game, a prosaic, unromantic roughness will. And, in a way, Spain fears Italy in the same way that a goalkeeper fears the penalty kick. For its part, Italy has no fears. Spain is unbeaten in nineteen games, but that's not significant now. No victory would matter more for Spain than one over Italy. And nobody would be surprised should Spain fail the test. This won't be a just a game, it will be a coming-of-age story that ends either in adulthood or a retreat into adolescence.

• • • • •

IT IS early afternoon in the heat, under clear blue skies. Around St. Stephen's Cathedral—the Stephansdom, a Gothic wonder, the mother church of Mozart and anchor of all that is Vienna— Spanish fans are dancing. A great conga line of a thousand swaying, singing teenagers goes around and around. A man in a matador's outfit pounds a drum. A tall, elegant, thirtysomething woman in a dress made from two flags of Spain—three horizontal stripes of red, yellow and red—her jet-black hair in a dramatic Spanish updo, stands nearby. She just stands there, her shopping bags from designer stores at her feet, waiting to be admired and photographed. There is a diva-esque quality to her pose, an operatic haughtiness. The Viennese take her picture—as they must, in this city of music and opera and grand, baroque design—and she smiles for each of them. "Look at the dance, listen to the drum, look at me," her expression says. "This is Spain."

Outside the stadium, I see a tall, handsome Italian youth with his arm around a young Spanish woman. He wears the blue shirt of the Azzurri over a rippling chest, and white shorts. She wears the red/yellow/red of Spain over her golden skin, and on her white skirt, by her left thigh, there's a drawing of a bull. They both wear reflective sunglasses that show you how ordinary you are in comparison. They are the sexiest couple on the planet at this moment. Everyone takes their picture. Even I do—as well as that of a very large-bellied Italian man who has Italy's colors and the word "mama" drawn over his exposed, heaving stomach. Two friends hoist him on their shoulders for the TV cameras. He is laughing his head off, amused and addled as a child.

In the stadium, there's a gymnastics display on the field. Flix and Trix, the tournament mascots, flounce about. Lusty chanting of "*Olé, olé, olé*" from the cheerful Spanish contingent during the gymnastics. Obscene remarks, too, probably. On the big screen, pictures of people in cool hats are featured. The Italians weigh the merits of the headgear on the screen with exaggerated seriousness, like a judging committee, modulating their cheers for the chic, the absurd, the original.

Italia. España. This is some kind of soccer heaven. It is the twenty-second of June. Spain has bowed out of three major championships on this date: the World Cups of 1986 and 2002 and Euro 96—all in the quarter-finals and always on penalties. Some say—with reason, obviously—that Spain is cursed on this day.

The teams are in the tunnel. The referee is Mr. Fandel of Germany. Spain goes with a 4–4–2 formation, Torres and Villa up front. Italy is going 4–3–1–2, Luca Toni and Antonio Cassano up front, Simone Perrotta holding behind them. And then it starts.

It's 0–0 at the half. And the chance of a goal looks extremely remote. Some nice moves from Spain, but Italy playing it tight at the back. Spain is too slow in moving the ball and getting into the goalmouth. Melodrama is coming, I can tell. Small grievances abound. Fabio Grosso trips David Silva in the penalty area—it looks like a nasty swipe at Silva's foot. The referee sees no reason to be concerned. There is much sulking from Spain. And yet, if coach Aragonés should tell the boys to move faster, Spain will have a goal coming, surely.

More falling and sulking in the second half. The Italians are the ones sulking this time. They pick up the pace a bit. It is only in the thirty minutes of extra time that the game opens up, becomes gripping and fast. Spain finally introduces its fluency and swift passing, and comes close twice. Italy responds with more verve, and coach Donadoni introduces the talismanic Alessandro Del Piero. But tired legs on both sides are causing countless mistakes.

The penalty shootout is what makes the game memorable. The goalkeepers, Spain's Iker Casillas and Italy's Gianluigi Buffon, are the two best in the world. Villa scores for Spain and Fabio Grosso for Italy, and then Santi Cazorla scores for Spain again. Then, when Casillas makes a spectacular dive to save from Daniele De Rossi, there comes the sound of fifty thousand people gasping. Time seems frozen as Italy's Buffon saves from Dani Güiza. But then it happens: Casillas repeats his extraordinary act and saves Antonio Di Natale's kick. All that is needed is for Cesc Fàbregas to beat Buffon, and he does. Then the dancing starts. Spain has erased a curse and decades of showing up, showing off and failing to hang in. Now it has fortitude as well as style.

The Spanish fans dance, endlessly. Fans of other countries sing and chant with gusto. They roar. But they don't dance. Spain plays a dancing sort of soccer, all energy, exquisite coordination and connection. The Italians don't; they usually crush others' hearts with skill, dour tactical aggression—and, sometimes, just aggression. Not now, not here. There should be no Italian tears after they've played a cynical game of maintaining possession and slowing the pace. Italy did nothing to add to the often superb, flowing soccer that has characterized this tournament. And yet, of course, the Italians are hurt, disappointed. Bitter, aggrieved Italian supporters loiter outside, slump on the subway, sit stone-faced in the bars and cafés. "Hush, hush, my darlings," I want to tell them. "Don't despair. Spain deserved this triumph for the breathtaking, dancing movement of its play in the tournament, and for old times' sake."

• • • • •

ON MY last day in Vienna I go to look at the Egon Schiele paintings, again. I feel like the male figures he draws—stark, skeletal, raw, yet bursting with life in the eyes. Outside the enclave called the Museum Quarter, there is a long stretch of grass. There are giant feet in soccer boots there. Art. Each is in the color of one of the sixteen countries that qualified to play at Euro 2008. I see two small boys kick a ball in an alleyway. An email from the nice woman at Vienna Tourism suggests I try champagne and elderberry syrup.

I'm shopping on the Mariahilfer Strasse when I see someone waving at me, I think. The young woman who has brought me coffee in the hotel restaurant most mornings for a week has ducked out of a coffee shop to wave and say hello, briefly. She's gone in a flash. Shy Viennese. The other day at breakfast, she said to me, "I didn't know there were so many Turkish people in Vienna. So many. My husband said I was foolish. Of course there are." I hadn't a clue what to say. I'd only slept for four hours anyway. She thinks I'm American and that I expect to hear "Have a nice day" every morning. I told her once that I'm from Canada. She gave me a look that said, "Yeah, right."

I find the place I've been looking for—an art "supermarket," filled with original art and arranged by price only. You get a shopping cart at the door. It's a Monday afternoon; there's nobody there. A young man asks if he can help. Then he assumes I'm

English—offers to bring me tea. I take the tea and sip it, reading email on the BlackBerry. A man from Spain, long living in Vancouver, has written to me: "That was the best post-match article I read, and actually as a Spaniard it made me cry, just a little, a little, little bit. Thank you."

On the tram that goes around the opera house, two Spanish women are trying, groggily, to take in the sights. One sees the flag of Spain attached to a railing, a remnant of the party the night before. She points. They both beam and stifle giggles. Stephen Brunt will soon be in to Vienna to cover a semifinal match and the final. In less than forty-eight hours I'll be back in Toronto, working at my day job. Today, I will remember everything. Everything.

· · · · ·

VIENNA IS still in my head when I watch Germany play Turkey in the first semifinal game. I'm watching it on TV in Toronto, but I can smell, taste and touch Vienna. In Vienna, too, they're watching it on TV, hundreds of thousands of people in the Fan Zone by the Hapsburg Palaces. The game itself is being played in Basel, in Switzerland, and it is a heart-stopping drama, a superb spectacle. Turkey takes a 1–0 lead, but Germany equalizes and then goes ahead 2–1. Turkey ties it with four minutes left. Germany wins 3–2 with what is almost the final kick of the game. Some people are saying, before the game is even over, that the first half was the finest forty-five minutes of soccer they had ever seen. Although defeated in the end, Turkey is the better team, magnificently unstinting, determined to score. A BBC commentator asks, "Will we see a better international tournament in our lifetimes? I hope so, but I'm not sure how you improve on this."

A very strange event occurs during the game. The TV signal disappears. There's a storm somewhere in Austria or Switzerland and the signal is disrupted. It comes, goes, then vanishes. Later, I read that in Vienna there were 250,000 people watching on the big screens in the city. When the signal vanished, they were asked to disperse and leave—the remainder of the game would not be seen. And leave they did, in quiet disappointment. No trouble, no scuffles, no fighting, no riot. I'm not surprised at all.

In the other semifinal, the next day, Spain dispenses with Russia, blithely. It's a 3–0 victory. There is the weight of expectation on Russia after their emergence as a team of shocking talent. But Spain is unfettered now, freed from a history of curses, timidity and underachievement. The second goal is breathtaking, balletic art. The ball goes to Fàbregas, who turns and simultaneously slips a perfect pass to Dani Güiza, who is in mid-stride but chests the ball down and nonchalantly lifts it over the Russia goalkeeper with a casual, side-footed strike.

The final is decided by a single goal: Spain 1, Germany 0. After thirty minutes, Spain pushes past an obstinate German defense. The goal happens when Fernando Torres races on to a pass from Xavi and, with an exemplary combination of speed and strength—the attributes that now encapsulate the Spanish team—lifts the ball over German keeper Jens Lehmann. Spain dominates throughout. Germany's only recourse is to run hard and tackle aggressively, but the squad is utterly outclassed. Spain absolutely deserves the victory and championship. Right to the end, they never stop playing their attacking game.

It is a fine end to an exquisite tournament, one that saw France, Italy and finally Germany slide down the list of great European teams. Holland brought the first part of the tournament alive with exciting, entertaining play, but it is Spain, from their opening game to the last, that is technically and artistically superior and always pleasing to the eye, the epitome of the sophistication that soccer can achieve.

As Euro 2008 ends, World Cup qualifying for South Africa 2010 is under way. While I was in Vienna, Canada had already beaten St. Vincent and the Grenadines in a qualifying game. Time moves on as the planet turns and as the ball rolls forward. As it must.

PART III

WORLD CUP 2010:
The TRIUMPH *of* GRACE *over* COERCION

CHAPTER 1

HOME

TEAMS REPRESENTING 198 national soccer associations from six continents participated in the qualification process for the 2010 World Cup in South Africa. In the end, thirty-two countries qualified—only one of which, the host country, had an automatic berth. It was a long, hard, winding road. I traveled to eight countries on three continents to see qualifying games, to find stories and to write this book. It seemed at times a crazy idea. I had no guaranteed accreditation for any of the matches, as I would at a tournament. There would be no translators or helpers on hand as there would at a tournament. I would do this over weekends, or using part of my vacation time. I would be a freelancer and often be the lone reporter from North America, the stranger hoping for refuge and camaraderie because soccer is international, all-encompassing and welcoming.

But, first, a diversion. It is a Thursday night in late November. I'm at home, a small house in downtown Toronto, tucked away in the west end on a street of little homes of red and yellow brick, most of them built to house soldiers in the 1870s. The neighborhood was working-class then and still clinging to it now. It's near 8 P.M., and I have to meet someone from work for a drink at a bar a few streets away. Winter is quickly descending, and I check the weather on TV before I head out. The temperature is sinking towards zero, with a bitter wind coming in off Lake Ontario. Snow flurries even, drifting in on the cold night air. I bundle up in an extra layer, a scarf and gloves. Down the street I walk, quickly, feeling the first, sharp shiver of winter.

At the end of the street I turn left, down Niagara Street. I'm fifty paces along when I slow the pace. I can hear it before I see it: the thump of the foot against the round leather ball. On a patch of Astroturf in a small, well-lit space beside Niagara Street Public School, ten boys are playing soccer—five a side. They're all in their early teens, wearing hoodies, sweaters, long pants, short pants over track pants. Some wear gloves. They've piled sweaters, in the traditional way, to mark the goal posts. They're deep into the game, I can tell. It's intense now—a competitive tactility hovers over it. There are shouts, a moan of frustration, orders barked to move it, pass it. I watch the skills—the long ball forward, a drag-back, the short pass, a glancing kick with the side of the foot to send the ball spinning. They've surrendered to the game. The darkness and the cold don't matter, even as small, white flecks of snow curl in on the cold wind and settle on the green turf. A man on the other side of the street, walking his two dogs, stops, lights a cigarette and watches.

This is a moment. A scenario, a few minutes of movement and drama that clarifies something intuited, nagging. I'm in Canada and here a defining vignette of the culture is an imagined picture of boys on a frozen pond in winter, skating, their sticks moving the puck. This small, intense drama I'm watching, on a winter's night, is like a response to that—boys in the city night, in early winter, oblivious to the cold, intent on the ball, the choreography of their play. Nothing exists beyond the touchline. This, too, is Canada, the drama tells me. I have no idea who these boys might be—Portuguese, perhaps, but it's been two decades since the neighborhood was all Portuguese. Everyone of every possible background lives here. I can't see the kids clearly, and it wouldn't matter anyway.

The trick about multicultural diversity is not to make a big deal over it. I've known, intuited, that this is now part of the place where I live, a place where soccer is what it is—football, futbol—and here, some hearts to one purpose alone are devoted.

The game, the simple pleasure of it, and then the enormously complex web of emotions and connections that link this little patch of Astroturf to the world, don't matter in any profound way. It just is. The ball turns here, as it does anywhere. Right here, where these young boys play, I no longer waste my sorry days away wondering what happens to teams in Ireland, England, Italy or Argentina. Here, I no longer need to search out bits of news, hints of schisms and changes, stories of glory and disgrace. Here, we are connected, and here, too, it happens: the essence of the world's game.

I know that right here at this spot on Niagara Street, on Saturdays—and sometimes Sundays or Wednesdays—one can hear it emphatically. I can hear it from my back garden: the roar of the crowd, the boasting, the berating, the manic, cheerful bellicosity of the crowd in full-throated blast. "This. Is. Our. House." We have a team. There's a league. After the World Cup was held in the United States in 1994, Major League Soccer moved, stealthily, into the U.S. and then into Canada. No fuss, no promise of has-been superstars and huge crowds. Just the game, loyal fans who understand, and a small, hard hope that the league would survive and grow. And it did. After the 2006 World Cup, Toronto FC appeared. It was a business, of course. Shrewdly planned, assessed for profitability in attendance and merchandising. In Toronto, the formula succeeded instantly. Games sold out, but of more consequence, the arrival of the local professional team seemed to touch something in the soul of the city.

Many months before this November night, it had been announced that David Beckham would be playing in the MLS. He'd play for the Los Angeles Galaxy, get paid big money and might draw big crowds, thanks to his skills, his reputation and the glamour that he embodied. And then Beckham came to my town. He was injured, unfit to play, so he sat on the bench in a nice suit and watched the Galaxy manage a 0–0 draw with Toronto FC. He chewed gum, walked gingerly along the edge of the artificial turf and waved to the sold-out crowd at BMO

Field, home of what some people hereabouts simply call "The FC." The next day, he went shopping and bought a vintage Iron Maiden T-shirt. The papers were full of news about the shopping. "Spend It Like Beckham," roared the inevitable headlines. In search of Beckham-mania, the *Toronto Star* discovered two fans waiting for an autograph outside the Galaxy's hotel. For this, Beckham had a bodyguard.

Here in Toronto, the biggest city in Canada and the most ethnically diverse city in North America, some people were really disappointed that Beckham didn't actually play. Most disappointed were the hard-core Toronto FC fans, the thousands who populate the south end of BMO Field (sponsored by Bank of Montreal) and call themselves the Red Patch Boys, even though they're not actually all boys. A whole lot of women congregate there too. They'd been waiting for months to greet Beckham. It's been known for ages that the Galaxy's away game in Toronto would probably mark Beckham's first regular-season MLS game. They wanted him to take a corner at the south end—then, you see, he'd get what all opposing players get in Toronto when they take a corner there: five thousand people screaming "Who are ya?" Instead, the tiny, whiny, baldy and snarky Landon Donovan was asked the question.

If Beckham had paid attention while here—and nobody is sure he did, because in press interviews he talked only about himself—he would have seen his own redundancy. This is the one MLS city that doesn't need David Beckham to sell soccer. No way. Toronto FC, in existence for mere months and laboring through its first season at the bottom of the Eastern Conference of the MLS (tied, mind you, with the Chicago Fire and with more points than the L.A. Galaxy), is an instant hit. BMO Field holds twenty thousand people and every game is sold out. Yes, even games against the most obscure American teams. There are fourteen thousand season ticket holders. After the first home game, every single Toronto FC scarf was sold out; they can't keep the merchandise coming fast enough to the team store. Long before Beckham was lured to the MLS, some genius figured out that Toronto was soccer heaven in North America. All you had to do was build a stadium, create a team and show up. They were right.

Oh sure, like everyone across Canada and the U.S., we were impressed that Beckham was coming. But this is Canada, not America. We're different here. We have our own kind of heroes. Here, we know that Beckham's supposed to be a beauty and all, but he's no Danny Dichio. Danny's our kind of guy. Dichio is a gangly, shaven-headed journeyman player, formerly of the unglamorous Sunderland and Preston North End in England. He's a striker who's all tenacity and enthusiasm. In Toronto, he's a god. He scored the first goal in Toronto FC history, and about twenty minutes later he received the first red card in club history. It was a game against Chicago Fire, and TFC's fifth game ever. The first three were away games, and TFC hadn't managed a goal, much less a point. Their fourth was the first home game and it provided a taste of what was happening here. It was on a cool Saturday in April, against the Kansas City Wizards. The noise from the FC fans was deafening. A Kansas City showboater named Eddie Johnson scored the only goal, in the eighty-first minute. Then he ran over to the south end to celebrate and was instantly drenched in beer.

Entering the home game against Chicago, the FC had run up the second-longest opening scoreless streak for a new club in MLS history. When Dichio broke the streak, that's when things got interesting. The game stopped for ages while the crowd went insane. They'd all been given seat cushions prior to the game, and several thousand of these rained down on the turf. Then streamers. Then a few guys leapt over the fence with the express intention of kissing Dichio. It was bedlam, and it was beautiful. There were also FC goals by Maurice Edu and Kevin Goldthwaite—the final score was Toronto 3, Chicago 1—but Dichio's goal and the red card sealed it: he was The Man. The Business. The face of Toronto soccer.

It was Mo Johnston who brought him here. The legendary Mo Johnston, the first player to play for both Glasgow Celtic and Glasgow Rangers, who ended his career with the Kansas City Wiz (wisely changed later to Wizards) of the MLS. He ended up as manager of the New York/New Jersey MetroStars, which became Red Bull New York. But he left. Never mind; he's here. In Toronto. He's ours now. Mo brought Danny Dichio here. That suited the locals just fine. Dichio was not the only non-Canadian on the team, of course. Welsh international Carl Robinson was brought from Norwich and works tidily in midfield. Collin Samuel, the Trinidad and Tobago international and Scottish Premier League veteran, arrived too. And Ronnie O'Brien, briefly one of the most famous Irish people on the planet, thanks to some Irish students' 1999 campaign to have the then Juventus reserve voted *Time* magazine's Person of the Century. He came here from Dallas and played the first games wearing a knee brace. After Dichio, he was the fan favorite because, well, he tore around in a knee brace.

Canadian Jim Brennan, formerly of Norwich and Southampton, was the team's first captain. But the local favorite among the Canucks became nineteen-year-old Andrea Lombardo, who played briefly for Italian sides Perugia and Atalanta before returning to his hometown. Why was he the favorite? Because he famously took the bus to work, that's why. Part of the TFC magic lies in that connection between the players, the fans and the reality of the city and soccer's role here. The players are not remote figures, multimillionaire superstars. Once, just down the street from where I saw those boys play on Niagara Street, I saw Jim Brennan. It was an odd but telling vignette. A Toronto FC game had ended a couple of hours before. Thousands of supporters were in the bars and restaurants in the neighborhood, decked out in their red shirts and scarves, talking the hell out of the game. As I waited to cross the street, a man on a bicycle passed by, and I recognized him as Brennan. Captain of the team, cycling home from work.

In other MLS cities, soccer barely registers. Here, there was immediate fanaticism. Nobody had to explain to the offspring of Italian and Portuguese immigrants (or those from England, Scotland, Ireland, Chile, Peru, Brazil or Poland—and you can keep going until you've got the most ethnically diverse mix imaginable) what to do at a game and how to enjoy it. A year before the team played its first game, potential fans gathered online, organized a fan base and began creating terrace chants. Because this is Canada and officially bilingual, there's even a French chant: *Qu'est-ce que vous chantez? / Nous chantons les rouges allez!* Nobody is sure how many Quebecers show up at games, but they're welcome. And the small group of FC fans who travel to away games in American MLS cities get a real kick out of performing the French chant for the Americans—it annoys and puzzles the heck out of them.

Fans who couldn't get tickets for the first FC games had to watch on TV. Other MLS teams are lucky if a game is shown on an obscure cable channel. Here, Toronto FC had an immediate TV deal with the Canadian Broadcasting Corporation, a national, over-the-air network, publicly funded, available to anyone in Canada for free. During those early games, the CBC's camera work was often shaky, because the entire stadium was vibrating from noise and foot-stamping. After a month, an army of workers had to tighten bolts throughout the stadium. Of course, during its first season, Toronto FC went into a major slump. The team went 462 minutes without scoring a goal. Dichio and five other starters were injured for weeks. Still, the momentum didn't stop. The faithful are truly that, not to mention fanatical, and the atmosphere at games is electric. Nobody expects TFC to be the equivalent of the local Major League Baseball, NBA or NHL team. The Toronto Maple Leafs are a storied, attention-grabbing team, but the players don't take the bus or cycle to work. There is a lucid authenticity to the soccer as it exists here now. This is real. The only thing that's artificial is the turf.

CHAPTER 2

AWAY

AUGUST 28, 2008, TORONTO
CANADA 1, JAMAICA 1

Ah jeez, that's a pity. We needed to win.

REMARKABLY, TO SEE MY FIRST World Cup 2010 qualifying game, I didn't have to start by going to the airport. I simply walked down the street and got on a streetcar that would take me, in minutes, to BMO Field. It's a warm August evening and, amazingly, there's excitement in the air. The idea is being floated that Canada can qualify for the World Cup. This is very confusing.

The tourists on the crowded Toronto streetcar heading for the stadium on the Canadian National Exhibition grounds are certainly confused. Two young women from Spain, heading for the carnival and fun fair that is the CNE, look around and see men and women in red and white shirts. Some of the shirts declare allegiance to Toronto FC. Others say CANADA. The thing is, there were as many men, women and children in green and yellow shirts emblazoned with JAMAICA. There is mild joshing going on between the two factions, and a bit of anticipation in the air. A man getting on the streetcar sees the Jamaicans and waves a red scarf that says ALLEZ LES ROUGES.

One of the Spanish ladies looks at me, an older guy standing on the crowded car, wearing some kind of official badge and carrying a laptop bag. "What . . . ?" she begins, but can't form the question. "It's a soccer game," I say. "Football. World Cup qualifying. Canada is playing Jamaica tonight." She looks at her companion and two pairs of eyes widen. "Football?" they ask each other in unison, with more question marks than can be expressed in writing. They expected lumberjacks, perhaps, but certainly not football fans.

They aren't the only ones confused. Canada hasn't played a World Cup qualifying game in Toronto in years. And it's an odd scene in this most culturally varied of cities where the visiting teams from the CONCACAF region are likely to have more supporters than the home country. There are thirty-four countries in CONCACAF, many in the Caribbean, and thirty-two of those countries have thousands of immigrants living here. For a start, the city annually stages Caribana, the largest Caribbean festival in the world. Only a game against the U.S. could possibly muster enough pro–Canada support to inspire the players on the field. Things are supposed to have changed now. Toronto has an MLS team, supported by loud and fanatical fans who can spook any visitors. TFC supporters have promised to show up, shouting, singing and urging Canada to victory through sheer strength of numbers and noise. And they do show up. If the Spanish visitors had taken a different route, they would have seen it: thousands of Toronto FC fans making a splendid, noisy march to the stadium, chanting for Canada, banging drums and waving flags. There are police officers lining the route, watching for trouble. The cops look bewildered. All that noise and color, and no trouble?

This is supposed to be Canada's time. The country hasn't qualified for the World Cup since 1986, but there's a new manager, Dale Mitchell, who says the right things. And there are good young players alongside a few sturdy veterans. Tomasz Radzinski, once of Anderlecht, Everton and Fulham, and now with some Greek club—Skoda Xanthi—that nobody has heard of, is on board and enthusiastic. Previously, he'd seemed surly about it. There's Dwayne De Rosario, currently with Houston Dynamo in the MLS, who can score from here, there and everywhere. There's Julian de Guzman, who spent three seasons with Hanover in the German Bundesliga and now plays for Deportivo in Spain. Among the old-timers is goalkeeper Pat Onstad, who stands six foot four and is forty years old. Onstad now plays for Houston Dynamo, and his career is a barometer of the changes in football in North America. He spent years playing for such teams as the Rochester Raging Rhinos or the Winnipeg Fury before having a high-profile job in the game. Like all forty-year-old goalkeepers, he's a sentimental favorite and is treated as a sage. This will prove to be a bit of a problem.

At a rocking BMO Field, with the carousels and thrill rides of the Exhibition all around, the thousands of Jamaican fans are cocky, as well they might be—Jamaica has just produced the fastest man and the three fastest women at the Beijing Olympics. For thirty minutes, Canada controls the game and Jamaica sits back, less the Reggae Boyz than the back-pass boys. Then Deon Burton wakes up. The much-traveled journeyman who has played for ten teams in England launches an attack, and Canada looks vulnerable. Nothing happens, though.

Canada comes out strong for the second half and looks set for a famous victory when De Rosario crosses from the right, Radzinski heads a ball beautifully to de Guzman in the Jamaican box, and he sends a left-footed shot past a diving Donovan Ricketts in the Jamaican net. The atmosphere, which has been loud, cheerful and endlessly noisy all night, becomes intense. Those thousands of TFC fans know how to chant, roar, mock the referee and taunt the opposing supporters. Now they sense a great victory for Canada.

And then—oh no. Five minutes later, a corner kick by Jamaica's Andrew Williams curls towards Pat Onstad. Somehow, Onstad deflects the ball into his net. An own goal by the old-timer, the famously reliable man. He looks mortified. My heart goes out to him, but a goal is a goal. The game is tied and, with Mexico and Honduras still to come, Canada needs to win here to have anything near a chance at qualifying for the World Cup. Canada pours it on. Ricketts is the busiest guy on the field, stopping shot after shot from Radzinski and de Guzman. The crowd screams. The tension is terrific. But it ends in a draw. A single point at home.

Canada goes on to lose to Honduras in Montreal, then to Mexico, Honduras again and Jamaica again. There will be one fine victory against Mexico, but it isn't enough. Canada will not qualify for the World Cup. Still, a seed has been sown. The game in Toronto was a revelation, even to many soccer fans here and to some of the players. Pure passion poured from the supporters in the stands. By the time the qualifying for the World Cup is complete, as I write this in 2009, De Rosario and de Guzman are playing for Toronto FC. There is the promise that a field of real grass will be planted in BMO Field for the 2010 season. Even better, for me, is the memory of walking home after the Canada–Jamaica game. A woman on a balcony sees me passing, spots the press badge still hanging around my neck, and shouts, "Who won?" It's not the baseball Blue Jays, the Maple Leafs or the Argonauts of the Canadian Football League she's asking about—it's the World Cup qualifier against Jamaica. "It was a draw, 1–1," I tell her.

"Ah jeez, that's a pity," she says. "We needed to win." She knew.

SEPTEMBER 10, 2008, CHICAGO
USA 3, TRINIDAD AND TOBAGO 0

My aunt thinks we're just here to see her. She can't really believe that we came to see a soccer game.

IT IS A MILD, mid-week September evening in downtown Chicago. The L trains move like rolling thunder over the streets, carrying people home at the end of the workday in this most old-fashioned and lovable of major American cities. In the crowded L car I'm standing in, no one is talking soccer. In September, this is a baseball town, and with both the White Sox and Cubs sitting on top of their respective divisions in Major League Baseball, the city is looking forward to a sweet September playoff series—maybe even a cross-town World Series. At the end of the line, waiting for the express game-day bus to Toyota Park in the suburb of Bridgeview, I begin to feel utterly absurd. I'm the only one waiting. Me, the idiot who came from Canada to Chicago for a World Cup qualifying game. It's ninety minutes before kick-off and there's not a supporter in sight. Most people in this town are obviously oblivious to any soccer action taking place. Not even the presence of the U.S. national team can make a dent in the local baseball bliss.

And then, minutes before the bus departs, they materialize, like magic. I stare at them, figuring they must be as rare as New York Yankees followers in this city. As the almost-full bus scoots through the bland suburb of Bridgeview, I'm hoping for some insight into the U.S. soccer fanatic. But most on the bus don't appear likely to chat. And there's no point in eavesdropping. Many are alone. Loners and eccentrics, I figure. Off the bus and on the long walk through the enormous, near-empty car park, I fall in with a thirtysomething couple, both draped in the U.S flag, who seem excited about going to the game. They've actually come all the way from St. Paul, Minnesota. A long pilgrimage, I suggest to them. "It's a long way and we can't really afford it," the guy says. "But we couldn't resist. We're staying with her aunt, so we're not paying for a hotel." His wife chimes in, "My aunt thinks we're just here to see her. She can't really believe that we came to see a soccer game." I ask if there are many soccer fans in St. Paul. "No," the guy says, with a rueful laugh, "but it's growing. Believe me, there are people I talk soccer with, every day. There are so many games on TV now. You can talk about Barcelona and Manchester United and AC Milan. But the U.S., that's our team. That's why we're here."

Toyota Park is a lovely stadium. Home to the Chicago Fire of the MLS, it holds twenty thousand people. The Fire is currently fourth in the MLS in average attendance with 17,339. They trail the Los Angeles Galaxy (25,648), Toronto FC (20,150) and D.C. United (19,746). Across the league, the average attendance at MLS games is 16,410. But how many have shown up for the USA versus Trinidad and Tobago in a World Cup qualifier? The announced figure is 11,452. The national team is drawing fewer fans than the local MLS team. It's an eerie, surreal experience to be watching the USA in a half-empty stadium in America's third-largest city. The atmosphere is weirdly relaxed, almost torpid. Only the few hundred fanatical U.S. fans at one end—chanting "USA! USA!" for ninety-plus minutes—keep the event from transpiring amid utter silence.

At halftime, I wander around and notice the food concession stands free of line-ups and a total of three people peering at the U.S. and Chicago Fire regalia for sale. Suddenly, there's a bit of a commotion. About thirty guys are on a march around the stadium, waving flags, singing. Up close, it's obvious they're all Chicago Fire fans and singing a Chicago Fire chant, over and over, in Spanish. Not a word about the U.S. national team, as far as my limited Spanish can interpret. Then it all makes sense: the bedrock of soccer support in Chicago is Spanish-speaking, mostly Mexican. A soccer game—any soccer game—will draw the die-hard ethnic fans. The rest of the city couldn't care less. The feat of transcending ethnic interest and achieving mass appeal has always been the core problem with soccer in America. As much as the MLS has succeeded in establishing a solid league with a reasonably good standard of play, and as much as the U.S. national team has played at six consecutive World Cup tournaments, mass interest is only slowly growing. The arrival of David Beckham has drawn media attention to the MLS, and nobody is going broke, but in terms of mass interest, soccer in America is a small-scale proposition. And that's fine, really. There's a purity in the fans' emotional attachment to soccer that sets it apart from the support for baseball, basketball and hockey. At the packed, raucous BMO Field in Toronto, the atmosphere was astonishing, and at times the sound of twenty thousand Canadians and Jamaicans was deafening. There was cheerful mayhem. Here, in Chicago, the 11,452 who turn up are the ones who care, deeply.

As for the game, well, the U.S. thumped Trinidad and Tobago 3–0, and T&T was flattered by the score—in fact, the U.S. should have won 6–0. The Soca Warriors played the entire first half in a sort of 6–3–1 formation and didn't have a single shot on goal. This team is a far cry from the one I saw in Germany. The U.S. scores after nine minutes, with Michael Bradley scoring the easiest of goals from a Landon Donovan free kick. Nine minutes later, Clint Dempsey makes it 2–0, taking advantage of chaos in T&T's defense. At this point, the game is essentially over and won. At the start of the second half, T&T looks a tad more lively; sub Anthony Wolfe dashes around the center area, eccentrically determined to get the ball to lone forward Cornell Glen. This lasts all of twelve minutes. In the fifty-seventh minute, Brian Ching pokes home a goal for the U.S. after yet another shambolic T&T response to a free kick. That's it. The Soca Warriors manage two shots on goal in the entire game.

Prior to the game, there'd been a fuss about whether Dwight Yorke would play. He played for T&T the previous weekend, but Yorke now plays for Sunderland in England and Roy Keane is the manager, his boss. There were suggestions that Keane had ordered Yorke not to play against the U.S. Then Keane and the wily FIFA vice-president Jack Warner, from T&T, began trading insults over Yorke's availability, or lack thereof, for the game in Chicago. Roy Keane usually gets his way. For a few minutes, while I'm talking to a local journalist about the fuss, I'm reminded that I've been writing about international soccer for a while now. A major figure from the 2002 World Cup is being talked about in Chicago in the context of the non-appearance of a major figure from my experience at the 2006 World Cup. Small world, and all that. Or maybe just the soccer in my head. Would the thirty-six-year-old Yorke have made a difference? Not very likely. It was a dominating, imperious performance by the U.S., a thrill to be savored by those followers of the national team.

At O'Hare airport the next morning, security is a bit tighter than usual, it being September 11. I am stopped and asked the purpose of my visit to Chicago. I explain that I'm a journalist and had been at the soccer game between the USA and Trinidad and Tobago. "Wow," the guy from Homeland Security says. "You got that assignment? Weird." As I mosey along, he calls after me: "Hey, buddy, who won?" But when I turn back to answer, he's already questioning somebody else. He didn't really want to know. Like most of Chicago. But at least he asked.

A month later, in a bizarre twist, T&T beats the U.S. 2–1 in Port of Spain. But the U.S. moves steadily down the long, complex route to qualifying from North and Central America. It will qualify ahead of Mexico.

It is heresy to say this in Canada—and indeed, in the rest of the soccer world—but I like the American team. I admire their style and guts. These players are not superstars. Clint Dempsey, who scored a goal in Chicago, learned his soccer growing up in a trailer park in Texas, playing with Mexican and Honduran kids. He progressed through the ranks to the English Premier League. Like most of his colleagues on the national team, and unlike his counterparts in baseball or the National Football League, Dempsey is unknown. The players are, in a way, similar to the fans, in that they're loners of a sort, forever encountering condescension in Europe and bafflement in the States. Hearts of oak these players have, and an intense love of the game that takes them out of America and into the world.

I identify with the American supporters too, because, in a way, I'm like all of them—the loners searching out a congregation of like-minded people. Uncaring about the relative obscurity of the game they care passionately about. When I was a young fella in Ireland, the Gaelic games commanded all the attention and soccer was almost hidden. Certainly, it was derided. Much as soccer fans find it in the United States today, with so much scrutiny and celebration devoted to baseball, basketball, football (in the case of the latter two, both pro and college) and hockey. They know the lonely days when the solace of soccer is strong, but private—clandestine.

The USA will qualify for the World Cup by beating Mexico, tying with Costa Rica, beating El Salvador, beating T&T again and beating Honduras 2–1. By the time that game is held, again in Chicago but at Soldier Field, 55,000 people will attend the game. Riddle me that.

OCTOBER 11, 2008, LONDON, ENGLAND
ENGLAND 5, KAZAKHSTAN 1

It is very important that the crowd help him and not boo him.

SOMEWHERE BETWEEN Toronto and London, something odd occurs. I'm writing for *The New York Times* now. I'm not quite certain how it happened. A man told a man who told a man, and I sent a note to the editor of the *Times*'s online soccer page. I'm in my parents' home in Dublin before going over to London, and there's an email from the *Times* on my BlackBerry: "John, what is your angle for the England–Kazakhstan game on Saturday?" I'm in—I have another outlet for my reports and stories. My dad tells someone in the pub, the night before I leave. I get a pint on the house.

I arrive in London for England's first competitive home game under the new manager, the famously intense Fabio Capello. I read the morning papers in London and watch the pre-game coverage on TV. What I see is war imagery. A sensible person would respond with one word: "Chill." Yes, it's a World Cup qualifying game, and a win is important. But, after all, it's only Kazakhstan. Yes, Kazakhstan the hopeless—the land of Borat, a country that just fired its coach and replaced him with the under-21 team's coach. Ranked 131st in the world—way, way below England's rank of 14th.

It's unlikely that even the most obsessive follower of English soccer could name a single player on the Kazakh team. Players from all over the world toil in the English leagues, but is there a notable chap from Kazakhstan? Not bloody likely. And yet, within hours of my arrival, I can see that the English anxiety is glaringly obvious. It's a toxic mixture of hand-wringing and hyperbole. There's the nagging worry about the home supporters at Wembley.

Will they boo if there isn't a rout of the minnows from Kazakhstan? In a crowd of ninety thousand, the law of averages says some hard-bitten skeptics are likely, expressing scorn if there isn't an honest endeavor. Worrying about it is pointless. Still, in the maniacally neurotic local press there's the suggestion that England just can't cut it at Wembley. *The Sun* quotes Capello as saying, "After failing to qualify for Euro 2008 we were full of fear. Notably when we played at Wembley." Even for a tabloid newspaper, the *Sun*'s "fear" theme is loaded.

Then there's the subtle war-like hyperbole. On Friday, in the print edition of the *Guardian*, there was a startling photo of the England team in training. In red shirts or rain jackets, running, arms swaying and fists at chest level, they looked eerily familiar to any student of English history. They are the Redcoats, soldiers from another century. You could plausibly Photoshop muskets into their arms. They are stout-hearted chaps, armed and ready for action. The iconography of the English set-up is so very weird, rich and layered. If war is the metaphor, then Capello, a pragmatic Italian, is with the program. He talks of discipline and purpose. There's the quality of a military officer to his piercing gaze and his obvious contempt for sloppiness. It's clear that Capello is all for the bulldog spirit.

England has played two qualifying games, both away—a labored 2–0 victory over teensy Andorra and an impressive 4–1 victory over Croatia in Zagreb (called "The Glory of Zagreb" in papers both sophisticated and silly). Theo Walcott, the nineteen-year-old kid, had scored a hat trick. For the game against Kazakhstan, Capello will play a 4–3–3 formation with Wayne Rooney, the lumbering Emile Heskey and young Walcott up front, ready for war.

Oddly, Walcott seems only a whimsical addition to the solid Rooney and Heskey. He's barely mentioned in the build-up. It is Rooney who was trotted out to meet the press early on. Rooney the bloke, the working-class hero, a goal-scorer but equally devoted to tracking back, defending corners, playing deep from the middle, helping others, doing yeoman service. All the papers, broadsheet

or tabloid, drew Rooney into contemplating the international success of his contemporaries—specifically Cristiano Ronaldo
(twenty-three years old, as is Rooney) and Lionel Messi of
Barcelona and Argentina (a mere twenty-one years old). Rooney,
blessed with both a great right foot and native cunning, plays
down his own celebrity status. "I always say it's about the team,
not individuals" blared a pithy headline, based on his remarks,
in the *Daily Express*, a paper that features a drawing of an English
knight, complete with chain mail, spear and shield, between the
words *Daily* and *Express* on its front page every day. Maybe
because I'm Irish, the military subtext is glaring to me. It is also
both weird and risible. It's crazy, this neurosis. It's a game, not a
war. Against tiny Kazakhstan, what can England be afraid of?

The trip to the new Wembley Stadium is a joyful journey that
diminishes the wariness about all that war imagery. Wembley
holds about ninety thousand people, and the London Underground
is packed with people going to the game. At Baker Street station
the platform is crammed, and there are countless announcements
about the soon-to-arrive express trains for Wembley, interspersed
with warnings about people being obliged to, well, behave themselves. The crowd begins to chant back, in good humor, at the
anonymous public address announcer. There's good cheer everywhere. I sit opposite two thirtysomething guys and listen.
One's a Chelsea supporter, the other follows Tottenham Hotspur.
They lament the rise in ticket prices, the cost of match-day pro-
grams and the complicated online system used to get tickets for
European competition games. They talk about how little it cost
to attend games when they were schoolboys. They shake their
heads in disbelief, like old codgers reminiscing about the price
of things decades ago.

At Wembley Park station I spot a group of England supporters that's growing by the minute. It turns out that, somewhere
in the middle, are two guys from Kazakhstan, both wearing
what I think are traditional Kazakh hats. A very friendly discussion is under way. The English fans want to know who is the
best player on the Kazakh team, whether there's a league in

Kazakhstan, whether the Kazakhs have an opinion on Wayne
Rooney and whether the English Premier League can be watched
on TV there. The two visitors look a little overwhelmed, but
are delighted to talk—and, I think, very relieved to find that
the English supporters are friendly, curious and deeply interested
in Kazakh soccer. Handshakes and cries of "good luck" abound.
One English guy, who has listened with deep interest, hand on
chin, asks the two visitors if they would like to go for a pint
after the game. While the visitors try to figure out what he's
saying, the English guy has a second thought. "Sorry, mate, I
forgot. Are you allowed to have a drink? Are you Muslim or
something?" Me, I have to leave to get my ticket before the
answer arrives.

England ends up with a more than adequate margin of victory
against Kazakhstan to maintain an excellent record in World Cup
Qualifying Group 6, but the scoreline should deceive no one.
England is at times dreadfully poor, and manager Fabio Capello
must wonder why the spark that so electrified the 4–1 win in
Croatia seems to have disappeared. Still, a win is a win, and
when the final table is compiled, three points and five goals at
home will not look so bad. Yet it takes Wayne Rooney's late
double and Jermain Defoe's injury-time effort to kill off spirited
opponents ranked 131st in the world after Kazakhstan rallies from
a breakthrough, headed goal by stand-in captain Rio Ferdinand.
There are plenty of negatives. Capello's plea for supporters to cut
out the booing of home players is ignored. England is jeered after
a goalless first half, and Ashley Cole is the target of abuse from
his own fans. It's a tough crowd at Wembley.

Kazakhstan tries to play elegant soccer and attack when possible, and shows plenty of enthusiasm if not much finesse, as half-
chances come their way thanks to some lackluster England
defending. But the gulf in ability is obvious from the outset, and
the crowd sits back and waits for the slaughter. It doesn't happen.
In fact, Kazakhstan goalkeeper Alexandr Mokin doesn't have a
shot to save in the first half, two punches to Frank Lampard free
kicks being the most exertion required of him. England's defense

lacks cohesion. In front of them, a midfield designed to get the best of Emile Heskey and Wayne Rooney repeatedly fails. England finally makes the breakthrough in the second half, profiting more from poor goalkeeping than design. Ferdinand has an empty net to nod the ball into. An own goal by Kazakhstan comes next. Then Cole aimlessly lofts a pass into the path of Zhambyl Kukeyev, who promptly scores. Cole is booed relentlessly by the England fans thereafter, and it is Wayne Rooney who cheers them up with his characteristic speed and aggression.

There's a surreal quality to the post-game press conference. Capello and the players know the team didn't perform well, but they decide to concentrate on the matter of the crowd's response. "I couldn't understand the crowd booing Ashley Cole after he made a mistake," Capello says. "It is possible for one player to make mistake. It is very important that the crowd help him and not boo him." Rio Ferdinand can't let it go, either, ranting, "As regards the booing of Ashley, a lot of the fans will go home—and I hope they will be ashamed of what they were doing. Everyone is human, and people make mistakes. We are big enough to hold our hands up when we have made a mistake, but it is not made any easier when you have got your own fans booing you. A lot of the fans did try to clap Ashley, and I think you've got to rally round as players and supporters when anyone makes a mistake."

The game provided fascinating insights, really: England is poor if Rooney isn't on fire; the supporters are impatient and suspicious of lazy players. It won't be the last time I'll see England play in its qualifying campaign.

OCTOBER 15, 2008, BRUSSELS, BELGIUM
BELGIUM 1, SPAIN 2

We are champions of Europe. We are better than Brazil.

SOMEWHERE BETWEEN Dublin, to which I returned after London, and Belgium, I've come down with a terrible cold. My voice is reduced to a rasp. I'm sniffling and coughing. It's a time when, getting by on cold remedies, I'm seeing events with a strange palpability. After the early-morning flight from Dublin, I land in Brussels unsure of how to get to my hotel. In the lineup at the airport subway station, I realize that I'm not the only one here for the game. A man in front of me, from Spain, is trying to find out the nearest stop to the stadium. The man selling tickets is surly. An argument breaks out.

The Spaniard eventually shouts, "I want to see the football!" I feel like shouting, "Me too!" Around us, almost all the customers look like they're here on official European Community business. They glare at the man from Spain. On the subway platform I ask him his prediction for the game. "Spain will win," he says. "We are champions of Europe. We are better than Brazil. But Brussels is the source of many of our problems in Spain. I don't like it here. I'm sure it will rain."

At my hotel, a tiny Hilton, the room isn't ready. The staff is most apologetic; I'm offered coffee, perhaps breakfast—free, of course. I opt for espresso and orange juice, as usual. I sit in the lobby and watch CNN on the big-screen TV. The U.S. election campaign is covered heavily. There's not a word about soccer. When the room still isn't ready after another couple of hours, the manager offers me more coffee, lunch, whatever I'd like. I ask, in my rasping voice, for a beer. He gives me a look but serves me a glass of cold beer, which I thoroughly enjoy. Then the manger asks me the nature of my business in Brussels. I tell him I'm here for the game against Spain. Oh, how he wishes he'd been able to get a ticket, he tells me. The chance to see Spain play!

Indeed. How sweet it is to see Spain play. Live. In person. It's not like it is on TV, where the camera follows the ball and the intricate orchestral maneuvers that ebb and flow around the play cannot be seen. There's going to be a full, expectant crowd of close to fifty thousand at Roi Baudouin Stadium. Most, of course, are here to support Belgium, which has made a vigorous and impressive start to its World Cup qualifying campaign, but even the most partisan supporter is also here to savor Spain's skills,

those of the European champion, unbeaten in twenty-seven
matches.

When I finally get my room and then leave the hotel, I see
that the Belgians are welcoming, in a commercial way. In the
city center, those stores that sell what the English call "tat" to
tourists are peddling giant Spanish flags to arriving supporters—as if, you know, many had not thought to bring one along
on the trip. It this city, where the European Union is adminis-
tered, it seems a very continental idea to provide, efficiently, all
necessary accoutrements for a big game. Small bars and restaurants offer paella for a mere ten euros (about sixteen dollars) and
a game-day special of Stella Artois beer for five. The few Spanish
fans I see downtown seem more interested in finding out when
the clubs that feature go-go dancers open for the night. They are
cocky, the Spanish, and interested in sexy things. As the world
knows now, their team plays sexy soccer.

But there is no welcome mat for Spain at the stadium. After
seven minutes, Belgian striker Wesley Sonck stuns the European
champions with a headed goal. The Belgian team and fans are
ecstatic. Before this, you see, Spain had not conceded a goal in
seven games, and goalkeeper Iker Casillas hadn't been beaten in
710 minutes playing for his country. For the next few minutes of
the game, played by both sides at a blistering pace, Spain looks
dumbfounded. There is more gloom when Fernando Torres leaves
the field with a hamstring injury. But then, as champions do, Spain
finds its extraordinary, defining rhythm and determination. Cesc
Fàbregas, who has replaced Torres, is superbly placed to pounce
on a loose Belgian pass and Andrés Iniesta, seeming to grasp the
coming move before it happens, is already in place to take the pass
from Fàbregas. He dances around two defenders, blithely rounds
Belgian keeper Stijn Stijnen and fires into the net from an acute
angle, the culmination of thirty seconds of breathtaking skill,
speed and perception.

Amazingly, it was mere months ago that Spain carried the tag
of eternal underachievers. A country with a bottomless supply of
talent, yet it always failed to win a tournament. Before last

summer, Spain's lone title was the 1964 European Championship. All that mythos evaporated at Euro 2008, when Spain beat Germany. After that, cranky old coach Luis Aragonés walked away to manage Fenerbahçe in Turkey. There were mutterings that Aragonés, an eccentric and devious motivator, had been the key to Spain's long-delayed success. Maybe Spain at Euro 2008 was a flash in the pan. But under a new coach, Vicente del Bosque, Spain had cruised to 1–0, 4–0 and 3–0 wins over Bosnia and Herzegovina, Armenia and Estonia. The flair is definitely still there. And especially so against a spirited, young side such as Belgium is now. This current Spanish team is a lethal mixture of Latin swagger and old-fashioned European toughness, and looks utterly unbeatable.

I'm reminded of the man from Spain on the subway this morning. What he said is true, not an empty boast. In world soccer, Spain is the new Brazil. Spain does now what Brazil did for decades—it enthralls. Just as those who were not soccer fanatics admired Brazil's joyous use of ball skills, the casual observer today is intrigued and entertained by Spain's incisive, speedy short-passing game and daring creativity. Spain does what both purists and the half-interested expect from soccer—it sends lightning attacks forward from midfield, playing with a balletic cohesion and confidence that is awe-inspiring. I wonder, too, if Spain's status must be a matter of particular chagrin to its neighbor Portugal. It was Portugal that stunned the soccer world at Euro 2000, all panache and keenness, resolutely determined to score often and in style. The Golden Generation of Portuguese players were talked of as Europe's answer to Brazil. But that team never mustered the muscle to accompany the skill and flair. At Euro 2004, the World Cup in 2006 and Euro 2008, Cristiano Ronaldo defined the team—gifted, capable of moving like a gazelle, but always ready to throw himself on the ground and claim a foul at the slightest touch.

Spain has the muscle. Always skillful and full of intricate movement, its play is simultaneously obdurate and resilient. The defining figure is Torres. He looks a delicate figure, and clearly takes delight in his own silky ball skills, but he can outmuscle a defender and a goalkeeper to direct the ball into the net. There is sweat as well as swagger in him.

And yet, even without Torres, Spain combines skill and stubbornness. In this game, Spain beats Belgium in the eighty-eighth minute on a glorious move from David Villa, who has been both tireless and creative throughout. Villa anticipates a cross from Dani Güiza and, with sublime appreciation of the space allowed him near the Belgian goal, darts instantly into position to head it into the net. Then he runs off the field, towards the thrilled Spanish fans who are chanting *"Olé, olé, olé!"* in his honor. When he strides back to the field, he walks like a matador. The Belgian team and fans look devastated. But that's what beauty does: it breaks hearts. And yes, the best of the beautiful game has moved from Brazil to Spain.

It's cold and raining steadily as I make my way back to the hotel. I've promised a story about the game to the *New York Times* and I'm running late, shivering, sniffling. When an editor finally reaches me by phone, my voice gives it away—I'm sick and suffering. I write and write, hoping it makes sense. Spain. Beauty. Brazil. Poor old Belgium gets a little left out.

Brussels barely registers with me. I get my sleep on the one-hour flight to Heathrow. As I'm boarding the flight to Toronto, my BlackBerry beeps. Questions, queries from New York. I'm madly typing insertions and revisions for my story when I have to stop because the plane is about to take off. This is a demented journey I'm on. I'm thinking that my devotion to soccer is irrational.

• • • • •

SPAIN WOULD breeze through World Cup Qualification in Group Five in Europe, with a perfect record of ten wins in ten games, scoring five goals against Bosnia and Herzegovina and five against Belgium in the return game in Spain. Belgium, with some of the best young players in Europe, imploded. Coach René

Vandereycken was replaced after a sudden burst of disastrous results and rumors of personal battles with the players.

APRIL 1, 2009, BARI, ITALY
ITALY 1, IRELAND 1

Can I have spuds with that?

THEY'RE QUITE USED to it at Dublin airport. Whenever Ireland plays away in a qualifying game, the Green Army follows. And the business people taking their early-morning flights to London, Brussels or Paris look at the sea of green shirts with envious smiles. There's going to be a *hooley* somewhere tonight. In a foreign city, the accents of Ireland will be heard, laughing, singing, roaring for more drink or just roaring drunk, celebrating a rare win—or, more likely, a tied game. Celebrating being there.

No, it's not like the Oranje Army or the massive groups who follow England to away games and tournaments. The Green Army is a ragged, tousled group. Ireland hasn't won a World Cup or even made it to the final game. It hasn't revolutionized soccer. The Green Army does have a nationalistic thrust, but is not arrogant or conceited. Ireland is too small for that. It doesn't seek to achieve the kind of bliss that the Dutch achieve in their mass celebration of everything orange-colored and the underlying assertion of the sophistication of Dutch society.

The Green Army isn't all male. Since Ireland first qualified for a tournament, entire families have traveled to support the country. The Green Army considers itself composed of "the best fans in the world," a term that means it is always cheerful, devoted to the team and dedicated to making friends. At first, this ideal was about distinguishing Irish supporters from the hooligan element of English supporters. But it has evolved. The Green Army's adventures abroad were once an escape from the glumness of Ireland, from Ireland's past and out into the larger world. Then it became, during the Celtic Tiger boom, an emphatic assertion of a new Ireland, unshackled from the past. That's why the fans dress ironically as leprechauns or priests. Now, as the Celtic Tiger economy seems to have evaporated, it is again about escape, ducking the problems of home.

The airport staff is prepared for the Army. An extra ten thousand or more passengers are expected and hustled through. "Now lads, if yiz are getting the flight to Rome, yiz had better get a move on. Join that queue there, will yiz? Good luck, lads." There are women too, of course—*lads* means anything you want in Ireland. In front of the entrance to the security checkpoint, a group of smiling young women who are trying not to giggle hand out little booklets entitled *A Soccer Fan's Guide to Bari*. It is, in fact, a small masterpiece of comic writing. Along with the ads for the betting company sponsoring it and a list of bars and restaurants in Bari, there are suggestions on how to use what's called "the local lingo." Helpful suggestions for ordering a meal in Italian are followed by the Italian phrases for "Can I have spuds with that?" and "I'm staying on Bono's yacht, by the way."

I've been in Dublin for days and I've seen how the country has been swept up in this mad enterprise. A few days in southern Italy for a Wednesday game. Everybody wants to go. The papers are full of feature articles about places to see and things to do. As if the Green Army was going to do much sightseeing. There isn't a hotel room to be had in Bari. Hasn't been for months. I know that. I'm going to be staying in Giovinazzo, about thirteen miles north of Bari—it was the only room I could find. It's going to be a long, long day: up at 5 A.M. for this early Tuesday morning flight to Rome, then another to Bari. All going well, I'll be able to get to the hotel, then scoot to the stadium for the pre-game press conferences. the *New York Times* wants a set-up piece for the game. No messing around today.

Off the plane in Rome, it's easy to find the next terminal and gate for the Alitalia flight to Bari. I just follow the green shirts. This pack is now, as some the green shirts declare, "Trap's Army."

The Irish fans worship Giovanni Trapattoni as they once worshipped Jack Charlton. (The fact that Trap's birthday is March
17, Saint Patrick's Day, adds to his appeal.) They understand there
is a small pool of Irish talent and what *Il Trap* has delivered—a
string of tied games, combined with an occasional 1–0 victory—
is, possibly, a steady course to the World Cup in South Africa.

Charismatic, charming and choleric when he feels like it,
Trapattoni is a maddening figure. A former player for AC Milan
and the Italian national team, he was manager of Juventus when
it won multiple Italian and European trophies in the 1970s. He
achieved similar success with Inter Milan before taking his skills
around Europe. He returned to Italy to manage the national team
in 2000. Me, I remember the 2002 World Cup, when Trapattoni
cemented his reputation as an adherent of defensive soccer as Italy
suffered that deserved but ignominious defeat to South Korea.
In that game, after Italy went ahead 1–0, he instinctively adopted
a defensive formation. At Euro 2004, when Trapattoni's team
stumbled through that 1–1 draw against Sweden, Trapattoni was
obliged to resign, his tactics under attack and his age an issue
with the Italian news media.

He was replaced by Marcello Lippi, who is also silver-haired
and is equally stubborn, oblivious to criticism and splendidly
pragmatic. Lippi, usually much less loquacious than Trapattoni,
took the helm in 2004, guided Italy to the World Cup in
Germany in 2006 and, after Italy beat France in the final, he
walked away. It was that time of scandal in Italian soccer, with
allegations of match-fixing against Lippi's former team, Juventus.
It was ugly, but Lippi was praised for uniting a team of traumatized players and steering them to the biggest prize. He molded
them into formations of defensive steel on the field, allowed the
occasional flare from the strikers, and it worked. After that,
former Italy player Roberto Donadoni took over, and when Italy
delivered that poor showing at Euro 2008, Lippi answered loud
calls for him to return. Now, Italy leads its qualifying group
over Ireland by two points. Much is being made of the game in
Bari being directed by two of the great Italian tactical masters;

Trapattoni and Lippi will do battle in an encounter between, on
the one hand, a striving and occasionally overachieving team
from an island where soccer was once despised as an English
game, and on the other, the world champions. And it is made
to look like a personal grudge match between Trap and Lippi.
It will be a game for the purists, for people who savor a chess
match of defensive maneuvers and containment.

Hours after I leave a cold, grey Dublin I'm in my hotel in
Giovinazzo, writing up the outline of the grudge-match, tactically intense encounter story. Then I take a taxi to the stadium,
an imposing building that holds sixty-five thousand people. The
Italian football authorities have been very accommodating. I have
a press pass giving me access to everyone and anything. I'm just
in time for Trapattoni's press conference. The room is packed.
Italian journalists clearly admire him as much as the Irish fans.
Little wonder: he gives good quotes. Asked about the utilitarian,
disciplined style he's imposed on Ireland, he shrugs and smiles.
"If I want to see a show, I go to the La Scala concert hall. I don't
go to the football stadium." This goes over well. The Italian press
understands the philosophy. Gaining a point from a tied game,
even if it's 0–0, is a pragmatic victory. "The objective is not to
lose," Trapattoni goes on. "This qualifying thing is draw, win.
But no lose." On a roll, and with the crowded room in the palm
of his hand, he adds, "The memory of beautiful football lasts for
a while. The result lasts forever."

When he's finished, I leave the room, waving at a few Irish
reporters who know me and are, at this point, none too surprised to find me turning up in the south of Italy for a game.
I use the BlackBerry to send Trapattoni's quotes to New York.
Next comes Lippi, who is a bit sullen. The odor of Trapattoni's
charm is still in the room. Lippi is deeply respectful. He admires
Il Trap, he knows the older man well. This will be a good game.
But Lippi knows what's coming: it's the Antonio Cassano question. The Bari-born striker is on a streak in Serie A, scoring
many goals. Yet Lippi declined to put him on the national team.
Cassano has played for Italy several times, but he developed a

reputation as a hothead and a troublemaker in the locker room.
He's older now, obviously more focused, and still gifted and
scoring goals. But Lippi won't budge. No Cassano. For this, he
is loathed in Bari. Lippi dodges questions, knows there's no
point in trying to justify the snubbing of the local hero. He
leaves, smiling tightly.

I finish writing my story and send it to New York. This time,
the story will be in the paper, not just the online edition. I am
foolishly impressed with myself. Serene. Not far away, I know,
thousands of Irish supporters are making Bari a lot less serene. It's
near 10 P.M. when I get back to the hotel. The restaurant is about
to close, but yes, yes, one last meal for me. It is one of the best
I've ever eaten. Simple enough: pasta and seafood, the local bread,
the local wine, some fruit. The elderly waiter, an enormous man,
shakes my hand at the end of the meal. Then he makes a speech
about Giovanni Trapattoni, who is, I gather, a truly great man.
An honest man. A working man who does not forget his roots.
In Bari, they like Trapattoni. This Lippi is a shit. I agree, heartily. I've heard that before. And I realize that I haven't been this
happy in my travels since Vienna.

• • • • •

WEDNESDAY MORNING, from the balcony of my room, I can hear
it—the accents, the joshing, the laughter. Part of the Green Army
has bedded down here. I'm looking at the clouds over the Adriatic
and wondering if the sun is trying to poke through. A man says,
in an accent that sounds like Tipperary, that there's a grand place
for drinks in the tiny port of Giovinazzo. He recommends it
strongly. "Sure, we're well known there," he concludes. A woman's
voice says, "How can ya be well known? Sure, ya only got here
yesterday." The man explains, with the air of a chap who knows
how to conquer places on behalf of the Irish, that all he did was
turn up with his pals, order something to eat and tell the owner
they were from Ireland. "Yer man brought out this bottle of
Jameson, gave us shots on the house, and we polished it off. Decent
man. Loves Trapattoni. We're well known. I'd go again."

Eventually, I go down to the terrace restaurant for coffee and join them. As I arrive, the elderly waiter from the night before comes into work. Still in his raincoat, he wanders onto the terrace and shakes hands with all of us. Me, he remembers. In fact, he remembers the meal I had last night—and the wine. Did I like? Assured that I did, he points to the "Trap's Army" T-shirt won by one of the Irish and tells us all, again, that Trapattoni is a great man. The man with the Tipperary accent looks at me, smiles. "It's a gas, isn't it? They love Trap here. They hate Lippi. Might do us some good tonight."

On a taxi ride into Bari in the afternoon, the driver informs me, in Italian only, and while moving at a terrifying speed past acres and acres of olive groves, that Antonio Cassano is a great son of Bari and a fine player. And Lippi is a shit. I get it. I get it. No translation needed. As we enter Bari's gorgeous old downtown, the driver sees a group of Irish fans outside a bar. We come to a screeching, heart-in-the-mouth stop. He leans out the window and bellows at the Irish: "Trapattoni! Trapattoni!" They cheer him with raised glasses of beer and wine. "Hey, hey, Trapattoni!" he chants on the rest of the ride, delighted with himself. He deposits me near the seafront. I pay him a huge sum for the ride and tell him, with a wink, "Lippi is a shit." He is very well pleased.

Here I am, in the south of Italy, on the day of a World Cup qualifying game. I have eaten well and slept well. I am utterly alone. Not a fan. A journalist, yes, but one from Canada. Of no consequence whatsoever. At around the time I'm being transported around Puglia at white-knuckle speed, *The New York Times* is landing on people's doorsteps across the United States, and, buried in there, is my story about Trapattoni and Lippi. But I'm certain that no one in Bari gives a damn. It feels like I'm twelve years old again, back in Dublin, endlessly in search of a game, a bit of beauty on the field.

I'm wandering around Bari for about five minutes when I see Tom Humphries sitting on a bench. It is both bizarre and gratifying to be greeted on the street in Italy, on the day of a big

game, with "Howya, John." He's got an enormous bag beside
him. Had to check out of the hotel at noon, so he's killing time
until the game. I ask if he plans to fly back to Dublin immediately after the game. Indeed he does—there's a plane carrying
the Irish team, and the press corps, leaving a couple of hours
after the game ends. I am too polite, too much the admirer of
Humphries's work, to just sit down beside him. I'm not going to
be on that special flight tonight, but no matter. I know I'll see
out the hours after the game, searching for a bus, a taxi, a way
back to the hotel. And I don't care.

Along the seafront of the ancient port, several thousand Irish
are relaxing and making friends. Great acres of pasty-white flesh,
stark against the green jerseys and the dark blue water of the
Adriatic, are exposed in the on-off sunshine. Flags and banners
declaring allegiance to Trapattoni are everywhere. The frolick-
ing on the seafront is the fun part. The game will not be wildly
entertaining. The Irish fans get the message from their Italian
leader: "No lose." In fact, they have gone Italian in spirit and
soccer attitude.

• • • • •

SOCCER IS a serious matter in Italy. You can be told that, and
get the idea, but it's only when you're here that the reality sets
in. It's a vitally important matter, nationally, emotionally. The
game itself against Ireland is messy and, in the end, only memorable for the stark mediocrity of the Irish attacks. But the theat-
rics are unforgettable. Before it starts, the Irish team warms up
and Trapattoni wanders around. He shakes hands with everybody. Even the obviously startled medical staff, the ones who are
there with a stretcher in case of a terrible injury. I'm sitting in
the stands, in an excellent seat, beside a man who represents
Agence-France Presse. Behind me are much of the Italian press.
They are hugely amused by Trapattoni's glad-handing. They rise
en masse and begin applauding him, sarcastically but affectionately calling out, "*Il Papa, Il Papa.*" That's what Italians call the
Pope. When The Italian team walks out, and Marcello Lippi's

name is announced, the entire stadium, all sixty thousand people, boo him with gusto.

For a few fleeting moments—shortly after the game opens, just after Italy's Giampaolo Pazzini receives a red card—it looks like the ten-man home team might be in for a desperate fight not to lose. But the Irish threat evaporates quickly. Thanks to a moment of sublime skill from Vincenzo Iaquinta, who breezes through a frightened Irish defense, Italy is ahead 1–0 at the eleventh minute. Then, long periods of superb, disciplined defensive work by Fabio Cannavaro and Giorgio Chiellini make sure that no amount of Irish pressure can seriously threaten a goal. It is easy to forget that Italy is playing with the disadvantage of one fewer man. As Ireland tries to take advantage of Pazzini's dismissal, the truth becomes apparent. Giovanni Trapattoni is rich in experience and skill, but he cannot make world-class players from journeymen and inexperienced kids. Sure, Ireland is without two of its best players—Damien Duff and Aiden McGeady are injured. But the mediocrity becomes highly visible against top opposition. The first forty-five minutes have almost elapsed before Gianluigi Buffon, in Italy's goal, has to make an effort to save a shot from an Irish player.

In truth, the second half becomes such a repetitive, tediously recurring pattern of failed Irish attack and blithe Italian skill that the home crowd becomes bored. For a long stretch, they sing songs about AS Bari, the local team, and, as if suddenly remembering an insult that had stung a lot earlier, they throw taunts at Lippi for refusing to include Cassano. At one point they sing Verdi—the Triumphal March from *Aida*. The crowd can hardly be blamed. There is little happening on the field and Italy looks secure.

Then Trapattoni throws caution to the wind. Unusually for him, throughout the game he makes decisive substitutions. Even more surprising, he puts strikers on the field. The big decision is to replace winger Andy Keogh with Caleb Folan. It's an any-port-in-a-storm decision. Folan is a tall and a physical presence, but far from prolific. He toils for Hull City in the English Premier League

and is rarely in the starting line-up there. He is not going to strike
the fear of an onslaught of goals into the Italian team. What he
does is to throw himself around and generally act as a nuisance.
It helps in the final ten minutes, when this game finally, and
delightfully, comes to life. The Italian defenders are tiring, the
absence of an eleventh player is at last an issue, and the Irish are
desperate to score. Folan heads forward a long ball from Irish
keeper Shay Given. It is a hopeful, not an expert, move. And
Robbie Keane, always quick, even after eighty-eight minutes, sees
it coming and rifles home the goal.

The Irish fans are delirious. "You'll never beat the Irish!"
they sing. In the dying seconds, Ireland almost grabs a winning
goal, but fails. Both sides seem happy when the game ends in
a draw. Trapattoni's real achievement is becoming evident: he's
brought back discipline and a never-say-die attitude to the Irish
team. The self-belief induced by discipline and spirit makes
players transcend mediocrity. The supporters of Italy have no
reason to be unhappy tonight. Their team did what the best
sides always do: spin creativity from a setback. The Irish attack
was blunted with aplomb. A goal was conjured from nothing.
A last blast of force from Ireland intervened at the end. Nothing
serious. Still, the Green Amy is rapturous. The thousands of
them stay and sing as San Nicola Stadium empties. They're singing for themselves. Then I hear it: "The Fields of Athenry."
Always that song. They sing it with a strange intensity. The
man beside me in the press area looks up from his laptop. "What
are they singing?" he asks. "It sounds sad, but they got a draw."
I tell him that, really, it's a long story, and explaining Irish history would take forever.

I'm allowed into the mixed zone where the players run a
gauntlet of waiting reporters. The area is supposed to be shielded
from the public, but somebody has torn a large hole in the covering that's been put over a tall fence. Thousands of Italians are
peering in. They're waiting for Lippi, to give him another blast
of abuse. Meanwhile, they rate the Italian players as they pass.
Some are jeered. Cannavaro gets mild applause and cheers. Buffon

gets prolonged applause. Someone shouts something very rude
at Simone Pepe, and the remark sparks laughter. Pepe glares and
makes a gesture. The crowd responds with what I know is prolonged mockery. It is an extraordinary scene, this. Very Italian.
The public enjoying the chance to hold forth. Two young guys
in tuxedos appear out of nowhere. They work at the restaurant
for VIPs, I reckon. They barge through the reporters and grab
Andrea Pirlo. Then manhandle him into posing for a photo with
them. Pirlo sets his face into a stony gaze and peers at the camera.
The guys then wave the camera at the crowd on the other side
of the fence, in triumph. There's a huge roar.

I find myself talking to Andy Keogh, the young Irish winger
who looks like he's about twelve years old. He seems taken aback
by the bedlam of the scene—the jeering and cheering Italians,
the hordes of reporters, some giggling at the running commentary from the gallery behind the fence. "Well," Keogh says, drawing a deep breath when I ask for his perspective on the game,
"the Italians did what they do well. Play the ground, hold the
ball. We did well to the get the equalizer. Not complaining."
He's correct, and channeling Trapattoni I'm sure. Inside,
Trapattoni gives a short press conference. He's pleased with the
result. A draw away from home against Italy. Could have got a
winner in the end. A point is a point. A good result. "No lose."
He walks out, waving and smiling at the Italian reporters. Lippi
gives a lengthy news conference and then stands in the lobby of
the media center, still talking to any reporter who shows up. I
get the feeling he'll talk to the local Boy Scout publication if they
want comments. Mostly, he issues variations on a thundering
denunciation of the German referee who dismissed Pazzini for a
clumsy challenge on Ireland's John O'Shea. He suggests that the
standard of refereeing is in crisis. Over and over, he does it.

I spend ages outside the stadium, which is by an expressway,
trying to get a taxi. I have several phone conversations with local
taxi companies, each of which concludes with implausible promises. I'm hoping the promise of a long trip to Giovinazzo will
tempt a driver to get to the stadium and take me. No luck. The

Irish reporters stream out, heading for a bus that takes them to
the airport for that flight. Paul Lennon of the *Irish Daily Star* sees
me and says, "John, you have to come to Sofia now." Ireland
will play Bulgaria there in June. I tell him no, I'm planning to
go to Buenos Aires to see Argentina play. He looks at me as if
I'm mad.

Eventually, I share a taxi into Bari with three people. The guy
squeezed in beside me, tall and bald as a billiard ball, says he
works at the Sheraton Hotel, where the Irish team stayed. He
shows me a photo on his cell phone of him with his arm around
an unsmiling Robbie Keane. Everyone in the taxi gets a look,
including the driver. They're all deeply impressed. Billiard Head
tells me that Keane once played for Inter Milan. "He played in
Italia. He is good."

After writing in the hotel room, I get two hours' sleep before
heading to the airport for the flight to Rome and then on to
Dublin. I share a taxi with the man from Tipperary and his cronies. They are very subdued. Seriously hungover. "Are you going
in to work tomorrow?" one asks another. "I am in me arse," is
the reply. "I think I have alcohol poisoning." "Better get yerself
a doctor's note," the Tipperary man advises. And we all guffaw.
Dawn is arriving. At tiny Bari airport, there is a stunning sight:
the floors are strewn with hundreds of sleeping Irish supporters,
most in their green regalia. I'm awed by it. The Green Army at
rest. Job done.

JUNE 6, 2009, BUENOS AIRES, ARGENTINA
ARGENTINA 1, COLOMBIA 0

Maradona, he's talking crazy-talk now.

FIRST, I SEND AN EMAIL to the Argentine Football Association.
Then I send a fax. Then I send another email. No reply. So I
send an email to the Argentine consulate in Toronto, asking for
assistance with arranging press accreditation for the World Cup

qualifying game between Argentina and Colombia in Buenos
Aires. The next day, I hear back. An official at the consulate
would like to meet me. At the appointed time, I meet Alfredo
Bascou, the deputy consul general, for coffee and a chat. It soon
becomes clear that my bona fides are being tested. Do I know a
damn thing about soccer and Argentina? I do. My ace is a mention of Vélez Sársfield, once a top club team in Argentina. I
explain that I have long been interested in the team, as I was
born on Sarsfield Street in a small town in Ireland. I am familiar
with the story of Patrick Sarsfield, the hero of Irish rebellion
against English rule. I've always assumed that Vélez Sársfield was
named after the man. Alfredo is sold. Everything will be arranged,
just leave it to him. He'll have his friend Carlos Pachamé, a
former player and once part of the coaching team for the Argentine
national team, take care of everything.

This is a great turn of events. Over the next few weeks, when
I try to confirm arrangements and get no response, it occurs to
me that it is ignoble to question anything I've been told. Things
will be taken care of. It is a matter of honor. I must find a translator, though. I mention this at work and to friends. Almost
immediately, I hear from a friend of a friend, a man from
Argentina, whose brother-in-law in Buenos Aires would be
happy to help. Then I hear from the brother-in-law, Marcelo
Burello of the University of Buenos Aires. We'll meet, he'll come
to the game, translate, help. Not a problem. I've had more diffi-
culty getting a ticket to a Toronto FC game.

It takes thirteen hours to fly from Toronto to Buenos Aires,
with a brief stop in Santiago, Chile. Me, I'm going for the weekend. At the airport in Toronto, I'm pretty sure I'm the only passenger going to see the soccer game. Must do, though. Diego
Maradona is now the manager of Argentina. He was the greatest
player of his time—infamous, iconic, probably a little mad.
Almost died once, but came back to do this job. He's one of the
most famous people on the planet.

Argentina has been in recession for a long time. The currency
collapsed twice, I think, and Buenos Aires is deeply melancholic,

I'm told. Turns out it is. Wary of being lost and out of the way, I stay at the Hilton in the Puerto Madero area, part of the old port that has been reclaimed and restored. When I check in, there are several messages in sealed envelopes. I open them in my room. Most are to tell me that Carlos Pachamé is waiting for me in the lobby. There, I ask one of the staff if he can tell me where Mr. Pachamé is waiting. He says the name aloud—a little too aloud. Every head turns. Pachamé is here! The famous Pachamé—footballer, coach, pundit, analyst. In this most soccer-obsessed of countries, I'm meeting an important man.

Carlos appears. A good-natured, gentle soul (famous as a player for his bone crunching tackles), he presents me with my game tickets and we have a beer. Maradona is what I want to know about. Carlos shrugs. He's cagey. Who knows what Maradona is doing? Carlos couldn't possibly speculate. No, he won't be at the game. Complicated reasons. Carlos Bilardo, who is officially part of Maradona's management team, a man who coached Argentina to victory at the 1986 World Cup, is an old friend and colleague of Pachamé's. Maradona is, perhaps, not listening to Bilardo. Pachamé will not be at the game, but, he assures me, we will have dinner afterwards. Before bed, I watch the sun set over Puerto Madero and the Bridge of Women. The BlackBerry doesn't work here—the Internet connection is a bit hit-and-miss. But I am in Argentina, and Argentina is playing Colombia in a World Cup qualifying match on Saturday night. It's all worth the time on planes and the money spent.

Like everyone coming here to see soccer—and soccer tourism is a growth business in beleaguered Argentina—I'd anticipated a fabulous atmosphere. Screaming, singing, chanting fans watched uneasily by police, just in case of real trouble. I see the police, for sure, and the fans, all forty-five thousand at River Plate Stadium, but the cops are relaxed and the fans are the edgy ones, not the enthusiastic rabble-rousers I expect. I learn a lot, but mainly this: in Argentina, nothing is what is seems. Everything in soccer here is loaded with local meaning—the grass on the field, the numbers on the players' shirts. The game unfolds on a chilly evening—it's winter here—but a true chill, an authentic sense of something ominous, is in the air as much as the cold wind that has many of Argentina's fans wrapping themselves in blankets. This is Diego Maradona's must-win game as coach of the national team. He is worshipped here, but for his playing skills. In truth, he has yet to convince anyone that he can coach the national team.

Argentina beats Colombia, 1–0. The home side gains two important points towards qualifying for the World Cup. The game is an improvement after Argentina's 6–1 loss to Bolivia in April. But in truth, it's an unconvincing win, marred by a raggedly chaotic display in the first half. This becomes clear as soon as I sit down in the stadium. Marcelo, my guide and translator, points at the field. "It's not as good as it looks," he says. "The grass was painted green the other day. It's in poor shape for an international game, so to make it look better they actually painted the grass. Maradona is supposed to be livid about it. But it's not just about that. This is the River Plate stadium. He's Boca Juniors." Maradona played for Boca Juniors, who have a long-standing rivalry with the River Plate club. "He can't say anything positive about River Plate or this stadium."

Ever since his surprise appointment to the helm of the national team in October of 2008, Maradona has said all the right things. To those who thought he was too much of a flake to hold the office, he answered by appointing a team of advisers, including Carlos Bilardo. To those who said he was too close to the nation's star players in Europe, he responded by fielding teams that also had several Argentina-based players. But the results have been erratic. After starting his reign with three consecutive wins, there was that thrashing by Bolivia, which jeopardized the country's natural assumption that it would be one of the four South American nations to qualify. Unease about Maradona surfaced, but quietly.

The first half shows why. Maradona's team, though filled with stars such as Lionel Messi and Carlos Tévez, looks unsure. There seems to be as much tension between the eleven players on the field as there is among the forty-five thousand supporters in the stands. Playing with a three-man defense, Argentina looks panicked every time Colombia mounts an attack down the flanks. Real Madrid defender Gabriel Heinze is assigned to mark the tall Colombian striker Wason Rentería, but he looks bewildered when Colombia's Juan Zúñiga turned up in his place. Colombia comes close to scoring twice in the first fifteen minutes. In reply, long balls from Juan Sebastián Verón in midfield are sprayed towards Messi, but Colombia's defenders can see the move signaled early and Messi quickly becomes redundant.

I'm interested in the five thousand visiting Colombian supporters. At the Hilton in the morning, the lobby lounge had been full of them—strutting men and their well-coiffed, large-breasted wives and girlfriends. The men drank cognac; the women sipped coffee or Champagne. I had the feeling I was witnessing some comic-book version of Colombian supporters. In the stadium, they cheer and sing with abandon, sensing, with reason, a possible upset victory like the infamous 5–0 triumph over Argentina in 1993, an event that still stings in Buenos Aires.

The game is goalless at halftime, but Colombia looks by far the more organized and dangerous team.

The most-repeated phrase among the Argentine fans at halftime is "I'm worried." Not shouted, but muttered, Marcelo tells me. It's the second-half display by Argentina that keeps alive the idea that Maradona is a good coach, a manager with acumen. What he does is simple enough: he reverts to a four-man defense. The goal, after fifty-six minutes, is no beauty, and it comes from a surprising source. Verón sends in a dipping corner that Colombia fail to clear and defender Daniel Díaz, who looks surprised to find the ball coming towards him, volleys it into the Colombian net. There is a massive sigh of relief in the stadium, and probably across all of Argentina. When the game ends, after some minutes of apparent indecision by the referee about the amount of added time, there is prolonged cheering in the stadium. But throughout the game there has been nothing of the electric atmosphere that one expects when Argentina plays in Buenos Aires.

The muttered phrase "I'm worried" sums it up, though nobody uses the phrase with Maradona afterwards. Instead he's asked, circumspectly, about the difference between the first and second halves. His answer is meandering: "I admit we weren't smooth in the first half. The loose balls fell for Colombia, not us. Messi is being roughed up by other teams, the referee allows it to happen and that's a terrible shame. In this situation, when we had a setback in qualifying for the World Cup, it's the result that matters, not the beauty of the game. In the first half, it was clear we underestimated Colombia. I was angry at halftime. I made substitutions. Some of my players on the field for the first half weren't fit. I realized this and took care of it. The substitutes did better."

And there, buried in the cocky rambling, is a rare admission. Maradona has—almost—admitted he made a mistake, that he's still learning this team-management thing. It's fleeting, and only a half-admission, but there's a sigh of relief in the room. Maradona has kind of, sort of, said he's no genius. This is an extraordinary moment. Diego Maradona is godlike here. The aura that surrounds him is unimaginable in other sports, other countries. Everyone knows his storied past, his fabulous ability with the ball. His success in Europe with Barcelona and Napoli. The game against England at the 1986 World Cup, in which he scored possibly the two most discussed goals in soccer history: one, the infamous "Hand of God" goal, when he palmed the ball into the opposition net; the other, from a stunning solo run past six English players. The cocaine addiction. The ballooning weight. The heart attacks. The official announcement warning that he would likely die within hours, followed by the news that he was going to recover. He is beyond special. He is worshipped, He cannot be questioned openly.

Eventually, he is asked why he played Heinze on the left of the defense, but before the question continues into more implied criticism, Maradona interrupts. "Because I decide," he shouts and then laughs, as if subtle criticism must be some sort of joke. And then, Maradona notes, with an air of exaggerated sadness, that he hadn't felt the home fans were helping the team. "You could hear the Colombians more than the Argentinians, and that shouldn't happen," he says. The reason why, of course, was that the majority of Argentina's fans were biting their nails, worrying and whispering about the faults they saw on the field.

The post-game press conference is a bizarre, bravura one-man performance. For a start, the press room at River Plate Stadium is, literally, a theater. The stadium is also home to a fully functioning school for trainee players and local kids, and this is where the kids put on their shows. There are rows of plush red seats sloping down from the back, and there's a stage big enough for a musical. I'm astonished to be here, in Maradona's presence. He looks so familiar—short, stocky, with the mullet hairdo, the diamond studs in his ears, the defiance in his eyes. Marcelo is translating for me, whispering into my ear in English as I write frantically. Maradona hears the ceaseless whisper and glares at us. I stare back at him, terrified he's going to point and make a scene. He seems to grasp the situation, though—a translator whispering and a reporter writing it down. There's a fleeting smirk on his face for a second. Then he begins ranting about the field. "The field was impossible," he says. "It was impossible to move the ball with ease. It was a field for horses, not football." Then he declares that River Plate could not continue to be the home ground for Argentina. "Unless there is a big change, we will demand another stadium."

"Maradona, he's talking crazy talk now," Marcelo whispers. "This is not about this game. It's about Boca and River Plate again." Then Maradona is gone. A bundle of manic rage, ego and defiance leaves the room and leaves it utterly empty. I think we all feel very, very strange.

• • • • •

LATER THAT night, in a Buenos Aires steakhouse, Marcelo and I have dinner with Carlos Pachamé. An enormous hunk of steak appears on the table. A bottle of wine. A teensy little salad. I am exhausted, jet-lagged and elated. I am very glad that I've decided to make these journeys, to write this book. "Does Maradona listen to Bilardo?" I ask Carlos, as a delicate way of suggesting that Argentina had put in a shabby effort against Colombia. A little unwilling to spill the beans about his personal chats with Bilardo, Carlos says, "Maybe he asks, but he doesn't listen. That is Maradona sometimes. He's Maradona. Does he have to listen?"

I mention how, late in the first half, with Argentina struggling to find a rhythm, one of three forwards, Sergio Agüero, was substituted. "Strange time to make a change," I say. "It's only five minutes to the break."

"Agüero is married to Maradona's daughter," Marcelo says. "Probably picked because he's the son-in-law. He looked useless; maybe Maradona was saving him from more embarrassment." I ask about Javier Pastore, a nineteen-year-old midfielder who is a scoring machine with Huracán in the Argentine Primera División. Pastore has reportedly attracted bids from Manchester United, Milan and Lazio. Couldn't he solve some of Maradona's problems, liven up the national team, as Maradona himself once did as a teenager? "First, he has to marry Maradona's other daughter," Carlos says, and we all laugh.

But, I press on, it was still shocking to see the utter redundancy of Lionel Messi, possibly the most skillful forward in the world. He was easily hustled off the ball by Colombia and looked deeply frustrated as seemingly every ball sent to him by Juan Sebastián Verón, in midfield, was anticipated. Messi, I note, now wears the number 10 shirt for Argentina. That was Maradona's number, and it carries a burden, right? In Argentina, the player who wears the number is simply called "Ten" because he's the playmaker, the magician who conjures chances from instinct. "Who should be 'Ten' now?" I asked. "Riquelme," Marcelo says, referring to Juan Román Riquelme. "But, you know, Riquelme fell out with Maradona a few months ago. They can't stand each other." Even I, an outsider, know Riquelme is a mercurial figure, given to public complaining. But he has been a startlingly inventive attacking midfielder for Villarreal and Argentina. Surely differences could be put aside and the man persuaded to play for his country. "No chance," Carlos answers. "It got personal."

Then Carlos begins explaining how Messi should be used, how the team should move in concert around him. He takes out a pen, turns over the paper place mat and begins drawing. Soon there is page after page of tactical suggestion on the table. Marcelo looks astonished. We are getting a private lesson in tactics. Carlos's pen moves deftly and swiftly, drawing orchestrations of movement for this, that and every possible situation.

To understand so much of soccer in Argentina requires insider knowledge. But Argentina's situation under Maradona is no joke. It is shaky and uncertain. Of that I was certain after a weekend in Buenos Aires. It was worth the trip. Argentina will, after this, lose to Ecuador, Brazil and Paraguay. Maradona will become even more defiant, his grip on Argentina more shaky, before two spectacular, strange games ensure that Argentina qualifies for the World Cup, by a whisker.

SEPTEMBER 5, 2009, BRATISLAVA, SLOVAKIA
SLOVAKIA 2, CZECH REPUBLIC 2

It's peaceful. Really, it's a peaceful rivalry.

I'VE SEEN A FEW international soccer games, obviously, but never in Eastern Europe. And rarely one as raw and rich in rivalry as the draw between Slovakia and the Czech Republic. The game is low in the international soccer hierarchy but promises a full measure of potential meaning and flavor. While much of the world may have been paying keen attention to the game between Argentina and Brazil on the same night, the one in Bratislava is its equal for pride and passion. Slovakia's current slogan to entice tourists is "Slovakia: The Little Big Country." A cute phrase, but it understates Slovakia's ambitions. In Bratislava, there is intense appetite to stop being the little brother to the Czech Republic, especially in sport. For the Slovaks, this is an emotionally charged, potentially myth-making game.

The tension between Czechs and Slovaks makes this one of the great rivalries in world soccer. The two countries used to be one. Since they split, in 1993, the Czechs have been a powerful force in European soccer. The very fact that the neighboring countries have been drawn together in a qualifying group, again, has been a source of excitement for the improving, anxious-to impress Slovaks. The same situation had arisen in qualifying for World Cup 1998 and Euro 2008, but Slovakia was always an also-ran. This time, it's different.

In April, Slovakia traveled to Prague and beat the Czechs 2–1. Czech coach Petr Rada was fired and six players were banned from the team for allegedly partying with local women of dubious repute. On the day of a defeat by the low-rent next-door neighbors, no less. Czech team captain Tomas Ujfalusi responded by announcing his retirement from international games. In Bratislava, they smiled.

The best way to get to Bratislava from the West is to fly to Vienna. The two capital cities are closer than any other pair in the world. And the best way to get from Vienna to Bratislava is to take the boat on the Danube. That's what I do. The journey, which takes an hour and a bit, takes me from laid-back Vienna—where, once again, there's more interest in the opera season than the soccer season—to a city where soccer is central to everything right now. When Austria co-hosted Euro 2008, there was enthusiasm and soccer talk everywhere in that country. Now, it has evaporated. In truth, ice hockey rivals soccer in popularity in Slovakia, thanks to the success of the Stastny brothers and several dozen others who have followed them to the National Hockey League. But on the morning I arrive in small, pretty Bratislava, Slovakia tops its qualifying group. The mission for the national side is to avoid defeat against the Czechs and keep the momentum going for a World Cup debut. Important as that ambition is, it matters even more that a win would ruin the Czechs' chances of qualifying. It seems that international soccer success is within reach for this nation of 5.5 million, and the interest is intense.

Still, they're really not used to that here, and it shows. On the Saturday afternoon of the game, a small contingent of visiting Czech supporters makes more noise in downtown Bratislava than the gathering group of locals headed to the game. A posse of Czech supporters leaves a bar and piles into a white stretch Hummer to get to the stadium. The locals stare, take photos. It looks arrogant and ostentatious to them. Even the Japanese tourists ambling down the cobblestone streets stop to take pictures.

The stadium itself, home to SK Slovan Bratislava of the Corgon Liga, is small, about the size of BMO Field in Toronto (only twenty-four thousand are crammed in here for the big game), and it's old and ramshackle. I can't find the media entrance, and two police officers I ask are also baffled as to its location.

The crowd at the game is almost entirely male, and much beer has been consumed in advance. As I search for the media entrance I see a long line of guys urinating against a wall, all the while cheering for Slovakia—I think. In the press seats, when I find them an hour later, it's a case of grab a chair and hold on to it. Nobody pays attention to the designated seat numbers on the tickets. There are cheerleaders performing suggestive dances before the game, to the Bryan Adams song *When You're Gone.* The crowd roars with pure lust. When Petr Cech, the Czech and Chelsea goalkeeper, leads his team on to the field—carrying a bouquet of flowers, as if to emphasize that Slovakia and the Czech Republic used to be married—he is heartily abused in a manner that involves the sort of language and gesturing that would probably get you jail time in Canada.

The game itself is tense and thrilling and a seesaw all the way. The upshot is that the Czech Republic twice comes from behind and squeaks out a point. That's not enough to bring them back into real contention for a place in South Africa, but it isn't the embarrassment that a loss would have been. It is a goalless first half, with the Czechs piling on the pressure, thanks largely to veteran Jan Koller (newly returned to international duty to help save the Czech prospects), but Slovakia holds firm. After an hour of play, Stanislav Sestak gives Slovakia the lead, but Daniel Pudil evens the score minutes later. The stadium erupts in loud and crazy joy when Marek Hamsik (an emerging star in Italy, playing for Napoli in Serie A) restores the lead with a seventy-third-minute penalty. Then it goes from mayhem to misery for the Slovaks as Hamsik gets two yellow cards within minutes of each other and is sent off. I can feel the cockiness evaporate in the stadium. And the crowd is nearly silent when Milan Baros comes off the bench to score the Czech equalizer in the eighty-fourth minute.

The Slovak press and the fans are woebegone. It doesn't matter that the country is still on course for World Cup qualification; they're depressed because the pesky Czechs weren't beaten. Slovak coach Vladimír Weiss (whose son played well in the game) tells us in the post-game press conference that it's "one game at a time" and that he's not worried.

· · · · ·

IN THE taxi back to the hotel, the driver unleashes a loud laugh when he determines I'm from Canada. Then he tries to charge me twenty euros for an eight-euro ride. No matter. It is the end of an excellent day.

I've arranged to meet Milan, a man from the office of the mayor of Bratislava, on the day after the game. "Obviously, every sports game between the Czech and Slovak republics since the 1993 Velvet Divorce of Czechoslovakia is cause for bedlam. Very emotional and enthusiastic," he says. "Much more for smaller Slovakia than for Czech Republic. It's peaceful. Really, it's a peaceful rivalry. I hope you didn't expect fighting. Now, we have the first real chance to qualify for the big sports event in the most popular game on earth. It is very, very important to us here."

I knew that. A total of forty-five World Cup qualifying games are scheduled to be played within a few days in Europe. There are some glamorous, headline-inducing games: Portugal, desperate for a point against Denmark; France, struggling behind Serbia for points in Group 7 and playing a strong Romania. But I chose the best one to attend.

• • • • •

SLOVAKIA WILL indeed qualify for the World Cup. A few days after the game against the Czechs, it will beat Northern Ireland in Belfast. It will later lose to Slovenia in Bratislava and, on a bitterly cold night in October, in a city in Poland, with heavy snow falling, it will beat Poland and be certain of playing in South Africa. I'll be in London on that night. I send an email of congratulations to Milan in Bratislava and the media officer for the Slovak national team. They send me thanks, and gifts. They've gone giddy in Slovakia.

OCTOBER 10, 2009, DUBLIN, IRELAND
IRELAND 2, ITALY 2

Hope.

DUBLIN AGAIN. Round Two of Ireland and Italy's battles. On this night at Croke Park, Italy qualifies for the World Cup, while the Republic of Ireland is guaranteed a playoff spot.

Some of the younger Irish players play the game of their lives. The odd thing is that, even before the thrilling, fast-paced game begins, Ireland knows it is certain of a playoff spot. Earlier in the day, Bulgaria collapsed against Cyprus in a 4–1 loss, and the hierarchy in Group 8 of European qualifying was solidified. The game could have been what the Italian daily *Corriere dello Sport* calls a *passeggiata*, a pleasant walk, for both teams. But it wasn't. Instead, the newspaper described it as "a heart-stopping match."

Oddly, given how things evolve later, I write this in my report: "Reaching the playoff is no guarantee of anything but potential heartbreak for the Irish. Now that FIFA has decided it will seed the playoff teams, Ireland is likely to find France, Russia or, possibly, Portugal blocking its road to South Africa."

On this night, for the Irish players, there is, possibly, the temptation to pull off a famous victory against world champion

Italy. But the Irish players are still professionals, not awed kids. They don't have to knock themselves out. Certainly the Italian media, not easily amused or impressed, are surprised by the Irish team's performance, and by the atmosphere in Dublin. Although Italy didn't arrive in Ireland until the last minute—they arrived the night before the game—Italian reporters were here for days before. What the Italian reporters discover, and remark on continually, is the cult that surrounds Giovanni Trapattoni in Ireland. As they keep mentioning, everything is about *Il Trap*, not the team. For a week, Dublin has been blanketed by striking billboards created as a pastiche of Barack Obama's presidential election campaign. Trap's face is shown in silhouette, drenched in the green, white and orange colors of the Irish flag. There is only one word on the billboards: Hope. It's unclear what is being advertised: the telecom company that sponsors the team, a fan website or tickets to the game. The only thing certain is that Trap is the man to sell it.

Simultaneously, another advertising campaign for a team sponsor features TV commercials that cheekily present Trap as an Irish Godfather. When the visiting Italian reporters ask Trapattoni about these images, he offers a long, rambling answer about the inevitability of national stereotypes, but makes it clear he isn't in the least bothered by the Mafia reference. Then he changes the subject and begins talking about Egypt's success at the Confederations Cup.

Trapattoni is not without his critics here. He has failed to persuade Manchester City's Stephen Ireland to return to the Irish national team. He decided not to include Andy Reid of Sunderland, a young, gifted attacking midfielder, in the team. Before each game, the local pundits bemoan the absence of those players and attack Trapattoni for being rigid and for choosing young players who, on the face of it, are not of international caliber. For instance, hardly anyone had paid much attention to the career of defender Sean St. Ledger of Preston North End, on loan at Middlesbrough. Then he turned up on Trapattoni's roster. After this game, a lot of people know St. Ledger's name. It is his

diving header that makes it 2–1 for Ireland and, for three minutes, it is St. Ledger who has all of Ireland believing that the
Italians are beaten. It takes a ninetieth-minute, last-gasp goal from
Alberto Gilardino to tie the game. Afterwards, Trapattoni reminds
everyone that his players are "young men, not old" and thus don't
yet know how to hold a one-goal lead for three minutes and not
squander it. He even suggests that his players are too inexperienced to indulge in "time-wasting play," as he calls it.

For me, sitting high in the stands at Croke Park, once the bas-
tion of Gaelic-only games, I see Ireland reborn, again. From the
opening minute, Ireland attacks. The crowd, nearly eighty thousand strong, is thrilled. The noise and enthusiasm are fierce. For
ages, it seems I'm watching what I believe is true—that in soccer,
a small country can conquer a big one through sheer determination and tenacity. It's what happens on the field that matters. The
field is a space in which dream-logic takes over, sometimes spurred
on by the roar of the crowd. I suspect that Trapattoni believes it
too, for all his pragmatism. It is understanding the game, the patterns, and applying discipline to the application of a game plan
that can force the game to become a fable where anything might
happen. *Il Trap* is the reason why ordinary youngsters play the
game of their lives here. Ireland now goes into that playoff setting, guided by Trap, who is no genial older guy out for a
passeggiata. He doesn't do gentle walks. He leads battling armies
of inspired young men on campaigns. On the evidence of this
game, I'm thinking that Ireland can squeeze out a victory against
any team in Europe.

· · · · ·

AFTER THE game I walk through the crowded, late-night Dublin
streets to meet my sister and her partner in a quiet pub. There,
the small crowd is glued to the TV showing the game between
Argentina and Peru. Soon, I am too. It's yet another must-win
game for Maradona and Argentina. The game is being played in
the River Plate Stadium in Buenos Aires. I know it well. It's
pouring rain there, with a hard, driving wind. I'm in time to see

Peru equalize in the dying minutes. An elderly man sitting at
the bar counter shouts out, "Yer man Maradona will be fired.
He's mad, that fella. Mad." Two minutes into stoppage time
Argentina scores for a 2-1 victory. Maradona runs and throws
himself on the ground, sliding in the mud and rain with relief,
with defiant joy. "Jesus mercy," the old man says. "He's mad.
But lucky." Days later Argentina will win again, against Uruguay
and finally be certain of qualifying. And Maradona will unleash
a torrent of pent-up invective against all the doubters.

OCTOBER 14, 2009, LONDON, ENGLAND
ENGLAND 3, BELARUS 0

You'll Never Walk Alone

ON WEDNESDAY MORNING, as I land in London at the start of a mild,
grey day, the final participant in the Fourth Plinth experiment in
Trafalgar Square has her say. The experiment—Antony Gormley's
project allowing 2,400 people to spend an hour each on the plinth
(a pedestal on which a statue usually stands) over one hundred
days—is eccentric, but it gives ordinary people the power to perform or preach in a great public space. While others have railed
against global warming or taken off their clothes, the final person,
Emma Burns, a thirty-year-old medical photographer, draped a
Liverpool FC banner over the plinth and read out the names of
the ninety-six Liverpool supporters who died in the Hillsborough
Stadium disaster in 1989.

I watch it on TV in my hotel, and hear the hundreds of people
watching Burns end the plinth experiment break into a sponta-
neous singing of the Liverpool supporters' song, "You'll Never
Walk Alone." It is a surreal, emotional scene. Soccer is bred in
the bone here. It was fitting and natural that this power-to-the-
people experiment would end with a soccer story, a tragedy from
the past. And then, on Wednesday night at Wembley, I see
England play Belarus in a game that is all about the future of

English soccer. England achieves a scrappy 3–0 victory over tiny Belarus, and some possible team members for England's trip to South Africa emerge, but it is a deeply unsatisfying, frustrating game to attend. All that talent in England. All that narcissism and confidence. All that money. All that English club success, and then this mediocre performance? England has already qualified for the World Cup. This game means little. But it is shockingly bad.

It's always about the past in England. One World Cup triumph and many tragedies big and small; that is England's encumbrance. The World Cup victory of 1966 is fetishized. And there's always the English cockiness, the military-spirit excitability. Then it fizzles out.

It's Fabio Capello's job to fix England, and he's doing a good job. Even he, though, the cagey, terse Italian, must be dismayed by the quality of the players and the public's extraordinary expectations. His job has always been to instill realism and discipline into his players, and now his job will be to persuade the great English public to have realistic expectations in South Africa. On both fronts, he has his work cut out for him.

But at least he has ensured qualification. England has won nine of its ten qualifying games. Mind you, the team was hardly tested by European soccer's great powers. The biggest threats came from Croatia and Ukraine, countries with teams in transition. Otherwise, England was up against the no-threat sides from Kazakhstan, Andorra and Belarus. Having seen England play twice against low-grade opposition, I think English soccer has reached its natural, second-tier level, a fact masked by the success of its club teams—Manchester United, Chelsea and Liverpool—in the European Champions League. The idea of the current England squad being on a par with Germany and Italy is farcical. Most of the players on England's national team are overrated and overpaid, but the news media here are over the moon about them. Most lack discipline, exceptional skills or cunning. Tellingly, few ever succeed when playing for European clubs. Some have done it—Beckham at Real Madrid, for example—but most, one suspects, are simply afraid of the rigors of playing in Spain or Italy.

Capello has fixed some things. He seems to have hushed players who mouth off about striding to easy victory in South Africa. That's key. Some, like John Terry did a few weeks ago, spew optimistic nonsense, and the tabloid press inflates it into a national fervor that is delusional. Capello prefers realism. The week I'm here, Frank Lampard talks about the players' fear of Capello's post-game analysis, his blunt anger and sarcasm about mistakes made on the field. Apparently, Capello has "laser eyes" for mistakes. That's the manager doing his job.

In public, at news conferences, Capello is an intriguing figure. He's intimidating without being dramatic. You can tell that a fierce temper and impatience lurk under his low-key demeanor. He's not a father figure or humorous in the style the English call "matey"—he's the boss who hounds you at work to do more and do better. And yet he can only work with the material handed to him. What is clear from this scrappy, meandering win over Belarus is that Wayne Rooney and Steven Gerrard are England's best attacking players, the ones who can set a game alight and strike fear into opponents. They are both missing from the game because of injury. There isn't a defender from a top-quality team like Italy or Spain who would worry about the skills of stand-in strikers Peter Crouch or the young Gabriel Agbonlahor. Stout-hearted Englishmen they might be, but world-beaters they are not.

One suspects that a pragmatist like Capello knows the strengths and weaknesses of England's situation. Playing at home, England always looks a tad stronger than it is. Even two-thirds full, Wembley Stadium is an intimidating home ground when the supporters sing "Rule, Britannia!" Sitting at Wembley before the game starts, my heart sinks when I see members of the British armed forces, in uniform, carry the flags of the countries into the field. England never lets go of the war imagery. For some national team managers, the crucial task is to inspire journeyman players into performing above their abilities when they put on the national team shirt. For Capello, the key is to acquaint some

players with the fact that they are journeymen, not superstars—
and that discipline and hard work bring victory. That's a tall order
in a country where soccer is bred in the bone and delusion is
rampant. England plays very badly against Belarus. Many in the
crowd begin leaving about fifteen minutes before the game ends.
I join them.

NOVEMBER 14 AND 18, 2009, TORONTO
IRELAND 0, FRANCE 1
FRANCE 1, IRELAND 1
FRANCE WINS 2–1 ON AGGREGATE

Cheat! Cheat! You're a fucking disgrace!

THE END, THEN. The last stop on the journey of qualifying games
for the 2010 World Cup. I'm in McVeigh's to see Ireland play
France in a playoff game to determine which country qualifies
for the World Cup. As I was to see Ireland play Iran in a playoff
series in 2001. The column I wrote about that confrontation
propelled me into eight years of travels and soccer writing.

I haven't been here, in this Irish bar, for several years. Each
time there has been a qualifying game for the big tournaments,
I've been away at the games somewhere around the world. When
I walk through the door of McVeigh's and wait to pay my
twenty-dollar fee to see the first game, I look at the posters and
photos on the wall. I realize that I'm staring at myself. The
column I wrote about the Ireland–Iran games has been copied,
framed and is on the wall. It's an honor, I know. But there is
today's game in Dublin and then the second game in Paris four
days later. These are what matters now.

McVeigh's is packed by game time. A family of nine and of
several generations, with the grandmother in a wheelchair, has
been here for hours, having lunch before the game starts. There
are many young Irish men, too—the ones just arrived from
Ireland. Irish emigration is back. A conversation takes place

behind me. One man asks another how long he's been in Canada. The answer is "twenty years." He asks the same question of a young guy on his other side. The answer is "since Tuesday."

From the moment the TV signal arrives from Dublin, we can tell that the Irish team is fired up even beyond anyone's expectation. While the Irish national anthem is being sung, Damien Duff belts out the Gaelic song, eyes closed and resolute. Of course, I'm reminded of Niall Quinn singing the same anthem with equal ferocity in Japan, years ago. Ireland has more than hope here. France has stumbled through its qualification campaign. A defeat by Austria, two tied games with Romania and another tie with Serbia left France far from automatic qualification. Only a 5–0 victory over the Faroe Islands and a solid 3–1 win over Austria in Paris got France to the playoffs. Serbia won automatic qualification from that group. There have been endless rumors of disarray in the French camp, with stories that the players have lost faith in manager Raymond Domenech and that Thierry Henry has had a falling-out with him.

Ireland starts at a blistering pace. Crunching tackles tell the French superstars they are playing hard men. There is not much evidence of great skill. No short passes or exquisite movements. But the belief and toughness are there. The players believe that the long ball and determination can win the game. France looks vaguely terrified for a while. No amount of skillful, orchestrated movement seems capable of breaking down Ireland. At halftime the score is 0–0 and everyone in McVeigh's is blindly optimistic.

A different French team seems to play in the second half. The Irish have more chances to score, but nothing clicks. Then fluid French passing comes to the fore and the Irish seem to tire. They've gone hell-for-leather all game, and the pace can't be maintained. They're chasing the game. The goal, when it comes, though, is a lucky break for France. Nicolas Anelka's shot deflects off Sean St. Ledger and past Given into the Irish goal. In the final minutes, Ireland races for an equalizer. The French defense is careless and Glenn Whelan almost scores but doesn't. This is far from an emphatic victory by France, but it has scored an away goal, which will count for extra if the game in Paris is tied. There's a deflated mood in McVeigh's. Ireland looked good, but not quite good enough. The game in Paris will be tough.

On Wednesday, I go into McVeigh's a realist. Ireland is unlikely to win this game and qualify for South Africa. Mind you, there's one intangible factor that could boost their chances: there is every likelihood of a huge Irish presence in Paris. The city is a short hop from Dublin or Cork. In 2004, when Ireland played a World Cup qualifying game in Paris, the Stade de France held twenty-five thousand Irish supporters making an extraordinary amount of noise. They sang the French anthem, *La Marseillaise*, with greater gusto than the French supporters. It was very sporting, very Irish and very canny. I'm thinking that Ireland's enthusiasm cannot be underestimated, and France's talent cannot be overestimated.

The first few minutes of the game change everything I've believed. Ireland completely dominates the game from the start. The players break up every French attempt to pass and move forward. Minute by minute, it becomes clearer. Ireland is looking more and more dangerous, resolved to score, treating the French with utter scorn. When the Irish goal comes, it is not unexpected, but it is beautiful. Kevin Kilbane plays a perfect ball to Damien Duff on the left wing and Duff takes it, but suddenly and perfectly pulls it back and feeds it to Robbie Keane. Keane blithely side-foots the ball beyond French goalkeeper Hugo Lloris. Now Ireland is in complete control, on even terms, and both the French team and supporters are utterly aghast.

The Irish domination continues into the second half. The crowd in McVeigh's is ecstatic. We all know that Ireland has the game by the throat and fully deserves to win. We can see Ireland, not France, playing in South Africa. Near-misses abound and Ireland can't quite find the winning goal, but France looks very unlikely to score. The game goes to extra time. Ireland presses. France presses. It's end to end, with Irish ferocity making it look less likely that France can find the way to another goal. Suddenly there's a scramble in the Irish goalmouth. It's hard to see what's happening, but it seems a French player has bundled the ball into the net in a confusion of bodies. Is it a goal? The Irish players run to the referee. They point and slap at their hands, the universal signal for an illegal handball. The referee waves them away. The goal is awarded.

And then comes the moment: the TV replay of the French goal. We all watch, horrified, as, from several angles, we see Thierry Henry handle the ball not once, but twice, to get control of it and pass it to William Gallas, who bundled it into the net. The goal should never have been allowed. Henry cheated, *twice*. It's so stunningly obvious. The referee, it seems, didn't see it. The linesman, it seems, didn't see it. But the whole world can see it.

There are only minutes left. The Irish players look devastated. They know they've been cheated. When the camera shows Thierry Henry, a man in McVeigh's breaks the awful silence by leaping from his chair and roaring, "Cheat! Cheat! You're a fucking disgrace!" We all join him in shouting it at the screen. Then it's over. Damien Duff is in tears. Some of the Irish players are white-faced, traumatized.

I leave McVeigh's immediately. I can't stand to be there—the talk, the anger, the rage at the cheat Henry. I feel I need strong drink, but I can't be drunk. On this evening, I have to write these last sentences in this book. I stand outside for a minute. The injustice was stark. And yet. And yet. The more one lives the more one knows how hope dies. The jubilation of the French players had been so cruel. The French. I remember the first game I covered as a sportswriter. I remember the day before it, in Seoul. Thierry Henry nonchalantly striking the ball at the crossbar and the upright. The arrogance of it. I remember the game against Senegal on the sweet green field in Seoul. I remember El Hadji Diouf and Papa Bouba Diop, the speed of them, darting from the sidelines, like deadly assassins in a sudden uprising against an old oppressor. The terror they caused. The frightened looks on the faces of the French defenders. Papa Bouba Diop dancing by the corner flag when he scored, hips swaying, arms waving, delight on his face. I close my eyes and think of this. I wish it on France again.

It's only a wish, and done with malice, but little do I know on this November evening, how France will reap what it sowed. South Africa will settle matters. Some strange force will take possession of France there, and it will be a bad end.

• • • • •

ON THE streetcar the rush-hour crowd is dense, packed. I close my eyes again and think of the field in Seoul. I must look strange, lost. A woman moving by accidentally brushes her soft fingers against my hard fist gripping the upright rail. She stops, shocked by the distraught look on my face and she's all apologies. I try to smile. The cell phone rings. A voice says, "Well?" And I whisper the score. "Oh," the voice says. "Oh, those poor boys in green." I say, "Boys no longer. The field is a space where we all grow up."

CHAPTER 3

SOUTH AFRICA

BEFORE IT KICKED OFF, I thought the first World Cup held in Africa would be very different compared to tournaments past. If the first World Cup held in Asia back in 2002 presented a template, I felt that upsets would happen. The traditional powers of Europe and South America would be playing in unfamiliar territory. Randomness would be increased in this new circumstance, and countries from the perceived margins of soccer might thrive. I was hopeful that 2010 would see a record six African countries at this World Cup, yet none benefited from the draw that determined their opponents, leaving all of them with a tough task to progress beyond the opening round. But as this book has made clear, factors beyond the truth of tradition and previous success can change the course of any game. The roar of the crowd and the fierce determination to prove the world wrong can and will change everything in some games. It would be winter in South Africa and, as it turned out, in the wet South African winter, the shape of the tournament would shift and twist like the wind on a winter night.

• • • • •

THE SOUNDTRACK in The Football Factory is reggae. Strictly so. If the game isn't on—and the games can be from any number of countries, most of the year—the music is reggae. That's just the way it is: Owner's choice. Roots reggae. Pop reggae.

Obscure, hard-thumping surreal reggae of the serious drugs variety. One minute you're aware of it, and then you're not. The rhythm just throbs.

It's late afternoon on a Thursday, a day of warmth and dappled sunshine in Toronto. A group of young Japanese women are in the Factory, finishing their pints. They've had a few. And they are all slight, chic figures, looking a little absurd waving big pint glasses around with their slim wrists. They clink them together, giggling. They are a little tipsy, and happy as the day is long. Behind them is a giant poster on the wall that they probably don't even notice. But I do. It features Bob Marley, toying with a soccer ball, over and over, in frame after frame. And it declares Marley's phrase: "Football is part of I. When I play, the world wakes up around me."

The afternoon hours have passed in a glorious tangle of images, feelings, squeals, groans, and all manner of responsiveness. The Danes came in first: Male, cocky, cheerful as they always are, and interested in beer. Group E's crucial game would begin soon: Japan against Denmark to determine who would follow the Netherlands into the last 16. At the last minute, some 60 or 70 Japan supporters arrived en masse. No one knows why or how they found this place, of all places, to see the game. No one asks. They probably found it on the Internet and "Football Factory" sounded nice and neutral, merely devoted to the game. Not some ex-pat hangout or phony Irish/English bar. This was a place to be.

If anyone stepped outside on the patios, they'd have heard the sound—that distinct sound of Toronto in these dreamlike days— of helicopters rattling in the skies, going this way and that with little apparent purpose. The downtown core is emptying, fenced-off, caged in. The G20 Summit is about to open. Already, the G8 Summit is underway an hour from here, and there's an aberrant mood downtown. In this hallucinatory period, two worlds keep on colliding and converging. Absorbing a good portion of the World Cup through the prism of the G20 tensions is like looking at a dreamscape. The conventional world—wherein police gather, huge dividing fences appear and tensions mount—is predictable, no matter how traumatizing the brute force of it might become. The dreamscape is a balm, but not an escape. It has sharp shifts in tone and its logic is flexible and infuriating, yet it has more consistency and holds more comfort because it has the texture of life lived, life felt. There is moral degeneration in the ostentatious signifiers of repression that are the hallmark of the summits, and conversely, there is a moral uplift in the World Cup.

Here inside the bar, we are simultaneously aware and dismissive of the slowly compelling coercion of the city. Up the street, at the corner of Queen West and Bathurst, two maroon-colored vans are parked. About twenty cops seem to have arrived at this, one of Toronto's toughest corners. They stand round with no apparent purpose. I notice that all the panhandlers, crack-addicts and other street denizens seem to have disappeared, except for one. He's passed out on the sidewalk, a little ways east. He has no idea. Neither do the cops. And, anyway, nothing much matters except what's unfolding here, in the bar. From a nearby alley comes the distinct odor of marijuana.

The Danes open strongly but, as in their previous two games, look unsteady in defense. Japan oozes confidence, blithely indifferent to the Danish threat. In the first half, two sublime goals from superbly-taken free kicks mean Japan has the game by the throat. The bottle-blond Japanese striker Keisuke Honda is electrifying. The ball bends and curls to his will. Japan looks utterly self-assured, uncaring about those tall Danes running around, chasing the ball. Each sweet movement is followed with gasps, squeals while the Danes, in the bar and on the field, look bewildered. On and on it goes, this mad dance. Near the end, Denmark is awarded a penalty. Japan's goalkeeper stops it with aplomb, but the Danish striker Jon-Dahl Tomasson meets the rebound and bundles it in. Hope for Denmark, but not for long: Honda sashays into the Danish penalty area, makes a dunce of goalkeeper Thomas Sorensen and, ever the gentleman, passes to Shinji Okazaki to score. It's done. The Danes are gone.

In the aftermath, the young Japanese men sit outside and

smoke. They sit in a circle on the ground, away from the patio where no one ever sits. They are as chic as the young women, all wearing expensive denim and t-shirts. One wears a Japan team shirt on his head and manages to look avant-garde and stylish while doing it. I recall my days in Japan in 2002, and all those delirious youths, frantically buying team merchandise, fumbling toward understanding the game and the torment of its significance. Here, they have submitted to it in their own way. Overhead, the helicopters go around and around, buzzing, rattling. Nobody pays any attention.

A minute's walk away, the Prague Deli is near empty but filled with the lingering feel of hard ardor. A man sits in the window seat, drinking coffee. He's been here for hours, smiling, and trying to sober up. The Prague is Czech, strictly speaking, but the Czechs and Slovaks had a soft, sweet divorce and the Slovaks hang out there for the tournament. Earlier in the day, little Slovakia threw Italy out of the World Cup. Since dawn, there's been a van with a Slovak flag on it parked across the street from my house. It belongs to a plumbing company, according to the name on the side. No one has come to drive it away, and no one will for another day. The driver is lost, understandably. Ten minutes' walk to the north, College Street, one of the Italian hubs, is subdued, and probably perplexed about the morning's defeat. I'm not going there, and neither is the man steadily drinking coffee and smiling at the world. The Slovak victory spilled onto Queen Street earlier, a great wave of delight you could taste and still sense, many hours later. Police cars go by, one after another after another, oblivious.

Back at The Football Factory, the last glasses clink to the sound of easy laughter. The reggae starts up. Bob Marley's Jamaican face gazes down as the last of the Japanese ladies leave. I write down the words to ensure I remember: "Football is part of I. When I play, the world wakes up around me." The helicopters are in the sky, buzzing, droning, still. No one looks up. The police cars go by. No one looks.

• • • • •

I'M NOT in South Africa, obviously. The recession and the rig-
marole of work—both professional and personal—prevent that
happening. Instead, I'm here in Canada, still and forever simultaneously the best and strangest place to experience a World Cup.
The country embraces the tournament, especially Toronto, and
all the attendant surface meaning, but animosity is spat out too,
infrequently but sharply. All of this tangled-up tension and joy
is captured for me on the morning that World Cup 2010 opens
in South Africa. It's very early, shortly after 6 A.M. and I'm walking the downtown streets on my way to a CBC radio interview
that is just one small part of a big World Cup party being thrown
outdoors by CBC. The broadcaster has invited the fans of each
of the 32 countries playing at the World Cup to come out, wear
their team shirts and scarves, and wave their flags. I can hear the
noise emanating from a few streets away, and I can feel the
BlackBerry buzzing in my pocket. There's a message—it tells me
that yes, actually, I can write about the World Cup for my paper.
First the plan was to have me write commentary for several
weeks—I'd written this book about soccer, after all—but that
plan was vetoed. Now the veto has been overturned. Talk about
complicated feelings.

There is a punchy, excited quality to the radio show and party.
Before I join the on-air discussion, two men from South Africa
are interviewed, one young and white, the other older and black.
The young man ended up in Canada through some quirk of work.
The older man, who had been jailed several times in South Africa
for being an anti-Apartheid activist, followed his family here. The
two talk eloquently about what the World Cup means to their
home country—an acknowledgment of South Africa's present, a
rejection of its past, and how the tournament has brought people
there together in an emotional way that promises a better future.
When they get up from the table and the microphones, both stand
near me and look up at the giant TV screen showing images of
the stadium in Johannesburg. The old man turns to smile at the

younger man, who puts his hand out for a handshake. The older man ignores the hand, swiftly embraces him and I can hear him say one word as he hugs hard: "Brother."

I watch the opening ceremony and the game between South Africa and Mexico in the company of Deon Meyer, the South African thriller writer. He's in Toronto at the end of a multi-continent book tour and the publishers have arranged for us to have breakfast while watching the TV images from Johannesburg. There's sparking wine, orange juice and lots of food. Meyer is a good-natured man. An impressive figure with cropped grey hair, he's the same age as me. But, having looked into his background, I'm startled by the vastly different lives we've had. He was a newspaper man, worked in advertising and became a writer of books, as I am. But he did military service and worked a good part of his adult life in a country that was an international pariah, a racist state. The year in which he published his first book, 1994, was the year that South Africa held its first universal-suffrage election and the African National Congress swept to power.

We watch the opening ceremonies in near silence. I can feel Meyer's excitement; he laughs and slaps his hand on the table when the TV shows Bishop Desmond Tutu dancing away to music in the VIP area. "Look at the Bishop!" he shouts. "A wonderful man, the Bishop." Meyer tells me that he has no patience for the pessimism about South Africa the country or South Africa the World Cup host. He was in Germany, France and England, he says, before arriving in Canada. "Negative, negative, negative" he says. "Almost every interview I did had this undercurrent of gloom. They all expect it to be a disaster. Soccer fans murdered on the streets. No transportation. The stadiums falling down. I almost lost it with this French reporter. I started counting. He made fourteen negative remarks about South Africa." So I asked him, "And in South Africa itself? He says "There is joy. It's palpable. We have all these problems, but this is something to celebrate. It's there on the surface, it's there in people's hearts."

Others come to join us for the opening game. Meyer is tense; I can tell he's trying not to choke up. The South African national anthem is a hard few minutes for him, with emotions close to overflowing. Mine are too. I've barely slept for several days, and in the past few weeks I've been to both coasts of Canada and to Montreal completing an endless series of interviews about the World Cup. And at last this glorious morning: I could get emotional here, on the spot. Then the game begins. The noise in the stadium in Johannesburg sounds like ecstasy. Both teams look nervous and play cautiously for a while. Mexico is the better team, with tightly controlled passing and an assuredness in possession. South Africa tries to keep up, all spirit and grit. At halftime, Deon Meyer, says, "I'm optimistic. They soaked up the pressure. Let's see what happens." Then he has to step outside. The tension is getting to him.

As the second half opens it's obvious South Africa has been told to run, play, and enjoy the game. There are long, sweeping passes and noise in the stadium goes up several levels. Then it arrives. Siphiwe Tshabalala races down the left flank, the ball played through to him. He takes it with poise, keeps going and fires in a thunderbolt with his left foot. The first goal of this World Cup has been scored. Deon is on his feet, shouting, "Yes, yes!" There's a fairytale air about the game now—the South African team, arguably the weakest of the six African countries in the tournament, could start with a glorious victory. But Mexico settles. The team is untroubled and begins to hold possession, moving the ball around the field with skillful ease.

The inevitable equalizing goal comes 11 minutes from the end via Rafael Márquez. This rattles the South Africans, and there is much running and chasing. Katlego Mphela breaks free in the dying minutes but hits the post with a well-taken kick. A draw is a fair result and everybody seems happy with it. Deon leaves to walk the streets, he says, soak up what he's seen and call home. In the afternoon, exhausted, I watch France and Uruguay play to a mundane goalless draw in the second game of this World Cup. There is nothing to savor in the game except Uruguay's firm determination and the ceaseless threat of Diego Forlan scoring. France looks hopelessly uncoordinated, and the players seem confused about their roles. If anything, they look worse than in the controversial playoff games against Ireland. There is, I think, the whiff of something rotten about France.

Some of the themes of this World Cup begin to emerge already. TV viewers are irritated by the tens of thousands of honking vuvuzelas in the stadium. South Africa looked like an enthusiastic team but couldn't really get a grip on the game. Will all the African teams be outclassed? Mexico looked surprisingly efficient and skilled. Uruguay was impressively unawed and anxious to score. Is this the time for Central and South American teams to rise up and eclipse Europe?

• • • • •

I SPEND ages trying to learn where Americans will gather to watch the US play England. I'm told that a non-descript, English-themed pub is the likeliest place because it's close to the American consulate in Toronto and is a regular haunt of the staff. In the cab ride to the bar, the taxi driver asks me what I do for a living and when I tell him I'm a journalist, he has twenty questions about the upcoming G20 Summit. Why does it cost so much? What possible security can be bought for $1 billion? Who are the twenty leaders, anyway? How many jobs could be created with $1 billion? Why can't it be held on a ship somewhere? Why is nobody willing to compensate people who will lose money, like cab drivers? The guy is so agitated that he makes two wrong turns, and I'm anxious about seeing the start of the game. As we pull up outside the bar, I ask him what team he is supporting in the World Cup. Argentina. Why? "Maradona. He's my guy. Doesn't give a rat's ass."

Inside, it's standing room only. All I can see and hear are people supporting England. I stand by the bar counter and, soon, two English guys stand behind me. One does an irritating running commentary, addressing the English players by their first names. "Come on John, get a foot in." "Alright Frank, take it easy. No need to panic, it's only the Americans." Every now and then, his companion cackles. After five minutes of typical England opening play—all speed and attack with gusto—England is ahead. Steven Gerrard looks sublimely confident and carefree as he celebrates the goal.

For a time, the life is sucked out of the game. The Americans regroup, settle and begin their methodical, spirited fight back, much like they always do. Underestimated and undeterred, they become grimly determined. Michael Bradley prowls the midfield, breaking down every England move and spraying the ball to the left and right. Not everything works smoothly but it soon becomes obvious that England is creakingly dull-witted. Especially Wayne Rooney. The English players are disappearing from the game as the first half draws to a close and the Americans' hard-won dominance becomes clear. Clint Dempsey tries a shot from long range. Robert Green in the England goal tries to stop it, but he doesn't. The ball seems to bounce, slip away from his hands and dribble over the line. There's a quiet, mass groan in the bar. A few titters from people who realize the goal is profoundly embarrassing and can't help but giggle in some kind of nervous embarrassment. Silence.

As I watch the slow-motion replay and we all see the ball dribble across the line, the silence is shattered. "Yes!" a voice roars. "Yes! Yes! Yes! USA!" Next there's a pause and, even louder, another shout: "U! S! fuckin' A!" See that? See that? That's the U.S. fuckin' A scoring. It ain't over!" I look at the guy doing the shouting: a short bespectacled figure in his late twenties, he has one arm in the air. He looks at his friends, four of them at the table, all grinning. He looks around him. "Limeys! Fuckers!"

The English guy behind me asks his companion, "Did he just call us "Limey fuckers?" There is no reply. It's all very, very embarrassing. A ridiculous goal, and the world knows it, but it seemed inevitable. The American players just kept going, maintaining their composure after that early England goal. Undiminished, shrewd and focused, they were already taking control of the game.

The second half unfolds as an excruciatingly tense drama. The

England fans in the stadium sing "God Save the Queen." The England fans in the bar urge Wayne Rooney and Emile Heskey on. Heskey, who had created England's goal, begins to look tired and defeated. The American attacks come in waves. Splendidly organized and with Michael Bradley as maestro, looking for opportunities, they look formidably cool. Jozy Altidore races forward like a sprinter and the England defence panics. No more goals come, but the end result is satisfying—a stuffy, unimaginative England pegged back by a hard-working, determined U.S. team.

This World Cup has put soccer strangely at the forefront of the more serious American media. The New Yorker published a lengthy story about the US defeating England at the World Cup in 1950, and goalkeeper Tim Howard is presented as a compelling, tortured figure heading to South Africa. This is a very American story—the urge to find a lone figure whose story can encapsulate everything. It is slightly spurious because this American team is very much a team, a group working in remarkable harmony and armed with awesome obstinacy. The New York Times instigates a debate between columnists in which "American insularity" and "parochialism" is mentioned. David Brooks writes this: "We in this country prefer pastimes that are rational and quantifiable. Football plays can be drawn up in a playbook and baseball lends itself to statistical analysis. But the rest of the world follows a sport that rewards resilience and neuroticism. Soccer is a sport perfectly designed to reinforce a tragic view of the universe, because basically it is a long series of frustrations leading up to near certain heartbreak." This is astute, and there is much more perplexing drama to come.

• • • • •

THE NEXT day, Ghana beats Serbia 1–0, a solid victory for one African team, though the soccer-watching world is more interested in the German team that trounces Australia 4–0. This is a new Germany, all speed and flair. Michael Ballack is injured and absent but it means little. Bastian Schweinsteiger controls the

midfield and the two newcomers, Mesut Özil and Thomas
Mueller, run rampant. All bets are off on Germany. The team
looks astoundingly precocious.

When I go to watch Italy play Paraguay in its first game, I
stay away from the Italian neighborhoods in Toronto. Instead,
I'm in a generic sports bar, with the game showing simultaneously on twenty-six TV screens. For company I have four guys
who say they're from Hong Kong, originally, but want to be
described as Canadian. Their interest in the game is perverse—
they loathe Italy. When Paraguay goes ahead after 39 minutes,
the bar is filled with the sound of their glee. These guys only
care about Italy being humiliated. They giggle at missed passes
and shout for Paraguay to move forward. Eventually Italy equalizes and the game ends 1–1. This is obviously an aging Italy, the
same basic team held to two tied games by Ireland. There is a
skilled methodology to their defense, but no imagination in
attack.

Before Brazil plays North Korea, no one knows how to read
the game. Some expect Brazil to cruise to a multi-goal victory,
while others expect the Koreans to be defensive, hard-tackling
and intent on destroying Brazil's rhythm. The game is a wonderful revelation. North Korea's star striker Jong Tae-se cries
during their national anthem and, minutes later, looks like the
architect of a phenomenal upset. His team play splendidly tidy,
superbly organized soccer, and the defenders aren't interested in
hacking at Brazil. For long periods the game is evenly balanced
and vastly entertaining. The Koreans are extraordinary tacticians,
managing to hold possession and keep Brazil at bay, a far cry
from the thugs some expected. They never argue with the referee and look embarrassed when a foul is called. In the end, it
takes a goal of magical skill to get Brazil ahead and the South
Americans win 2–1, but the game stands out for multiple reasons.
Brazil looked beatable; the pure tactical skill by North Korea
made the game utterly absorbing to watch. It was a chess match,
with Brazil unable to use its flair to breeze past the opposition.
And while it has become common among pundits to note that

Brazil no longer plays in the rhythmic, fluid style sometimes called Samba Soccer, this team looks shackled, without cadence, range or liberty.

The day after Brazil's uneasy win, Spain puzzled me and countless others, losing to Switzerland in their opening game. It's an early morning game and I watch alone at home. The European champions take total control of the game but fail to find the sharpness needed to score a goal. They possess and pass slickly, but the Swiss defend stubbornly. There is profound tension in the game, an uptight thrill. It is the antithesis of the Spanish style that is the deciding factor—a long, hopeful ball finds its way through to Swiss player Gelson Fernandes, and, after awkward errors by Spain's defense, he bundles it into the net. Spain looks rusty, smug even. I sense that this is the wake-up call, the reminder that Spain needs resolve as well as skill to win at a tournament. The result puts pressure on Spain and throws the expected pattern of the World Cup into doubt. If they finish second in Group H, they'd be forced to face Brazil in the second round.

The game between the U.S. and Slovenia is thrilling, but for very different reasons. I watch it in the same nondescript sports bar where I saw Italy play Paraguay. The handful of people present are neutral observers. Slovenia takes charge and then the Americans, as they must, come battling back. For the second time, the American team fails to coalesce and settle quickly. Slovenia takes swift advantage, blunting any growing American power of attack. At half-time, Slovenia leads 2–0. The second half is vastly different. Manager Bob Bradley makes two changes to give the Americans greater speed and a cutting edge. They roar back. Landon Donovan is a dynamo and scores superbly off a Slovenian mistake. Michael Bradley looks even more impressive than he did against England. The Americans swarm Slovenia, determined, driven and shockingly resilient. Its 2–2 when Bradley scores in the 82nd minute, but the Americans want a winner. Maurice Edu is on the field for the U.S., a strapping, likeable young man who was a familiar figure—he played for Toronto

FC back in 2007. The crowd in the bar, whom I imagined to be
subtly anti-American, respond to that. Edu is American but in
the way of soccer these days, ours too. He worked within shouting distance of here. He collects a free kick from Donovan and
thumps it high into the net. It's a glorious goal. The referee dis-
allows it, but it's not clear why. Edu was onside. If there was
pushing and tugging, it was by the Slovenians and the U.S. had
the advantage. The small crowd in the bar mutters about bad
luck. I leave and minutes later, at home, I'm watching the replay
footage alone and I'm outraged, mystified. I curse and wake up
my cat who paces, back and forth, eyeing me suspiciously, sensing conflict. Inside 24 hours it seems that half the population of
the U.S. is outraged and mystified too. The inevitable fury
unfolds. Why is there no video replay?

Sepp Blatter, the president of FIFA, is steadfastly against the
use of video technology in soccer. No video replay to determine
if a player was offside, and no little microchip in the ball to
determine if it crossed the line. Arguing against Blatter and those
who agree with him is rather like arguing about religious faith.
Leave logic out of it; this argument is about the soul of soccer.
Does a "soul" exist? Not in a real, tangible way. In sport, though,
it surely does.

I'm with Blatter, though I know it makes no sense. It's a question of faith. I don't believe in God but I do believe in the soul
of soccer. A week before this World Cup started, Blatter again
dismissed the introduction of video or microchip technology.
"Society is not perfect, football is not perfect, it must retain its
human face," he said. In this matter, Blatter is not just adhering
to a sort-of religious faith in soccer. He's taking a fundamentalist
view. The issue is particularly difficult for followers of North
American sports to understand. Games followed here—NHL
hockey, NFL football, baseball and so forth—are driven by technology these days. A controversial incident happens and the game
stops. Somebody looks at the video replay. Viewers watching on
TV see the slow-motion replay. A decision is made and eventually, the game goes on.

Soccer, on the other hand, is not a stop-start game. It flows. As some people see the matter, it's bad enough when an already slow-moving, defensive game is frequently interrupted by fouls. To have more stoppages would be unacceptable. I know, I know: Go tell the Americans who saw they were obviously denied a good, winning goal against Slovenia. And there's part of the problem, maybe—the Americans. Blatter, like FIFA chiefs before him, would like soccer to have a bigger presence in the U.S.. But, really, he doesn't care that much. In fact he's probably proud of the fact that FIFA is so powerful without the U.S. being a dominant influence.

And I know what Blatter means when he talks about the "human" face of the game. Soccer is a brutal game. Not because players kick each other on the field, but because it's like life, as brutal, illogical and transfixing as life itself. Disappointment lurks. Sorrow is under the surface. All adults know that. Sometimes, but not always, cheaters get their come-uppance, like the French are at this World Cup.

The referee can be fooled into believing what everyone else knows is not true. That's also part of life. To believe in the purity of the game as it is, without the benefits of technology, is to believe that things even out in the end. It's to believe, I suppose, that Karma exists. That might seem naive, but in the soccer world it's the North American sports fans that are naive. They believe, with an admirably youthful sense of right and wrong, that justice always prevails. It doesn't in real life. Injustice happens, but time passes, the world turns just as the ball does during the game. The whole point of the game is that the ball turns, moves forward, much like we do. Call it illogical, and I do, but there's a reason why video technology is not used in soccer. It's rather like the reason for a religious belief.

• • • • •

AFTER SEEING the U.S. held to a draw against Slovenia, I go out to see England play Algeria. I meet up with my friend Simon, an Englishman to the core. We are in a phony Irish bar. There's a gaggle of us who all know each other, vaguely. When the game starts I realize that many of the crowd are women and in their twenties. This is an illumination of the soccer nation here. They're hardcore Toronto FC fans, connoisseurs of Italy and Portugal, knowledgable and resentful of the space taken up by England in the media. David Beckham sits on the bench in a good suit, looking worried. As well he might. A young woman leans in to me and says, "Have you seen Beckham's bitch-face? It's hilarious." Soon enough, the "bitch-face" is donned. England looks hopeless, adrift and second-rate. Beckham, who is nothing more than a mascot, glares. The crowd in the bar lose interest. The G20 Summit is days away. Everyone has a day or two off work because downtown will be closed. There is excitement as people plan their days off around the games. "Fuck me! I can watch Brazil play Portugal!" England earns a 0–0 draw with Algeria.

The shape of the World Cup shifts. It seems like old Europe is wilting in South Africa. Italy sneaks a 1–1 draw with New Zealand. The French team implodes in feuding and rage at Raymond Domenech, newspapers full of all the sordid stories. Nicolas Anelka unleashes foul-mouthed fury at Domenech and is sent home early. The other players decline to train, supporting their exiled friend. France loses to South Africa. The team is out of the World Cup, without winning a game and after scoring a single goal. It is ignominy not predicted, but deserved. There is a rank sourness about France, as there was on that November night when the team sealed its place in the World Cup.

Argentina, with Maradona dancing, waving and pouring forth passion on the sideline, looks unbeatable. On that sunny day when I end up at The Football Factory to see Japan play Denmark, Slovakia tosses Italy aside in a thrilling game. I remember the Slovakian supporters in Bratislava the night I was there—the incandescent male cacophony of insults and beery camaraderie. What Bratislava must be like on this summer night. Spain finds its feet, after that shocking loss to Switzerland and defeats Honduras. The game that sticks, mind you, is the Americans' thrilling, dying-moments defeat of Algeria. Watching alone at home, I realize I have been smitten by the Americans since that night in Chicago when the team and the fans showed up in the middle of baseball fever, to do their jobs, and win. I saw more than moxie there. It was true American optimism, determination and daring. The players at the World Cup are good, only a handful are as yet great. They are undervalued by the opposition, and they don't care.

It is a breathtaking thing: Altidore races down the right and crosses to Dempsey, who has never ever stopped running. Dempsey meets it cleanly. It's a point-blank shot but parried by the goalkeeper. The ball slides into the path of Donovan, who hammers it into the net and all those worried Americans into rapture. This is a hardboiled team.

• • • • •

OFF TO a place called the Plaza Flamingo, on a Friday afternoon, to see Spain play Chile. The city has become a maze. Some streets closed, others partially open but you don't want to go there. There are 15,000 police officers in the downtown core for the G20 thing. The police move in packs, on foot, on bikes and in cars. There are special, temporary laws for these days, the TV news says. The police can detain, question and search you for any reason. Mass demonstrations are expected. The police, the city and all levels of government have formed a deliberately hostile face to the world. No one seems to be coming or going to work. Helicopters rattle all day in the sky. And still all the talk on the street is of this, the intricate drama that radiates from South Africa.

The Flamingo is a sprawling place—dining, dancing and live entertainment. A sign says that salsa lessons are offered, but that's not traditional salsa booming out of giant speakers. It's crashing guitars followed by the throbbing beat of Latin disco. The mood, before you even enter in broad daylight, is feverish, lightheaded.

There's a fuss getting in. About thirty Chilean supporters arrive just before me, and inside, the place already looks packed.

The person I'm meeting calls on the cell phone: "I can see the top of your head out there. There's a seat for you." The man at the door is frazzled. Inside, the music is ferociously loud, bone-shaking. There's a giant screen showing the end of the Cote D'Ivoire/North Korea game. Nobody is paying attention. Two young women in teensy Brazil shirts are dancing by the bar for themselves only, two brunette Shakiras.

A drink ordered, I look around. There are hundreds of women of all ages in Chilean shirts, many waving Chilean flags. Some are busy painting each other's faces in Chile's colors. It's like a beauty salon in the middle of the supporters at a stadium. Nobody can hear anyone talk. People shout. The women take pictures of each other and their newly-painted faces. I'm sitting across from a man who looks vaguely amused. A handshake. Can't hear anything he's saying. Can't hear my friend either. We point and gesture.

Game time. The music stops. On the giant screen the footage from the Spanish-language channel shows the players in the tunnel. There's a deafening roar. Everyone stands for the national anthems. Everybody. No Anglo gets away with being a mere observer. While the referee calls the team captains together, the singing starts: *"Olé, Olé, Olé, Olé, Chile!"* Two young women stand on their chairs and roar "España!" over and over. The crowd, it seems, is two-thirds Chilean and one-third Spanish. I'm staring at the brazen Spanish women standing on their seats, and the Chilean guy who shook my hand is laughing at me, the gawking tourist who wandered over from the other part of the World Cup, absurdly concerned with England or Germany. No dancing over there, his laugh says, no sea of women who look like this, sound like this, or dance like this.

Spain needs to win. Chile needs to win. But it all depends on the result of the other game—Switzerland plays Honduras, and a tied game there will see both Spain and Chile advance. Chile starts brightly, all attack and gusto. Short passes, darting runs. A shiver of delight goes through the mass of people around me whenever Alexis Sanchez has the ball. The pace is furious; goals are imminent and everyone knows it. In the tightly packed crowd, people grip each other, instinctively, to express the tension. We have all vanished into it, the endless running, the one-two passes, the sliding tackles, the goalkeeper soaring to get a fingertip to the ball. This is happiness. This is packed, frantic euphoria.

Referee Marco Rodriguez of Mexico, barrel-chested and stern-faced, comes and goes amid the flowing drama, sometimes as a hero waving off claims for fouls, and sometimes as a villain. Now he's giving out yellow cards to Chile. Marco Estrada's got one and Estrada is fiery. A mass of people by the bar scream insults at the referee. Spain is getting a grip on the game now. Sharp, sweet passing movements. Fernando Torres is on the move. The Chilean keeper panics, clearing the ball to David Villa who is far, far from goal but Villa hits it sweetly, stroking it firmly from distance. Goal! Beautiful one. The heaving mass, undaunted, roars Chile on and, yes, yes, Chile race forward. Then madness and chaos as Spain score again from another exquisite passing move. Emotions are flaring on the field. The referee reaches into his pocket and, cruelly, issues another yellow to Estrada. Two yellows is one red, and so Estrada's dismissed, leaving Chile down to ten men. The referee, I am informed, is commonly known as "Dracula."

At halftime, nobody's interested in the punditry on the screen. The music starts up again. Seeking air on the tiny front patio I find four guys smoking in one corner and three girls dancing in the other. The guy manning the door looks exhausted now. Not the Chilean team. Back on the field, they lay siege to Spain's goal. A man down but seething with lust to score, they quickly do as Rodrigo Millar tries a what-the-hell shot from a distance. Spain's defenders are unsure, and the ball is deflected into the net. Pandemonium. I notice that everyone around me has changed places. Friends to be hugged, smiling faces to be kissed. The young Spanish ladies are in front of me again, standing on their chairs and shouting. No one can hear them, or anything else.

Chile defends. Spain makes substitutions. Cesc Fabregas comes on. There's a roar for that from somewhere. The score from the other game is flashed on the screen: Switzerland 0, Honduras 0. If it stays that way, both Spain and Chile survive for the next round. This game slows, languorously, maddeningly. Spain passes the ball endlessly in the middle, declining to move forward. No one is sure what's happening but the euphoria never evaporates. Just stay here and everything will be alright. Move the ball, here, here, stay in possession. Caress it. Tense, hot minutes elapse, and then it's over. Spain wins 2–1. The music—some serious rock 'n' roll with big guitar sounds and major chords—rises up. Something about España. A march starts onto the street. Honking horns and waving flags. Dozens of women are dancing on the sidewalk. Hip-shifting, lascivious dancing. What a party this is. Doesn't matter who won or lost.

Down the street, I stop for coffee. I'm not drunk but feel the need to sober up. Across the street, a young man in a Spain shirt with Torres on the back kisses his girlfriend, a young woman in cut-off jeans and a yellow t-shirt that just says "Spain." She shimmies. Then he pulls her into the doorway of a sushi restaurant and kisses her again. The kiss lasts a full seven minutes, by my watch. The cops arrive, to no point. Isn't there a G20 protest somewhere? There isn't, because the city is near-empty. I walk back to the Plaza and watch. Hulking and grumpy, the cops wave people off the street and onto the sidewalk. The young women keep dancing, all thighs and hips. The cops are impatient but they stall, baited and hooked. Old men in Chile shirts smoke cigarettes and stare hard at the cops who are staring at the women. Their faces betray nothing, yet their eyes betray everything. The cops go away, as they must. The dancing goes on. No army of police in the city, no razor wire or fences can stop this, the languid dancing in the dreamscape.

• • • • •

WHEN I walk into The Football Factory to see the Second Round game between Ghana and the U.S. I'm amused to see a table full of media-types there. All news editors from the two major papers are supposed to be working on this Saturday afternoon as the G20

Summit finally opens and all those world leaders are in the near-empty city. The editors are here though, just not at work. In the 77th minute of the pulsating game, when it's tied 1–1, the text crawls suddenly across the TV screen. G20 protests, violent clashes. Some people look at their iPhone or BlackBerry. Some glance out the window. No one moves. No one changes the channel.

It was happening, is all, the customary theater of the protests. Without even seeing the footage, we could all picture it—kids in black hoodies and bandanas throwing stones, breaking windows, and probably setting a police car on fire. Of course, that's precisely what it was. For four days, first as Toronto is traumatized by the lockdown and then as the police react in panic and confusion to the stark violence against the lockdown, the city teeters, unsure. The leaders of the twenty most powerful countries in the world are here doing who-knows-what, and mass groups of people wander the streets, trying to assert control. Some of us, in our hearts, know why it all feels so addled. It is winter in South Africa. Sometimes, on TV, you can see the rain pouring down. Always you see people bundled up against the cold. Here, in mid-summer, we are unsure of where the reality is anchored. Ghana wins 2–1. As ever the U.S. fails to settle together and allows a goal after five minutes. The fight-back is epic and intense, and the game is tied with a penalty awarded to the Americans. In extra-time the winner from Ghana is a lesson in strength and composure—Asamoah Gyan meets a long ball downfield, controlling it on his chest before striking it with exemplary composure into the American net. The packed bar is in love with Ghana and feeling condolence toward the Americans. It's fairness, everybody feels. When people step outside the bar, they can smell burning and can see acrid smoke in the sky.

On Sunday morning, Germany wipes the floor with England, beating them 4–1. At halftime, because there is endless news of riots and arrests, there is news coverage on TV, not soccer punditry. In a small pub we watch an awkwardly-staged scene of British Prime Minister David Cameron sitting down with German Chancellor Angela Merkel to watch the game. They are on TV, seeming distant despite being just a few minutes' walk away. England limps home. Merkel, I remember from Vienna, had finger-pointing discussions with the German manager Joachim Loew. Knows the game, Angela. I have a feeling I know where she's going from here. The inevitable pull of South Africa will draw her in.

For a few days, there is an idea at large that this is South America's World Cup. A Brazil-versus-Argentina final is touted. Uruguay is still in it, fearsomely disciplined in the way of small countries on this great stage. Diego Forlan, blond-haired god of the attack and the free kick, looks inviolable. Around him, young men, picked for South Africa and classified by the soccer world as innocents and mediocrities, sniff immortality in the air. Where I observe it unfold in Canada, the country seethes in a sullen argument with itself. The police went too far at the G20 summit. The police didn't do enough. A photo in the newspaper shows police officers on horseback standing in an empty street, watching World Cup soccer on a giant TV screen. Diego Maradona is shown on TV constantly, an excited man in his ill-fitting suit, hugging his players, smiling, shrugging. An adorable madman.

In the quarterfinals, Germany breezes by Argentina with the speed and incisiveness of youths unimpressed by the reputation of others. Argentina has no midfield formation or tactics, and it shows. The Germans have placed a very capable Bastian Schweinsteiger in the midfield role usually taken by Michael Ballack, who is injured and misses the entire tournament. The young Germans Muller and Ozil are imperious in their counter-attacking speed. Angela Merkel is indeed there, delighted. After, Maradona is inconsolable. There is a scene of him hugging his daughter for a long minute while Joachim Loew waits to shake his hand. Shockingly, Brazil self-destructs against Holland. The Dutch are well-organized in defense while the Brazilians are not. When the Dutch take the lead, Brazil looks strangely unable to respond. There is no plan, only desperation, and all their skill and composure evaporates.

There's a reason why the South Americans crashed out, and it's a tale of tactical innocence and cynicism. Maradona was revealed to be tactically naïve.

After that endlessly fraught qualifying campaign, it seemed that a chastened Maradona managed to forge a very male, very intense bond with the players in preparation for the World Cup. All enthusiasm, but no tactical plan. Crucially, Argentina lacked a principal midfielder, a playmaker to propel the team, to feed the ball to Lionel Messi and Carlos Tevez. An attacking midfield player, the engine of any team, is essential to take advantage of the natural skills of both. Argentina's success at the World Cup in 2006 was largely due to Juan Román Riquelme playing this role—fluent passing, setting the tempo and acting as a fulcrum. Without Riquelme, Argentina looked ungainly. Maradona decided to have Juan Sebastian Veron try the midfield playmaker role, but Veron couldn't do it. Javier Mascherano, essentially a more defensive midfielder, was tried in that role, but couldn't do it. In fact, at times, Lionel Messi himself was playing the role—playing deep, hence his lack of goals at this World Cup. This was a waste. Against Germany, the lack of any midfield plan was all too clear.

Remembering the memorable night in Buenos Aires, I put this theory in an e-mail to Marcelo, my translator then. And he replies, "If you say "tactically naive" you really fall short. We never had tactics at all. It was a question of trying to score spontaneously and defending miraculously, no matter what. Wonderful players, isolated on the field, "sweating the shirt" (it's a favorite local expression) but with no team concept." That's a damning indictment, but accurate. If a lack of tactics was Argentina's downfall, then a far too rigid tactical blueprint was Brazil's downfall. In fact, the reality is just mundane.

Unusual for Brazil, Manager Dunga was firmly committed to a traditional 4–4–2 formation. Given the array of talent available, this wasn't just a rejection of free-flowing soccer, it was absurdly limiting. Essentially, it meant that Kaká formed a kind of attacking triangle with Robinho and Luís Fabiano, his role being largely defined by the forward movement of two attacking defenders—Maicon to the right and Michel Bastos on the left. This very European style aims to suffocate attacking teams with a rock-solid, four-man defense and two defending midfielders who cut off passes and block opposing attackers from going anywhere. Scoring comes on the counter-attack, when space suddenly opens up. In the long marathon that is European league soccer, this formation will work, grinding out victories here and there by small margins, but in the sprint that is the World Cup, an instant flexibility is required. Dunga abandoned all signs of "Samba Soccer" for ruthless pragmatism on the field. For Brazil, there was no flexibility, no preparation for a Netherlands team that relied not on a 4–4–2 formation but depended on the abilities of Arjen Robben and Dirk Kuyt to move ceaselessly on the wings and switch positions from left to right. As soon as Brazil fell 2–1 behind against Holland, all the limitations of Dunga's plan became glaringly obvious. He had no midfield maestro to conjure attacks. He had wingers and no middle. He was out-maneuvered.

• • • • •

URUGUAY'S DEFEAT of Ghana on penalties is an epic battle, one that causes considerable fuss. With the game tied in the last minute of extra time, Uruguayan striker Luis Suarez uses his hand to stop the ball in a goalmouth scramble. The referee sees it, uses the red card and dismisses Suarez. Ghana gets a penalty kick that will, if converted, take it to the semifinal. The kicked ball skims the crossbar, and with the game still tied, it must be decided on more penalty kicks. Ghana fails and the last African team in the tournament is out. Suarez is villified for his handball and he's an easy target—young, mouthy and unapologetic. The North American press show a curious disappointment about Ghana's exit. There is a kind of guilt to the coverage—if only an African team had got to the semifinals, then everybody would have felt better. It's all too easy to see Suarez as a villain.

All along, though, there has been a subplot in the tournament. Spain gets stronger with each game and has an emphatic mastery of the short-passing technique. Their intricacy of movement is mesmerizing to watch and can easily intimidate opposing teams, who know they are doomed to spend long periods in a futile pursuit of the ball. When Spain plays, the game is one long buildup toward a goal; time rife with tension as the Spanish players engage in steady, ceaseless movement while in possession. The method is sometimes called tiki-taki soccer, but that doesn't do it justice. The manner of Spain's play has the beauty of a tightened string instrument, waiting to burst into soaring music. The crazy thing about Spain is their tendency to try to walk the ball into the net. Time after time, players confidently attempt to move past several defenders and be alone against the goalkeeper. It's a matador thing, I'm sure—the urge to be one-on-one with the beast, the keeper. The style of rhythmic possession and darting movement is about thought. Spain relies little on the possibility something accidentally arising from a long kick forward, a rush toward the opposing goal. Spain's game is a thought-out narrative based on possession skills and tactical acumen. If this move goes well then the next move will connect and, inevitably, the goal comes. The style has taken Spain past Portugal, Paraguay and Germany. It meets The Netherlands in the final. In essence, Spain's tactic is midfield-anchored. It has a midfield as supple as a snake, with three players connected to control movement. The Netherlands, too, is midfield-based but the tactic involves a midfield that serves as a hard spine to the rest of the team. While Spain is seductively supple in the middle, the Netherlands is rock solid.

Spain beats The Netherlands 1–0 in a game that is persistently scrappy until extra time. There are countless fouls. The main Dutch plan, facing Spanish artistry, is to kick at ankles, tug shirts, and manhandle opposing players. But Spain wins—a victory of lithe grace and technique over muscle and force. It is no epic and thus disappoints casual soccer fans. For me, as usual, the entirety of the tournament is defined by a key element of the final, and the context of where I watch and absorb the tournament. Just as the 2006, the final was defined for me by being in Germany and then by Zidane's perplexing head-butt and the mystery what triggered it, this one captured me in Holland's fruitless attempt to impose violence on the harmonious, confident and collectivist style of Spain. Watched and enjoyed in a city temporarily transformed into a place where authority seemed to wage war on peaceful citizens, the tournament is the triumph of ductile grace over gratuitous cruelty and coercion.

It doesn't matter that superstar players failed to perform at this World Cup as expected. It doesn't matter that soccer didn't leap in popularity in the United States and Canada, as the purpose of the World Cup is not to sell the sport to people normally devoted to the NFL, the NHL, NBA or Major League Baseball. Major League Soccer exists and flourishes at its own level. It doesn't matter that some people were lividly indignant about incidents of diving or play-acting by a handful of players. It doesn't matter that the lack of video-replay technology confuses an audience that expects such things when watching sport on TV. None of these things fundamentally diminish the sport. It matters more that the world outside North America was again completely transfixed by the World Cup, linked by it, and that soccer was again a vast, shared experience. Anyone who paid attention knows that Spain won by dint of dexterity and in winning represents the triumph of skill and finesse over ruthlessness, and that's all they need to know.

At The Football Factory, for the final, there is a huge Oranje Army. Among them, one of the staff, Hugo, marches about with the flag of Spain wrapped around his neck. He is Spanish; he is Captain Spain. He smiles and jokes as the Dutch fans become uneasy and then, some of them, very drunkenly uneasy. Afterward, I see a young man dressed in orange stumbling down my street. He eventually stops and, white-faced, stretches out in someone's front garden. A sense of numb pain hovers around him.

If I could, I'd tell him this: Everything I've thought about the joy, madness and meaning of soccer has come under confused scrutiny in my head, on this very street. On the day not long ago that France beat Ireland and qualified for this World Cup, it became clear. The game goes beyond logic. Nothing matters beyond the touchline. The game is like life. The referee's decision is final, even if he's wrong and the whole world knows it. The game brings joy and kills it. It is so mercurial it transcends ideals of "sporting" and "fair play." Cheating happens, and just as in life itself, an injustice unfolds, flourishes. Then, not always, but often enough, justice prevails.

I have traveled the world to watch soccer and write about it, and celebrate it. Yet it was here, near my home, that I knew, heart-scalded, the terrible meaning of it all. The game brings joy, breaks your heart, brings joy, breaks your heart, brings joy, breaks your heart . . . The meaning whirls and turns as the ball does—as the world does.

ACKNOWLEDGMENTS

MY THANKS TO JOHN FITZGERALD, who first invited me to write for the *Globe and Mail* and thus made me a writer. Thanks to my agent, Denise Bukowski, who saw it through with aplomb. Tim Rostron became my editor at Doubleday Canada and showed exceptional patience and skill, which saved the day. Martha Kanya-Forstner took it on first, and said, "Ooh-ah, Paul McGrath" when I proposed this book, and that made it all OK. At Rodale Books in the U.S., John Atwood supported the book's development with great care. Thank you all at Rodale for unleashing a book about soccer in the United States. At the *Globe and Mail*, my profound thanks to Neil Campbell whose idea it was that I write about soccer. This was all his doing. Steve McAllister, a fine man and editor, tolerated my mad reports and let it be, over and over through the years. Phillip Crawley, the boss, was unswerving in his support, which mattered most. And then at one point I fell happily into the arms of the *New York Times* and Jeffrey Marcus became my wonderful editor, game for anything.

In Toronto, Theresa McVean was indispensable, providing suggestions and support in the way that the best people do. Alison Gzowski, Simon Beck (QPR Reserves), and Sarah MacWhirter at the *Globe* were so good to me. Michelle Johnson, Lori Spring, Alan Round, Isabella Cattelan and Roland Schlimme took good care. Darryl Wiggers is the most reliable man I know and saved me over and over. Steve Petherbridge, Heather Mallick, Linden MacIntyre, Carol Off, David Studer, Alison Pick, Kevin Quain and Mike Clattenburg aided and abetted. Paul Beirne at Toronto FC is a fine fella and Richard Scott of the Canadian Soccer Association was helpful. Don Taylor sat with me in McVeigh's at unholy hours to see history unfold. Chris Young and Cathal Kelly of the *Toronto Star* were exceptional pals on the road. Tom Humphries of the *Irish Times* and Paul Lennon of the *Irish Daily Star* were indulgent.

On my travels, Gerry McDermott and then Lynne D'Arcy took care of access in Ireland; Anna Pitcher at the Football Association in England, Geert Paternoster in Belgium and Simone Orati of the Football Association in Italy were welcoming. In Slovakia, Janka Perackova of the Slovak Football Association was terrifically helpful and Milan Vajda of the Mayor's Office of the City of Bratislava was bountiful with his time. In Austria, Eva Draxler of Vienna Tourism became my ally and my friend. In the matter of Argentina, Alfredo Bascu of the Consulate of Argentina in Toronto took charge, made it happen and also became my friend. Carlos Oscar Pachamé, a great player and a great man, took grand care of me. Robert Devereux kindly introduced me to Marcelo Burello of the Universidad de Buenos Aires, who was so gracious and a good companion.

My mother, Mary Ahern, gave me this attitude and my father Sean Doyle had the grace and courage to take off his Fáinne and accompany me to my first international soccer match. My sister Máire and Stephen McBride were kindness itself. My man Mick and Rita (Ittybitty) were so loyal and, of all, the Mott was so patient and tolerant that thanks are not enough.